From the Comic to the Comedic

From the Comic to the Comedic

The Traditions of Comedy of Bhāsa and Shakespeare

Sudha Gopalakrishnan

1993
Sharada Publishing House
DELHI-110052

SHARADA PUBLISHING HOUSE
(Publishers on India's Past and Pressent)
E-239, Shastri Nagar, Delhi-110052
Phone : 7516539

First Published 1993
ISBN 81-85616-11-6

Published by B.L. Bansal for Sharada Publishing House, E-239, Shastri Nagar, Delhi-110052 and Printed at Garg Offset Works, B-76, Naraina, Industrial Area, Phase I, New Delhi.

CONTENTS

PREFACE		vii
CHAPTER I	INTRODUCTION	1
CHAPTER II	THE AESTHETICS OF COMEDY	8
CHAPTER IIJI	THE THEATRE OF COMEDY	29
CHAPTER IV	THE THEMES OF COMEDY	60
CHAPTER V	SITUATIONS IN COMEDY	71
CHAPTER VI	CHARACTERIZATION IN COMEDY	89
CHAPTER VII	IMAGERY IN COMEDY	104
CHAPTER VIII	THE USE OF LANGUAGE IN COMEDY	119
CHAPTER IX	COMEDIC VISION OF LIFE	132
	GLOSSARY	141
	BIBLIOGRAPHY	145
	INDEX	158

PREFACE

THIS BOOK is an attempt to compare the theory of classical Indian drama with that of Western drama insofar as they relate to the modes of comedy. At an elementary level, the theory of comedy in the two traditions may be considered similar on the ground that it operates primarily through laughter. The laughter in comedy produces a particular kind of aesthetic response often characterised by carefree and irresponsible mirth. At a higher level, however, Indian and Western theories accept the fact that comedy is an attempt to transcend the cares and anxieties of life while presenting an affirmative approach to experience. Beneath the establishment of an atmosphere of celebration, an attitude that goes far beyond the temporality of life is visible in both the comic traditions.

In this discussion, the works of Bhāsa and Shakespeare are taken to represent the dramatic theories of classical Indian and Western comedy respectively. Since dramatic theory is usually grounded on theatrical practice, the devices of enactment in comedy are examined in some detail. Modern experimental drama in the West which moves closer to the non-illusionistic theatre of the Orient is not taken up for discussion here. The theatric form of Kutiyattam is given a special mention because it seems to be the only form of extant Sanskrit theatre.

The introductory chapter of this book tries to explore the similarities along with the differences between Western and Sanskrit aesthetics. On a comparative analysis, the differences between the two are as striking as the similarities. Chapter II, "The Aesthetics of Comedy", is a comparative study of the classical Indian and Western theories of comedy. The discussion is based on a comparative analysis of the nature of laughter, the classification of the comic modes and the different levels in the experience of comedy in both the traditions. Chapter III, "The Theatre of Comedy", analyses the stage devices employed in the Western and Indian theatre of

PREFACE

Comedy and these are explained in relation to the origin and evolution of comedy in the two traditions. Chapter IV, "The Themes of Comedy", is an examination of the themes that seem to recur in both Western and Sanskrit comedies. The continuity of the cycle of life and the part played by fortune in it are taken up as the most persistent themes in comedy. Chapter V, "The Situations in Comedy", is an analysis of the comic element involved in some of the basic situations in the plays, as well as the devices employed to enhance them, while chapter VI, "Characterization in Comedy", is devoted to a discussion of the methods of characterization employed in both dramatic forms. The different manifestations of the comic protagonist in drama are examined in some detail. The next chapter, "Imagery in Comedy", seeks to bring out the significance of imagery in projecting the comic element in a play. Chapter VIII, "The Comic Use of Language", underscores the importance of language in comedy. Both Indian and Western comedies display similarities in the blending of prose and verse, the use of dialectic variations to suit the occasion and the use of common linguistic devices. The last chapter, "The Comedic Vision of Life", deals with the philosophic dimension of comedy. The ultimate end of comedy seems to be a state of serene calmness which both the comic traditions have aspired to achieve this is a state of blissful repose which may be defined as "comedic".

A glossary of the terms in Sanskrit used in this thesis is given at the end.

I would like to acknowledge my gratitude to the University of Kerala which offered me a research fellowship to undertake this study. I am grateful to Dr. K. Ayyappa Paniker, my professor and guide, for his invaluable help and suggestions. I am indebted to Shri Satkari Mukhopadhyaya, the members of his family and Shri S. Jithendra Nath for their help in bringing out this book. It would be audacious on my part to attempt to thank Shri D. Appukkuttan Nair who provoked and sustained my interest in classical theatre with parental care.

Sudha Gopalakrishnan

CHAPTER I

INTRODUCTION

A COMPARATIVE STUDY between Western and Sanskrit theatre seems relevant in the present situation, when writers and commentators in the field of aesthetics in general and drama in particular are attempting to establish many points of correspondence between them. At a superficial glance, the differences between the two are more striking than the similarities. Sanskrit drama, unlike the Western, is not today a live mode of expression. Montgomery Schuyler records that "the age of Sanskrit drama may roughly be given as extending from A.D. 400 to 1100. This period does not, of course, include the earliest efforts at dramatic composition, nor take in a large number of late and inferior plays."[1] It does not take into account the possible dates of dramatists before Śūdraka, like those of Aśvaghoṣa and Bhāsa. Bhāsa's plays came to light as late as 1912 with Ganapati Sastri's publication in Trivandrum of the thirteen plays ascribed to him. A.B. Keith comments that "the first century B.C. can with fair certainty be assumed to be the very latest period at which the appearance of a genuine Sanskrit drama can be placed."[2] Thus, according to the data available today, the best of Sanskrit drama seems to have been written approximately during the first thousand years of the Christian era. In the West, drama had its origin from ancient Athens, and developed as a full-fledged branch of literature by the association and infiltration of various cultures and systems of thought. As a result, the religious, moral and aesthetic precepts of associated with classical Western drama have tended to be greatly diversified. Even today, Western drama is being subjected to be a lot of experimentation and transformation, through the use of new forms and precepts, thus reflecting the conflicting drives and struggles of

[1] Montgomery Schuyler, *A Bibliography of the Sanskrit Drama* (1906; rpt. Delhi: Asia Education Publication Services, 1977), p.6.

[2] A. Berriedale Keith, *The Sanskrit Drama in its Origin, Development, Theory and Practice* (Oxford: Oxford Univ. Press, 1924), p. 72.

Western thought. But in Sanskrit theatre as well as in ancient Indian society, there seems to have been an accepted code of *dharma* or moral and ethical code. J.A.B. Van Buitenen observes that in the classical drama of India, "there is a curious intermixture of the simplicities of dharmic life and the complexities of courtly or urban life."[3] The dramatist thus draws his plot and characters out of the hierarchic scheme of this society. But, in spite of these differences in age and culture between the two dramatic traditions, there are striking similarities which, according to Henry W. Wells, "mark the essentials of all good drama."[4] The similarities may be observed in the areas of aesthetic theory, theatrical practice and elements of dramatic composition.

In considering the nature of aesthetic experience, the importance of language as a medium of expression should be taken into account. The word 'language' in this context applies to all the verbal and non-verbal elements that aid communication like speech, gesture, painting, music, which are all included in the word. The connection between a word and its sound has been subjected to analysis by thinkers in the West as well as in India. G. Hanumantha Rao finds a resemblance between Merleau-Ponty's theory of expression and Bhartṛhari's theory of word. According to him, "Merleau-Ponty considers original expression alone as true expression. In cases of all original expression which art is presumed to be, the original thought is discovered only when it bursts into expression."[5] Bhartṛhari explains this communication through his theory of *sphoṭa* according to him, *sphoṭa* is the eternal and imperceptible elements of sounds and words and the real vehicle in communication, which bursts or flashes on the mind when a sound is uttered. The full import of a sentence or a word strikes the hearer with a sudden force after the whole extent of the sound is uttered – thus invariably a connection is established between the speaker and the hearer. Bhartṛhari speaks of the tonal meaning in artistic expression which

---

[3] J.A.B. Van Buitenen, 'The Classical Drama,' *The Literatures of India: An Introduction*, ed. Edward C. Dimock et. al. (Chicago: Chicago Univ. Press, 1974), p. 85.

[4] Henry W. Wells, *The Classical Drama of India* (Bombay: Asia Pub. House, 1963), p.6.

[5] G. Hanumantha Rao, *Comparative Aesthetics: Eastern and Western* (Mysore: D.V.K. Murthy, 1974), p. 158.

is similar to the reverberation of a bell and calls it *dhvani* (*Vākyapadīya*, I.102).[5a] *Dhvani* may roughly be described as the suggestive power in poetry. In a poem, the sound as well as the superficial sense becomes subordinated to the suggested sense, which Anandavardhana calls *dhvani.*[6]

The Indian theory of aesthetics recognises the nature of aesthetics experience in terms of *rasa* or the pure and untainted pleasure derived out of one's artistic identification with a poem or a play. Ananda Coomaraswamy equates *rasa* with Ideal Beauty. In his words, "aesthetic experience . . . arises from a self-identification of the spectator with the presented matter."[7] He offers a translation of the passage relating to *rasāsvāda* in *Sāhityadarpaṇa* thus: "Pure aesthetic experience is theirs in whom the knowledge of ideal beauty is innate; it is know intuitively, in intellectual ecstasy without accompaniment of ideation, at the highest level of conscious being; born of one mother with the vision of God, its life is as it were a flash of blinding light of transmundane origin, impossible to analyze, and yet in the image of our very being." (III.2-29). It is a subjective feeling affording unique pleasure, and its ultimate effect is one of repose or *śānti*. In Western aesthetic thought, writers are increasingly aware of this condition of serene calmness, which the arts are capable of conveying to the reader or spectator. Regarding this, I.A. Richards observes: "The arts are our storehouse of recorded values. They spring from and perpetuate hours in the lives of exceptional people, when their control and command of experience is at its highest, hours when the varying possibilities of existence are most clearly seen and the different activities which may arise are more exquisitively reconciled, hours when habitual narrowness of interests or confused bewilderment are replaced by an intricately wrought composure."[8] This state roughly corresponds to the state of the experience of *rasa*. The experience of ultimate joy derived out of

---

[5a] *Vākyapadīya*, I.102

[6] Anandavardhana. *Dhvanyāloka*, trans., E.V. Damodaran (Kottayam: National Book Stall, 1973), p. 101.

[7] Ananda K. Coomaraswamy, *The Transformation of Nature in Art* (Delhi: Munshiram Manoharlal, 1974), p. 51,

[8] I.A. Richards, *Principles of Literary Criticism* (1924; rpt. Bombay: Allied Publishers, 1967), pp. 22-23.

poetry and drama which is termed *rasānubhava* is subjected to a close analysis by commentators like Bhaṭṭanāyaka, Bhaṭṭatauta and Abhinavagupta, who expound the theory of *sādhāraṇīkaraṇa*. The experience of *rasa*, according to Abhinavagupta, is different from the enjoyment of pleasure in the ordinary world because it is impersonal and detached. The experience reveals or strikes itself on the reader or spectator in an idealized or exalted form – its idealization makes it equivalent to *brahmānanda* or the joy derived out of the perception of the Absolute Self (*Brahman*). Thus, irrespective of the nature or the situation evoked, the experience is one of pleasure because it is in a state of *sādhāraṇīkaraṇa*. This idealization of nature in art is similar to the central thought in Aristotle's doctrine. S.H. Butcher, while commenting on the function of poetry with reference to tragedy, says that "imitative art in its highest form, namely poetry, is an expression of the universal element in human nature."[9]. The term 'catharsis' suggests purification – in drama, it is the purification and idealization of the spectator's emotions. On seeing a tragedy, the feelings of pity and fear are aroused in the mind of the spectator, but this has no correspondence with the world of everyday reality. Butcher explains it thus:

> . . . this fear, unlike the fear of common reality, is based on an imaginative union with another's life. The spectator is lifted out of himself. He becomes one with the tragic sufferer, and through him the humanity at large. One effect of the drama, said Plato, is that through it a man becomes many, instead of one, it makes him lose his proper personality in a pantomimic instinct, and so prove false to himself. Aristotle might reply: True; he passes out of himself, but it is through the enlarging power of sympathy. He forgets his own petty sufferings. He transcends the narrow suffering of the individual. He identifies himself with the fate of mankind.[10]

Thus *catharsis* and *sādhāraṇīkaraṇa* seem to be similar in their effect, because both lead to a state of blissful repose, due to the exaltation or transcendence of the personal self through aesthetic experience.

The dramatic practice in India is markedly different from that in the West, because unlike the Western which mostly depends on the

---

[9] S.H. Butcher, *Aristotle's Theory of Poetry and Fine Art* (1907; rpt. Delhi: Lyall Book Depot, 1967), p. 150.

[10] *ibid.*, p. 266.

realistic technique, Indian theatre is nonillusionistic and formalistic. Indian drama draws heavily on classical and primitive mythology for its theme. The audience in India favours a theatre which incorporates all the elements of dramatic art. In other words, it incorporates tauryatrika – *gīta* or vocal music, *nṛtta* or dance and *vādya* or rhythmical accompaniment. Thus it is a stylized mode of theatre which caters to an idealized audience. In the West, it seems the producers are getting increasingly aware of the advantages of stylization, and they are trying to discover new forms and a fresh approach. The experiments in this direction have brought the Western mode of production closer to the Indian. For example, the "Epic theatre" of Bertolt Brecht, the "Poor theatre" of Grotowski and the "Theatre of Cruelty" or Artaud are a few attempts in this direction. All these modes of theatrical representation avoid a realistic technique and opt for stylization, because the latter affords more scope for suggestiveness. Instead of presenting the play in a rigid and concrete manner, stylized acting involves a free play of the spectator's imagination – it is thus creative rather than imitative.

The dramatic genre of comedy adopts an affirmative approach to life. In a very general way, comedy may be described as a play with a happy ending. Primarily, it operates through laughter. In a comedy, laughter produces a particular aesthetic response which entertains and delights the reader or spectator. It is also an expression of carefree and irresponsible mirth. William E. Gruber equates comedy with wildness. According to him, "the essential dramatic form of the comic hero follows not from his familiarity, but from his undifferentiated wildness – or, more precisely, his dramatic form follows from human understanding of such wildness."[11] This feature is perhaps best illustrated in conceiving the figure of Falstaff as he appears in the two parts of Shakespeare's *King Henry IV.* Falstaff symbolises a way of looking at life. C.L. Barber observes on this point that "his [Falstaff's] extraordinary meaningfulness comes from the way he manages to live 'out of all order', out of all compass, by his wit and his wits; and from the way he keeps reflecting on the rest of the action, at first indirectly by the mock roles that he plays, at the end directly by his comment at the battle."[12] Beneath his

[11] William E. Gruber, "The Wild men of Comedy: Transformations in the Comic Hero from Aristophanes to Pirandello', *Genre* XIV (Summer, 1981), p. 214.

irresponsible extravagances, he has a stalwart adhesion to life, which according to Robert M. Torrance is "the essence of comic heroism."[13] When Falstaff, through his verbal skill, rises above the embarrassing situation of his discomfiture at Gadshill robbery, and when on the battle-field of Shrewsbury, he prefers a bottle of sack to a sword, he stands for the gratification of physical impulses as opposed to abstract concepts like honour, so that life to him becomes an endlessly joyous activity. Amidst the tension and din of the battle-field, Falstaff's longing for "I would 'twere bed-time, Hal, and all well" (1 *Henry IV.* V. i. 124-25) sums up his outlook on life. Upon seeing the dead body of Sir Walter Blunt, he observes: "I like not such grinning honour as Sir Walter hath. Give me life . . ." (V. iii. 59-61). At a higher level, comedy suggests a way of transcending despair and misery by rising above itself, a level where the joys and sorrows of everyday existence are replaced by a serene calmness and blissful repose. *Hāsya* or the comic, according to Indian thought, can act as a means to achieve this level of *śānti.* To quote P. Pancapagesa Sastri, ".... the Yogin finds the world a bundle of incongruities. Laughter *(hāsa)* is the 'sthāyin' that leads to renunciation and so to the seeking after eternal truth which leads to eternal bliss."[14]

An analysis of the plays in the Western and Sanskrit dramatic repertory reveals the fact that the comedies of Shakespeare and Bhāsa are worthy of a deeper study, because they seem to encompass within their sphere a wide variety of levels and perspectives of comedy. Their dramatic milieu is similar because their comedies seem to evoke humour rather than display wit. The plays of Bhāsa have been subjected to a lot of discussion and controversy regarding their authorship, authenticity and the approximate date of composition. A.D. Pusalker writes that the date of Bhāsa "is one of the most vexed questions in Indian chronology and one is surprised to find a difference of over fifteen hundred years in the earliest and latest

---

[12] C.L. Barber, *Shakespeare's Festive Comedy: A Study of Dramatic Form and its Relation to Social Custom* (Princeton: Princeton Univ. Press, 1959), p. 198.

[13] Robert M. Torrance, *The Comic Hero* (London: Harvard Univ. Press, 1978), p. 132.

[14] P. Pancapagesa Sastri, *The Philosophy of Aesthetic Pleasure* (Annamalainagar: Annamali Univ., 1940), pp. 272-273.

dates ascribed to him by different scholars."[15] After discussing the problem in the light of both internal and external evidences, he places the date of Bhāsa's plays in the fourth or fifth century B.C.[16] Similarly, critics hold contrary opinions regarding the common authorship of the thirteen plays ascribed to Bhāsa. But inspite of this, their authenticity and Bhāsa's authorship of the plays have come to be accepted today. In subjecting the plays of Bhāsa and Shakespeare to a closer comparative study, the most obvious similarity seems to be their approach towards the comic – both Bhāsa and Shakespeare do not limit themselves to any particular perspective on comedy, or advocate any particular branch of philosophic thought. The humour derived out of the plays is spontaneous, free and devoid of malice. The similarities also pertain to their theatrical effectiveness, methods of employing plot, situations, themes, characterization and language. Inspite of the differences in spirit and culture, there seem to be striking similarities between the two dramatists in the form as well as the content of their respective plays.

---

[15] A.D. Pusalker, *Bhāsa: A Study* (Delhi: Munshiram Manoharlal, 1968), p. 63.

[16] *ibid.*, p. 81.

CHAPTER II

THE AESTHETICS OF COMEDY

IN THE WEST, the word "comedy" is often used to refer to a particular type of drama which adopts a more or less affirmative approach to life. The origin of comedy, according to Aristotle, is obscure because it was not highly valued.[1] But later writers have traced the origin of comedy to Greece. The root of the word is Greek "komos" or the revel-rout of Dionysiac worshippers. *The Oxford English Dictionary* states that "comedy" is derived from the Greek "comoedia", which also means "revelling" or "merry-making". It defines comedy as "a stage-play of a light and amusing character, with a happy conclusion to its plot."

Comedy can be defined as a play which evokes the aesthetic response of delight in the spectator. It expresses the basic impulse of life-affirmation, which Susanne K. Langer describes in the pithy phrase "human life-feeling." According to her, "comedy sets up in the audience a sense of general exhilaration, because it presents the very image of livingness, and the perception of it is exciting."[2] In comedy, unrestrained pleasure serves to evoke natural impulses like liberty, mirth and vitality. It is a celebration of the atmosphere of festivity translated into drama. The word "festive", as used by C.L. Barber in his statement "much comedy is festive",[3] implies a saturnalian release from the cares and anxieties of everyday life. The temporary escape into freedom and release is a basic feature of the experience of comedy. One of the most obvious examples of the festive element in comedy may be observed in the theatric form of the Italian Commedia dell'arte. The festive strain in this mode of

[1] Aristotle, "Poetics" in *Theory of Poetry and Fine Art*, trans. S.H. Butcher (London: Macmillan, 1907), p. 21.

[2] Susanne K. Langer, "Feeling and Form," in *The Comic in Theory and Practice*, ed. John J. Enck, Elizabeth T. Forter and Alvin Whitley (New Jersey: Prentice-Hall, 1960), p. 84.

[3] C.L. Barber, *Shakespeare's Festive Comedy: A Study of Dramatic Form and its Relation to Social Custom* (Princeton: Princeton Univ. Press, 1959), p. 3.

dramatic presentation is pure and absolute, since constraints like plot, characterization or theme have only a minimal role here. It presents vividly how a group of stock characters related to a stock situation becomes the source of entertainment and comic pleasure. The interest of the drama is built up with techniques ranging from improvization to acrobatics, and it reveals festive liberty at its best. This feature also connects comedy to the instinct of play. Both have their origin in saturnalia and carnival custom. Play is primarily rejoicing or celebration, and so is comedy. John Huizinga defines play as "a free activity standing quite outside ordinary life as being not serious, but at the same time absorbing the player immensely and utterly."[4] The spirit of freedom or "a stepping out of 'real' life into a temporary sphere of activity with a disposition all of its own"[5] is a feature common to both comedy and play.

In Sanskrit drama, comedy encompasses a large sphere. Tragedy as a rule is avoided by Indian dramatists unlike their counterparts in the West, so that in Sanskrit it may be said that comedy constitutes the only serious dramatic genre. In Sanskrit, the word *nāṭya* corresponds to "dramatic art". Bharata's *Nāṭyaśāstra* is an attempt to celebrate theatre as a way of life. The primary objective of *nāṭya* is to provide entertainment. In the *Nāṭyaśāstra*, the gods are depicted as approaching their head, Brahma, and requesting for a play-thing – "something pleasant to look at and something pleasant to hear"[6] –. Brahma creates *nāṭya* primarily to fulfil their desire. *Nāṭya* refreshes the mind of the spectator and diverts him from the cares and anxieties of daily existence – it is a release from tension. This primary motive of entertainment relates the concept of *nāṭya* directly to the concept of comedy in the West, because both imply a release from tension and the consequent experience of pleasure. According to Bharata, "the theatre is a means of creation and rest for those bowed down by sorrow, engaged in ascetic endeavours or weary after long labour."[7] The element of entertainment also con-

---

[4] Johan Huizinga, *Homo Ludens: A Study of the Play-element in Culture* (Boston: Beacon, 1955), p. 13.

[5] ibid., p. 8.

[6] K.P. Narayana Pisharoti (ed.), *Bharata Muniyute Nāṭyaśāstram* (Trichur: Kerala Sahitya Akademi, 1971), p. 6.

[7] *Nāṭyaśāstra*, I. 87.

nects *nāṭya*, as it does comedy, to the instinct of play. According to Pramod Kale, "the *Nāṭyaśāstra* views theatre primarily as a recreational, leisure-time activity resembling a game or sport."[8] The dramatic device of *prastāvana* or prologue in Sanskrit drama offers a good illustration of the recreational aspect of drama. In *prastāvana*, the stage-manager or *sūtradhāra* appears and directly addresses the audience. Then he engages in a conversation with the *naṭi* or actress, in the course of which he introduces the playwright, the play, and the other details of presentation. This device establishes that drama is only a sport, a temporary escape from reality to an imaginary world of make-believe. For example, in *Abhijñānaśākuntala*, the stage-director explains to the actress what she has to do:

> STAGE-DIRECTOR: My lady, this audience is for the most part composed of learned men. Today we intend to entertain them with a new play, composed by Kālidāsa; so please bestow care on every part.
>
> ACTRESS: As your arrangements are well-made, nothing will be wanting.
>
> STAGE-DIRECTOR: My lady, I will tell you the truth; until the wise are satisfied, I cannot feel that my knowledge of acting of sound; the mind of even the best-trained (persons) is loth to trust itself.
>
> ACTRESS: So it is. Let my lord now command what is to be done next.
>
> STAGE-DIRECTOR: What other than to please the ears of the audience? Therefore, sing about this very summer season (so), enjoyable, which has just begun.

This is perhaps not the sole purpose of *nāṭya*, because it also has a didactic motive. But the ultimate experience in drama is one of pure joy – it is an act of celebration. Thus the primary objective of drama as understood by the Western and Sanskrit playwrights seems to be identical – the celebration of life through the experience of pleasure.

It is usually assumed that comedy is inseparable from laughter, and so discussions on comedy are generally linked with discussions on laughter. It is beyond doubt that comedy has a lot to do with laughter, because the "comic element" in comedy usually gets expressed through laughter. In the West, many writers have tried to

---

[8] Pramod Kale, *The Theatric Universe: A Study of Nāṭyaśāstra* (Bombay: Popular Prakashan, 1974), p. 45.

analyse the causes and effects of the phenomenon of laughter. George Meredith observes that "the test of true comedy is that it shall awaken thoughtful laughter."[9] The word "thoughtful" in this definition highlights the intellectual quality associated with the mental process by which laughter is derived. Charles Baudelaire points out another cause which arouses laughter. According to him, "human pride, which takes the upper hand . . . is the natural cause of laughter in the case of comic."[10] In this case, laughter is an expression of superiority. It arises out of a sudden sense of superiority which one feels in relation to the object at which laughter is directed. One is moved to laughter on seeing the antics of a clown, or hearing absurd talk, because one instinctively feels superior to him. Similarly, the juxtaposition of two incongruous ideas gives rise to a sudden pleasure which gets expressed as laughter. Sigmund Freud points to the effect of incongruity as promoting comedy in the theatre: "A person appears comic to us if, in comparison with ourselves, he makes too great an expenditure on his bodily functions and too little on his mental ones."[11] The idea of the physical when confronted with the mental is a permanent source of the comic in the theatres of all countries. The theatrical institution of the clown is founded on this principle.

In Indian aesthetics, discussions of the comic come under *hāsyarasa*. According to Bharata, the word *rasa* suggests delight.[12] In poetry and drama, *rasa* is experienced through the union of *vibhāva*, *anubhāva* and *vyabhicāribhāva*. Dhanañjaya states that "*rasa* results when a *bhāva* produces a pleasurable sensation through the operation of *vibhāvas*, *sāttvikabhāvas* and *vyabhicāribhāvas*." [13] *Bhāva* is the means to develop *rasa*. Bharata states that *bhāva* is termed so because it makes the meaning of the play intelligible through the various forms of *abhinaya*. *Vibhāva* is described as the

[9] George Meredith, "An Essay on Comedy and the Use of the Comic Spirit", *The Comic in Theory and Practice*, p. 36.

[10] Charles Baudelaire, "On the Essence of Laughter", The Comic in Theory and Practice, p. 36.

[11] Sigmund Freud, *Wit and its Relation to the Unconscious* (London: James Strachey, 1960), p. 145.

[12] *Nāṭyaśāstra*, VI. 35.

[13] Dhanañjaya, *Daśarūpaka*, trans. George C.O. Haas (Columbia: Columbia Univ. Press, 1912), p. 132.

cause or condition which determines the mode of *abhinaya*. Bharata sees that word "*vibhāva*" as synonymous with "cause" or "stimulus". *Vibhāva* is divided according to its nature into *ālambana* and *uddīpana*. The former is the object responsible for exciting the dormant *sthāyībhāva* and the latter signifies the external conditions responsible for its development. In *Abhijñānaśākuntala*, for the King afflicted by the shafts of love, Śakuntala becomes the *ālambana vibhāva*. He addresses the God of Love with the words: "Your having flowery shafts and the Moon's having cool beams – both these are observed to be untrue for such as me. For the moon sheds fire (on them) with her dewy rays; and you make your flowery-darts hard and adamant" (Act III. verse 3). Here the flowery shafts of the God of Love become the *uddīpanavibhāva* to evoke the *sthāyībhāva* of rati or love. *Anubhāva* is the external manifestations of the emotion excited by the *vibhāva*. Bharata explains that *anubhāva* makes the spectator experience the meaning through the mode of *abhinaya*. *Vyabhicāribhāva* is a subsidiary or transient *bhāva* that accompanies and highlights *bhāva*. Bharata analyses the root "*vyabhicāri*" as "*vi*", "*abhi*" and "*cara*". It moves in relation to the *sthāyibhāva* and helps to make the *rasa* manifest itself. Bharata states that *vibhāva*, *anubhāva* and *vyabhicāribhāva* exist in relation to or dependent on the *sthāyībhāvās*, which are permanent, innate impulses or states of mind in human nature.

The *sthāyībhāvās*, which are eight in number, with the association of the other *bhāvās* develop into *rasās*. Like the *sthāyībhāvas*, Bharata mentions eight rasas – *sṛṅgāra*, *vīra*, *karuṇa*, *adbhuta*, *raudra*, *hāsya*, *bībhatsa* and *bhayānaka* – but later writers recognize *śānta* as a ninth rasa. Thus *hāsyarasa* or the comic is one among the eight *rasās* discussed by Bharata.

In *Nāṭyasāstra*, Bharata defines *hāsa* or laughter as causing amusement through one's own or another's strange appearance, words, attire or action.[14] *Hāsa* is the *sthāyībhāva* of *hāsyarasa* – so *hāsya* is the development of *hāsa* which is caused by strange appearance etc. Bharata states that *hāsa* or laughter is produced by imitating the actions of others, by indulging in absurd talk, baselessly accusing others and behaving in a ridiculous manner. One is also

[14] *Nāṭyaśāstra*, VI. 60.

moved to laughter on seeing weaknesses such as greed, inpudence, tendency to quarrel and physical defects. Laughter is also caused by tickling a person. These are the *vibhāvas* of *hāsyarasa* – the one at whom people laugh for his strange appearance, etc. become the *ālambana vibhāva* and his actions become the *uddīpana vibhāva* of *hāsya*. The *anubhāvas* of *hāsya* are narrowing of eyes, smiling, throbbing of the lips, the nose, and the cheek, perspiration, colour of the face and taking hold of sides. In other words, these are the external features by which laughter is manifested. The *vyabhicārībhāvas* of *hāsya* are sleep, indolence, stupor, dream and jealousy. The colour ascribed to *hāsya* is white and the deities ascribed are the attendants of Lord Śiva.

Thus *hāsa* or laughter is derived out of incongruity – it arises out of comic appearance, speech or manners of a person. This feature makes the concept of *hāsya* in Indian aesthetics equivalent to the concept of laughter in the West. Both relate laughter to the incongruous, or the disconnecting of one idea from another, which produces pleasure and gets expressed as laughter. *Nāṭyaśāstra* also provides one of the causes by which *hāsya* is produced. Bharata observes that imitation of *sṛṅgāra* becomes *hāsya*. He also states that *hāsya* is derived from *sṛṅgāra*. This implies that the imitation of a lofty subject makes it ridiculous and invariably produces *hāsya*. This fact is especially true in the case of *sṛṅgāra* because it has no trivial associations with it. In the theatrical form of *Kūṭiyāṭṭam*, the traditional Sanskrit theatre of Kerala, the Vidūṣaka or comic character deliberately imitates the sentimental extravagance of the hero – the hero's passion for his beloved finds a parody in the Vidūṣaka's panegyric on the attributes of Cakki, the paragon of ugliness and deformity. In *Subhadrādhanañjaya*, the hero reflects that all the qualities characterising a woman have been abundantly showered on his beloved so that Brahma, the Creator, has exhausted everything. If Brahma has to create another woman, he has now to beg her for getting the virtues back. In a parody of this romantic exaggeration, the Vidūṣaka also elaborates on the "attributes" of Cakki, his "beloved", who is characterised by her foul smell, cruel glances, dirty hair and rash talk. All these "virtues" are so abundantly showered on her that Brahma, if he has to create another such woman, has to beg these of her. Thus it is a burlesque on the hero's romantic extravagance. Not only *śṛṅgāra*, but any other *bhāva* can be rendered comic through a deliberately comic imitation. In Bharata's definition of *hāsya*, laughter is seen as a reaction to human weaknesses and also as a case of incongruity, where a feeling of superiority is implicit. Thus an analysis of the cause of laughter in Western and Sanskrit aesthetics seems to bring out their essential similarities.

In the West, just as "comedy" is a broad and general term for a genre of drama, "the comic" is a broad sphere which includes a variety of modes ranging from delicate humour to severe invective. Very often, the partitions that divide one from the other are thin and the modes seem to overlap. These can be classified broadly into three divisions – verbal, thematic and situational.

Verbal humour refers to the humour produced through verbal exchange and other forms of speech. Comic modes like wit, humour, repartee, sarcasm, jest and pun belong to this group. *Wit* appeals by the pleasurable sense of shock due to a verbal expression that is deliberately uttered to achieve this effect. It results from a sudden perception of similarity in things dissimilar. Usually, a witty expression is short and pithy, and has an intellectual quality. For example, in the dialogue between Jacques and Rosalind in *As You Like It*, Jacques boasts that he is a traveller and has a lot of experience in the affairs of the world. when Rosalind remarks: "And your experience makes you sad. I had rather have a fool to make me merry than experience to make me sad – and to travel for it too" (IV. i. 24-25). Humour is a generic name that appeals to the genially comic in man's disposition. It arises out of a comic speech, appearance or mannerism. Humour is not deliberate like wit, but is spontaneous. Unlike wit, it is not intended to be comic. For example, in *King Henry IV*, when Glendower declares that he has magical powers by which he can call spirits from the vasty deep, Hotspur replies: "Why, so can I, or so can any man: But will they come when you do call for them?" (III. i. 53-55). *Repartee* is a witty remark in which a person tries to cap the remark of another, and turn it to his advantage, thus ensuing in a skirmish of wit. A typical example is the merry war between Benedick and Beatrice in *Much Ado About Nothing*, in Act I, Scene i:

BEN: What, my dear lady Disdain! Are you yet living?

BEAT: Is it possible Disdain should die while she hath such meet food to feed it as Signior Benedick? Courtesy itself must convert to disdain if you come in her presence.

BEN: Then is courtesy a turncoat. But it is certain that I am loved by all ladies, only you excepted; and I would I could find in heart that I had not a hard heart, for, truly, I love none.

BEAT: A dear happiness to women . . . (101-108)

Jest is a witty remark intended to arouse laughter – it is synonymous with a joke. It can vary from a mocking or jeering speech to a piece of raillery to banter. In *Much Ado About Nothing,* when Claudio insistently asks Benedick what he thinks about Hero, Benedick replies: "Why, i' faith, methinks she's too low for a high praise, and too little for a great praise.." (I.i.147-49). Here Benedick is jesting on the sentimentality of Claudio's love. *Sarcasm* is a subtle expression of verbal sneer, while *pun* is a figure of speech which involves a play on words. Usually, pun involves the association of a single phonetic term with double meaning. For example, Mercutio's words in *Romeo and Juliet:* "Ask for me tomorrow and you shall find me a *grave* man."

By thematic humour is meant the humour that is inherent in a theme – that is, humour which operates as the central theme of a given work. The comic modes like burlesque, satire and invective come under this group. *Burlesque* consists in "the use of imitation of serious matter or manner made amusing by the creation of an incongruity between subject and style."[15] John D. Jump classifies burlesque into four types:

(1) *Travesty,* the low burlesque of a particular work, achieved by treating the subject of that work in an aggressively familiar style.

(2) *Hudibrastic,* the low burlesque of a less confined material.

(3) *Parody,* the high burlesque of a particular work or author achieved by applying the style of that work or author to a less worthy subject.

(4) *The mock-poem*, the high burlesque of a whole class or literature achieved by lavishing the style characteristic of the class upon a trifling subject. *Satire* is a deliberate attack

[15] John D. Jump, *Burlesque, The Critical Idiom* (London: Methuen, 1961), p. 1.

> on a subject. It is intended to expose and ridicule the subject and evoke the attitudes of contempt and derision towards it. *Invective* is a speech or writing that is denunciatory, abusive and vituperative. The plays of Aristophanes have plenty of instances of invective.

The modes which express the author's comic vision of the world – that is the comic perspective which the author or the characters adopt as a view of life – belong to what may be called situational humour. Among these the irony of fate or cosmic irony is a mode by which God or Destiny or the Universal process is depicted as deliberately contriving events to mock and frustrate the protagonist. Irony in this sense borders on tragedy. It can be seen as a method of reconciling despair and happiness. According to David Worcester, "it tends to neutralise all passions and turn all men into the spectators of the human comedy. . . when the mind is paralysed by conflicting drives, irony offers a way of escaping from the conflict and rising above it."[16] This is a positive aspect of irony. Secondly, "if it is taken playfully in a comic milieu, it is comic irony. For example, it affords scope for the radical contrast between fact and fiction which is at the heart of the comic."[17]

Bharata analyses the phenomenon of laughter by its context and its manifestation. According to the situation involved, *hāsya* is classified into two types – *ātmastha* and *parastha*. If a person laughs by himself, it is *ātmastha*, and if he makes others laugh, it is *parastha*. According to its histrionic manifestation, *hāsa* is classified into six varieties. In *smita*, the eyes are made wide open and in *hasita*, the teeth are shown a little. *Vihasita* is followed by a sweet sound, and *upahasita* by the shaking of the head. In *apahasita*, the laughter becomes so intense that tears well up in the eyes. *Atihasita* is uproarious laughter, with the shaking of the whole body. The first two are associated with the higher, the third and fourth with the middling and the last two with the lower characters respectively. In Kathakali, the sacred dance-drama of Kerala, for instance, the gentle smile characterising women and other mild characters comes

---

[16] David Worcester, *The Art of Satire* (Cambridge: Harvard Univ. Press, 1940), p. 141.

[17] Elkin Calhoun Wilson, *Shakespeare, Santayana and the Comic* (London: George Allen & Unwin, 1973), p. 58.

under the category of *smita*, and the loud shouts of demons and other cruel characters are included in *atihasita*.

The claim of *śānta* as the ninth rasa has been the subject of a lot of discussion. Bharata's *Nāṭyaśāstra* mentions *śānta*."[18] *Śānta* is acceptable as a poetic rasa, but its worthiness as a dramatic or *nāṭya rasa* is held to be doubtful. There is a lot of controversy regarding the *sthāyībhāva* of *śānta*. Bharata has not mentioned the *sthāyībhāva*, *vibhāva*, *anubhāva* or *vyabhicārībhāva* of *śānta*. *Śama* or quietism, *nirveda* or renunciation, *tatvajñāna* or the perception of the Supreme Truth – all these can be considered the possible *sthāyin* of *śanta*. Ānandavardhana regards yet another – *tṛṣnākṣayasukha*, or the pleasure derived by the absence of all desires – as the *sthāyin* of *śānta*.

It is also possible that any one of the other eight *sthāyībhāvas* can be a *sthāyin* for *śānta*. Thus *hāsa*, or laughter has a claim. For a detached person who has perceived the absurdity of the material world, the ordinary man's anxieties and worries over trivial matters appear ridiculous. The actions of the world are just sport (*līla*), and their absurdity evokes nothing but laughter. Nārada, the mythical sage, is a good example to illustrate this point. A sort of play-instinct underlines Nārada's hāsya. It is as if the means by which he achieves his end is hāsya. Basically, Nārada is a sage who has renounced all worldly pleasures, but he is always engaged in the pursuit of "mischief" – his chief device is the surfacing of discord among people. Still, beneath this, he has absolute detachment, for he is totally unaffected by the result of his actions. From such a perspective, even hasa could be regarded as one of the *sthāyins* of *śānta rasa*.

The comic, in the Western sense of the term, has a broad span which includes variety of modes; though comedy is usually linked with laughter, the provinces of the two are not entirely identical. There are many varieties of laughter that do not bear a comic vein. Laughter is sometimes employed as a mask to cover some unpleasant feeling. In this case it has no affinity with the comic. Similarly, the sarcastic smile and the sardonic grin are not positive gestures of comedy. This is not the case with the concept of *hāsya*

---

[18] V. Raghavan, *The Number of Rasas* (Madras: The Adayar Library and Research Centre, 1940), p. 15.

in Indian aesthetics. *Hāsya* seems to be more in the nature of free and merry laughter derived from man's perception of the absurdity of things. In this sense it has a radically "comic" approach to life – as far as definition is concerned, the nearest equivalent to *hāsya* seems to be humour. Both are ascribed to the genially comic in human nature, and both have a spontaneous quality about them. They also share a common point in having a sympathetic or positive approach to life.

The term "catharsis" as used by Aristotle in *Poetics* signifies the purification of the mind through emotional release and the attainment of a level of composure or tranquillity. The word is derived from the Greek "kathairo" which means "to cleanse". Originally, Aristotle uses the term catharsis only with reference to tragedy. In his interpretation of the theory of catharsis, S.H. Butcher observes:

> Tragedy . . . is a vent for the particular emotions of pity and fear. In the first instance, it is true, its effect is not to tranquillise but to excite. It excites emotion, however, only to allay it. Pity and fear, artificially stirred, expel the latent pity and fear which we bring with us from real life, or at least, such elements in them as are disquieting. In the pleasurable calm which follows when the passion is spent, an emotional cure has been wrought.[19]

Though Aristotle refers to *catharsis* only in relation to tragedy, the ideal of *catharsis* can be applied to comedy also. In the theatre laughter is seen as purging the spectator of the vices that are exposed to ridicule on the comic stage. Lane Cooper in his attempt at the reconstruction of Artistotle's discussion of comedy observes that "if you succeed in making an angry or envious man laugh with pleasure, he ceases for a time to be angry or envious. Thus anger and envy might be said to be purged away by comedy."[20] He also says that "comedy is an imitation of an action that is ludicrous and imperfect... through pleasure and laughter effecting the purgations of the like emotions. It has laughter for its mother."[21]

The idea of *catharsis* is developed by Freud in his discussion of the nature of the comic. Eric Bentley sums up Freud's ideal of *catharsis* saying, "Freud carried the idea of Catharsis further than

---

[19] S.H. Butcher, *Aristotle's Theory of Poetry and Fine Art*, p. 246.

[20] Lane Cooper, *An Aristotelian Theory of Comedy* (New York: Harcourt, Brace, 1922), p. 67

[21] ibid., p. 224.

any Aristotelian commentator had ever dreamt of... For Freud, jokes are fundamentally cathārtic: a release, not a stimulant."[22] The aim of humour being the gratification of some forbidden wishes, the idea of the joke reveals itself to the hearer as a sudden shock, and this produces a gush of pleasure. "Inhibitions are momentarily lifted, repressed thoughts are admitted into consciousness, and we experience that feeling of power and pleasure, generally called elation."[23] Thus *catharsis* is effected.

In ordinary social interaction, the fear of laughter or ridicule imposes a sort of restraint on people. In such a context, laughter has a social function – to correct the vices of society. The corrective function of comedy is also traced by Cooper to Aristotle:

> As men in daily life are accustomed to suffer from a sense of disproportion, it is this that is relieved or purged away by the laughter or comedy... By contemplating that disproportions of comedy, we are freed from a disproportion in life, regain our perspective, settling as it were into our proper selves. To Aristotle, the process of settling into our true selves is pleasure; that is his definition of pleasure.[24]

But, to confine comedy to its strictly corrective function through *catharsis*, would only serve to limit the sphere of comedy, because the range of comedy is richer and more extensive than mere social correction.

The effect of *catharsis*, whether it appeals to tragic emotions like pity and fear, or to comic emotions like pleasure and laughter, is one of joy and freedom. This is also the level of experience described by Indian aestheticians as *rasāsvāda*. Irrespective of the nature of the emotion aroused in the mind of the spectator, the ultimate experience in artistic communication is one of aesthetic rapture. Writers on aesthetics have tried to interpret the nature of this aesthetic experience and put forward several theories.

Bharata's dictum "*Vibhāvānubhāvavyabhicārisaṁyogādrasaniṣpattiḥ*" (*rasa* is manifested through the union of *vibhāva*, *anubhāva* and *vyabhicāribhāva*) has led to a lot of discussion on the exact meaning of the terms "samyoga" and "niṣpatti". According to the definitions

---

[22] Eric Bentley, *The Life of the Drama* (London: Methuen, 1965), pp. 228-29.

[23] ibid., p. 230.

[24] Lane Cooper, *op. cit.*, p. 181.

of these two terms, aestheticians interpret the nature of *rasāsvāda* differently. Among these, Bhaṭṭalollaṭa, Śaṅkuka, Bhaṭṭanāyaka and Abhinavagupta represent four different schools of interpretation.

One of the earliest commentators on Bharata who tried to offer a solution to the controversy over Bharata's definition is Bhaṭṭalollaṭa, who represent the *rasotpatti* school. He interprets the term "*niṣpatti*" as "*utpatti*" – "generation of something which develops into *rasa*."[25] To take an example, Duṣyanta who meets Śakuntala in Kaṇva's hermitage is possessed by love and Śakuntala is in a state of mind to return the love. The love at this stage can be termed as *prīti*. This *prīti* under favourable conditions develops into *rati*. The *rati* is *generated* in the lovers due to these *vibhāvas*, and so "*niṣpatti*" corresponds to "*utpatti*". Through *anubhāvas*, this *sthāyībhāva* gets expressed, and it is inferred by the other person. Through the *vyabhicārībhāvas*, this *sthāyībhāva* is intensified. Thus, the term *samyōga* does not merely mean the union of *vibhāva*, *anubhāva* and *vyabhicārībhāva*. It means generation in the case of *vibhāva*, inference in the case of *anubhāva* and intensification in the case of *vyabhicārībhāva*.

In the theatre, the spectator has a mistaken cognition that the actor is the original character himself. So, owing to invalid perception, the actor's gestures and movements are taken to be those of the original character. The spectator is so absorbed in the representation that he enters into the mood of the actor, who, according to him, is the original character, and as a result, he experiences *rasa*.

Bhaṭṭlollaṭa's argument that the spectator experiences *rasa* due to invalid cognition is not satisfactory, because *rasasvāda* is a purely personal experience. Further, Bhaṭṭalollaṭa recognizes different grades in the development of *rasa*. This is a totally mistaken conception of the nature of *rasa*, for *rasa* is a blissful state of mind, and does not allow different gradations. So Bhaṭṭalollaṭa's theory fails to convince.

---

[25] P. Panchapagesa Sastri, *The Philosophy of Aesthetic Pleasure* (Annamalai Nagar: Annamalai Univ., Press 1940), p. 32.

Saṅkuka who puts forward *rasānumitivāda* or inference theory states that *rasa* is not generated as *sthāyībhāvas*, but is inferred, because it has the nature of *anumiti* or inference. When the actor plays the role of Rāma, the spectator assumes that he is Rāma himself – Śankuka equates this idea with the idea of a painted horse (*citraturaganyāya*) in which the painting is taken to be the real horse and not a painting. The actor skilfully represents the character of Rāma by means of *vibhāvas*, *anubhāvas* and *vyabhicāribhāvas*. Though they are unreal (for they do not belong to the actor, who is only imitating Rama), they appear to the spectator as really belonging to the actor because the spectator has the delusion that he is the original character himself. This inferential knowledge of the *sthāyībhāva* in the actor causes the spectator to experience *rasa*.

The description of *rasa* as an imitation (*anukaraṇa*) of *sthāyi* has been subjected to criticism by Bhaṭṭatauta, and this is cited by Abhinavagupta in his *Abhinavabhārati*. According to Bhaṭṭatauta, this statement is wrong from the point of view of Bharata. Śaṅkuka's presumption is that *rasa*-realization is the result of a series of influences, prompted by a desire for further inference, as a result of which the spectator derives pleasure for a considerable time. But this is erroneous, because a desire for further inferences distracts the mind and obstructs the experience of *rasa*.

Bhaṭṭanāyaka describes *rasa* as an inward experience that leads to aesthetic enjoyment (*bhoga*). Artistic expression, as different from linguistic expression, has three different functions – *abhidha*, *bhāvakatva* and *bhojakatva*. *Abhidha* or the primary denotative power makes the meanings clear and makes the spectator acquainted with *vibhāva*, *anubhāva* and *vyabhicāribhāva*. *Bhāvakatva* is a peculiar power in poetry and drama which "serves at once to make the reader or spectator forget himself and transcend his environment and be prepared to enjoy what is toward and to universalize what is going on the stage."[26] The reader or the spectator, who at first recognizes the actor as the character, gradually gets lost in it. This makes him think of the situation in an abstract way, through the operation of *bhāvanā*. This has the effect of a purgation in the

[26] ibid., p. 131.

spectator, and so it is capable of *sādhāraṇīkaraṇa*. Thus, *vibhāvas* and *sthāyi* are also perceived in this general way. By *bhōjakatva*, the attribute of *sattva guṇa*, the generalised *sthāyībhāvas* are enjoyed along with generalised *vibhāvas*, *anubhāvas* and *vyabhicārībhāvas*. Then the spectator derives pleasure, whatever be the emotional quality of the object of perception. This pleasure is different from ordinary pleasure because it is impersonal, but it is also different from the *yogin's* perception of pleasure, because it is derived from objects on the stage – that is, it accepts plurality. The word "*samyōga*", thus, means the cognition of things in a generated form and the word "*niṣpatti*" means enjoyment (*bhoga*). The *sthāyibhāva* is enjoyed as *rasa*, through the operation of *vibhāva*, *anubhāva* and *vyabhicāribhāva*.

Abhinavagupta who contradicts this theory recognizes *vyañjanā* or the suggestive power as competent to do the functions of both *bhāvakatva* and *bhōjakatva*. Also, the term *abhidha* relates to word and not sense – the reader or the spectator comes to understand the mental conditions of the characters through the power of suggestion. According to Bhaṭṭanāyaka, the spectator's pleasure is not personal, it is universalized. This statement is also defective, since *rasāsvāda* must also be the result of an inward experience.

Abhinavagupta who contradicts the theories of his predecessors puts forward his own theory of *rasa*-realization. He says that the minds of all *sahṛdayas* are endowed with certain latent impressions (*vāsana*), and these are *sthāyībhāvas*. While seeing a play or reading a poem, these *sthāyībhāvas* are suddenly awakened by the generalised *vibhāvas*. Here, generalisation (*sādhāraṇīkaraṇa*) means the detachment from ordinary life – that is, they bear no relation to any particular person or circumstance. The *sthāyībhāvas* thus evoked are also in a generalised form. This process makes the spectator transcend his own self, and he is elevated for the time being into a higher plane of consciousness. Thus by suspending his personality in a higher form of bliss, the spectator derives pleasure. It is as if a screen has been lifted off the region of supreme bliss. Bharata's term "*samyoga*" is interpreted to mean "the relation (1) of the Suggestor and Suggested, so far as the *Bhāvas* of the original characters are concerned; (2) of the Revealer and Revealed, so far as the *sthāyībhāvas* of the spectator."[27] Abhinavagupta's theory also explains pleasure in scenes of pathos, because the experience of *rasa* has no connection with the mundane world, but only dormant *sthāyībhāvas* awakened under certain conditions. So, whatever be the nature of the *sthāyībhāva*, the result is supreme pleasure – the experience of *rasa*.

The concept of *sādhāraṇīkaraṇa* expounded by Bhaṭṭanāyaka, Bhaṭṭatauta and Abhinavagupta marks the supreme level of *rasānubhava* because at the height of aesthetic experience, the spectator "loses" himself in the poem or play and is lifted out of his narrow personal self. At this level the experience has no connection to his private self or even to the nature of emotion evoked by the context of the play. The pleasure derived is unique, because being disinterested, it is pure. This experience is equivalent to that of *catharsis*, because both transport the spectator to a region of untainted bliss. Thus *catharsis* and *sādhāraṇīkaraṇa* seem to be identical in their effect, because both lead to the experience of transcendental aesthetic rapture.

The tragic and the comic are two basic impulses in man's nature. In the West, Aristotle considers comedy to be inferior to tragedy. According to him "comedy ... is an imitation of characters of a lower type – not in the full sense of the word bad, the ludicrous being merely a subdivision of the ugly. It consists in some defect or ugliness, which is not painful or destructive."[28] While tragedy deals with a dignified theme, comedy only serves to excite laughter through the exhibition of folly. Further, tragedy deals with the lives of men of high rank, such as kings and aristocrats, while comedy is confined to the lower strata of society.

Aristotle's criticism of comedy applies even today, because it is generally assumed that comedy cannot attain the height achieved by tragedy. On this point, Howarth observes: "one of the clearest distinguishing features of comedy seems to be its lack of that metaphysical dimension which is of prime importance when we come to define tragedy ... here, fate is replaced by a more trivial, a

---

[27] ibid., p. 194.

[28] Aristotle, "Poetics", p. 21.

more impersonal chance."[29] But such views offer only a limited scope for comedy. Once the objective of comedy is accepted as a celebration of life, it attains the grandeur of tragedy. Comedy looks through the cares and anxieties of the mundane world, and is able to overcome them through a spirit of affirmation and reconciliation – this is perhaps what Barber implies in his phrase "the experience of moving to humorous understanding through saturnalian release."[30] In this sense "humour" is not mere ridicule or laughter, but is a way of looking at life – it is an acceptance of life on its own terms. In Western drama, Falstaff perhaps best embodies this larger sense of life itself as a mode of comedy. His extraordinary meaningfulness comes from the way he manages to live defying all the normal rules of social decorum. The very introduction of Falstaff establishes asking Prince Hal, "Now, Hal, what time of day is it, lad?" to which Hal replies: "... What a devil hast thou to do with the time of the day? Unless hours were cups of sack, and minutes capons, and clocks the tongues of bawds, and dials the signs of leaping-houses, and the blessed sun himself a fair hot wench in flame-coloured tafetta, I see no reason why thou shouldst be so superfluous to demand the time of the day" (I Henry IV. I. ii. 8-14). Falstaff flouts the established norms of morality. He represents the triumph of festive liberty over everyday restraints. This attitude to life is best summarised in the meaning of the word "*bhoga*" in Sanskrit which literally means "indulgence in worldly pleasure". Monier Williams in his *Sanskrit-English Dictionary* defines *bhogin* as "having or offering enjoyments", or "a voluptuary". Falstaff is a *bhogin* in that sense. The entire range of Sanskrit dramatic repertory seems to lack a composite figure like Falstaff who encompasses in his own person so many different roles. But the conception of the figure of Kṛṣṇa in the epic *Mahābhārata* illustrates the concept of *bhōga*. Kṛṣṇa, as seen in the epic, is deeply rooted in the affairs of the material world – he is always involved in *karma* or action. But beneath his adherence to life, there is absolute detachment, and this gives a unique dimension to his personality. This could also be the reason why Kṛṣṇa is deified in the legends – he incarnates the basic

[29] W.D. Howrath, *Comic Drama: The European Heritage* (London: Methuen, 1978), pp. 1-2.

[30] C.L: Barber, *op. cit.*, p. 2.

feature that moulds Indian philosophy. The aesthetic transcendence over misery exalts comedy to a level higher than that achieved by tragedy. Eric Bentley regards "misery as the basis of comedy and gaiety as an ever-recurring transcendence."[31] This points to a level in which, after indulging in this life and undergoing all the experiences of life, one rises so high as to perceive the absurdity of material life and is able to view it with philosophic detachment.

Bharata regards *rasa* as the soul of poetry. Later writers on aesthetics have also stressed the importance of *rasa* in artistic experience. The major commentators on Bharata tried to interpret aesthetics in the light of the schools of philosophy to which they were attached. The most important of these are the *Nyāya* school represented by Śaṅkuka, *Sāmkhya* school by Bhaṭṭanāyaka and *Vedānta* school by Abhinavagupta.

Advocates of of *Nyāya* system of philosophy believe in the logical proof, to prove the existence of the objective world. So it is a realistic system, *Nyāya* believes in the multiplicity of souls. There are as many souls as there are subjects capable of cognition. But the cognition is effected through the mind and the senses.

K.C. Pandey summarises the basic precepts of this system:

1. The conditions of knowledge.
2. Means of right knowledge.
3. Theories of error, doubt and knowledge based on similarity.
4. Theory of recognition.[32]

The conditions of knowledge include (1) a cognising subject (2) the object of cognition (3) the resulting state of knowledge (4) means of knowledge, and (5) the connecting links between the subject and the object. The objects of knowledge are infinite – everything in the world except the means of knowledge is the object of knowledge. There are four means of knowledge: (1) Direct perception (*pratyakṣa*), (2) Inference (*anumāna*), (3) Comparison

---

[31] Bentley, *The Life of the Drama*, p. 301.

[32] K.C. Pandey, *Comparative Aesthetics* (Varanasi: Chaukhamba Sanskrit Series, 1959), p. 40.

(*upamāna*) and (4) Verbal testimony (*śabda*). Error or illusion (*vyābhicārijñāna*) in *Nyāya* is a term by which an object is taken to be what it is not. It is a subjective feeling, which lasts only until it is set aside by the right perception. Doubt (*samasya*) is a mental activity by which a person is unable to decide which is the stimulating object -- it is a state of oscillation. Recognition (*pratyabhijñāna*) is a kind of qualified perception. It gives us knowledge of things as qualified by the past.

Śaṅkuka utilises this system of philosophy in his theory of aesthetics. He says that the *sthāyībhāva* is cognisable through inferential knowledge by means of three types of inferential reasons – *vibhāva*, *anubhāva* and *vyabhicārībhāva*. The inference of love from imitative representation on the stage would be, "Rāma, the happy person, is this." The spectator has the mistaken cognition that the actor is the hero himself. According to Śaṅkuka, this is not an erroneous judgement, because the spectator's judgement is aesthetic — not practical, and it is not later contradicted by a subsequent knowledge. There is also no doubt or *samasya* in this aesthetic judgement. The two images, the standard of comparison and the subject of comparison, are fused in the mind of spectator, as in his theory of the painted horse (*citraturaganyāya*). Thus, according to Śankuka, the experience of *rasa* has the nature of an imitation derived through inferential knowledge.

The *Sāmkhya* system is built up on the concept of dualism. It starts with two absolutes – *prakṛti* and *puruṣa*. *Puruṣa* or self is awareness and *Prakṛti* is the external world constituted of the five elements. *Buddhi* enables *puruṣa* to realise the two ideals of life – *bhoga* and *apavarga* – that is, to experience pleasure or pain or to attain spiritual elevation through right knowledge. The theory of the three *guṇas* also belong to *Sāmkhya*. The three *guṇas* are *sattva*, *rajas* and *tamas*, which constitute the effects *sukha*, *dukkha* and *moha* respectively, but each mind has impulses that can transform them into *rājasic* and *tāmasic*. The experience of pain or pleasure is the result of the interaction between *prakṛti* and *buddhi*. What causes pain to one may cause pleasure to another. One who transcends the sphere of pain and pleasure is the one who is capable of recognising the essential disparateness between *prakṛti* and *puruṣa*.

He attains the level of detachment and serenity. But this is not attainable to the ordinary man who cannot transcend his *buddhi*. He can do this temporarily by resorting to the realm of art, for it is a temporary release from the physical world.

Bhattanāyaka advocates the *Sāmkhya* concept of *rasa*. He conceives the experience of *rasa* as enjoyment (*bhoga*). Unlike ordinary conditions of existence, this is impersonal. It is also a temporary transcendence from ordinary life. The terms *abhidha*, *bhāvakatva* and *bhojakatva* have also a direct bearing on the *Sāmkhya* system. Bhaṭṭanāyaka also illustrates the three *guṇas* – during *rasānubhūti* (the experience of *rasa*) *sattva guṇa* predominates, and the other two are temporarily suspended. Thus, according to him, *rasāsvāda* is a temporary transcendence from ordinary life, but also different from spiritual experience.

Vedānta, the monistic and idealistic philosophy, regards *Brahman* or Absolute self as the one and only reality. *Brahman* is of the nature of Bliss or *Ānanda*, because it comprehends the unity behind apparent diversity. Man in ordinary life strives for the possession of material ends – he is kindled by desire. One who is able to transcend desire through the perception of the Final Truth is *jīvanmukta* – a level impossible to attain while one is in the world of illusion (*māya*). When once this *maya* is unveiled, the real nature or *ātman* or Supreme Bliss asserts itself. This is not expressible in words or through any other means of objective knowledge – it can only be realized.

Abhinavagupta discusses the nature of *rasa*–realization through the *Vedāntic* perspective. From the point of view of the spectator, the theatric performance is total impersonal, because there are no personal gains to be achieved in its experience. It is an idealized world, where absolute concentration is possible through the theory of *sadhāranīkarana*. The *sahṛdaya's* mind is absorbed in the dramatic situation, and is free from all distractions. At the summit of this concentration, the evoked *sthāyībhāvas* lift the screen off the region of bliss and *rasa* is revealed (*abhivyakti*) to the spectator. This revelation corresponds to *ātmānanda* or Supreme Bliss.

Jagannatha carries Abhinavagupta's analogy further. He asserts that the experience of *rasa* is the experience of blissful *ātman* itself (and not just experience *similar* to it). But it is also different in the sense that the spectator has the aids like *vibhāva* and *anubhāva*, to kindle the *sthāyi*, so as to obtain pleasure, while the *yogin's* experience is unique. But aesthetic experience, irrespective of the form, is the experience of *ātmānanda* itself, and the *sahṛdaya* has equal status with the *Vedāntin*.

Texts on Sanskrit dramaturgy shun tragedy in the Western sense of the term. Violent scenes like battle, bloodshed and death are also avoided by the canons of aesthetics (*Nāṭyaśāstra*. XX. verse 24). Though there is a lot of conflict and struggle, Sanskrit drama, as a rule, does not end on a tragic note. The ending is always affirmative.

H.W. Wells remarks on the affirmative quality of Indian theatre: "The stage was a ritual to frustrate the malignity of events... The theatre was one of the disciplines by which peace was established within the soul."[33] The insistence on an affirmative ending traces drama to the foundations of Indian thought. Tragedy or gloom has no place in the affirmative quality of Indian philosophy. According to Wells, the emphasis "is not on optimism, but composure."[34] Sanskrit drama provides a lot of scope for pathos and tragedy, but it is never left at the darkest spot – the ending is always on a note of poise. A play begins with a *nāndi* or prayer, usually directed towards the prosperity of the human race. The drama usually portrays the achievement of something that the hero has been aiming to get -- so it is "action with a purpose", the subsequent efforts to achieve it, and the final achievement.

Daśarūpaka states that dramatic action is composed of the following stages – the *bīja* (germ) sets the action. The action has a beginning, and it passes through three stages – *yatna* or efforts, *prāptyāśa* or the prospect of success, *niyatāpti* or the certainty of success and *phalāgama* or the attainment of result. In such a steady course, there is no room for frustration. Between the second and third stages, there is *apāyaśamka* or fear of failure, but it is set right by the attainment of result. Thus any possibility of a calamitous ending is ruled out in Sanskrit drama.

---

33 H.W. Wells, *The Classical Drama of India* (Bombay: Asia Publishing House, 1963), p. 12.

34 ibid., p. 11.

CHAPTER III

THE THEATRE OF COMEDY

A THEATRICAL PERFORMANCE is the temporary construction of an imaginary situation which creates an artistic illusion of reality. The nature of reality to be represented in drama depends on the age in which it is produced, the locale and the taste of the audience. In attempting a comparative study of the theatre of the West and that of Sanskrit, all these factors have to be taken into account. Considering the vast difference between the two theatres in their spirit or inner meaning, Wells has observed: "The likeness between the two theatres defines the essentials of all good drama, the differences describe outstanding distinctions between East and West and so delineate the peculiarities of each."[1]

In India, there have been several attempts to define the idea of the theatre and its relationship to life. According to Sanskrit aesthetics, the theatre does not merely constitute a few hours spent at the play-hall. It has a greater appeal – there is an attempt to equate it with its larger counterpart, namely, life. For example, *Nāṭyaśāstra* declares that the objective of *nāṭya* is to "portray the manners and actions of the people of all the three worlds." (Chap. 1. verse 79). Brahma, the creator of *nāṭya*, also explains it thus: "This *nāṭya* which I have created is enriched by the different moods and situations of the various people of the world. It is an imitation of the ways of the world" (Chap. 1. verse 84). Thus, *nāṭya* has the nature of an imitation. In the West, Aristotle also observes that all fine arts, including tragedy and comedy, are in the nature of "imitation" (*Poetics*, I. ii). But the word "imitation" in these assertions does not seem to imply a photographic copy of life, but an artistic re-creation of life. Butcher, discussing the significance of Aristotle's use of the term "imitation," sees it as the expression of the universality of human experience: "Imitation ... is a creative act. It is an expression of the

---

[1] Henry W. Wells, *The Classical Drama of India* (Bombay: Asia Publishing House, 1963), p.6.

concrete thing under an image which answers to its true idea. To seize the universal and to reproduce it in simple and sensuous form is not to reflect a reality already familiar through sense perceptions; rather it is a rivalry of nature, a completion of her unfulfilled purposes, a correction of her failures."[2] This universality is precisely the objective of the concept of *nāṭya* in Indian aesthetics. The experience of drama is one of pure joy – it is an act of celebration. Pramod Kale describes this experience thus: "The pleasure in drama is not mere sensuous pleasure – epicurean pleasure in its highest sense, which liberates rather than enslaves the body and the soul."[3] In short, it leads the spectator to *rasāsvāda*, the experience of aesthetic rapture.

The theatrical practice of the West and that of India reflect the culture or spirit of the civilizations to which they belong. Broadly examined, the two theatres present enormous diversities and glaring contradictions. Classical Indian drama mostly exploits myth from the two epics, *Rāmāyaṇa* and *Mahābhārata*. Stories are also adapted from the popular legends; mostly they are court comedies. Thus it is completely different from the classical Western practice, which freely incorporates any exploitable source – like folk tales, stories of popular imagination and stories invented by the dramatist himself. To translate the mythical, incantatory experience of Indian drama into the theatre, a powerful medium which integrates all the elements of theatric communication is essential. So, unlike the classical Western theatre which mainly resorts to the verbal medium for theatric conveyance, Indian drama exploits all the verbal and non-verbal aids like music, rhythmical dance and gesture.

The ultimate aim of the theatre according to Sanskrit classicists being *rasāsvāda*, this *rasa* has to be effectively conveyed to the spectator. The medium through which this is done is termed *abhinaya* in Sanskrit, which literally means "to lead towards". According to the manner of representation involved, Bharata has classified abhinaya into four categories:

---

[2] S.H. Butcher, *Aristotle's Theory of Poetry and Fine Art* (London: Macmillan, 1907; rpt. Ludhiana: Lyall Book Depot, 1967), p. 154.

[3] Pramod Kale, *The Theatric Universe: A Study of the Natyasastra* (Bombay: Popular Prakashan, 1974), p.4.

1. *āṅgika*, in which the actor communicates through the effective use of the organs of his body. *Āṅgikābhinaya* gets expressed by hand gestures, facial movements and the like.

2. *Vācika* is verbal communication. The speech uttered by the different characters in a play, as well as the rythmical and musical elements in the play constitutes *vācika*.

3. *Āhārya* relates to the communication through decorative aspects like costume and make-up.

4. *Sāttvika*, the fourth element, is the highest form of *abhinaya* in Sanskrit aesthetics. It is the expression of the actor's mind which has reached a sublime level of existence through his artistic identification with the state of mind of the character he represents. In this condition, he can bring out the essence (sattva) which the character stands for.

Abhinaya or theatric communication can be in the nature of *lokadharmi* or *nāṭyadharmi*, the former standing roughly for a realistic, and the latter for a stylized, representation. According to Bharata, when the *abhinaya* depicts the acts and activities of the people of this world, without employing decorative movements, gestures and postures of the body; when it contains natural or realistic feelings, pure and undistorted... it is said to be *lokadharmi* (*NŚ*. Chap. XIV. verse 64) and when "a performance has an abundance of passionate, spirited speeches and actions, when it is made attractive by the use of theatrical devices, when the *abhinaya* is through decorative movements, gestures and postures of the body; when musical ornamentation is added and when the characters in it are heavenly men, it is known to be *nāṭyadharmi*" (XIV. 65). Bharata also states that *nāṭya* should always be in the mode of *nāṭyadharmi*, because without the use of music, body movements, rhythm, etc., the spectators do not derive theatric pleasure.

Comedy as a theatrical form has had a great appeal in India. Though there are not many accounts giving the details of stage representation of the plays during the time in which they were written, there are some clues supporting this conclusion. The evidence of details texts on dramaturgy like Bharata's *Nāṭyaśāstra*, Nandikeśvara's *Abhinayadarpaṇa* and Śārṅgadeva's *Saṅgītaratnākara* themselves testify to the fact that the drama was intended to be performed. The device of the play-within-the play employed in Bhavabhūti's *Uttararāmacarita* and Harsa's *Priyadarśika* throw some light on this aspect. Many Sanskrit plays are supplied with clues for their acting. There is evidence in all the three plays of Bhavabhūti that they were performed during the festival of Kālapriyanātha – he has exploited the device of the Sūtradhāra to convey this information. *Kuttanīmata*, composed by Damodara Gupta (A.D. 10th century), has a detailed account of the stage-enactments of the first Act of Harṣa's *Ratnāvali*. Kūtiyāṭṭam, the existing form of traditional Sanskrit theatre in Kerala, and Kṛṣṇāttam, the sacred dance-drama of Kerala, are two instances of the stage-enactment of Sanskrit drama.

In Western theatre, comedy encompasses a large sphere. It takes a different direction from tragedy, because it emphasizes the ridiculous side of man's nature, while tragedy idealizes and exalts human behaviour. The comic actor laughs at humanity, and exposes the vanities and pretensions of man. So the acting style emphasizes the ridiculous, physical and commonplace details of everyday life, in an exaggerated manner. So, perhaps, comedy is no more a realistic representation of life than tragedy because, while tragedy exalts and dignifies human nature, comedy exaggerates its triviality. While tragedy remains a fascinating medium to reveal man's quests and inner anxieties, comedy is perhaps the preferred theatric form to cater to all classes and all tastes. This fact seems to be true of the theatre of any country or region in the world. For example, it is true of the theatric form of Old Comedy in Greece as well as that of Kūṭiyāṭṭam in India. Popular taste prefers the oral speech or *vācika* of the Vidūṣaka in Kūṭiyāṭṭam to the elaborate abhinaya of the hero. One of the reasons of this preference may be the fact that it makes the audience feel superior to the comic character. For example, the amusement derived from seeing a stock character like Pantalone or Harlequin on the stage springs from the fact that the audience set themselves mentally on a higher plane than these comic characters and expect them to perform in such a way as to make them laugh. The continued appeal of the clown in the theatre is because of this principle.

The origin of comedy in the West is traced back to Greece. Aristotle's *Poetics* devotes only a few lines to comedy, in which he states that comedy has had no history, because it was not taken seriously. According to Aristotle, "it was Homer who laid down the main lines of comedy by dramatising the ludicrous instead of writing personal satire."[4] In Greece, the first expression of comedy is connected with the worship of Dionysus, the God of wine and fertility. In *Comus*, or the procession of folk-worshippers of the god, the performers, dressed in extravagant costumes, danced, sang lampoons against the chance by-standers and even on public characters. This was gradually elaborated through parody and clowning. The Satyr play is another form which began as a kind of phallic mummery. The performers were dressed as half-men, half-goats, called Satyrs. Gradually, these became the chorus, and stock characters, fitted out with grostesque masks, were added, who burlesqued some legendary situation. Euripides's *Cyclops* is a complete Satyr play.

In contrast to the situation in the West, there is no direct evidence on the origin of drama in India, and so the problem is steeped in conjecture. According to Bharata's *Nāṭyaśāstra*, drama had a divine origin. It was created by Brahma at the request of the Devas and was first staged in heaven at the Indradhvaja festival. It was later transmitted to the human species through Sage Bharata. Despite this theory, Sylvain Levi seeks the origin of drama in the dialogue-hymns of the Vedas, in the dramatic dialogues in the epics *Rāmāyaṇa* and *Mahābhārata*, in the Kṛṣṇa cult, in the puppet-shows which were popular in India, etc. European Orientalists like Weber, Pischel and Windisch suspect the possibility of Greek influence on Indian drama. In a comparative study of Indian and Attic comedies, Levi quotes Windisch who states that "this type of comedy could find an echo everywhere, in Ujjainy as well as in Rome, for it is based on the daily life of ordinary man and possesses many features common to universal mankind."[5] He points out as evidence such dramatic conventions as the division of a play into acts, the soliloquy, aside and the use of curtain. The plot of the play, *Mṛcchakaṭika*, also bears similarities to a typical plot of New Comedy. The play

[4] Aristotle, *Poetics*, in *Aristotle's Theory of Poetry and Fine Art*, p. 17.

[5] Sylvain Levi, *The Theatre of India* (Calcutta: Writers Workshop, 1978), II, p. 56.

has a young man falling in love with a courtesan. The blending of the political and domestic themes is also a typical feature of New Comedy. But according to Levi, all these characteristics do not establish any possible influence, because all these features are common to any drama, not necessarily the Greek alone. Refuting the points of Windisch, Levi observes:

> In spite of its general human appeal, the Attic comedy had to undergo considerable changes to adopt a Roman garb, although Greek civilization had penetrated deeply into Roman life. Plautus and Terence had to practise what they called 'contaminatio' i.e. the combination of the plots of the two plays to make one of their own. If Rome, close as she was to the Greek spirit and temperament, was unable to absorb them without tampering with them, what shall we say of India, so distant from Greek in taste, doctrines and institutions? How could the social conditions depicted in the Greek comedy be assimilated by Indian artists?[6]

Thus, any influence of Greek comedy on Sanskrit drama seems improbable. Sanskrit drama seems to be closer in spirit to Elizabethan rather than Greek comedy. For example, all the three plays of Kālidāsa – *Śākuntala*, *Vikramorvaśīya* and *Mālavikāgnimitra* – fit into the spirit of romantic comedy and in this respect they can be compared to the middle comedies of Shakespeare – *Much Ado About Nothing*, *As You Like It* and *Twelfth Night*. They deal with courtship and romance, and they conclude with the happy union of the lovers. Each of the plays of Kālidāsa has a Vidūsaka employed in the service of the king, a stock figure who is responsible for much of the humour of the play. The Vidūṣaka's task in the play is to provide fun and advise the king on his romantic fancies. These features find a parallel in Shakespeare's comedies also. They revolve around the theme of love. The hero who mostly belongs to the upper class of society is often provided with the comic character of the fool who is responsible for much of the humour of the play. Similarly, Kālidāsa also exhibits skill in providing low comedy. In *Śākuntala*, the scene in which the policemen interrogate the fisherman taken captive for the suspected theft of the royal ring is a scene taken raw from life. The scene is introduced mainly for the purpose of comic relief. The absurd comments of the policemen and their treatment of the case is reminiscent of Dogberry and Verges in *Much Ado About Nothing*. Kālidāsa's plays abound in rich poetry and pic-

---

[6] ibid.

turesque imagery. They are a blend of prose and verse. All these features find a parallel in Elizabethan drama also. Thus classical Indian drama bears many striking points of resemblance to Elizabethan drama.

In ancient Athens, writers of comedy were accorded extreme licence to attack whatever incongruity or folly they saw around them. On the freedom of the comic writer, Lucas Collins observes that "the satiric writer must have felt that his popularity depended upon his aiming his blows only where the popular feeling held them to be well-deserved."[7] He equates the free speech of the comic writer to the freedom of the press in our own age. Thus Aristophanes, the vigorous satirist, who is the most representative writer of Old Comedy holds up to ridicule everything that his eyes behold as incongruous. In the extant eleven plays, he has dealt with a variety of themes, in which he attacks institutions and even living persons. In *Clouds*, the satire is directed against the new school of philosophy that developed in Athens, of which Socrates is the best representative. *Wasps* ridicules the Athenian passion for leadership, while in *Ecclesiazusae,* the satire is upon the ideal republic founded on communistic principles, like the ideal republic of Plato. Aristophanes frequently directs his satire on contemporary persons such as Socrates, Euripides and Cleon. In *Frogs,* the contest between Aeschylus and Euripides, the two tragedians, in the presence of Pluto, with Dionysus acting as the middle-man, is depicted. This theme serves the dual purpose of parodying the lyrics of the two masters, and also ridiculing the genre of tragedy itself.

In Indian drama, it is difficult to discover the sharp sarcasm or severe invective that characterise Aristophanic comedy. Wells notes that in Indian drama, "... in the field of comedy, Gupta sophistication notwithstanding, there are no formulations of specifically comic attitudes, as Aristophanes' sensualism, Cervantes' romantic dualism, Molière's urban materialism, or Machiavelli's calculated satire."[8] An obvious exception to this rule perhaps is seen in *Mṛcchakaṭika* in the character of Maitreya, the Vidūṣaka. Maitreya stands apart from the common rut of Vidūṣakas, because he is more individualised.

---

[7] Lucas Collins, *Aristophanes* (London: William Blackwood, 1907), p. 9.

[8] Wells, p. 8.

Maitreya is a keen observer of the world around him and he subjects to sharp criticism the foibles of society. He levels his attacks on the institutions of wealth and prostitution. He warns Cārudatta that the love of a courtesan could be as fickle as a torch that has no oil in it. Just like a courtesan, the oil-less torch will not burn for the impoverished (Act I). He is moved to wonder at the wealth and splendour of Vasantasenā's mansion, but on seeing the brother of the courtesan clad in expensive clothes and ornaments, he remarks that "he is like a *campak* tree, lush, graceful and perfumed, but growing along the roadway of a cemetery and, therefore, to be shunned by all" (Act IV). Seeing the enormous size of Vasantasena's mother, he sarcastically remarks that "surely they could not have built that magnificent gateway until after they had carted her in like a colossal statue of Śiva" (Act IV).

The satiric or corrective strain in Sanskrit drama is developed in the theatric form of Kūṭiyāṭṭam in the verbal elaboration of the Vidūṣaka who, in the course of interpreting the *śloka*, subjects himself as well as the world to ridicule. The vacika employed by the Vidūṣaka, tinged with humour and sarcasm, is intended to correct the vices of society and lead to the path of virtue. In this respect, he has the licence to dwell upon and ridicule any person, subject or institution that his shrewd eyes behold as foolish or incongruous. In the past, the *cākkyār* or actor was afforded official sanction to criticize on the stage anybody, including the king himself, and no person, however high his position in society, had the right to question the validity of the criticism. During the days when the rulers retained the authority to lay down the law, such liberty on the part of the *cākkyār* imposed some restraint on tyranny or absolutism. This spirit is, thus, closer to the freedom enjoyed by the comic playwright in ancient Athens. The *cākkyār* indulges in satire by discovering new shades of meaning other than the textual, thus elaborating on the subtext. Ideas and situations are exaggerated and magnified, so that he fully exploits the possibilities of every single word. While the incidents are related to contemporary affairs and refers to contemporary persons, the theatric illusion is kept up by treating them as though they are part of the story itself. Thus this method gives the *cākkyār* enormous freedom to make fun of anybody in the theatre.

In Greece, the satirical element in comedy disappears with Menander (324-291 B.C.), the most representative writer of New Comedy. The reconstruction from the fragments of the three extant plays, *Samia, The Shorn Lady* and *Arbitration,* – reveals that they conform to a similar pattern. The basis of each play is a love-story – a young man's love for his neighbour's daughter, or for a mistress whose identity is later revealed. The main characters are upper middle class citizens, but there is also a vivid portrayal of the lower strata of society, like servants, slaves, cooks and courtesans. He takes the audience into confidence about facts of which the characters are ignorant. In *Arbitration,* Charisus's rage at his wife bearing a child as a result of his own violation of her before their marriage, and in *The Shorn Lady,* Polymon's jealousy at Glycera's affection for Moschion, who later turns out to be her own brother, are comically ironic. Katherine Lever remarks that "Menander's view of life is comic not because it is joyous, but because it is satisfying. His comedies present us with an illusion of life."[9] New Comedy lost some aspects of stylization that marked Old Comedy. The costumes, for instance, became more realistic.

The theory of comedy in Plautus and Terence is based on the social and domestic side of man. The intention of comedy is not to degrade or satirize. Even rascals and villains are described not with malice, but with indulgent humour, projecting the ridiculous side of their nature. In the plays, misapprehension or mental error on the part of the characters leads to the confusion in the plot. The superior knowledge of the audience enables them to appreciate the intrigues. For example, the warrior in *The Braggart Warrior* has an exaggerated idea of his personal charm. The primary objective of comedy in Plautus and Terence is not to lecture, but to amuse. The playwright laughs with the characters rather than at them. In this respect, it is comparable to Shakespearean comedy. This is also the spirit behind a major part of Indian dramatic repertory. For example, many Sanskrit plays have the typical motif of the love between the king and a maiden of mistaken identity, who later turns out to be of divine or noble origin, and the play ends with their happy union. Thus the theme of love as intrigue is handled by many

---

[9] Katherine Lever, *The Art of Greek Comedy* (London: Methuen, 1956), p. 200.

dramatists like Bhāsa, Kālidāsa and Harṣa. In Bhāsa's *Avimāraka*, the position is reversed – it is the hero who is mistakenly assumed to be of a low caste, but is actually a prince who is temporarily subjected to a curse.

In the three plays of Kālidāsa, it is seen that he has employed a few devices repeatedly for the creation of humour. In *Vikramorvaśīya*, the love-note written by Urvaśi is misplaced by the carelessness of the Vidūṣaka. The queen herself happens to come across it and she presents it to the king. The discomfiture of the hero, pining for his beloved, at the sudden appearance of the queen is a device repeated in *Malavikāgnimitra* also. The love-intrigues and the mutual jealousies of the queens are also presented with delicate humour. Harṣa models the plots of his plays *Priyadarśikā* and *Ratnāvali* on Kālidāsa's *Mālavikāgnimitra*. Wells prefers to call them "comic romances" because their emotional content is slight."[10] The play-within-the-play in Act III of *Priyadarśikā* is comically ironic, for, in the play-acting, the king himself decides to take the role of the king. Araṇyaka, his sweetheart, poses as Princess Vāsavadatta, while the real Vāsavadatta, unaware of the fact that her husband himself is playing the role, looks on as the spectator. The scene is well-managed, and the comic situation brought about in this way is cleverly manipulated.

Viśākhadatta's (c. 9th century) *Mudrārākṣasa* is a sharp deviation from earlier drama in subject-matter and temper, because the subject is taken from history. The action takes place during the time of Chandragupta Maurya, who ascends the throne after defeating the Nandas, with the help of his able minister Cāṇakya. The play has, thus, a political theme – it portrays Cāṇakya's attempts and his final success in winning over Rākṣasa, the minister of the Nandaṣ, to the Maurya side. Wells sees this play, built up on intrigues and counter-intrigues, as coming close to a problem-play,[11] while Krishna Chaitanya sees "tragic arrest in this well-knit drama of intrigue."[12] Though the play ends as a comedy according to conventional stand-

---

[10] Wells, p. 86.

[11] ibid., p. 63.

[12] Krishna Chaitanya, *A New History of Sanskrit Literature* (New Delhi: Manohar Book Service, 1977), p. 323.

ards, Rākṣasa emerges as a tragic figure, for he has to sacrifice his oath for the sake of personal friendship. Thus the interest of the play is centred not on the plot, but on the development of character. In the West, the interest in character in comedy is most markedly seen in Molière (1622-73), the comic dramatist of France. The most significant comic device is derived from the interaction of a central character who has a dominant obsession and a trickster who exploits this weakness. Sometimes, the trickster-figure is absent, and the hero, by his eccentricity, brings about his own downfall. In *L'Eccle des Femmes,* the plot is conventional. but Arnolphe, the central character, is individualised by his eccentricity – the fear of being made a cuckold. *Amphitryon* mocks the rich and powerful nobles, the rivals of Louis XIV, while *Tartuffe,* presents the irrational, intense fascination of Orgon for Tartuffe, and his exploitation of this weakness.

The comic drama in England has a rich and varied tradition, and it is possible to detect various strands in it. Religion was at the root of medieval English drama. The church exploited drama to propagate faith in the people. At first, drama was presented in the church itself. When the technique of presentation became more elaborate, it moved outdoors, and acquired the support of secular people like guildsmen. In this drama, there were a lot of visual effects to exploit the comic element. At first, the minor clergy were allowed to indulge in satire on the masses and also on the superior clergymen. It is possible that the rigorousness associated with the church is a later development. In the earliest religious performances, Lucifer and Adam were represented as comic and ludicrous, because they brought about their own downfall by revolting against God's omnipotence. The Devil of the Miracle play and the Vice of the Morality play are presented more or less as comic characters. The growing interest in classical drama as well as the changes in social structure affected the nature and form of medieval drama. During the reign of Elizabeth I, religious plays were suppressed. With the Reformation, English comedy assumed a moralistic strain. Sydney defends poetry by asserting that the prime function of comedy is correction. He also asserts that comedy has pure joy, which he calls "delight", but finally opts for didacticism in comedy. English comedy also comes under the influence of the Latin drama of

Plautus and Terence – Nicholas Udall's *Ralph Roister Doister* is indebted to Latin drama in its form and treatment. In *Gammer Gurton's Needle*, this influence is more striking. The plays of John Lyly are different since he exploits the theme of romantic love. He also establishes prose as a medium of drama, but his style is artificial and euphuistic. The double strains of romanticism and didacticism are seen existing side by side in the masters, Shakespeare and Jonson. Shakespeare intersperses high comedy and low comedy, since he wrote for a mixed audience. Shakespeare's comedy is not critical – it is emotional, imaginative and human. It is a blend of many dramatic forms and devices, but Jonson's comedy is realistic and satiric. Jonson takes upon himself the task of correcting folly and attracting hypocrisy. The prologue to *Every Man in His Humour* makes his aim clear:

> ... deeds and language, such as men do use,
>
> And persons, such as comedy would choose,
>
> When she would show an image of the times
>
> And sport with human follies, not with crime.

During the Restoration period, comedy assumes a realistic strain. The action takes place in London, and the characters and situations in the drama are typical. The characters belong to the superior class of society. The dialogue is witty and anti-sentimental. Restoration comedy is marked by detachment, intellectualism and sophistication. The reaction to this comedy of manners comes in the form of Sentimental drama. The advocates of this form attack the Old Comedy as lacking in morals. In Sentimental drama, comedy begins to adopt some of the functions of tragedy. It sentimentally exalts virtue. Its significance is only as a corrective to the restoration comedy of manners.

The plays of Goldsmith and Sheridan are important mainly because they attempt to revolt against sentimentality, and try to revive the old comic traditions on the stage. In the Preface to *The Good Natured Man* (1768) Goldsmith declares himself "strongly prepossessed in favour of the poets of the last age. The term 'genteel comedy' was then unknown amongst us."[13] *The Good Natured Man*,

---

[13] Oliver Goldsmith, *The Good-Natured Man* (London: Macmillan, 1890), p.i.

the first of the comedies that he wrote, pivots on the psychological study of the young Honeywood who is endowed with an excess of good nature, which he carries to a ridiculous excess. This peculiar nature provides the many comic situations in the play. In *She Stoops to Conquer,* Goldsmith continues his attack on Sentimental Comedy. In Tony Lumpkin, the boorish squire whose supposedly dull wit succeeds in throwing every other character into confusion, and who is responsible for most of the comic twists in the plot, Goldsmith has presented the very antithesis of Sentimental drama. Tony, with his double-edged humour, as being a wit and a butt, is reminiscent of Falstaff. Goldsmith's tirade on sentimentality is followed up by Sheridan. In his Prologue to *The Rivals,* Sheridan directly challenges the goddess of the woeful countenance, the sentimental muse, thus offering the defence of his drama. In *The Rivals,* the typical heroine of Sentimental Comedy is satirised in the heroine Lydia Languish, whose fancy is fed on the sentimental novels from the circulating library. Mrs. Malaprop, the stern guardian whose "nice derangement of words" has added another word to the English language, is equally comic. In *The School for Scandal,* Sheridan finds the theme of the gossip-mongers fit for satirical comedy.

Towards the last part of the nineteenth century, Bernard Shaw introduces a new form – the comedy of ideas – to suit his purpose of social correction. Shaw's plays are anti-emotional, anti-romantic, and are interspersed with wit and intellectualism. He attacks hypocrisy behind the social institutions by turning established ideas topsy-turvy. Fred Mayne comments thus: "Shaw continually converts the great into the small, the romantic into the prosaic, the solemn into the frivolous.... or, to generalise the transposition of the comic formula – the expected into the unexpected."[14] This basic paradox is integral to Shaw's treatment of comedy. In *Man and Superman,* the main theme is a paradoxical view of courtship with woman as hunter. Tanner, the idealist, who regards himself as an enlightened crusader finally falls a victim to the woman's chase. In *Candida,* the stronger of the two men turns out to be a domestic pet. In *Arms and the Man*, Shaw deflates the romantic attitude adopted towards the themes of military heroism and love. Shaw expects the reader

[14] Fred Mayne, *The Wit and Satire of Bernard Shaw* (London: Edward Arnold, 1967), p. 54.

or spectator to use his intellect rather than emotion. He is opposed to laughter for its own sake. In this respect, his perspective towards the comic is different from that of the Restoration dramatists.

During the twentieth century, with its breakdown of values, comedy, paradoxically, seems to have established itself as the preferred mode of expression in drama. Inspite of the disasters that have overtaken the world during the twentieth century – like the two world wars, economic depression and the invention of sophisticated weapons of warfare – comedy seems, strangely enough, to have become meaningful in the life of the modern man. It has attained a wide significance, and encompasses the spirit of a new generation. The disillusioning atmosphere makes tragedy an impossibility, because the milieu of tragedy is idealized or exalted.

W.D. Howrath terms this new trend towards comedy as "a new comic response, palpably different from the past." This shift, according to him, works in two ways: "Internally, the distinctions between the various branches of comedy have weakened; high comedy mingles with farce, satire frequently intrudes. Externally, the realms of comedy and tragedy now share certain border territories or coalesce."[15] Thus terms like "dark comedy" and "black humour" come into vogue. J.L. Styan defines dark comedy as "drama which impels the spectator forward by stimulus to mind and heart, then distracts him, muddles him so that time and again he must review his own activity in watching the play."[16]

The plays of Ionesco, Beckett, and Genet share a common experience, which may be said to have evolved into the concept of the Absurd. This seems to equate comedy with farce, thus revealing the comic discovery of man's absurdity of existence. The Absurdists see man's predicament as totally hopeless. The only way to keep sane in this purposeless world is by being passive, by accepting the world as it is. Beckett's application of this concept in his *Waiting for Godot* has had a powerful impact in the post-war world.

---

15 George Brandt, "Twentieth Century Comedy" in *Comic Drama: The European Heritage*, ed. W.D. Howrath (London: Methuen, 1978), p. 168.

16 J.L. Styan, *The Dark Comedy: The Development of Modern Comic Tragedy* (Cambridge: Cambridge Univ. Press, 1968), p. 262.

In India, Kūṭiyattam, the mode of theatre which claims to have an antiquity of about two thousand years, emphasizes the imaginative use of all the visual and aural elements of drama. This theatric form chiefly resorts to the *nāṭyadharmi* mode of *abhinaya*, incorporating *tauryatrika*. Thus it is the art of elaboration moving towards perfection through stylized acting. The text of the play serves only as a bare skeleton to provide the basic material which the actor has to elaborate through his skilful *abhinaya*. Kūṭiyāṭṭam employs all the four modes of *abhinaya*, namely *āṅgika*, *vācika*, *āhārya* and *sāttvika*, in order to achieve effective communication with the spectator. Thus, by an imaginative use of all the elements of drama, the play transcends the limitation of the text, gains a multi-dimensional significance, and the experience attains a level of sublime joy. This mode of theatric communication is completely different from the Western theatre which mostly depends on the *lokadharmi* mode of *abhinaya*. In the West, the actor chiefly resorts to *vācika* or the oral rendering of passages in the text. The other devices only support and re-inforce this chief device of acting. This may be seen with reference to Bernard Shaw's concept of dramatic practice. On seeing John Barrymore's production of Shakespeare's Hamlet in performance, Shaw criticises Barrymore for editing the play and "filling it up with an interpolated drama of your own in dumb show". He says: "My own opinion is ... that of an author. I write plays that play for three hours and a half even with instantaneous changes and one short interval. There is no time for silences or pauses: an actor must play on the line and not between the lines, and must do nine-tenths of his acting with his voice."[17] This method of acting seems completely different from the traditional Sanskrit dramatic practice represented by Kūṭiyāṭṭam, in which the actor is encouraged to resort to an elaborate method of improvization. This may be compared to the phenomenon of the ice-berg. The text of the drama in Kūṭiyāṭṭam is like the tip of an ice-berg, in which only one-tenth of the whole is visible from the surface. All the potential resources are embedded deep inside the text, and the actor's task is to unravel the hidden meaning effectively to the spectator. Thus,

---

[17] Bernard Shaw, "A Letter to John Barrymore," in *Shakespeare's Tragedies: An Anthology of Modern Criticism,* ed. Lawrence Lerner (1963; rpt. London : Penguin, 1964), p. 87.

the effective script is one in which the author has said very little, leaving the major share to the actor who has to improve upon and fill the gap in the author's version. This may be one of the reasons why Bhāsa is theatrically more effective than Kālidāsa. While Kālidāsa describes in detail each shade of meaning and explicates each emotional variation in a richly poetic language, Bhāsa's drama is devoid of such poetic embellishments. The dialogue he employs is often short, but intensely dramatic. Western drama, on the contrary, is a theatre mainly of words. Applying the ice-berg phenomenon, it is seen that almost nine-tenth is visible on the surface, only one-tenth being left to the imagination of the actor.

Indian theatre draws heavily upon the epics and mythical legends for its plot. So a degree of stylization seems to be essential to make it credible in the theatre. This may be one of the reasons why Indian drama resorts to the *nāṭyadharmi* method of dramatic presentation. Another reason could be the nature of the demand on the spectator – for example, the theatre of Kūṭiyāṭṭam or Kathakali presupposes a certain kind of spectator. The Indian texts on dramaturgy have set down the specific characteristics of the ideal spectator or *sahṛdaya*, "the one with a good heart". In the tradition of Indian drama, the action does not interest the spectator on account of its plot-development, because he is already familiar with the story. His interest is in watching the elaboration of certain high points of histrionic skill and also in the total experience, and so a knowledge of the dramatic conventions like the use of gesture, music and other elements of dramatic presentation is essential for him.

Kūṭiyāṭṭam, thus, exploits all the elements of *abhinaya*. In *āngika*, the meaning of the *śloka* is interpreted through gestures and facial movements, so as to bring out the multiple dimensions of meaning. First he orally recites the *śloka*, accompanied *mudra* or gesture. Then he analyses it according to its verbal meaning, thirdly enacts the superficial meaning, and lastly, dwells at length on the meaning. This method gives it an elasticity not attainable in Western drama. The actor who describes heaven, deep sea or mountain does not need visual embellishments like stage-setting to re-inforce his theme. He recreates the splendour of heaven or the loftiness of a mountain before the spectator, who is able to recapture in his mind the scene;

and this elaborate acting strikes him much more forcefully than the unidimensional physical setting. In the same way, *vācika* is also subjected to transformation. In Kūṭiyāṭṭam, the Vidūṣaka's oral rendering of *nirvahaṇa* or *puruṣārthas*, especially his presentation of *Mantrānkam* (the third Act of Bhāsa's *Pratijñāyaugandharāyaṇa* illustrates the elaboration of action through the medium of *vācika*. The *puruṣārthas* of Kūṭiyaṭṭam are a comic imitation of the original *puruṣārthas*. The Vidūṣaka's task is to unravel the full possibilities of this basic idea. In *Mantrānkam*, the Vidūṣaka in the guise of a jesting beggar narrates his previous story and reflects upon the possibilities of saving his master from prison. In *Bhagavadajjukīya*, the speech of the Vidūṣaka includes a tirade on Buddhist philosophy. These speeches, lasting for several days, digress from the main theme and touch on various subjects. Several stories, maxims and proverbs are cited with great elaboration and a lot of humour. Thus, here too, the unidimensional plot of the story attains a multidimensional significance. The *āhārya* is also stylized, since most characters have fixed patterns of costume and make-up. Kūṭiyāṭṭam employs a specialised kind of drum called *miḻāvu*, which is a big bronze pitcher, the mouth of which is covered with leather. Kūṭiyāṭṭam, being a ritualistic form of drama, is originally connected with the temple, and perfdrmed in the theatre-house called Kūttampalam.

Kūṭiyāṭṭam was remodelled into its existing form during the time of Kulaśekharavarman (A.D. 10th century) who, with his friend Tōlan, introduced many improvizations in it. He introduced detailed texts on choreography called *kramadīpikas* and *āttaprakārams*. *Āttaprakāram* describes the *ślokas* and illustrates the methods and means by which the actor can elaborate them. *Kramadīpika* is a practical guide which deals with other relevant details which the playwright has not communicated. For example, it deals with details of make-up, production, stage-setting, etc. Kulaśekharavarman also introduced the elaborate mode of *abhinaya* of the hero. In order to break the monotony of *āṅgika abhinaya*, he introduced the comic character of the Vidūṣaka and gave him the right to speak in the vernacular. He also introduces the convention of the narration of *puruṣārthas* by the Vidūsaka.

Kūṭiyāṭṭam treats the Acts or *ankās* of Sanskrit drama as full-fledged plays, and subjects them to elaboration. For example, Śaktibhadra's *Āscaryacūḍāmaṇi* is a seven-act play in which each act has the status of an independent play – Act of the Hermitage (*Parṇaśālāṅka*), Act of Śūrpanakhā (*Śūrpaṇakhāṅka*), Act of the Illusory Sītā (*Māyāsītāṇka*), Act of Murder of Jaṭāyu (*Jaṭāyuvadhāṅka*), Act of the *Aśoka Garden* (*Aśōkavanikāṅka*) and Act of the Ring (*Aṅgulīyāṅka*).

Similarly, based on Bhāsa's *Abhiṣekanāṭaka*, there are three plays in vogue in Kūṭiyāṭṭam – *Bālivadhāṅka*, *Tōranayuddhāṅka* and *Māyaśīrṣāṅka*.

An example from *Tōraṇayuddhāṅka* will illustrate the method of elaboration in Kūṭiyāṭṭam. The scene shows Rāvana deeply immersed in thought after he learns that Hanumān, a mere monkey, has destroyed the Asoka garden and killed many of his people, including his son.

> Rāvaṇa: (Deep in thought. Reflecting) What a pity! Even if the Devas and Asuras combine their forces, it is difficult to even think of conquering Lanka. In such a place, a monkey has entered disregarding Rāvaṇa's prowess.

The description of Lanka

> How is that Lanka? (If you ask so) With forts, high walls, flag-posts, array of elephants and horses, rows of chariots, gardens, bathing-places, eating-places, fortresses, places of worship, courts, temples (depicts each of these elaborately by means of gestures accompanied by appropriate body movements and facial expressions).
>
> It is with protected by trenches loaded with weapons and by armed Rāksasās. In such a palace, it is a pity that a monkey has broken in.
>
> I had once overcome all the three worlds in battle. I attacked Kailāsa, frightened Parameśvara, Pārvati and their *bhūta* escorts. When I started to go back, I had behaved disrespectfully to Pārvati and Nandikeśvara, and they cursed me. Can all this be the result of that curse?
>
> Earlier, I became haughty after conquering all the three worlds. I attacked Mount Kailāsa inhabited by Pārvati and a host of *bhūtas*.
>
> If you ask how,
>
> One day, adorned with ornaments like the crown, bracelets, etc. and attended by Rāksasas holding the royal umbrella and other royal insignia, I was occupying the throne in my court, when
>
> (Seeing a messenger)

A messenger is coming. What does he say, after offering a piece of silk and the bracelet?

(In the guise of the messenger) I am the messenger of Vaiśravana. You must discard your unholy ways . The Devas and the sages are thinking of ways to destroy you. Vaiśravana sends you this message.

(In the guise of Rāvaṇa) You say so? (Gets angry, takes the messenger by the hair, draws sword and kills him. Then with the Rāksasa army reaches Alakapuri and challenges Vaiśravaṇa. Then the Rāksasas and the Yaksas are engaged in war, when Vaiśravaṇa arrives in the Puṣpaka plane, catches hold of him and is about to behead him, stops, reflects, decides not to kill him and throws him away. Takes the Puṣpaka plane, boards on it and starts his travels. The way is blocked at Kailāsa.)

(To the pilot) Ho, pilot! Why has the plane stopped?

(Acting as though he has heard him) Blocked on the Kailāsa peak? Ask Kailāsa to move out of my way.

(As pilot) Master, Śri Parameśwara resides on this mountain.

(As Rāvaṇa) Is it a sufficient reason to block my way? Ask him to move away.

(Hearing, again) What? No movement? In that case, just watch. Let me displace it.

(Gets down from his seat stool and takes a good look). This mountain is not too trivial.

Description of the displacement of Kailāsa

(Standing low, looks slowly from one side to the other – takes a view around the valleys, looks straight up for the lofty areas. Looks with a small leap for the rocks, etc. Glances backwards for peaks).

This mountain is not insignificant. (Acts out in detail peaks, bulges, sides, caves, top, trees, streams, lions, elephants, etc.).

O Wonder! Never seen a mountain like this before.

O Kailāsa! You must move out of my way. What? No?

(Gets ready to move the mountain. Strikes at it. Slips his hands under it. Sways it, lifts it and throws it up into the sky. Throws it up five or six times. In between plays chess).

Like this, I threw up Kailāsa and thus pleased Śri Parameśwara. How is that?

The Description of the Separation of Pārvati

When Śri Parameśwara is sitting with Pārvati, Pārvati observes Ganga on Śiva's head:

(Rāvana enacts this *śloka* by taking the roles of both Śiva and Pārvati).

(As PĀRVATI): Maheśa, what is there on your head?

(As ŚIVA): Lady, it is water.

PĀRVATI: There is a face.

ŚIVA: That is a lotus.

PĀRVATI: I see curls of hair.

ŚIVA: They are small waves in the water.

PĀRVATI: I see eyes.

ŚIVA: Aren't they black fish?

PĀRVATI: Those two breasts?

SIVA: Cakravāka birds.

At this stage, Pārvati is displeased and annoyed, gets angry with her husband, and starts to leave, when Kailāsa moves.

Pārvati is frightened, and embraces Śiva. In order to calm her down, Siva applies a slight pressure on Kailāsa with his toes.

When Śiva does that, Rāvaṇa's twenty hands get stuck under Kailāsa and he cries out aloud, and all the three worlds are filled with the noise.

Then Śiva appears before him and says: "Because you filled all the three worlds with your voice ("rava"), you will be renowned as 'Rāvaṇa.'"

Siva blesses him and bestows on him the sword Candrahāsa. Then Pārvati also wants to give some blessing. Rāvaṇa refuses the offer by saying that he will not accept anything from a woman. Then Pārvati curses him with the word "May a woman be the cause of your destruction".

Nandikeśvara, the servant of Śiva, appears by the side of Rāvaṇa in the guise of a monkey and asks, "What favour shall I bestow on you?" Then Rāvana jeers at the appearance of the monkey, and Nandikeśvara curses, "May your race be destroyed by monkeys." Can this be the effect of that curse?

The elaborate *abhinaya* sketched above is based on a single *śloka*. This is an occasion when the play gets a multi-dimensional significance, and the production becomes a work of art much more important than the text itself. So the successful text in Kūṭiyāṭṭam is one in which the author has provided a lot of gaps to be filled with action on the stage.

In Kathakali, *abhinaya* is effected mainly through *āngika*, because *vācika* is rendered by singers standing behind the actors. The actor resorts to an elaborate code of *mudras*, and this is reinforced by facial expressions and the movements of parts of the body. The oral rendering of the text is the task of the background musicians who set the lines to rhythmical music, and the actor has to operate within this framework. But once the passage is rendered, the actor has the freedom to improvize and elaborate on the theme, and here he gets a chance to exhibit his knowledge and skill. This situation also helps to unearth the subtle shades of meaning in the text, when there are voids to be filled in by action on the stage, and these are later summarised in *ślōkas*. The costume and make-up of Kathakali have no correspondence with realism – they are symbolic, and represent fixed psychological traits. For example, the facial make-up of *katti* is different from that of *pacca*. In addition to royal grandeur, *katti* is also suggestive of traits like valour or prowess. *Pacca*, though it is used for kings, is suggestive of mild characters. Thus, Duryōdhana, Rāvaṇa and Kamsa belong to the first category, namely *katti*, while Dharmaputra, Naḷa and Kṛṣṇa belong to the second, that is *pacca*. Like Kūṭiyāṭṭam, Kathakali also invokes a supernatural atmosphere, for its characters and story are based on supernatural legends. The stage-setting is almost nil – with only a brass-lamp provided with two wicks, one directed at the actor and the other at the spectator – and the actor conveys the feelings of character through his elaborate abhinaya.

Thus in Kūṭiyāṭṭam and Kathakali, the action takes place in the mind of the spectator through the histrionic skill of the actor, rather than just on the physical stage. Their scope becomes unlimited, because there is no limitation to the capacity of imagination of the human mind. This technique makes these two styles unique. and establishes them as highly advanced forms of theatric art.

Though there may be a lot of disparities between Western and Indian drama with regard to their theatrical practice, there are striking similarities in the form as well as the content of the two theatres. One such area pertains to the prevalence of farce in the Western theatre and prahasana in Sanskrit theatre. In the West, farce is a form of drama which has the sole purpose of creating mirth in the theatre. It is a simple and direct expression of riotous fun, unrestrained by reason. On the nature of farce, K.M. Lea observes that "when we care for neither characters nor motives, but

[18] K.M. Lea, *Italian Popular Comedy* (Oxford: Oxford Univ. Press, 1934), pp. 184-85.

are content to be amused by whatever absurdity may be trumped up, it is farce."18 Farce is in the first place, unliterary and theatrical. It avoids a convincing plot and consistent characterization. The audience is provided with a rapid series of laughs. Often the laughter produced in farce is attained by the juxtaposition of mutually contradictory elements, so that the effect is comically startling. The plot has only a nominal value. The spectator is not concerned with the progress of the plot or its consequence – the interest is only in the creation of fun. Allardyce Nicoll distinguishes farce from formal comedy: "In comedy, laughter is present, but only within measure: indeed seldom do we find any of the comedies keeping the house in a roar of merriment, which is precisely the effect aimed at in any farcial entertainment."[19]

The beginnings of farce may be traced back to France. Medieval French drama had farcical elements. It is lacking in religious or didactic motive, and shows the ridiculous depravity of man. Probably, one of the best examples is *Pierre Patelin,* an anonymous French play of the fifteenth century. It depicts the story of the lawyer Patelin who manages to outwit a merchant to whom he owes some money. The plot is of little consequence, and it shows a series of knaves outwitting each other.

The Italian Commedia dell'arte of the sixteenth century relies on the farcical technique. This theatrical form, absolutely theatrical rather than literary, appeals to all classes of people with different tastes. This is adaptable to any theatrical environment, and introduces a set of stock characters. Evert Spinchorn, in his Introduction to Giacomo Oreglia's *Commedia dell'arte*, says that it was "Entertaining for both high-brow and low-brow, comprising tried and true situations, endlessly varied, always undemanding intellectually, often raunchy and vulgar, and at its best, vigorous and spirited as only popular art can be."[20] This mode of theatre is purely the creation of the actors. Their action, with a lot of acrobatics and improvization, has more meaning than words. Among all the masked characters, the figure of Harlequin became the most popular. He has no direct

---

[19] Allardyce Nicoll, *The Theatre and Dramatic Theory* (London: George Harrap, 1962), p. 88.

[20] Evert Spinchorn, *Commedia dell'arte* (London: Methuen, 1968), p. i.

bearing on the drama, but his task is to keep the interest alive through wild acrobatics and parodies. Moreover the Pantalone, the Doctor, the Scaramouche, Brighella, Zanni or servants – all these are assigned fixed roles. Felicity Firth observes that "it is the pleasure of knowing and not knowing, of watching a predictable figure with familiar, even loved, idiosyncrasies, in an unpredictable figure or fantastic situation. It was probably the speciality of the commedia clown which was responsible for his life-span over 300 years, and for the spread of his fame over the whole of Western Europe."[21] Thus this theatrical form combines all the features of farce.

The dramatic category of *prahasana*, in which *hāsyarasa* predominates, is of popular origin and vogue. Unlike what happens in the other dramatic forms in Sanskrit, the subject-matter of *prahasana* is the dramatist's invention, and so there is considerable freedom for the writer. *Daśarūpaka* classifies *prahasana* into three – *śuddha* or regular type, *vikṛta* or modified, and *samkīrṇa* or mixed.[22] *Śuddha prahasana* is full of comic speeches and is performed with appropriate costume or language. It contains heretics, brahmins or low characters like servants and parasites. The *vikṛta* type is represented by eunuchs, chamberlains and ascetics. In *samkirṇa*, rogues dominate the scene. Thus it deals with the tricks and characters of every kind, but violent manners are excluded. *Daśarūpaka* says that the laughter in *prahasana* is six-fold – it ranges from gentle smile (*smita*) to the uproarious laughter (*atihasita*).

Among the *prahasanas* in Sanskrit, Mahendravikramavarman's *Mattavilāsa* and Bodhāyana's *Bhagavadajjukīya* are the most popular and both have been adopted to the Kūṭiyāṭṭam style of presentation.

In *Mattavilāsa*, the scene is laid in Kānci, and it severely ridicules the degenerate religious practices of the time, including those of Buddhism. The Śaivite Kapālin and his wife hold the stage from beginning to end, and their absurd, drunken revelry constitutes the entire action of the play. The Buddhist mendicant Nāgasena, on account of his greed for food, his desire for a voluptuous life-style

---

[21] Felicity Firth, "Comedy in Italy" in *Comic Drama*, p. 74.

[22] George C.D. Haas, trans., *The Dasarupaka of Dhanamjaya* (New York: AMS Press Inc., 1965), p. 99.

and his weakness for women, represents degenerate Buddhism. Bahrukalpa, the *pāśupata*, and the madman who possesses the skull belonging to the Kapālin, are portrayed with humour. The language of the play is also suited to its theme. The liquor-shop is compared to a sacrificial ground, and even minute details of the comparison are vividly described.

In Kūṭiyāṭṭam, *Mattavilāsa* undergoes a wide deviation from its text. The Kapālin, accidentally having committed the murder of a *brāhmin* boy, worships Lord Śiva, who, pleased with the austerity of his penance, grants him Oneness (*sārūpya*) with Himself. After this, he decides to become a Kapālin and please people by dancing, till he comes One with the dancing God. The performance is intended to make the spectator aware of the two levels of meaning embedded in the play – the obvious superficial level constituting the low comedy arising out of the drunken revelry of the Kapālin and the inner philosophical level which equates his nonsensical extravagance to the self-absorbed dance of Lord Śiva, who is "himself a spectator and who dances seized of emotions and portraying sentiments comprising the course of three worlds by speech and dress, by action and feeling."[23] He is intoxicated not with the effect of liquor, but with the experience of the Supreme Truth – here laughter serves as an exterior sheath to cover up a deeper philosophical idea.

The title of the play *Bhagavadajjukīya* is itself suggestive of humour, because of the curious juxtaposition of two types of characters with seemingly contradictory attributes – "*bhagavān*" meaning a saint, and "*ajjuka*", a courtesan. The chief device employed by the dramatist is the interchange of souls between a courtesan and a saint, thereby evoking an extremely hilarious situation when the saint adopts the manners and language of the courtesan and vice versa. The sage's disciple named Śāndilya who has the characteristics of a typical Vidūṣaka is another source of humour, and the two threads are cleverly interwoven to produce a totally comic effect. The Sūtradhāra announces the superiority of *hāsya* among the *rasas*, and the Vidūṣaka paradoxically announces his ignorance of the dramatic form of *prahasana*. The play exploits language to increase the comic

---

23 N.P. Unni, Trans., *Mattavilasa Prahasana of Mahendravikramavarman* (Trivandrum: College Book House, 1974), p. 71.

effect, when the yōgin, after the interchange of souls, starts speaking in the manner of the courtesan, and vice versa – the courtesan beckoning Śandilya to study and even exposing the ignorance of the physician.

This *prahasana* in Kūṭiyāṭṭam presentation takes thirty-three days, the Vidūṣaka taking up a major share of the action. With humorous anecdotes, Śāṇḍilya narrates his life-story up to the time he joins his present *guru*. He touches on various fields and subjects many institutions to sharp ridicule. It is here that he attacks Buddhist philosophy. The Vidūṣaka's speech has a double meaning, the superficially farcical and the deeper philosophical. When the Vidūṣaka says that he joined the Buddhist order to get an early breakfast, he means that he set out in quest of spiritual food. Not finding satisfaction in the Buddhist theory which accepts seeing as believing, he has come to his present *guru*. Thus here too laughter serves only as a cover for a deeper metaphysical meaning.

The *prahasana* the Indian drama has similarities with the farce in Western drama. In both, there is a deliberate attempt to provoke laughter. The characters mostly belong to the lower classes and their extravagant frolics constitute the theme of the play. In both, the story is imaginary. The main device to provoke laughter is the creation of an incongruous situation, which is by its very nature funny. But there seems to be an obvious difference. In farce, the laughter is for its own sake. There is no other purpose in farce than arousing laughter. But *prahasana* as is seen from the two plays *Bhagavadajjukīya* and *Mattavilāsa*, has a deeper layer of meaning embedded in the obviously farcical. In *Bhagavadajjukīya*, through the medium of laughter, the author seems to probe into man's quests and innermost needs. The problem is unresolved even at the end of the play. After the action is over and the souls re-enter their respective bodies, the confused Śāndilya asks his *guru*: "master, what is all this?" to which he gets no definite answer. Thus the play leaves its characters and the spectators in doubt about the fundamental issues of human existence. This metaphysical dimension is totally lacking in Western farce, which is intended merely to provoke laughter.

The association of comedy with ridicule has had an impact on the way comic characters are judged in drama. Aristotle considers comedy to be inferior to tragedy because comedy represents men as worse than they are, while tragedy represents them as better. But once the experience in comedy is accepted as the affirmation of a positive approach to life, a completely different picture emerges. The comic protagonist in drama, who adopts a subversive way of life, by turning established ideas topsy-turvy, becomes a figure not of derision, but of admiration. He attains the stature of a hero – a comic hero. On this point, Robert M. Torrance observes that the concept of comedy as derision was largely adopted by the culturally upper class of society: "But from this altered vantage point of the lower classes, looking at society from the bottom up, a radically different, if largely inarticulate, conception of comedy begins to emerge. The comic opponent of established authority, however knavish or buffoonish his character, however ludicrous or indecorous his activities, is no longer primarily a butt of mockery, but a vessel of sympathetic identification – when the invincible underdog of fantasy enters a world we recognise as our own... he assumes the dimensions of a comic hero."[24] His recklessness and libertine fatness become a virtue rather than a flaw in his character, because they bestow on him the licence to utter truths that are otherwise concealed.

Another basic feature of the conception of the comic hero is his freedom from restraint. The comic protagonist is not shackled by the ordinary norms of society – he distorts and disrupts the established order of things. He regards the world as patterned to serve his will. William E. Gruber calls him an "anarchist" in the sense that "he represents forces not within *any* plan; he is the wild man, the being who can never be absorbed even as a scapegoat in any system whatsoever."[25] In short, he is an 'outsider' as far as the established traditions of society are concerned. The institution of the fool in Western theatre and of the Vidūṣaka in Sanskrit theatre has relevance from this perspective, because of their affirmation of a

---

[24] Robert M. Torrance, *The Comic Hero* (Cambridge: Harvard Univ. Press, 1978), p. 8.

[25] William E. Gruber, "The Wild Men of Comedy: Transformations in the Comic Hero from Aristophanes to Pirandello", *Genre*, XIV (Summer 1981), p. 210.

subversive way of life, because it affords them protection for the audacities that others lack.

The Oxford English Dictionary offers a threefold classification of the nature of the fool: "(1) One who is deficient in judgement or sense, one who acts stupidly, a silly person, a simpleton (2) One who professionally counterfeits folly for the entertainment of others, a jester, a clown (3) One who is deficient in, or destitute of reason or intellect, a weak-minded or idiotic or mad person, or one who is made by circumstances to appear a fool, or a person who imitates for the non-fools the foolishness of being innately silly." These sum up the basic traits in the conception of the fool, who has antecedents and relatives in all parts of the world.

In the West, the history of the figure of the fool is an ancient and complex one. Barber records that there were festivals dedicated to the inversion of the normal social order, the most important of them being the Feast of Fools, Shrovetide and Carnival. The figure of the fool became an indispensable element during the Renaissance. Fools were attached to the household of great lords and also to the court, and were accepted and popular figures of the stage. Thus he was in real life, and more especially in the theatre, an expert and witty commentator on the follies of mankind. The status of being a professional fool gives him a new dimension that is denied to the ordinary man. The motley invests him with the freedom to "speak wisely what other men do foolishly."[26] The fool has an advantage over the others in anticipating the reaction of the audience. His primary concern is to divert the mind of his audience, and so he has to train his intellect in such a way that new ideas and intuitions strike him much faster than others.

The problem of the origin of the Vidūṣaka has been a subject of controversy in Sanskrit drama. His origin is traced by Windisch to Greek drama and the Roman mime. According to Lindenau, he is derived from the figure of Vṛṣākapi in Ṛg Veda. A.B. Keith discovers his origin in the Vedic ritual, that of the Mahāvrata ceremony in which a *brahmin* and a courtesan are introduced as engaged in coarse abuse of each other.[27] G.K. Bhat seeks his origir from the

---

[26] *As You Like It,* I. ii. 79.

[27] A. Berriedale Keith, *Sanskrit Drama in its Origin, Development, Theory and Practice* (Oxford: Oxford Univ. Press, 1924), p. 30.

evidence in the *Nāṭyaśāstra* of the conflict between the Devas and the Asuras. According to him, the earliest representation of a comic character is the figure of the Asura, a symbol of evil, whose discomfiture became a matter of amusement.[28] I. Sekhar maintains that the fore-runner of the Vidūṣaka is the *Cākkyār* or his type in Dravidian theatre, for in this he is given wide freedom to indulge in the witty, humorous, silly and even vulgar.[29]

The Vidūṣaka appears in Sanskrit drama as a stock character with stock traits. Minute details regarding his speech, manners and dress are recorded in texts like *Nāṭyaśāstra* and *Sāhityadarpaṇa*, and the Vidūṣaka should be able to impart *hāsyarasa* by all these means. Bharata describes him as a dwarfish, deformed person (XIII.110). *Sāhityadarpaṇa* sees his "*svakarma*" as creating comedy through his actions, physical appearance, dress and speech (III. 48). His fondness for quarrel is also a significant trait. Corresponding to the four types of heroes, there are four types of Vidūṣakas also. The one who attaches himself to the Gods is *Lingi*, an ascetic, to the king is *Dvija*, a brahmin, to the minister if *Rājajīvi*, an employee of the king, and to the *brahmin* is *Śiṣya*, a pupil. Nārada who appears in Bhāsa's *Bālacarita* and *Avimāraka*, who prides himself as a mischief-maker, instigating quarrels among the Devas and the mortals, is an example of the first type. The *brahmin* who appears as a companion – *narmasaciva* or minister in sport – of the king in the romantic plays like *Avimāraka* and *Abhijñanaśākuntala* come under the second category. The third division includes Vasantaka, who appears as Yaugandharāyaṇa's friend in Bhāsa's *Pratijñāyaugandharāyaṇa*. Śāndilya, the disciple of the yōgin in *Bhagavadajjukīya*, represents the fourth type of Vidūṣaka.

The humour of the Vidūṣaka is multi-faceted. He subjects himself and the world around him to ridicule. Thus self-derision and satire are the two techniques for evoking fun. This dual role of being a butt and a wit makes him a favourite with the audience.

The institution of the Vidūṣaka as well-established during the time of Aśvaghoṣa, because in his Buddhist play *Śāriputraprakaraṇa*,

---

[28] G.K. Bhat, *The Vidushaka* (Ahmedabad: The New Order Book Co., 1959), p. 23.

[29] I. Sekhar, *Sanskrit Drama: Its Origin and Decline* (New Delhi: Munshiram Manoharlal, 1977), p. 78.

the Vidūṣaka is introduced as a comic character. But Bhāsa's plays seem to establish his traits and fix him as a character. Vasantaka in Bhāsa's *Pratijñāyaugandharāyaṇa* and *Swapnavāsavadatta* and Santuṣta in *Avimāraka* are responsible for much of the humour of the plays. In Bhāsa's *Cārudatta* and Śūdraka's *Mṛcchakatika*, the Vidūṣaka, named Maitreya, serves as a dramatic necessity to balance the sorrowful condition of Cārudatta's poverty. He is also an irresistible epicurean who prefers food, drink and physical well-being to a pious life. He is characterised by absolute loyalty to his master even during times of distress. Each of the three plays of Kālidāsa has a Vidūṣaka employed in the service of the king, and his task in all of the three plays is to provide fun and advise the king in his romantic dalliances. He offsets the sentimentality of the king by his realistic and even indecorous expressions. In the hands of Harṣa, however, the Vidūṣaka deteriorates provoke only cheap humour. In Bhavabhūti's plays, the Vidūṣaka is conspicuous by his absence. In the plays dealing with the life of Rāma – *Uttararāmacarita* and *Mahāvīracarita* – a Vidūṣaka may not be strictly relevant, but his omission in the romantic play *Mālatīmādhava* seems to be deliberate. V.V. Mirashi explains that the dramatist, being a learned brahmin himself, may not have liked to introduce a clumsy and gluttonous Vidūṣaka, a brahmin only in name, and a disgrace to his caste.[30] In the same way, Viśakhadatta's *Mudrārākṣasa* is also too serious to provide any light comedy. In Kulaśekharavarman's *Tapatīsamvaraṇa and Subhadrādhanañjaya*, the Vidūṣaka degenerates into a stupid brahmin with stock characteristics and attempts at evoking humour.

The Vidūṣaka holds a vital role in Kūṭiyāṭṭam – place is more important than even that of the hero. The Vidūṣaka, unlike other characters, has the right to indulge in *vācika* throughout. In addition to his Prākṛt speech, he also speaks in Sanskrit, and interprets the meaning of the *ślōkas* in Malayalam. Thus unlike the hero and the other major characters in the play, he has access to all levels of spectators. Perhaps the reason for fixing the medium of *vācika* for the Vidūṣaka may be that it is closer to realism than the *āngika* of the hero, and so it is more appealing to all.

---

30. V.V. Mirashi, *Bhavabhuti* (Delhi: Motilal Banarsidas, 1974), pp. 328-29.

The Vidūṣaka is both inside the drama as a character and outside it as a commentator. He pictures himself as a foolish brahmin in the service of the hero, providing companionship and entertainment. In the context, he is a character inside the story. But he also interprets the Sanskrit *śloka* which the hero renders through elaborate *abhinaya*. The Vidūṣaka's task is to unravel the full possibilities of the idea of the *ślōka* and interpret it in Malayalam. While doing this, he steps back into his dramatic role as the companion of the king, and indulges in jokes, mildly ridiculing the king. But side by side with this, he is also free to ridicule the audience – this feature of adopting dual roles is unique to Sanskrit theatre.

The scene is *Subhadrādhanañjaya* between Arjuṇa and the Vidūṣaka named Kaundinya illustrates this point. Arjuna dwells at length on the beauty of the maiden he has just saved from a monster. He reflects that all the virtues characterising a woman have been abundantly showered on this beautiful maiden so that Brahma, the Creator, has exhausted everything. If he has to create another such form, he has to come and beg of her for the virtues. The Vidūṣaka repeats this *śloka* and explains the various shades of meaning of the apparently synonymous words describing the virtue of the maiden. He defines each virtue and subjects them to a scholarly interpretation.

The hero's romantic extravagance finds a parody in the Vidūsaka's description of his woman, appropriately called Cakki. Just as Arjuna praises the maiden, the Vidūṣaka praises Cakki. He acts as a foil to the hero in everything – like an inverted reflection of the hero's personality. It is also intended as a burlesque to deflate the romantic excess of the hero's infatuation for his beloved. There is no empathy on the part of the audience on the Vidūṣaka's "eulogy" of his sweetheart, as in the case of the hero's. The audience is detached, because they are aware of the fact that it is only a comic imitation of the hero's passion.

Another device used by the Vidūṣaka to arouse laughter is self-mockery. He reflects on the impoverished state of affairs at home. Objectively, this self-exposure has a tinge of pathos, but through his comic perspective he transforms it into a hilarious experience. In Kūṭiyāṭṭam, this is a conventional pattern of the Vidūṣaka's nature.

For example, in *Subhadrādhanañjaya* Kauṇḍinya reflects how he turned destitute and sets out to seek a generous king. He was impressed by the mighty and dignified Yudhiṣṭhira, and he managed to please the king by his witticisms. The Vidūṣaka, thus, subjects himself to mockery by revealing his ignorance and lack of proficiency in everything, but all this self-depreciation is turned to a comic end.

CHAPTER IV

THE THEMES OF COMEDY

DRAMATIC THEME has been defined by Elizabeth Burns as "a sequence of acts, interpretations and responses reinterpreted as a whole, by the spectator. It is ... recognised in the overall pattern of events, not in a single event but in the relationship between events."[1] This definition establishes the fact that drama is primarily the interaction between the actor and the spectator. The reaction of the audience to the action is conditioned by the nature of their response to the action and also by their social context. The motives of action, when they are reduced to certain symbolic and collective modes of experience, constitute the themes of drama.

The theory of *rasa* in Sanskrit dramatic criticism perhaps helps to elucidate the significance of themes. Aesthetic experience or *rasāsvāda* is not a negation, but an acceptance of life. Rasa, as a state, is the end-product of an aesthetic process, and a peculiar form of consciousness characterised by pleasure or beatitude. It is the realization of some persistent modes of experiences called *sthāyibhāvas* which exist as latent impressions in the mind of every human being. Raniero Gnoli, while explaining Abhinavagupta's thesis on *sthāyibhāva*, observes thus:

> Indeed every creature from its birth possesses these nine forms of consciousness. In fact, on the basis of the principle that all beings 'hate to be in contact with pain and are eager to taste pleasure', every one is pervaded by sexual desires (Delight); believes himself to be superior to others, whom he is thus led to deride (Laughter); grieved when he is forced to part from what he loves (Sorrow); gets angry at the causes of such separation (Anger); gets frightened when he finds himself powerless (Fear)—but still is desirous of overcoming the danger which threatens him (Heroism); is attacked, when judging a thing to be displeasing, by a sense of revulsion directed just towards this ugly object (Disgust); wonders at the sight of extraordinary deeds done by himself or others (Astonishment); and lastly, is desirous of abandoning

[1] Elizabeth Burns, *Theatricality : A Study of Conventions in the Theatre and in Social Life* (London: Longman, 1972), p. 218.

certain things (Serenity). No living creature exists without the latent impression of these mental movements.[2]

These latent impressions, under favourable conditions, and with the union of other factors like *vibhāvas*, and *vyabhicāribhāvas*. develop into the corresponding *rasas*, which are also nine in number. In the process of transmutation, these modes of consciousness lose their personal meaning and attain a universal significance. This process is called *sādhāraṇīkaraṇa*.. Thus the *sthāyībhāva*, which are latent impressions in the mind of every spectator, correspond to themes, which are also symbolic and collective modes of experience recognised by the spectator under conditions of *sādhāraṇīkaraṇa*.

Langer's remark that comedy is "an art form that arises naturally when people are gathered to celebrate life, in spring festivals, triumphs, birthdays, weddings or initiations"[3] explains the origin of comedy from seasonal festivities. The continuity of the rhythm of life and its need for constant renewal constitute the most persistent theme of comedy. Susan Snyder observes that "comedy celebrates the flexibility that ensures a new life."[4] Thus the favourite topic of comedy is usually that of love leading to marriage, because it symbolically represents the theme of rebirth and the perpetual renewal of life. This fact seems justified in the comedies of both the Western and Sanskrit dramatic repertory. Northrop Frye calls Shakespeare's comedy "the drama of the green world" and states that "its theme is the triumph of life over the waste land, the death and revival of the year."[5] The connection between comedy and fertility rites is symbolically manifest in Shakespeare's *The Winter's Tale,* in which Perdita greets Polixenes and the other guests with flowers at the sheep-shearing festival. In Kālidāsa's *Śākuntala*, there is a reference to spring festival, and the worship of Kāma, the Deity of Pleasure,

---

[2] Raniero Gnoli, *Aesthetic Experience According to Abhinavagupta* (Roma: Is. M.E.O., 1956), p.91.

[3] Susanne K. Langer, "Feeling and Form", *The Comic in Theory and Practice* (New Jersey: Prentice-Hall, 1960), p. 218.

[4] Susan Snyder, *The Comic Matrix of Shakespeare's Tragedies* (Princeton: Princeton Univ. Press, 1979), p. 46.

[5] Northrop Frye, "The Argument of Comedy", *Shakespeare's Comedies,* ed. Laurence Lerner (London: Penguin, 1967), p. 321.

with sprouts of mango-blossom with the words: "O mango blossom, a little pink and green and pale, the very essence of the life of spring, thou art seen by me, and I beg thee to favour (me), thou blessing of the season" (Act VI. verse 2). Similarly in *Mālavikāgnimitra*, there is a mention of the ceremony by which a young beautiful maiden strikes at the *aśoka* tree with her foot. It was a popular belief that at the touch of the feet, the longing of *aśoka* is gratified and it blooms forth in full splendour. All these are symbolic representations of the triumph of life with its rhythm of recurrence and renewal, and the inevitable principle of the victory of youth over age.

The theme of love which appears as the central motif in many of the plays of Western drama has been variously handled by dramatists from Aristophanes to those of the twentieth century. In Aristophanes the satirist, love takes the form of gross, sexual humour. Aristophanes is completely uninhibited in speaking about sex. In *Lysistrata,* in the confrontation between Kinesias and Myrrhine, sexuality is introduced as a device for promoting humour. Equally hilarious are the sexual consequences of Praxagora's revolution in *Ecclesiazusae.* But in Aristophanes, this is not the most important theme – he directs his satire at the different institutions of society of which love forms only a part. In New Comedy, the concept of the collective aspect of man's personality vanishes, and the interest of comedy shifts from the social to the personal. New Comedy concentrates on household matters like love affairs and the arrangement of marriages. Leo Salinger observes that in Menander's plays, "the implicit theme of most of the comedies is their sexual initiation."[6]

Shakespeare's comedies are so varied in matter and spirit that they cannot be classified under a common formula. This resistance to definition has led Kenneth Muir to remark that "there is no such thing as Shakespearian Comedy; there are only Shakespearian comedies."[7] Nevertheless, it is possible to identify certain themes that he

[6] Leo Salinger, *Shakespeare and the Traditions of Comedy* (Cambridge, Cambridge Univ. Press, 1974), p. 122.

[7] Kenneth Muir, *Shakespeare's Comic Sequence* (Liverpool: Liverpool Univ. Press, 1979), p. 1.

continuously highlights in the plays. The most recurrent theme is that of romantic love. All the other themes subserve and support this central theme. On the theme of love in Shakespeare, Salinger observes that "his comedies... are essentially celebrations of marriage, which he presents in a social and personal aspect."[8] Thus they are variations on the theme of love. Courtship and romance become the mainspring of action, and the young lovers usually attain their desired end. In the idealised world of love, impediments are overcome and the opponents of romantic love have to give in. In this respect, they are quite similar to the romantic comedies in Sanskrit literature. Sanskrit drama usually is a celebration of two dominant attitudes to life – the simplicity of the *dhārmic* life and the splendour of a courtly life. The first one involves a heroic theme in which *vīrarasa* predominates and the second one, an erotic theme which has *śṛṅgāra* as its basic *rasa*. The first category includes plays like *Mudrārākṣasa*, and *Pratijñāyaugandharāyaṇa*. Romantic comedies like *Śākuntala*, *Avimāraka*, and *Swapnavāsavadatta* come under the second category. They conform to a similar pattern in the invocation of a romantic world, the possibility of disorder and chaos and the final attainment of harmony.

In Sanskrit drama, the plays dealing with love differ in their treatment of the theme. For example, *Śākuntala* deals with the love-at-first-sight motif presented in a delicate manner and developed through the mutual infatuation of King Duṣyanta and Śakuntala. Kālidāsa also seems to excel in the elaboration of the theme of separation and reunion which promotes love. In Sanskrit, the motif of love in separation is named *vipralambha śṛṅgāra*, which is love in its fulfilment. Since the delicate emotion of *vipralambha* has abundant theatric scope or appeal, the Indian dramatists have portrayed it in all possible variations. Thus the mutual longing of Vāsavadattā and Udayanna in *Svapna*, of Kurangi and *Avimāraka*, of Vasantaśenā and Cārudatta in *Mṛcchakaṭika*, the conscience-stricken yearning of Duṣyanta for Śakuntalā in *Śākuntala*, etc. are examples. In *Svapna*, when the Vidūṣaka asks the King who between the two queens is dearer to him, the King very touchingly reveals the depth of his attachment and affection for the dead

[8] Salinger, *Shakespeare and the Traditions of Comedy*, p. 17.

Vāsavadattā: "Padmāvatī I much admire for her beauty, charm, virtue, and yet she has not won my heart still bound to Vāsavadatta' (IV. verse 4). The comic irony of the situation arises from the fact that both the wives hear his remarks, Padmāvati who hides in the bower of creepers, and the disguised Vāsavadattā who keeps her company. Vāsavadattā, on hearing this, is so overjoyed that she muses: "This is the reward for all my sufferings." But side by side with idealizing this love, Bhāsa also emphasizes the nobility of the character of Padmāvati, so that there is no place for disapproval or jealousy on the part of Padmāvatī.

The dramatic motif of *vipralambha* or love in separation is seen in some of the comedies of Shakespeare also. For example, in *As You Like It,* the love between Rosalind and Orlando is developed through their separation and mutual longing. Orlando is depicted as composing songs on Rosalind during his separation from her, and hanging them on the trees of the forest of Arden. Similarly, the disguised Rosalind is so overwhelmed on hearing the news of Orlando's arrival in the forest of Arden that she exclaims: "Alas the day! What shall I do with my doublet and hose?" (III. ii. 203-4).

In Shakespeare's comedies with Italian plots, love is treated mainly as intrigue. These plays have the typical Italian motifs like mistaken identity, cross-wooing and deceit. The love of Lucian in *The Comedy of Errors* and the courtship of Anne Page and Fenton in *The Merry Wives of Windsor* mark Shakespeare's gradual development of romantic comedy. In the later comedies, the concept of love is transformed from a mere intrigue to that of a romantic ideal. Shakespeare's celebration of courtship and romance is most vividly expressed in the middle comedies, *Much Ado About Nothing, As You Like It* and *Twelfth Night.* These plays seem to be very much closer in matter as spirit to the romantic comedies in Sanskrit, because they present an idealized world of love where impediments are overcome and love finally triumphs. In the last plays, love is treated as an affirmation of the reality of the perpetual renewal of the cycle that constitutes life. Love is thus a blissful experience for young people who are ready to risk anything to fulfil their wishes. Against this picture is a character representing the older generation.

who is chastened and subdued with experience, and who has learned to accept life and its rhythm of recurrence with indulgence, understanding and philosophic detachment.

Side by side with exalting the theme of love, Shakespeare also ridicules and deflates the excess of romance. It is amusing that Shakespeare endows some of the lovers with a dimension by which they are made aware of the absurdity of high-flown love. For example, Rosalind knows that "men have died from time to time, and worms have eaten them, but not for love" (IV. i. 92-94). Similarly, the "merry war" that ensues between Benedick and Beatrice in *Much Ado About Nothing* runs counter to all established ideas of romance. Beatrice declares at the very outset that "I had rather hear my dog bark at a crow than a man swear he love me" and Benedick mockingly replies: "God keep your ladyship still in that mind" (I. i. 111-13). In spite of this, they are tricked into believing that both are madly in love with each other; but even at the close of the play, their mutual revelation of love is far removed from the traditional idea of romance:

BEN: Do you not love me?

BEAT: Why, no, no more than reason.

BEN: Why, then your uncle, and the Prince and Claudio have been deceived; they swore you did.

BEAT: Do not you love me?

BEN: Troth no, no more than reason.

BEAT: Why, then my cousin, Margaret and Ursula, are much deceived; for they did swear you did. (V. iv. 73-80).

This strain of anti-romanticism seems to be absent from the idealised milieu of Bhāsa's plays. Bhāsa, in his plays, highlights the power and intensity of love in all its variations. Apart from the plays in which Bhāsa treats love as the main theme, there are those in which he portrays the nature of true love with subtle touches. In *Pratimānāṭaka*, Rāma, referring to the nature of his relationship with Sīta, says that "rarely are couples born with natures so alike" (Act I). In *Pratijña*, the depth of the love between Princess Vāsavadattā and King Udayana appears vividly from the conversation between the disguised Yaugandharāyaṇa, Vasantaka and Rumanvān. Though the hero and the heroine do not even appear in the play, the extent of their mutual love and their elopment are clearly brought out. In the *Madhyamavyāyoga*, Hiḍimbā whispers something to the mystified Bhīma who is being brought to her, and he praises her worth in a telling phrase, "a demoness only by birth, not by nature".

Of the theme of family relationship other than that of love, Bhasa provides only a few examples. In the *Madhyamavyāyoga*, Ghaṭotkaca becomes a touchstone to test the bond of love and cohesion in the brahmin family. The predicament by which the father has to choose the elder son and the mother the younger son leaves out the middle one as a castaway. Though this sin is not deliberate, Ghaṭotkaca seems to scoff at the brahmin couple for their base conduct. When the boy cries out, "unwanted by my parents, who will care for me?" Ghaṭotkaca replies that he would do so. His own affection for the mother whom he cherishes and the father whom he worships as a deity although he has not yet seen him, are evident from his words and actions. Though he is not willing to kill a *brāhmin*, he does not hesitate to do so at his mother's bidding. When Bhīma orders him to release the brahmin boy, his reply is: "even if my sire should sternly bid me to release him, I would not obey, for he is seized by the order of my mother" (verse 36). Bhīma is touched by his filial obedience, for, according to him, "a mother for humans is the deity of deities", and is reminded of the fact that the Pāṇḍavas have come to this condition by honouring their mother's command. Rāma in *Pratimā* also shows filial obedience and respect, for he willingly throws away the kingdom and sets out to the forest, to keep his father's promise to his step-mother. Thus family relationship is exalted in Bhāsa, for children are portrayed as willing to lay down even their lives for the sake of their duty towards their parents.

In Shakespeare's plays, since love often leads to marriage, family relationship plays an important part. Salinger writes that "the cohesion of the family, as expressed through the dramatic motif of separation and reunion of parents and children"[9] is a theme of emotional importance to Shakespeare. This theme is employed in his first comedy, *The Comedy of Errors* and also one of the last plays, *The Winter's Tale*. In addition to this, he finds the comic possibilities of the theme of family life in *The Merry Wives*. In the play, Ford's disguise as Brook and his jealousy at Falstaff's boasts about Mrs.

---

[9] ibid.

Ford's attentions are comically ironic, since Falstaff himself is finally brought to ridicule and humiliation by Mrs. Ford and Mrs. Page. Similarly, the plotting and consequent blunder of Mr. Page and Mrs. Page over their daughter's marriage are also presented in a mildly humorous vein.

Shakespeare seems to idealize the theme of friendship in *The Merchant of Venice* in the intimate relationship between Antonio and Bassanio. Antonio prepares to forefeit his life to Shylock as a price for the generosity of Bassanio. But in *The Two Gentlemen of Verona,* he brings down this theme by stressing on the frailty of friendship. Muir writes that the "climax of this play is surely a sardonic comment on the popular idea that friendship is superior to love."[10] Proteus proves himself false, disloyal and totally unscrupulous, but since the play is a comedy, his sin is forgiven and he is redeemed to the former status as a friend of Valentine. Unlike Shakespeare, Bhāsa has provided very little scope for the discussion of the theme of friendship. But it is treated elaborately in *Mudrarākṣasa* in the character of Rākṣasa, the minister of the Nandas. In order to save his friend, he goes as far as changing sides and coming to the Maurya camp to serve as Minister after Kauṭilya retires from duty.

The play *Mudrarākṣasa* also seems to be an illustration of the theme of honour, because Kauṭilya through his superb intellect and clever strategy manages to win Rākṣasa over to the Maurya side. Thus he preserves his dignity, but Rākṣasa too is at peace with himself, because though he sacrifices his honour by joining the enemy camp, it is done for what he thinks is a better cause, saving his close friend from execution. Similarly, in *Pratijña*, Yaugandharāyaṇa swears to save his master Udayana who is taken captive by Mahāsena, the King of Avanti. To achieve his purpose, the disguised Yaugandharāyaṇa reaches Avanti along with two other ministers and through trickery, manages to set Udayana free, along with Princess Vāsavadattā. Thus he preserves his honour by retrieving his master, King Udayana. In Bhāsa's *Karṇabhāra*, Karṇa is depicted as being too eager to confront Arjuna and kill him in war, and thus attain honour, but circumstances conspire against this. In

[10] Muir, *Shakespeare's Comic Sequence,* p. 31.

order to protect his honour, he has to sacrifice even his divine ear-rings and armour to Indra. But out of this apparent failure, Karṇa seems to grow in stature, and he undergoes a process of purgation and rediscovery of his identity. The growth takes place within the play itself, and it becomes another interpretation of honour. He is ready to accept whatever fate that awaits him, since both are commendable – the honour of ascending heaven by death on the battlefield or the honour achieved in this world by killing Arjuna in war.

Karṇa's concept of honour as seen from the *Karṇabhāra* seems to be identical with that of Hotspur in Shakespeare's *King Henry IV*. To Hotspur, honour is a matter of personal pride or valour. He, like Karṇa, equates it with victory in the battlefield. In his words,

> By heaven, methinks it were an easy leap,
> To pluck bright honour from the pale-faced moon,
> Or dive into the bottom of the deep,
> Where fathom-line could never touch the ground,
> And pluck up drowned honour by the locks;
> So he that doth redeem her thence might wear
> Without corrival all her dignities. (I. iii. 201-7)

The ultimate test for Hotspur is the confrontation with Prince Hal in the battle of Shrewsbury, but here he fails to protect his honour and meets with his death. But this provides an occasion for Hal to retrieve his honour, for he shows that though he appears to be an irresponsible epicurean, he can rise to any situation. When his father points out Hotspur's heroic demeanour and the Prince's comparative insignificance, Hal flouts Hotspur with the words:

> ... every honour sitting on his helm
> Would they were multitudes, and on my head
> My shames redoubled. For the time will come
> That I shall make this northern youth exchange
> His glorious deeds for my indignities.
> Percy is but my factor, good my lord,
> To engross up glorious deeds on my behalf...
> (III. ii. 142-48).

At the end, the merits acquired by Hotspur are transferred to Hal through his killing of Hotspur, and his words are proved right.

Characteristically, Shakespeare views honour from different perspectives. Side by side with exalting, he also degrades it. He scoffs at this high-flown idea through Falstaff's subversive interpretation of it. Falstaff's perception of the absurdity behind such vague concepts like honour, and his zest for life are expressed in his words "give me life; which if I can save, so; if not, honour comes unlooked for, and there's an end" (V. iii. 58-60). His catechism on honour is another instance of his comic approach to the theme – he looks for personal safety even during times of war, and is prepared to admit it himself. Muir, who seems to appreciate the point of view of Falstaff, puts it sarcastically when he writes that "the end tries all. Falstaff comes with 'honours' from Shrewsbury, Hotspur is left there a corpse."[11]

In his plays, Shakespeare does not seem to be as fond of discussing social themes as a playwright like Aristophanes. Rather than discussing the problems of a society at large, he was interested in discussing the intricate working of the heart, that is, the psychological aspects of human nature. In this respect, his plays come closer to Sanskrit drama in which social criticism is subservient to the other themes. An exception to this is perhaps the character of Maitreya in Bhāsa's *Cārudatta*, who is provided with a few pieces of dialogue having a satirical strain. For example, he declares in Act I of *Cārudatta* that "there is no oil in the lamp as there is no love in a courtesan." But in the theatric form of *Kūṭiyāṭṭam*, the Vidūṣaka's rendering of "*Puruṣārthās*" in plays like *Subhadrādhanañjaya* and *Tapatīsamvaraṇa*, which is an elaboration of the subtext, becomes an occasion for the actor-protagonist to hold the individuals and the society at large up to ridicule and criticism. This is an occasion when the subtext becomes more important than the text itself. Originally, the *puruṣārthas* constituted for the enlightened brahmin the four purposes of life, *dharma* (piety), *artha* (wealth), *kāma* (desire) and *mokṣa* (salvation). But in the reversed context where a deterioration in values has occurred, the four purposes are replaced by *vinoda* (entertainment), *vañcana* (deceit), *aśana* (eating) and *rājasevā* (service under a king), and so he dwells at length on each of these. This speech is rendered in a language so rich in comic appeal that it caters to all types of audience.

---

[11] ibid., p. 201.

The theme of fortune affecting the life of a person, family or society is a recurrent theme in classical drama. Unlike what happens in tragedy, fortune plays a favourable part in comic drama. The convention of happy ending in comedy suggests the benevolent aspects of fortune and the consequent mood of celebration or rejoicing. The theme of fortune affecting the life of characters in Shakespeare's comedy is characterised by its benignity. Salinger writes that fortune in Shakespeare follows a cycle – adversity leading to loss of identity, which is disguise, which results in mistaken identity. But complications are cleared in the end, and it leads to the comic resolution or happy ending. Plays like *The Comedy of Errors* and *Twelfth Night* seem to follow this pattern. In *A Midsummer Night's Dream* and *The Tempest* divine intervention also becomes responsible for promoting the theme of fortune. For example, Puck who complicates the errors of pouring the magic juice supposed to create love in the wrong persons, also amends his error by doing it in the right couple, and this brings the play to a happy conclusion. Supernatural spirits pervade *The Tempest* also, and they are the agents of comedy, because Ariel as Prospero's servant and a "minister of fate" contrives the tempest which becomes an occasion for the meeting of Ferdinand and Miranda. In the same way, in Sanskrit drama, the role of fate that shapes human destiny is ultimately beneficient. In *Śākuntala*, the separation between Śakuntala and Duṣyanta takes place through a series of accidents, but the play is brought to a comic resolution by the discovery of the ring, because fate proves benevolent. In *Avimāraka*, the series of complications are resolved by the intervention of Sage Nārada, a divine agent to provide comic retributive justice. According to Van Buitenen, "The Indian Theatre takes the final view that inspite of all its apparent capriciousness, the world makes sense ... And it is a sensible world in which harmony finally prevails. Virtue necessarily triumphs over evil."[12]

[12] J.A.B. Van Buitenen, "The Classical Drama: Background and Types" in *The Literatures of India: An Introduction*, eds. Edward C. Domock Jr. et al. (Chicago: Chicago Univ. Press, 1974), p. 88.

CHAPTER V

SITUATIONS IN COMEDY

IN THE HIGHEST form of comedy, there is usually an attempt to adopt an affirmative approach to life through a broadly comic understanding of the world. Comic drama primarily deals with a plot evolving through specific situations. There situations may be seen to play a vital role in bringing out the comic element. For the enhancement of the comic, the playwright adcpts diverse perspective and employs a variety of devices.

Since classical Western drama originated from religious celebrations like the worship of Dionysus, it often exploits legends and mythical tales for its plot. It draws from the classical Greek legends, various tales of divine intervention in human affairs and histories of royal houses. While tragedy presents a serious treatment of these classical stories, comedy takes the form of satire against authority; personalities including the gods themselves are viewed from a comic perspective. In Aristophanes' *Birds,* the gods are portrayed as ludicrous, and as being subject to all the passions and weaknesses of men. In the play, a delegation of gods including Neptune, Hercules and a Barbarian god are sent by Zeus to Pithetaerus, the leader of the birds, to settle the quarrel between gods and birds, and establish peace in the world. Among the three gods in the committee, the Barbarian god is pictured as stupid and dull-witted, and Hercules as a glutton. Pithetaerus tempts the three with sumptuous food, and Hercules readily relents and accepts the peace-treaty by which Zeus has to hand over his sceptre and his daughter Iris to Pithetaerus. During the course of the talk, Pithetaerus also reveals the fact that Hercules is the illegitimate son of Zeus, and this creates another scene of mirth. Thus in Old Comedy, the playwright enjoys unlimited licence to ridicule even the gods. This freedom seems to have been lost in later times. On this point, Peter Arnott comments:

> There has been no later parallel to the way in which the Greeks permitted their gods to be shamelessly mocked on the stage. The mediaeval mind permitted the leavening of Bible stories with topical, often broad, humour, but even this broad-mindedness would not have been equal to the spectacle, say, of the Twelve Apostles engaging in knockabout comedy. Yet this would not have been but a mild equivalent of what the Greeks tolerated and frankly enjoyed.[1]

In Sanskrit, the dramatic category known as *nāṭaka*, like classical Greek drama, takes its plot from the epics or *purāṇas* in *Nāṭyaśāstra* Bharata states that *nāṭaka* has a plot dealing with a well-known episode – it is the imitation of things done in the former times by gods and mortals, by kings and other *dhīroddhata nāyakas* (XX. 8-10). In Sanskrit dramatic repertory, five plays of Bhāsa – *Abhiṣekanāṭaka*, *Bālacarita*, *Avimāraka*, *Pratimānāṭaka* and *Svapnavāsavadatta* – and Bhavabhūti's *Uttararāmacarita* belong to the category of *nāṭaka*. Bhāsa's indebtedness to the epics is evident from the fact that out of the thirteen plays ascribed to him, six – *Madhyamavyāyoga*, *Karṇabhāra*, *Dūtavākya*, *Dūtaghaṭotkaca*, *Ūrubhaṅga* and *Pañcarātra* – are drawn from the *Mahābhārata* and two – *Abhiṣeka* and *Pratima* – are based on the *Rāmāyaṇa*. The source of *Bālacarita* is the legend of Kṛṣṇa. *Pratijña* and *Svapna* seem to be adopted from Guṇādhya's *Bṛhadkathā* and the remaining two – *Cārudatta* and *Avimāraka* – seems to be the dramatist's own invention.

Though Bhāsa has drawn the plots of some of his plays from the epics, he has modified the basic material by subjecting the story to his own imaginative interpretation. Bhāsa does not seem to have followed the precepts laid down by texts on dramaturgy like *Nāṭyaśāstra* on the treatment of *purāṇic* sources. Though this fact has been utilised as a clue to fix the date of Bhāsa as prior to Bharata, it has made his plays singularly interesting in Sanskrit dramatic repertory. Sanskrit aesthetics prohibit the enactment of death, fight, etc. on the stage, but Bhāsa's drama offers abundant instances of the transgression of these rules.

In the plays based on the two epics, though Bhāsa is indebted to the source for the main story, he has deviated from the original

---

[1] Peter D. Arnott, *An Introduction to the Greek Theatre* (London: Macmillan, 1959), pp. 27-28.

source where it suits his dramatic interest and given it his own interpretation. Bhāsa's taking liberty with the epic story may be due to the fact that, at the time he was writing the plays, the epics composed by Vyāsa and Vālmīki might not have assumed their final form, and Bhāsa might have based the stories of his plays no one of the many existing versions. It is also possible that Bhāsa consciously deviated and gave his own dimension to the epic story, and in doing so, modified the spirit of the epic to a degree more suitable to dramatic treatment and theatrical presentation.

It may be seen that Bhāsa's treatment of the epics is unique in Sanskrit drama, for he usually takes a short episode and freely dramatizes it according to his own imaginative interpretation. The limitation imposed by the fact that he is adapting an already well-known subject is surmounted by the dramatist's inventiveness. Bhāsa's deviations from the epic may be classified under the following heads:

(1) A completely new situation is invented: For example, the plot of Bhāsa's *Dūtaghaṭotkaca* is his own invention. There seems to be no evidence in the *Mahābhārata* of Ghaṭotkaca going to the Kaurava court an as envoy of Kṛṣṇa after the death of Abhimanyu. Similarly, *Madhyamavyāyoga* presents the episode of the re-union between Bhīmasena and Hiḍimba, which is not found in the epic. In *Pancarātra*, Bhāsa has depicted Droṇa acting as a catalyst for establishing peace between the contending families of the Kurus and the Pāṇḍavas, and it ends with Duryodhana's promise of half the kingdom to Yudhiṣṭhira, its rightful heir. By contriving a happy ending, Bhāsa has omitted the battle of Kurukṣetra which is the main incident in the epic. Though the story obviously suffers in such a situation, the drama is interesting in itself, and the characterization is consistent with that conceived in the epic.

(2) New situations are contrived in a play that is based on an episode from the epic: In *Pratima*, which depicts the life of Rāma from his exile to the forest till his coronation, the incident of Bharata learning about his father's death from

the statue put up at the sculpture gallery – which gives the play its title – is not found in Vālmīki's epic. Similarly, the incident of Duryodhana's ordering the picture of Draupadi's humiliation to the Kaurava court in *Dūtavākya* has no parallel in the epic.

(3) Telescoping and condensing the story by omitting irrelevant details: Bhāsa reveals skill in carefully selecting the material from his source so that the play gains in dramatic force. This can be seen in *Abhiṣeka* – the necessities of the drama saved Bhāsa from the elaboration of the epic style. Keith notes that in *Rāmāyaṇa*, Vālmīki has illustrated the sorrow of Sīta in captivity through 29 similies, while the dramatist is content with only one.[2] In *Bālacarita*, Bhāsa has done considerable selection of detail depicting Kṛṣṇa. The dramatist's motive is to prepare the spectator for the final event, the slaying of Kamsa.

Bhāsa's adaptation of the *puraṇas* may be compared to that of Bhavabhūti in *Uttararāmacarita*. Bhavabhūti derives the plot of his play from the *Rāmāyaṇa*. In the play, he distorts the tragic ending of the final separation of Rāma and Sīta, and contrives a happy ending for the story by means of the union of the hero and the heroine. In transforming the original story in order to manipulate a happy conclusion, Bhavabhūti seems to be merely following the prescription of Sanskrit dramaturgy, which prohibits a tragic ending. But this appears different from Bhāsa's *Pancarātra* which also contrives a happy ending, because in the latter play, there is no feeling of inconsistency or irrationality – it is a natural development born out of Droṇa's attempt and final success in revealing the identity of the Pāṇdavas within five days. Thus Bhavabhūti appears to be a more conventional writer than Bhāsa because he sacrifices dramatic decorum for the sake of dramaturgical rules.

Bhāsa's adaptation of his source story may be compared to that of Shakespeare in Western drama because both follow a common pattern. Shakespeare borrows the basic plot of his plays freely from a variety of sources. But he transforms the original story by his own creative imagination. The merit of the drama lies in his own creative

[2] A. Berriedale Keith, *Sanskrit Drama*, pp. 114-15.

reinterpretation of the original story. He elaborates and complicates his story by infusing the elements of romance, wit and humour. Ideas, situations and even expressions are freely taken from other sources. He also compresses his material and omits a lot of irrelevant details. Thus he utilises his source story as a repository of narrative, and also explores it for general motifs to be manipulated in the course of his own re-creation.

The earliest influence on Shakespeare's comedies is that of Italian comedy. Shakespeare has directly borrowed from Italian sources in five of the twelve comedies he wrote from 1592 to 1604. He uses Plautus in *The Comedy of Errors* and *The Merry Wives of Windsor*. He uses Aristo's *Suppositi* for the Lucenti-Bianca plot of *The Taming of the Shrew*, and is indebted to an anonymous *Gl 'Ingannati* for the story of Julia in *The Two Gentlemen of Verona* and the main plot of *Twelfth Night*. The Italian setting of Shakespeare's plays provides them with a romantic milieu suitable for the enhancement of the comic spirit. Shakespeare uses many Italian motifs such as innocent mistakes, guileful deceptions, misapprehensions, disguise, recognition and double-plot. In *The Comedy of Errors*, which is a re-handling of Plautus's *Menaechmi*, the scene is laid in Ephesus and the play portrays merchant-life. The farcical situation of the play is summed up by Ruth Nevo thus: "A husband has lost a wife, a wife a husband, parents their children, their parents and brothers each other." [3] To increase the absurdity of the situation, Shakespeare has provided identical twins as servants to the twin masters. For this, Shakespeare is indebted the Plautus's *Amphitruo* – in fact, it is an attempt to outdo the original by an effective synthesis of the two plays.

The Taming of the Shrew is mainly based on another play entitled *The Taming of A Shrew*. Leo Salinger observes that this play is "not a mere imitation of New Comedy or Italian plots but the application of Italian methods to new purposes."[4] Shakespeare skilfully handles the three strands in the play – the gulling of Christopher Sly, the

---

[3] Ruth Nevo, *Comic Transformations in Shakespeare* (London: Methuen, 1980), p. 23.

[4] Leo Salinger, *Shakespeare and the Traditions of Comedy*, p. 225.

taming of the shrewish Katherina and the wooing of Bianca. Among these, the first two are radically comic situations, while the third is a comedy of intrigue very much in the tradition of Italian drama. Apart from introducing the play, the Induction is humorous in itself, for Sly, the tinker, is made to believe that he is a lord. In the taming of Katherina, Petruchio has to resort to the same technique adopted by his shrewish wife. He pays her back in the same coin, forcing her to self-revelation, and thus "kills her in her own humour" (IV. i. 183).

The Two Gentlemen of Verona has similarities with *The Comedy of Errors* since its plot corresponds to the pattern of Roman comedy. The story deals with two pairs of lovers in complicated, criss-cross relationships with each other, but the confusion is cleared in the end and symmetry is re-established. *The Merry Wives* is unique in Shakespeare's comedies because it alone has a realistic contemporary English setting. The influence of Latin comedy is evident in the main plot consisting of the farcical discomfiture of Falstaff and the jealous suspicion of the husband. The mistaken wooings and disguises, the braggart warrior, the device of the outwitting of men by women through resorting to trickery – all these elements have a Latin tradition. In *Twelfth Night,* Shakespeare has employed similar devices like the twins of different sexes, the woman's disguise as a man and shipwreck on a strange land.

Shakespeare's handling of Roman themes and techniques is unique because it is not a mere imitation, but an adaptation and an elaboration of the source. Shakespeare's versatility cannot be confined to one source alone. Salinger observes:

> As Shakespeare is such a complex author, even in his lightest comedies, it is impossible, or at least, artificial, to isolate one thread in the composition of his plays from the others. The richness of his mental world, the sense it gives of familiarity-together-with-strangeness, springs from his extraordinary power to bring out parallels and affinity between stories and dramatic devices from separate tragedies.[5]

Shakespeare's comedy is a blend of many dramatic types and devices. After the early explorations in the classical tradition, he evolves his own style. Shakespeare does not follow a particular

---

[5] ibid., p. 190.

theory in comedy – his comedy is too subtle to be pinned down to a single theory. But it is possible to identify several ideas and devices that he repeatedly uses in his plays.

C.L. Barber, who relates Shakespeare's comedies to holidays and pastimes, argues that his comedies are more Aristophanic than Terentian or Plautine: "Shakespeare's comedy is like Aristophanes' because its expression of life is shaped by the form of feeling of saturnalian occasions."[6] In this sense, it may be called festive. In Shakespeare's comedies, the whole experience of the play is made equivalent to that of a revel. Shakespeare seems keenly sensitive to this tradition – titles like *Twelfth Night, A Midsummer Night's Dream* are significant, because they reveal the association of comedy to festivity. In *A Midsummer Night's Dream,* Theseus' order to "awake the part and nimble spirit of mirth" (I. i. 13) sets the mood of the play. The comic mistake of Puck, who pours the magic-potion supposed to create love for the wrong person, begins the complications of the plot. This mischievous spirit knots and unknots and intrigues, and his comic disposition is summed up in his remark, "Lord, what fools these mortals be!" (III. ii. 115). In the same vein is the trick played on Christopher Sly in *The Taming of the Shrew*. Sly the tinker is made to believe that he is a lord who has fallen asleep for a long period of fifteen years. The huntsmen play their part and convince Sly so well that Sly begins to believe that he is a lord. In order to provide him entertainment, the players set themselves to act a "pleasant comedy". Sly asks whether a "comonty" (that is, comedy) is "a Christmas gambold or a tumbling trick", to which he gets the answer that it is more pleasing stuff, " a kind of history" (Induction, Scene ii. 133-38). Thus the play is introduced as an impromptu pastime, and so, in keeping with the light, merry tone, it has a lot of knockabout humour. This concept of comedy as entertainment directly relates it to the festive tradition. Barber equates the dominant mood of these festive comedies with that of a holiday or release. *As You Like It* provides the best example to illustrate the festive atmosphere of Shakespeare's comedies. The forest of Arden is a place of freedom and liberty as opposed to the anxiety and tension of the court. Barber says that "the feeling of

---

[6] C.L. Barber, *Shakespeare's Festive Comedy,* pp. 7-8.

freedom comes from the release from tension in the first Act at the jealous court."[7] The forest of Arden is a place where "they live like the old Robin Hood of England" (I. i. 106-9). It is also a place for unrestrained freedom for the young lovers. The disguised Rosalind asks Orlando (who does not know her identity) to woo her "for now I am in a holiday humour, and like enough to consent" (IV. i. 61-62). It is significant that Salinger notes that the festive element in Shakespearean comedy is derived more out of situation than character. He observes that it is a "social spirit, arising in part from the interplay within a group of characters and in part fortuitously from the circumstance."[8]

In Sanskrit dramatic repertory, Bhāsa's drama is unique because of its intense dramatic quality, and also because he has oriented his drama to a comedic perspective, that can be termed festive. He uses the resources of the theatre to exploit an attitude of celebration and gaiety. This justifies Jayadeva's description of Bhāsa as the laughter of poetry. His plays are rich in situations that create his comic artistry. In the low-comedy scene of the cowherds in *Pañcarātra* and in the carefree revelling of Kṛṣṇa and the cowherdesses in *Bālacarita*, there is a mood of holiday and festivity. The old cattleman in *Bālacarita* excitedly describes the scene: "Ready with all preparations and clad in fine dresses and with drums, we shall now go for an amusement" (Act III). Samkarṣaṇa sums up the mood of the celebrants thus: "Some of them are making a resonant melody with pleasant flutes and drums in delight and some others having their eyes and faces as lovely as lotus petals are plays in manifold ways, while others who remained wakeful and overdelighted in the hamlet are singing, equally overjoyed, in the Vṛnda forest filled with the cattle's bellowing sound" (III. verse 3).

Bhāsa has manipulated a radically comic situation in the clash between the father and son in *Madhyamavyāyoga*. In the play, Ghaṭotkaca, intending to address his culprit (the middle one among the brahmin boys), calls out for him and Bhīmasena (the middle one among the Pāṇḍavas) appears. During the course of their talk, Bhīma comes to know that Ghatotkaca is his own son, and his

[7] ibid., p. 224.

[8] Salinger, p. 16.

attitude becomes one of loving indulgence. When Ghaṭotkaca asks him if he knows who he is, Bhīma humorously replies that he is his own son, and this enrages Ghaṭotkaca, but Bhīma pacifies him by saying that warriors address all people as their sons. The conversation continues in this strain – Ghaṭotkaca on the offensive, and Bhīma in a mildly humorous and playful mood, till Ghaṭotkaca accuses Bhīma of cowardice and Bhīma retorts that he is unaware of the existence of fear, and would gladly take a lesson or two from him on what fear is.

Regarding the situation of the confrontation of Hiḍimba and Bhīma, Keith has observed: "Quiet humour is shown in the episode of bringing Bhīma by Ghaṭotkaca to his mother Hiḍimba. Ghaṭotkaca has difficulty in describing his victim and is much amazed to find his mother whose curiosity is aroused by his lack of precision, finding him to be his deity, and hers in his capacity as a husband and father."[9] His description of the victim coincides with her intention of finding out her husband. By looking at him, she is satisfied and introduces him to her son. She whispers something to her husband, who is taken by surprise at seeing her. The gist of the whisper is left to the imagination of the audience, but it satisfies the husband who praises her worth. Such situations rich in comic appeal abound in Bhāsa's drama.

There are a few instances in Sanskrit drama where drunkenness, a close ally of unrestrained liberty and release, is introduced for the creation of humour and mirth. In Bhāsa's *Pratijña,* the Gātrasevaka who appears as Vāsavadattā's elephant-keeper offers a panegyric on drinking and drunkenness, and it can be regarded as an example of the drinking songs in Sanskrit drama:

> Blessed are they that are drunken with wine;
> Blessed are they that are anointed with wine;
> Blessed are they that have bathed in wine;
> Blessed are they that are scuppered in wine.
> (IV. verse 2)

He goes on to say that "wretched are they who hear the misery of their son's wives and never try a cask of liquor." Another such instance occurs in *Mattavilāsa* when the Kapālin who gives himself

---

[9] Keith, p. 109.

up to drunken release and merriment compares an alehouse to a sacrificial ground. Even minute details of the comparison are vividly brought out, and it increases the comic appeal of the situation. Similarly in Harṣa's *Nāgānanda*, there is a scene between the intoxicated Viṭa and the Vidūṣaka in which the Viṭa under the spell of liquor, indulges in non-sensical extravagance. At the very outset, he declares that "these are the only two gods for me – the one who is always drinking and the one who brings lovers together – Baladeva and Kāmadeva." The spirit seems very close to that of Falstaff in *King Henry IV*. There are plenty of references in the play of Falstaff's addiction to liquor and women. When Falstaff asks Prince Hal, "Now Hal, what time of day is it, lad?" Hal humorously replies, "Thou art so fat-witted drinking of old sack, and unbottoring thee after supper, and sleeping upon benches after noon, that thou has forgotten to demand that truly which thou wouldst truly know. What a devil hast thou to do with the time of the day? Unless hours were cups of sack, and minutes capons, and clocks the tongues of bawds, and dials the signs of leaping houses, and the blessed sun himself a fair hot wench in flame-coloured taffeta, I see no reason why thou shouldst be so superfluous to demand the time of the day" (I. ii. 2-10). Elsewhere, Poins asks Falstaff: "Jack, how agrees the devil and thee about thy soul, that thou soldest him on Good Friday last for a cup of Medeira and a cold capon's leg?" (I. 109-112).

A close analysis of Western and Sanskrit drama reveals that the playwrights have used a few devices repeatedly for the creation of humour. The most important among these is perhaps the use of dramatic irony. According to Bertrand Evans, dramatic irony consists in "the exploitation of discrepant awareness,"[10] that is, the exploitation of a gap in awareness between the characters and the audience. The audience's superior knowledge of facts that are concealed from the characters is a technique adopted by Shakespeare to promote comedy. For example, in *A Midsummer Night's Dream*, Puck's application of the magic judice on the wrong persons creates the comic errors in the play, but the audience knows the cause of the confusion. Similarly in *Twelfth Night*, the audience knows the truth about the letter contrived by Maria, but Malvolio, ignorant of

[10] Bertrand Evans, *Shakespeare's Comedies* (Oxford: Oxford Univ. Press, 1960), p. ix.

this scheme, is made a butt, for he thinks that Olivia is deeply in love with him. In *The Tempest*,Prospero, who actually contrives the meeting between Miranda and Ferdinand, pretends that he is unaware of the relationship. The eavesdropping scenes of Benedick and Beatrice in *Much Ado About Nothing*, when both of them are tricked into believing that one is madly in love with the other, are also comically ironic. In *King Henry IV*, Falstaff's distorted account of the Gadshill robbery provides another instance. Falstaff elaborately describes the scene in which he was attacked by four people, and he fought with all of them single-handed. During the course of the description, his imagination runs riot and the number of people whom he is supposed to have overpowered increases accordingly. But the comic irony of the situation arises from the fact that Falstaff is speaking to the very same persons – Prince Hal and his company – who had attacked Falstaff and overpowered him. But Prince Hal feigns ignorance and leads him on with his tale – this is a situation rich in comic dramatic appeal, where the audience and some of the characters are aware of the fact that is concealed from Falstaff. As a result of this device, repeatedly employed in Shakespeare, his comedies do not surprise the audience. Elkin Calhoun Wilson quotes E.E. Stoll who attributes this device to the suspense of form, as against the suspense of plot: "Suspense of form is the excited expectation not of the answer to the puzzle, or of the disclosure of a mystery, but – under the spell of illusion – of the rounding out of a harmony, like the rime to come at the end of a verse or the rest tone at the end of a song."[11]

There are plenty of instances in Sanskrit drama where dramatic irony is manipulated to enhance a comic situation. The confrontation between Ghaṭotkaca and Bhīma in Bhāsa's *Madhyama*, and between Arjuna, Bhīma and Abhimanyu in *Pañcarātra* are radically comic situations when the son fails to recognise the father. In both these situations, the father identifies his son and so the latter mistakes the former's merry, bantering attitude for sarcastic taunts. In *Pañcarātra*, Bhīma calls Abhimanyu by his name, and he takes offence at this transgression of decorum. When Arjuna in the disguise of Bṛhannala asks him about his mother's well-being, his anger

[11] Elkin Calhoun Wilson, *Shakespeare, Santayana and the Comic* (London: George Allen & Unwin, 1973), p. 58.

mounts to such an extent that he sarcastically asks him if he is King Yudhiṣṭhira, Bhīmasena or Arjuna to take such liberties. The comic irony of the situation arises from the fact that he is addressing the very persons mentioned by him. When Bṛhannala further excites his rage by asking him "Kṛṣṇa, the son of Devakī", his anger mounts to such an extent that he retorts that if Kṛṣṇa is his friend, he must be doing well. Similarly in Kālidāsa's *Abhijñānaśākuntala*, the final scene of the meeting of King Duṣyanta and Śakuntala is contrived through a highly ironic situation. The king after his sojourn in heaven stops by the hermitage of Kaśyapa, where he meets a smart boy engaged in the dangerous task of counting the teeth of a young lion. The king feels attracted to this boy and he muses: "If it gives me such a delight to touch the limbs of the child who is the scion of some stranger's family, what rapture will arise in the heart of that happy man from whose body he sprang?" (VIII. verse 19). The irony of the situation is derived from the fact that he himself is the father of the child. He is led to doubt for the first time when the child bursts out with the words "where is my mother?" at the reference to a *śakunta* bird. Further evidences support this probability and thus, through the son, the couple is re-united.

Another device invented by Bhāsa to promote comic irony is the sudden appearance of a character who seems to answer an unfinished dialogue (or question) on the stage, but is actually in the process of carrying the report of an incident that has occurred off-stage. For example, in *Pratijña* during the course of the dialogue between King Pradyota and the Queen in Act II, where they discuss the possibilities of the marriage of their daughter Vāsavadatta, the King ruminates over the worthiest person for the betrothal of Vāsavadattā, when the Chamberlain hastily appears and announces "the King of the Vatsas". It seems as if he is answering the king's question, but he is actually conveying the news of the capture of King Udayana. This device is repeated in *Abhiṣeka* also.

In the dialogue between the Chamberlain and the King Pradyota regarding the capture of Udayana in *Pratijña*, Bhāsa uses another oft-repeated device for the enhancement of the comic. When the king hears the news, he is so overwhelmed with joy and surprise that he cannot believe what he has heard. The Chamberlain is made to repeat it several times before it registers on the king's perplexed mind. The device of repetition is seen in the last scene of *Avimāraka* also, where the facts of the relationship of Kurangi and Avimāraka are disclosed to King Kuntibhoja. The king is so confused that he cannot grasp the situation, forgets his own capital, and even his own self. He has to be politely reminded of his own identity, and the situation is genuinely humorous.

Another device employed by Western and Indian dramatists is the use of disguise. During the Elizabethan period, the device of disguise was helpful to the actors, when boys had to take the role of women. But in Indian theatre, as in Kathakali, though the female roles are usually played by men, the transformation is done through the skilful manipulation of *āhārya*. This is cleverly effected because as far as *āhārya* is concerned, Kathakali has no pretention to realism. The costume and make-up, for example, concentrate on highlighting certain vital organs necessary for *abhinaya*, like the eyes and lips, and concealing some unnecessary organs like the ears or the hair. So the device of disguise in Indian drama is not as much a theatric necessity as in Western drama.

The technique of adopting disguise also endows the character with a dual perspective. It affords scope for seeing things that may otherwise be concealed from the character. On the question of multiple awareness, Susan Snyder remarks: "Comedy must embrace more realities, more truths, than one. The single action, the single social level, the single perspective – these are not enough. Comedy must open out to find a more comprehensive view." It is this double identity that is achieved by the characters who adopt disguise in Shakespeare's comedies. For example, Rosalind in the guise of Ganymede is both the woman deeply in love with Orlando and the witty lad who is conscious about the absurdity of the sentimental exaltation of love. It is significant that Shakespeare never allows her to overstep her basic womanly nature. Her first reaction when she knows about Orlando's arrival in the forest of Arden is, "Alas the day! what shall I do with my doublet and hose?" (III. ii. 204-5). Similarly, on seeing the blood-stained handkerchief belonging to Orlando, she faints, thus revealing her actual womanly self. In *Twelfth Night*, Viola is also trapped into an ironic situation when Sir

Toby persuades the cowardly Sir Andrew into a duel with Cesario. The disguise of Rosalind and Viola in the two plays also puts them in more absurd situations when Phebe falls in love with Ganymede, the disguised Rosalind, and Olivia falls in love with Cesario, the disguised Viola. Viola's predicament of having to adopt disguise to her own disadvantage – for she has to see her lover offering himself up to another woman – finds an exact parallel in Vāsavadattā of *Svapna*, because she too, like her counterpart in Shakespeare's drama, "Sat like Patience on a monument, smiling at grief" (*T.N.* II. iv. 113-14). Just as Viola has to woo Olivia for her lover's sake, Vāsavadatta has to act the part of a bridesmaid to her husband's second marriage to Padmavati, and she even has to tie the wedding-garland for the couple. But her perseverance is rewarded at the end of the story by the solving of the problems and her union with her husband.

In the tradition of both the Western and Indian drama, the dramatists have made abundant use of the dramatic device of comic relief, or the practice of providing humorous interludes in serious action. It is a dramatic necessity in the interest of the audience. It was a part of the dramatic practice during the Elizabethan times, and Shakespeare often makes use of it. The comic chatter of Dogberry and Verges serves not only to impede the action, but also to relieve the tragic tension of the previous scene in which Hero is subjected to slander. In *Macbeth,* the scene in which the porter appears in Act II, which comes after Duncan's murder-scene, is deliberately introduced, and it also serves the same purpose of relief from tension. Romantic excesses are also deflated by the device of introducing comedy. George Gordon observes that in the romantic comedies, the double strands of love and laughter are balanced against each other: "The solemnity of love is relieved by the generosity of laughter, and the irresponsibility of laughter by the seriousness of love."[12] Gordon cites the example of *Twelfth Night* in which the first two scenes deal with the chief characters Orsino and Viola, and the next scene introduces the humorous sub-plot, with characters like Sir Toby, Maria, Sir Andrew and Feste. In *As You Like it,* the love of Touchstone and Audrey off-sets the high flown

[12] George Gordon, *Shakespearian Comedy* (London: Oxford Univ. Press, 1945), p. 49.

romance of Orlando and Rosalind, because Touchstone believes that "we that are true loves run into strange capers; but as all is mortal in nature, so is all nature in love mortal in folly" (II. iv. 49-52).

The practice of interspersing the comic and the serious elements is repeatedly seen in Sanskrit drama also. In the course of developing his comedies, Bhāsa indulges in humour even in the most serious situations. For example, in Act III of *Pratijña*, the Vidūṣaka tells the ministers at their secret conference that the elaborate plan invented by Yaugandharāyaṇa for the release of King Udayana is bound to fail. When Yaugandharāyana replies that he does not see any reason why it should fail, the Vidūṣaka humorously answers that he understands his thoughts first, and hints at the king's new-begotten love for Vāsavadatta.

Bhāsa employs the device of comic relief to mellow tragic tension. He does this by providing humorous interludes between scenes of serious action. The interlude of Act III in *Pratima,* which introduces the keeper of the sculpture-gallery, though it appears to be absurdly comic, has a tempering effect, because it comes after the pathetic scene of Daśaratha's parting from Rāma and his subsequent death. The interlude of Act IV in *Pratijña* also introduces comic scenes as a means of comic relief. The conversation between the soldier and the Gātrasevaka disguised as Vāsavadattā's elephant-keeper, who is actually a spy employed by Yaugandharāyaṇa, is almost farcical. The Gātrasevaka acts as if he is drunk. He also cleverly dupes the soldier into believing that he has pawned the elephant Bhadrāvatī to the liquor-shopkeeper. The Interlude of Act II of *Pañcarātra* depicts pastoral life. The merry-making of the cowherds with the lads and lasses clad in colourful attire and offering themselves up to dance, music and song, is a folk pastime that provides holiday licence. It is an occasion for festival revelry, since it is the King's birthday – an auspicious day when the king gives away the cows as gifts. The device of comic relief is employed by other dramatists also. For example, Kālidāsa introduces the scene in which the policemen seize and interrogate the fisherman who is supposed to have stolen the royal ring. The scene comes just after the pathetic scene of the repudiation of Śakuntala and so it has a tempering effect on the audience. Similarly in *Uttararāmacarita*, the scene were the students at Sage Vālmīki's hermitage discuss the culinary tastes of Janaka and Vasiṣṭha, is a scene deliberately contrived to provide some relief from the tension of the preceding scene of pathos at the separation of Rāma and Sīta.

Bhāsa's plays are unique in Sanskrit dramatic repertory because of their intense theatrical quality. Bhāsa has created many situations in his plays for their theatrical effect. In *Pañcarātra*, the dramatist has provided the stage-direction "they dance" and the specific name of the dance is mentioned as "hallisaka" dance. There is the depiction of this dance allied with music in *Bālacarita* also. In the personification of Kṛṣṇa's weapons in *Dūtavākya* and *Bālacarita*, Bhāsa has resorted to fantasy as a theatrical device. In *Dūtavākya*, the scene in which the picture of Draupadi's humiliation is brought to the Kaurava stage is dramatically very effective. The description of the picture does not mention the miracle by which Kṛṣṇa lavishes garments on her. According to Keith, this may be due to "the difficulty of exhibiting this by the painter's art."[13] But Bhāsa seems to have deliberately kept this open for the resourceful director to interpret it according to his imagination. Instead of bringing the picture-scroll to the stage, an imaginative representation resorting to gestural language would be more effective on the stage. Bhāsa's personification of the Chanḍāla maidens clad in black hovering over the sleeping-chamber of Kamsa in *Bālacarita* and his depiction of the mystery of sleep, dreams and waking are relevant as stage-devices and also for developing the theme of retribution. M. Winternitz observes: "this scene alone which hardly has any parallel in the dramatic literature of India would prove the Bālacarita to be the work of some good dramatist."[14] In this respect, Bhāsa's plays may be compared to Shakespeare's, because, the effect of the comic element in Shakespeare is visual rather than literary. The oral and visual elements dominate in his plays – masque, dance, play-within-the-play, song and brilliant dialogue. Barber observes that pastimes like dances, disguisings, games, shows and pageants were a regular part of marriage-celebrations during Elizabethan England. The en-

[13] Keith, *Sanskrit Drama*, p. 98.

[14] M. Winternitz, "Bhāsa and the Mahābhārata and Kṛṣṇa Plays" , *Bulletin of the Rama Varma Research Institute*, 5, No. I (1974), pp. 1-15.

ding of Shakespeare's comedy, which is usually a celebration of marriage, provides scope for all these. The supernatural element in *A Midsummer Night's Dream and The Tempest* have a highly visual effect. In these, the supernatural is given a comic treatment, for, Puck, the nimble spirit of mirth, and Ariel are responsible for much of the comic action. The popularity of the fool in Shakespeare's drama is also significant, for his costume, words and actions are manipulated to promote comedy in the theatre.

Shakespeare often intersperses the comic and the tragic elements – his tragedies include the comic and his comedies often shift towards the tragic. The tendency is derived from Shakespeare's refusal to draw a rigorous distinction between the two dramatic genres. To Shakespeare, the comic and the tragic are not mutually exclusive impulses. Mercutio in *Romeo and Juliet* and Polonius in *Hamlet* are characters who belong to tragedies, but they are also figures of high comedy. Their presence puts the action in the play on a certain perspective – that of life-affirmation. Their death is symbolic of the death of comedy itself. Thus comedy serves to re-inforce the theme of tragedy.

Another common ground between comedy and tragedy has been pointed out by Susan Snyder: "The formulas of comedy and their underlying assumptions can serve as the foundation of tragic dilemma: deeper probing reveals that the accepted comic goods like multiple awareness and self-completion through mating have their paradoxical shadow-sides."[15] Hamlet's pose as a madman is an example of the multiple awareness operating in his character. This endows him with an alternate identity, but unlike Rosalind's disguise as Ganymede, Hamlet's pose only deepens his tragic torment. Similarly in *Othello,* "Shakespeare subjects the comic assumptions about love, union, nature and reason to a radical reassessment, and in so doing, exposes the roots of tragedy."[16] Shakespeare here portrays the inadequacy of romantic love. The irrationality of the love of Othello and Desdemona is juxtaposed against the rational view of Iago, the villain, and this causes the tragedy of Othello. The

---

[15] Susan Snyder, *The Comic Matrix of Shakespeare's Tragedies* (Princeton: Princeton Univ. Press, 197), p. 5.

[16] ibid., p. 73

encounter between Hamlet and the grave-diggers reaches the level of black humour, because Hamlet is taken aback by the cool indifference of the grave-diggers in their profession. Death is the ultimate leveller, and is indifferent to both Yorick, the king's jester and Caesar, the emperor – it is the termination of life that makes every life, trivial and noble, equally absurd. The same spirit may be observed in *Ūrubhaṅga* – when Durjaya innocently insists on accompanying Duryodhana on his last voyage, Duryodhana asks him to go and seek the help of Bhīma in the matter. This sardonic statement which at the superficial level sounds like a humorous piece of advice deepens the sense of irony of Duryodhana's predicament, because it suggests the waste and absurdity of all that has happened before. This situation, though rare in Bhāsa, deepens the tragic predicament of Duryodhana's condition, and so his final transcendence of misery through the purification of evil thoughts becomes all the more significant.

CHAPTER VI

CHARACTERIZATION IN COMEDY

DRAMA, according to Eric Bentley, "presents human relationships"[1] – that is, the things men do to each other. The interaction between the dramatis personae is of vital significance in a play. Characterization in comedy, unlike that in tragedy, is usually not idealized or exalted. L. J. Potts is of the view that "the characters of comedy are not superhuman or subhuman, but on a level with the generality of mankind."[2] This may be due to the fact that comedy admits and even demands greater realism than tragedy. Characterization in comedy should, therefore, aim at highlighting the social side of a man's personality. The Vidūṣaka in Kuṭiyāṭṭam, for example, has access to all levels of spectators, because of his use of the vernacular and his freedom of speech. Similarly, in Aristophanic comedy, there is the convention that the characters, while engaged in dialogue, suddenly turn to the spectators and address the audience to make fun of some person or affair of topical interest. Thus it may be argued that in comedy, there is more realistic than tragedy, which by nature is more idealized or exalted so as to handle more complex psychological states.

Coleridge recognises the importance of characterization in drama. In this analysis of the characteristics of Shakespearean drama, he points out the limitations of interest in the plot as such. According to him, "the plot interests us on account of the characters, not vice versa; it is the canvas only."[3] Coleridge cites the example of *Much Ado About Nothing* which has characters like Benedick, Beatrice and Dogberry who may not be strictly relevant to the main plot, but are interesting in their own right. Shakespeare

---

[1] Eric Bentley, *The Life of the Drama*, p. 62.

[2] L. J. Potts, *Comedy* (London: Hutchinson, 1949: rpt. 1963), p. 115.

[3] Samuel Taylor Coleridge, *Shakespearean Criticism* (London: J.M. Dent, 1960), p. 199.

seems to be more interested in the depiction of the intricate working of the minds of his characters rather than the complications of plot.

Shakespeare's drama offers a wide range of characters. His skill in characterization is illustrated by the numerousness and diversity of his people, who belong to all sections of society. The world of his characters ranges from kings, aristocrats and soldiers to servants, menials and professional jesters. The comic protagonists of Shakespeare, as a rule, do not advocate any particular theory of comedy – the interest in them is for their own sake. Leo Salinger refers to "a fundamental innovation which distinguishes Shakespeare's plays from all previous comedies, that he gives his people the quality of an inner life."[4] Shakespeare's characters have the capacity to react to situations. They pass through new phases of experience, and grow in stature as the play proceeds – thus they are thoroughly humanised.

In Sanskrit drama Bhāsa's plays are unique because he, like Shakespeare, offers a wide range of characters. Unlike other dramatists who were content to write only a few plays, Bhāsa is credited with having composed thirteen plays, which have characters from varied walks of life. In addition to the human race, Bhāsa has incorporated characters from the superhuman and subhuman worlds as well. The world of his characters includes gods, sages, brahmins, kings, ministers, demons, servants and jesters. More than this, Bhāsa has personified other species like animals and birds who appear as characters in the plays. He has also personified the weapons of Kṛṣṇa and given concrete form to abstract concepts like curse and prosperity. In portraying this multitude of characters from such varied sources, Bhāsa has individualised most of them, and made them credible in the theatre.

Indian and Western drama often draw their plots from popular legends and other mythical tales. During the course of adaptation from the original source, character is subjected to transformation. In Old Comedy, because of its licence and topsy-turvy values, sometimes even the gods are depicted in a humorous light, projecting the weaker side of their character. In *Frogs,* Dionysus himself, the deity of drama in Greece and the leading character of the play, is

[4] Leo Salinger, *Shakespeare and the Traditions of Comedy,* p. 222.

portrayed as a coward and a fool. Though he comes to Hercules clad in a lion-skin and armed with a club similar to that of the latter, he is very much unlike Hercules in the matter of bravery. He asks Hercules the easiest way to reach Hades, so that he can bring Euripides from the underworld.

HERCULES	Come now, which of them shall I tell you first? Which? For there is one way by a rope and a bench, if you hang yourself.
DIONYSUS:	Come now, you tell me a choking one. Do you mean hemlock?
HER:	Certainly.
DIO:	Aye, a cold and chilly one, for it immediately benumbs the shins.
HER:	Would you have me tell you a speedy and down-hill road?
DIO:	Yes, by Jove, for I am not good at walking. (119-27)

In order to re-inforce the extent of his desire for Euripides, Dionysus brings in the comparison of the pea-soup which might move Hercules to desire, and immediately Hercules grasps the depth of Dionysus's need. Dionysus here is portrayed as being foolish and cowardly, and Hercules as a great glutton.

Shakespeare borrows freely from other sources and basic plot and character of his plays. The general frame-work of the characters being settled by the source-story, he sets out to re-create them in his own works. For example, the character of Falstaff is adopted from that of Sir John Oldcastle in *The Famous Victories of Henry V.* On this point, Geoffrey Bullough observes: "It is not easy to see why Sir John Oldcastle becomes a comic character, for he was tragic rather than a humorous figure."[5] Shakespeare seems to have taken merely the hint for this character, and he developed it transforming him into a genius of comedy. C.L. Barber, who identifies in Falstaff, a strain on saturnalian release, observes: "In creating Falstaff, Shakespeare fused the clown's part with that of a festive celebrant, a Lord of Misrule, and worked out the saturnalian implications of both traditions more complexly than anywhere else."[6] In *Romeo and Juliet,* Shakespeare develops the character of the Nurse and also that of Mercutio. In *As You Like It,* Shakespeare seeks a symmetry and close relationship between the characters, which is not found in the

[5] Geoffrey Bullough, *Narrative and Dramatic Sources of Shakespeare* (New York: Columbia Univ. Press, 1967)., IV. p. 168.

[6] Barber *Shakespeare's Festive Comedy*, p. 13.

source. Shakespeare in adapting the story makes his characters more credible and subtle than in the source-story. The character of Shylock is drawn from Marlowe's *Jew of Malta,* but Shakespeare's characterization is far more convincing, for he selects only the necessary shades of character from Marlowe's Jew, thereby making him more credible in the theatre and more amenable to the spirit of comedy.

In Sanskrit, the poets have dramatized ancient legends to suit their own imaginative interpretation. Thus Bhāsa's skill in characterization is evident in his treatment of the epics, which serve as the main source of the plays. Though he has taken a lot of liberties with the epic story, the characterization is consistent with that conceived in the epic. That is to say, there is no psychological violation of their basic conceptions. But in many cases, though keeping strictly within the frame-work of the epic, he has gone beyond it and given his own interpretation to the characters. He has elevated the character of some, by making them superior to their conception in the epic. For example, he attributes virtuous qualities to some of the characters who are portrayed as wicked in the source story. Thus he has softened the wickedness of Kaikeyī in *Pratimānāṭaka* and of Duryodhana in *Ūrubhaṅga*. They are portrayed as innately good – Kaikeyī's evil treatment of Rāma is the result of a verbal error, because her uttering "fourteen years" is a slip of her tongue – she had meant to say "fourteen days". Similarly, Duryodhana is presented in the epic in an unfavourable light, by stressing his villainous qualities, but Bhāsa portrays him as heroic and noble. In *Pañcarātra*, Duryodhana keeps his word to Drōṇa and willingly bestows half the kingdom on Yudhiṣṭhira, its rightful heir. In *Ūrubhaṅga*, Duryodhana has reached the level of high wisdom and serene calmness achieved through the cessation of desire and the purification of the heart – thus the conception of this figure in Bhāsa is an improvement upon that in the epic. In the same way, Bhāsa has made full-fledged characters out of some sketched only in outline in the epic story. Hidimba in *Madhyamavyāyoga* and Ghaṭotkaca in *Madhyamavyāyoga* and *Dūtaghaṭotkaca* are examples of Bhāsa's development of some minor characters of the epic. Hiḍimbā, though the demoness, is a pious woman; she is also a dutiful wife and a good mother. Bhīma is so much moved to admiration at her virtues that he remarks that she is "a demoness only by birth, not by action". Ghaṭotkaca also lacks the ferocious qualities of a demon. He is innately good – he resorts to terrorize the brahmin family only because he is eager to fulfill his mother's wishes.

Kālidāsa, in his adaptation of the source, subjects the characterization in his play *Śākuntala* to dramatic modification. *Śākuntala* is the dramatic version of an episode discussed in the Adiparva or first book of the *Mahābhārata*. In the original story, King Duṣyanta and thus the wife and the son are accepted. But Kālidāsa transforms this crude version of the story into a masterpiece of love. The time-span is cut short, and Śakuntala, while going to the court, is pregnant with Duṣyanta's child. Kālidāsa subjects the character of Duṣyanta to a psychological transformation. By introducing the curse of Sage Durvāsas and the loss of the ring which becomes responsible for his loss of memory, Duṣyanta's innocence is established and so he is exonerated in the end.

The protagonists in comedy are motivated to action by a certain attitude to life and things characterised by life-affirmation. The comic character is one who departs from the established norms and society with a specific purpose in mind. His non-conformistic and even subversive actions establish him as different from the other characters in the play. Life with all its incongruities is appealing to him, and he accepts it without fear or failure. For the same reason he attracts and entertains the spectator who may not himself share his values, but is willing to draw fun out of him. Viewed in this way, his actions can be seen as heroic rather than ridiculous, and he attains the stature of a hero – a comic hero. William E. Gruber refers to the many manifestations of the comic hero and observes that "it has been the specific role of this figure heroically or craftily or magically to disrupt the ordered society in which he finds himself."[7] Thus he is not a mere nonconformist, but a wild man – "not anti-, but simply alien, beyond definition."[8]

Discussing the comic character in Shakespeare, Barber argues that the saturnalian pattern came to Shakespeare from the theatrical

---

[7] William E. Gruber, "The Wild Men of Comedy: Transformation in the Comic Hero from Aristophanes to Pirandello", *Genre,* XIV (Summer 1981), p. 210.

[8] ibid., p. 214.

institution of clowning. He observes that Shakespeare used "the resources of a sophisticated theatre to express, in his idyllic comedies and in his clown's ironic misrule, the experience of moving to a humorous understanding through saturnalian release."[9] From his very first comedy onwards, Shakespeare incorporates the figure of the fool, who is mainly responsible for the comic action of the play. William Willeford in his analysis of the characteristics of a fool defines him as "a silly or idiotic or mad person, or one who is made by circumstances (or the action of others) to appear fool in that sense, or a person who imitates for nonfools the foolishness of being innately silly or made to look so."[10] This definition applies to the conception of the fool in Shakespeare's drama. The two extremes in the conception of this figure are the fool or professional jester and the clown or simpleton who becomes the object of laughter. The former is a quick-witted, professional entertainer who deliberately covers up his wisdom in the garb of simplicity, while the latter is an idiotic half-wit who is a butt of ridicule. All the comic characters who appear in Shakespeare's plays have either of these or a combination of these traits.

The comic characters of Shakespeare, unlike the trickester-servants of Roman Comedy, sometimes stand outside the main action of the play. Even if they get involved in the action, the participation is only incidental, and it does little for the development of the plot. For example, Touchstone in *As You Like It* is not directly relevant to the story, but his role is important, because he is responsible for most of the humour of the play. His task is the comedy is to "speak wisely what wise men do foolishly" (I. ii. 78-79). Thus the fool in Shakespeare as a rule is not involved in the complication of the action – he views it from the outside, as a spectator, and comments wisely on it. In this respect he is comparable to Bhāsa's character of the Vidūṣaka in his plays. Bhāsa provides a catalyst of the comic disposition in the Vidūṣaka who appears in all his three romantic comedies – *Avimāraka*, *Svapnavāsavadatta* and *Cārudatta* – and also in *Pratijñayaugandharāyaṇa*. Like his Shakespearean counterpart,

---

[9] Barber, pp. 3-4.

[10] William Willeford, *The Fool and His Sceptre: A Study in Clowns and Jesters and Their Audience* (London: Edward Arnold, 1969. 1969), p. 10.

the Vidūṣaka in Bhāsa is primarily a laughter-producer, and seeks to entertain the other characters as well as the spectators. He is a brahmin employed in the service of the hero. He diverts the hero with his witty speech and non-sensical actions. He also performs the functions of a "narmasaciva" or "minister in sport". But apart from this, he is different from Kālidāsa's Vidūṣakas – Gautama in *Mālavikāgnimitra* and Māṇavakā in *Vikramorvaśīya*. In *Mālavikāgnimitra*, Gautama is the chief agent who promotes the romantic affair of the king – he is a ready-witted, scheming person who resorts to a number of ways to secure Mālavikā for the King. He devises a plan for the meeting of the lovers by contriving a quarrel between the dancing masters, causes Queen Dhāriṇī to fall from a swing and pretends that he is bitten by a snake, so that he secures the ring from the queen to release Mālavikā from prison. Thus he has an important role to play in the development of the plot. But in Bhāsa, the Vidūṣaka stands outside the main action. Even Maitreya in *Cārudatta*, who is more individualised than the other two, is not directly involved in the story. The Vidūṣaka in Bhāsa has the dramatic duplicity of being a wit and a butt, as one who ridicules others and one who becomes the object of ridicule. A.B. Keith remarks on Bhāsa's employment of the Vidūṣaka thus: "The Vidūṣaka in his hands attains the characteristics which mark him in the later drama, and, though much was doubtless traditional, it may safely be assumed that he tended by his example to stereotype this figure."[11]

The essential purpose of providing fools, according to Ruth Nevo, is to create a detachment or aesthetic distance, since "identification with a protagonist would short-circuit a fully intelligent participation."[12] Comedy, unlike tragedy, need not conform to a single perspective – it can entertain multiple levels of thinking. For example, the fool's observation of life may be different from that of the hero or the heroine, and in a comedy, the audience is given intelligence of both. Many of the fools in Shakespeare are aware of the absurd dimension behind the man-made convention of marriage. Thus Speed in *The Two Gentlemen of Verona,* Touchstone in *As You*

---

[11] A.B. Keith, *Sanskrit Drama*, pp. 107-8.

[12] Ruth Nevo, *Comic Transformation in Shakespeare* (London: Methuen, 1980), p. 11.

Like It, and Feste in *Twelfth Night* have the comic function of offering an alternate conception of the established idea of romance. The fool in *King Lear* paradoxically has a saner perspective towards life, and his jokes are intended to make the king aware of his folly. In Shakespeare's comedy, he intersperses the action of lovers, kings, magicians and the actions of the low characters. Since comedy does not conform to a single perspective, no perspective is allowed to hold sway for long. In Sanskrit drama, the Vidūṣaka also serves as a foil to the hero – he complements the hero's "heroic" qualities – in this sense, he may be called a comic hero. For example, the hero's passion for his beloved finds a substitute in the Vidūṣaka's love of food. In *Svapna,* the king after great deliberation confides in Vasantaka that though he deeply admires Padmāvatī for her noble qualities, his heart still belongs to the dead Vāsavadattā. After this, the king in his turn asks Vāsavadattā. After this, the king in his turn asks Vasantaka: "Which is your favourite, the Vāsavadattā that was, or Padmāvatī of today?" After a great deal of hesitation, Vasantaka replies: "Lady Vāsavadattā I greatly admired. Lady Padmāvatī is young, beautiful, gentle, free from pride, gently spoken and very courteous. But there is one great virtue, Vāsavadattā used to come to me with delicious dishes, saying, "Where has the good Vasantaka gone to?" (Act IV). Thus, as befitting the spirit of comedy, he brings the high-flown idea down to earth, because it is almost a parody of King Udayana's sentimental passion for his beloved.

Shakespeare, in drawing humour from his comic characters, caters to all levels of spectators – satire for the sophisticated and slapstick for the simple tastes. The former category includes fools or the witty commentators on the follies of mankind. Among the long list of comic protagonists who use their wit to entertain the characters as well as the audience, Touchstone in *As You Like It,* Feste in *Twelfth Night* and the fool in *King Lear* stand out, for their task in the respective plays is to "shed the light of reality and common sense"[13] on the fanciful figures on the plays. The best account on the traits of a professional fool is summed up by Viola in *Twelfth Night.* She approves of Feste's intelligence and remarks

---

[13] John Palmer. *Political and Comic Characters of Shakespeare* (London: Macmillan. 1964). p. 384.

that "this fellow is wise enough to play the fool" (III. i. 56-57). Then she dwells at length on the fool's profession:

... to do that well craves a kind of wit.
He must observe their mood on whom he jests,
The quality of persons, and the time,
And, like the haggard, check at every feather
That comes before his eye. This is a practice
As full of labour as a wise man's art;
For folly that he wisely shows is fit;
But wise men, folly-fall'n, quite taint their wit.

(III. i. 58-65)

Thus Touchstone accompanies Rosalind and Celia to the forest of Arden, deflates the romantic excesses of the lovers by his account of the wooing of a dairy-maid called Jane Smile, and offers a burlesque on romantic love by his courtship of Audrey. After his encounter with Jacques, the latter is captivated by his superb flash of wit, and observes that he "used his folly like a stalking-horse, and under the presentation of that he shoots his wit" (V. iv. 100-102). This tradition is carried on by Feste, who, according to Nevo, is "the most detached, observant (his livelihood depends upon it) and ironic of Shakespeare's fools."[14] He is not involved in the course of the action, but is a keen observer who is wittily aware of the absurdity of the confusion arising out of the plot. He ridicules Malvolio after his discomfiture by parodying his absurd speeches. Besides, his brilliant jests unmask the true selves of the chief characters in the play – like Orsino, Viola, Olivia and Sebastian. He indulges in wit-combats with each of these people, and directs the dialogue to his advantage. The Fool in *King Lear* is a combination of the professional court jester and a faithful servant. His comic function has been summarised by Susan Snyder as "first to joke the king into an awareness of his folly, and then the joke away the pain caused by that awareness."[15]

The clowns or butts in Shakespeare's drama cause amusement at their own expense. They are often idiotic and silly – their ugly face, incongruous action and stupid, nonsensical talk are exploited to

---

[14] Nevo, *Comic Transformations,* p. 215.

[15] Susan Snyder, *The Comic Matrix of Shakespeare's Tragedies* (Princeton: Princeton Univ. Press, 1979), p. 148.

evoke laughter. In Shakespeare, clowns usually belong to the lower class of society – servants and menials like the Dromio brothers, Speed and Launce come in this group – but exceptions like Sir Andrew Aguecheek, Dogberry and Verges are not rare. The appeal of these clowns is often visual rather than literary. George Gordon records that "Richard Tarleton the comic actor created the part of the Clown, and created it so effectively – so completely captured the age – that writers of comedy had to provide him with a part whether they wished to or not."[16] During Shakespeare's time, the main actors proficient in taking the part of the clown were Richard Tarleton, William Kempe and Robert Armin. In addition to their skill in creating fun, they could play on tabor and the pipe. John Russell Brown observes that "they were active and nimble, Tarleton being fencing master and Kempe a notorious dancer."[17] Thus the clowns manipulate all these devices to create comedy in the theatre.

Unlike Shakespearean drama in which there is the categorization of the comic character into a wit and a butt, Indian drama has its counterpart in the figure of the Vidūṣaka who combines in his person these two roles. This may be seen in the character of Maitreya in *Cārudatta* and *Mṛcchakaṭika*. Maitreya is a keen observer of the society in which he finds himself, and he subjects to severe ridicule and satire the faults and foibles of the people around him. He expresses doubt at Vasantasena's loyalty by saying that "there is no oil in the lamp at Cārudatta's house, as there is no affection in a courtesan." Though he is taken aback at seeing the wealth and splendour of Vasantasena's mansion, he is not captivated by it, and views it with derision and contempt. His shrewdness and wit place him equivalent to Touchstone in *As You Like It.* But he is also pictured as a foolish and ridiculous brahmin, fond of food and engaged in ridiculous talk. For example, Cārudatta entrusts the casket containing Vasantasena's jewels to Maitreya for safekeeping, and Maitreya assumes charge of the casket, but goes to sleep. Meanwhile a burglar breaks inside the house, and is on the look-out for valuable things, when Maitreya starts sleep-talking. He blurts out

---

[16] George Gordon, *Shakespearian Comedy* (London: Oxford Univ. Press, 1945), p. 68.

[17] John Russell Brown, *Shakespeare's Plays in Performance* (London: Penguin, 1969), p. 107.

about the golden casket and thrusts it on the burglar, who things that the brahmin, having found out his identity, is taunting him. But Maitreya, mistaking the burglar for Cārudatta, presses him to accept the treasure: "My friend, if you do not take this casket, you will sin as sins the man who curbs a cow or refuses the wish of a brahmin" (Act III), and thus forces it on the burglar.

Another source of laughter in Bhāsa's Vidūṣaka is his physical and mental deformity, whether real or assumed. The Vidūṣaka projects a ridiculous image of himself. He is portrayed as a glutton, coward and idiot. There are also many references to his physical deformity and illiteracy. Santuṣṭa defends himself, saying, "why am I not a Vedic scholar? Listen to the *Rāmāyaṇa*. There are five verses in it, and I have read them within less than a year" (Act III). During the course of the talk, he also reveals the fact that he is illiterate, because he cannot read a single letter in a seal, but he again justifies himself, saying, "this letter is not found in my dictionary". His physical deformity is another device for producing comic pleasure. On Bhāsa's employment of the characters of the Vidūṣaka, A.S.P. Ayyar writes: "The object of having these jesters is to keep the kings human, instead of making them degenerate into pompous and conceited fools, by supplying a kind of licensed criticism from these boon-companions."[18] The maids are also portrayed in Bhāsa as having a delicate sense of humour – they serve as the female counterpart of the Vidūṣaka, by advising the heroine, diverting her attention from her love-sick condition, and even mildly ridiculing her. Among them, Madanika in *Cārudatta*, the servant-maid of Vasantasenā, is individualised. She persuades her lover to give back the ornaments he had stolen from Cārudatta for her ransom, and is rewarded for her loyalty by not only securing her freedom, but also her marriage to her lover Sajjalaka. Her vivacity and devotion to her mistress set her equal to Maria in *Twelfth Night*.

Among the different manifestations of the comic hero in Shakespeare, the figure of Falstaff is unique, because he is the most consummate embodiment of festive liberty. Falstaff, with his multifacetedness defies an exact definition. He has been subjected to many interpretations – this composite figure has been labelled as a

---

[18] A.S.P. Ayyar, *Bhasa* (Madras: V. Ramaswamy Sastrulu, 1957), p. 433.

fool, buffoon, thief, glutton, coward, boaster and misleader of youth. This multiplicity and resistence to definition make him unique. His celebration of a subversive way of life also gives him sanction for audacities that others lack. In sharp contrast to the troubled realm of *King Henry IV,* the world of Falstaff is one of carefree licence, occupied by cups of sack, capons and wenches in flame-coloured taffeta. He expresses the hope that "Marry, then, sweet wag, when thou art king, let us not that are squires of the night'a body he call'd thieves of the day's beauty. Let us be Diana's foresters, gentlemen of the shade, minions of the moon, and let men say we be of good government, being govern'd, as the sea is, by our noble and chaste mistress of the moon, under whose countenance we steal" (I. ii. 21-26). Elkin Calhoun Wilson emphasizes this radically comic strain in Falstaff, and hails him as " a king, every pound of him, of the comic, the humorous and the witty alike."[19] Falstaff combines in him the attributes of a wit and a butt. In his own words, "I am in other men" (2 *Henry IV.* I. 11. 10-12). Hal, Poins and the rest of the group fall under his spell, and they extract pleasure out of him. Falstaff falls a victim to ridicule after the Gadshill robbery, but he cleverly extricates himself through his verbal skill from the compromising situations. Even his physical appearance is manipulated to produce laughter–references to his grossness are abundant – "plump Jack", "huge hill of flesh", to cite a few. Shakespeare has conceived Falstaff as the embodiment of unrestrained comic spirit.

Śakāra, who appears in *Cārudatta*, has been described by Ayyar as "the Indian Falstaff".[20] But Śakāra does not seem to be as infinitely resourceful or as complex as Falstaff. He is portrayed as vicious, but he is also a coward, because though he attempts to seize Vasantasenā, he gets frightened and slips away at seeing the Vidūṣaka's lamp. This curious mixture of villainy and buffoonery makes his personality ludicrous. His position is secure as the brother-in-law of the King of Ujjainy, and this gives him licence for libertinism. His particular way with language, and his speech full of malaproprisms and misquotations also render him comic. For example, he addresses the fleeing Vasantasenā with the words "you

---

[19] Elkin Calhoun Wilson, *Shakespeare, Santayana and the Comic* (London: George Allen & Unwin, 1973), p. 132.

[20]. Ayyar, *Bhasa,* p. 423.

must fall into my power, because even Kuntī was captured by Rāvaṇa" and "soon I shall overcome you with violence, even as Hanumān seized Subhadrā, the sister of Viśvavasu" (Act I). Though he is not as multi-faceted and vivacious as Falstaff, he is an interesting character in his own right.

In Shakespeare, apart from the stock comic characters, there are some others who create fun, but are themselves unaware of their comic dimension. Polonius in *Hamlet* and the Nurse in *Romeo and Juliet* provide typical examples of this feature. Polonius is a figure of comedy, because his vanity and garrulity are in sharp contrast to the troubled world of *Hamlet*. The Nurse is rendered comic because of her grossness, slow-wittedness, vulgarity and arrogance. The comic role of the Nurse in *Romeo and Juliet* may be compared to that of Dhātrī in *Avimāraka*, because they have essentially the same functions to perform – promoting the marriage of their mistresses. But Dhātrī is more refined than the Nurse because she understands, sympathises and even helps Kurangi to achieve her desired end, the union with Avimāraka.

At times, comedy is manipulated by an agent who guides the action and brings it to its happy ending. Sometimes, the agent stands apart from the action, like the Duke in *Measure for Measure* or Nārada in *Avimāraka*. For example, like the Duke, Nārada is not involved in the story or fortunes of Avimāraka. But he acts as the agent of retributive justice by resolving the identity of Avimāraka. But in some cases, the agents themselves are deeply involved in the action – they are participants in the happy finale of the story – Portia, Rosalind and Viola, for example, are responsible for promoting the comedy, but themselves experience the consequences of the action.

Some of the characters in Shakespeare are endowed with the power to view life in its totality – Rosalind in *As You Like It* and Prospero in *The Tempest* best embody this power. Rosalind is both inside and outside the action, because she is deeply in love with Orlando, but is also aware of the fact that love is a mere madness. In her three-dimensional existence – as Rosalind, as Ganymede, and as Ganymede who acts as Orlando's Rosalind – she exhibits the multiple layers of her personality, and in this role–playing, she seems to rise above the common level of human activity. Prospero also has this lofty existence, because he holds the thread and directs the action to suit his own end. In this process he has control over supernatural powers as well. His attitude towards life is one of reconciliation – his forgiveness is based on an awareness of the truth that "the rarer action is in virtue than in vengeance" (V. i. 27-28). This is a level of high wisdom through overcoming selfish desires – in other words it is a level of philosophic non-attachment.

In Bhāsa's *Ūrubhaṅga* and *Karṇabhāra*, Bhāsa seems to project his world-view in the protagonists Duryodhana and Karṇa respectively. In *Ūrubhaṅga*, Duryodhana's inimical attitude towards the Pāṇdavas is transformed into one of repentence at his past evil deeds, He says that Bhīma's resorting to deceit on him is fully justified, because he has inflicted several injuries on their minds, by subjecting Pañcālī to shame, by killing Abhimanyu and by banishing the Pāṇdavas to the forest. Thus he accepts his fate by rising above himself, and the tragedy transforms itself into a comedic vision. In *Karṇabhāra*, Karṇa forsakes like in this world in pursuit of a larger objective – that of everlasting glory and gladly gives away the ear-rings and armour to Indra. He heroically meets with his death, which is a hero's death. In this case also the play goes beyond tragedy and spiritual salvation is achieved through the transcendence of selfish desires and the experience of bliss.

The final effect of dramatic characterization, according to Bentley, is one of mystery: "A mysterious character is one with an open definition — not completely open... as, say, a circle is open when most of the circumference has been drawn."[21] The character of Kṛṣṇa as it emerges from the plays *Bālacarita* and *Dūtavākya* may be relevant from this perspective. Kṛṣṇa is hailed in the plays as the Destroyer of *adharma* and Preserver of *dharma*. Nārada who descends from heaven to worship Kṛṣṇa, pays obeisance to him with the words:

> Here is Lord Nārāyaṇa,
>
> Whose valour is interminable and whose large eyes resemble the lotuses, and who is the supreme lord of the ruler of the Gods — the destroyer of the prowess of the demons, the flag-staff of the triple world, the creator of the universe, the supporter of mankind, the Primeval Man. (Act I. verse 7).

[21] Bentley, *The Life of the Drama,* p. 69.

In *Dūtavākya*, he is referred to as "Puruṣottama" or the best among men, but Duryodhana mockingly rejects this term and contemptuously refers to him as Damodara (one who has a rope around his belly), Gopālaka (cowherd) and Kamsabhṛtya (the servant of Kamsa). During the course of talk between Duryodhana and Kṛṣṇa, he abuses Kṛṣṇa and starts to fetter him, when Kṛṣṇa assumes *viśvarūpa*, a symbolic manifestation of the unity behind the apparent diversity of the world. Thus Kṛṣṇa's character is exalted in the two plays.

CHAPTER VII

IMAGERY IN COMEDY

IN DRAMA, imagery is one of the means by which the dramatist conveys an idêa effectively to the reader or spectator. Imagery refers to the symbolic use of words or ideas which bring out the deeper layer of meaning of the context of the play. In drama, imagery has a deeper significance than in poetry. W.H. Clemen writes that "imagery necessarily suggests to us the fundamental problems lying beneath the complex construction of a play."[1] It makes the play subtle and powerful by enriching the content and implications of the play. R.A. Foakes in his "Suggestions for a New Approach to Shakespeare's Imagery" observes that "dramatic imagery should include reference to the subject-matter and object-matter of poetic imagery, to visual and auditory effects, iterative words, historical and geographic placing, and to both the general and particular uses of these things."[2] This definition extends the scope of the image and gives it a wider dimension than its being confined to poetry alone. Any reference that stands not just by itself, but for something else and helps to unravel an idea, can be termed an image. This images suggest and re-inforce and idea through likeness, association, repetition or contrast.

Imagery, when it becomes an integral part of the play, increases dramatic concentration and deepens its imaginative significance. Through imagery, the dramatist knits together the apparently disconnected strands of thought and presents the central idea in a consistent and effective manner. In drama, imagery has multifarious functions. It can be used to describe an event or situation, to provide information, to establish a setting, or to fix the traits of a character. When describing an event, the dramatist conveys the message by

---

[1] W.H. Clemen, *The Development of Shakespeare's Imagery* (1951; rpt. London: Methuen, 1977), p. 4.

[2] R.A. Foakes, "Suggestions for a New Approach to Shakespeare's Imagery", *Shakespears Survey,* 5 (1952), 90.

invoking a mental picture which embellishes and reinforces the idea. To create a setting, the dramatist employs iterative imagery – that is, he keeps the mood of the play by repeating the same images that reflect the underlying idea. Una Ellis-Fermor in her essay, "The Functions of Imagery in Drama", observes that imagery in this case "not only knits the play together but emphasizes by iteration – and by iteration whose appeal is always to the emotions – the idea or mood which had guided the poet's choice of theme and shaping of form."[3] This feature is seen mainly in Shakespeare's *A Midsummer Night's Dream* and *The Tempest.* In these plays, imagery is one of the chief means for creating the background and atmosphere, and also for emphasizing the dreamy and enchanted quality of the plays. *A Midsummer Night's Dream* evokes woodland beauty through a series of images from nature – thus images referring to the moon, star, animals, birds, flowers and dew-drops are abundant. This may be compared to Kālidāsa's use of imagery in *Śākuntala* by which he establishes the pastoral setting of the hermit-grove. The world of Kaṇva's hermitage is occupied by objects from nature like creepers, fawns and bees. King Duṣyanta appreciates the beautiful form of Śakuntalā through images drawn from nature: "Even with the water-weeds entwined, the water-lily shows her charm. The dusky spot upon the moon elevates her splendour more. The dress of bark imparts a charm far greater on the slender maid. What may not, in truth, be called an ornament to lovely forms?" (Act I. verse 20).

Imagery can also be used to individualize character. Ellis-Fermor writes that "characters reveal themselves by their instinctive choice of subjects in which to image their thought and also by the form of the image, by their relation, that is, between subject and theme."[4] For example, as Clemen has observed on *Romeo and Juliet,* "the contrast between Mercutio's and Romeo's language is also a contrast between their different uses of imagery."[5] Mercutio, being a comic character, employs more or less realistic imagery, while Romeo's is more subtle and spiritualized. For example, Mercutio humorously remarks that Romeo is "stabbed with a white wench's black eye: run through the ear with a love-song; the very pin of his

[3] Una Ellis-Fermor, *The Frontiers of Drama* (London: Methuen, 1964), p. 83.

[4] ibid., p. 87.

[5] Clemen, *The Development of Shakespeare's Imagery,* pp. 68-69.

heart cleft with the blind bow-boy's butt-shaft" (II. iv. 14-16). In contrast to this, Romeo's imagery is more idealized. Romeo's words, "... her eyes in heaven/Would through the airy region stream so bright/ That birds would sing and think it were not right" (II. ii. 20-23), are less concrete and more subtle than Mercutio's. In *King Henry IV,* Prince Hal whose deeper layer of character is revealed by a soliloquy through a powerful image provides another instance of the use of imagery for establishing traits of character:

> ... herein will I imitate the sun
> Who doth permit the base contagious clouds
> To smother up his beauty from the world,
> That, when he please again to be himself,
> Being wanted, he may be more wonder'd at
> by breaking through the foul and ugly mists
> Of vapours that did seem to strangle him.
>
> (I. ii. 190-96)

The aid given by imagery in the rapid revelation of a character is seen in the figure of Nārada in *Bālacarita*. With a few touches, Nārada emerges as a pious yet humorous character. He states that he has come to earth to worship Lord Nārāyaṇa who is born on earth assuming a human form. Further, "the hostilities between the gods and the demons having waned, I do not take delight in an atmosphere permanently tranquil and hence in the intervals of my Vedic study I stir up strife as well as the wires of my lute" (Act I. verse 4). Moreover, "I possess supreme faith in the words of Brahman and hold all the penance groves in high esteem. Yet I speak the truth that the lute struck by my fingertips, hostilities and disputes dreadful and stiff are dear to me" (verse 5). The analogy between discord and the notes of a lute brings in a powerful image which reflects the personality of Nārada, and establishes him as a comic character.

In comedy, imagery is put to a variety of uses. Here, dramatists often employ imagery for a purpose different from that of tragedy. Unlike tragedy, comedy represents the condition of life as it exists in the present – it seems to proceed from an acceptance of life as it is. The indulgence in, and the enjoyment of, life triumphing over the stresses of circumstances is the first prerequisite of comedy. So the primary function of imagery in comedy may be said to highlight this feature. In Shakespeare, Falstaff, as he appears in the two parts of *King Henry IV*, provides a good example. Life to Falstaff is a most exciting experience – in his own words, "young men must live" (II. ii.88). He defends himself from the charge that he is "a villainous, abominable misleader of youth", with words that emphasize his zest for life: "If sack and sugar be a fault, God help the wicked: If to be old and merry be a sin, then many an old host that I know is damned; if to be fat is to be hated, then Pharaoh's lean kine are to be loved" (II. iv. 452-56). The imagery used in this context throws the ordinary norms of life into insignificance, because Falstaff celebrates an alternative way of life; he declares, "banish plump Jack, and banish all the world" (462-63). But this is exactly what happens in the end, and so these words of Falstaff become highly ironic.

The entire range of Sanskrit dramatic repertory seems to lack a character with the multi-facetedness and uniqueness with which Falstaff is conceived. In Bhāsa's *Bālacarita*, which is a celebration of the exploits of the youthful Kṛṣṇa, comedy is not of a subversive nature, as in the case of Falstaff. Kṛṣṇa is depicted as the joy and pride of the Gopa race, but he is also idealized and exalted as a paragon of virtue. This becomes clear in Act III through the conversation that ensues between an elderly cattleman and his young nephew. The latter, named Damaka comments that "ever since Nandagopa's son was born, the cows have remained free from all diseases. Certainly, the satisfaction of all the herdsmen is growing more and more. And moreover, there are vegetable roots in every furrow and fruits in every thicket." He goes on to describe the abundance of other products like honey, milk and butter. The prosperity of the Gōpa clan is thus revealed through a series of images from the objects of nature, and it is ascribed to the birth of the son of Nandagopa. The welfare calls for a celebration, and so the cowherds, along with Kṛṣṇa, Saṅkarṣaṇa and the lasses, amuse themselves by revelling. Dāmodara surrounded by the cowherds is compared to a lion in a cave. The cowherdesses themselves are as fair as the golden *campaka* flowers, with their faces and eyes resembling pink and blue lotuses in full bloom (Act III. verse 2). Thus the imagery in this context is in keeping with the festive atmosphere, as well as the mental condition of the lads and lasses clad in fine attire, giving themselves up to fun and frolic.

Apart from establishing an atmosphere of celebration, imagery serves to enhance the comic spirit by exposing ironic situations. This may be observed in Bhāsa's *Avimāraka* in which Avimāraka, disguised as a thief, breaks into the palace of Kuntībhoja. The palace appears impenetrable and frightful due to the darkness, and even trees seem as if they are swallowed up by the dense darkness around. The city as it appears in the dark night is compared by Avimāraka to a stream, through a series of images relating to the river: "Streets in the form of rivers waft in darkness, rows of mansions appear to resemble sandy banks, and the ten quarters are sunken in the dark. Thus this blinding darkness requires to be crossed over, as it were, by a ferry-boat" (Act III. verse 4). Avimāraka is able to take in all the sights and sounds of the palace because he has adopted the disguise of a thief, and is also protected by the darkness. His situation is highly ironic, because he meets another thief who has come to rob a house, and he manages to avoid him, though his own predicament is similar to that of the thief himself. He also sees a man who is engaged in trying to soothe his sweetheart: "While uttering the words 'what am I to you', not fully yet through her affection and in a manner by which her stammering is even hindered and dulled by tears and her neck is bent, she speaks unfavourably through her feminine nature, though she has become submissive to the wish of her lover out of her timid disposition" (verse 7). But as this scene progresses, she hears the crowing of an owl, gets frightened and embraces her lover. The uniqueness of Bhāsa's imagery lies in the fact that it is highly dramatic, and is adaptable to an elaborate style of acting.

Shakespeare often employs imagery to promote the comic irony of a situation. *Much Ado About Nothing*, in which Benedick and Beatrice are tricked into falling in love with each other by the merry company of Don Pedro, Claudio, Hero and Ursula, is a typical example. Leonato acts as though he has not seen Benedick (who is in hiding, but nevertheless is within hearing distance), and conveys to the rest of the group the news that Beatrice is deeply in love with

Benedick. Claudio, in between this conversation lowers his voice and whispers, "Bait the hook well; this fish will bite" (II. ii.109) and so the plan is well laid out to make Benedick believe in the truth of the report. A similar scene ensues in Leonato's orchard between Hero and Ursula, to make Beatrice believe that Benedick is strongly attracted to her. During the course of the talk, Hero notices: "... look where Beatrice, like a lapwing, runs/ Close by the ground to hear our conference", and Ursula, again by a striking image from angling, describes her plan to hook Beatrice: "The pleasant'st angling is to see the fish/ Cut with her golden oars the silver stream,/ And greedily devour the treacherous bait./ So angle we for Beatrice" (III. i. 24-29). The analogy between angling and the situation in the context is evident, and increases the comic irony of the situation. A more or less similar situation arises in Kālidāsa's *Mālavikāgnimitra*, when the king appears before Mālavikā to woo her, and the king's lawful wife named Irāvati, who has been hiding behind a tree, suddenly makes her appearance. Mālavikā has been sent by the Queen to strike at the *aśoka* tree so that it bears flowers, and the king addresses her with the words, "I too have not for a long time borne the flower of happiness; with the nectar of touch do you satisfy the longing of one who has relish left for nothing else now" (Act III verse 19). At this, Irāvati reveals herself and pursues the same imagery used by the king: "Satisfy, satisfy; the *aśoka* may or may not bear blossoms; but this on the other hand not only flowers, but also bears fruit." Thus the imagery in this context enhances the comic irony of the predicament and the discomfiture of the king and Mālavika.

More than any other verbal expression, the use of appropriate imagery enables a play to extend its scope and strengthen its quality. It is often employed in satiric writing, because its suggestiveness makes it far more powerful than descriptive writing. Aristophanes, the vigorous satirist, employs imagery to different purposes. In *Frogs,* he directs his ridicule at the great tragedians, including Euripides, and the satire is put into the mouth of Bacchus who is engaged in a conversation with Hercules:

HER: Are there not therefore here more than ten thousand other more lads who compose tragedies, more loquacious that Euripides by more than a stadium?

BAC: These are small fry, and chatter-boxes, 'twittering places of the swallows,' disgraces to the art, who vanish speedily, if only they receive a chorus, after having once piddled upon tragedy. But a poet of creative powers you would no longer find, if you searched, who uttered a noble expression.

HER: How creative?

BAC: So creative as to utter some venturous phrase as 'Aether, the little mansion of Jove', or 'Foot of time', or 'The mind which was not willing to swear by the victims, and the tongue which swore apart from the mind.'

HER: Do these please you?

BAC: Nay, but they please me to more than madness.

(*Frogs,* 88-104)

The tragic writers in general, and Euripides in particular, are subjected to vigorous satire – even the imagery used by Euripides is mocked.

Shakespeare only seldom indulges in satire – his plays are very different in matter and spirit from those of Aristophanes. Kenneth Muir, however, observes that his comedies make a relevant comment on life: "In all of them", Muir says, "he shows us some characters behaving foolishly or sinfully and others wisely and virtuously, and he does not leave us in doubt as to what we should be thinking and feeling."[6] Sometimes, human weaknesses like vanity, pedantry and fickleness are brought in for mild, good humoured ridicule. Touchstone in *As You Like It,* for example, provides an instance in his description of a typical courtier. Jacques is moved to admiration at his wisdom and intelligence, and introduces him to the Duke: "This is the motley-minded gentleman that I have so often met in the forest. He has been a courtier, he swears" (V. iv. 39-40). Touchstone humorously supports this statement, and his defence offers a comment on the life-style of a typical courtier: "If any man doubt that, let him put me to my purgation. I have trod a measure; I have flatter'd a lady; I have been politic with my friend, smooth with mine enemy; I have undone three tailors: I have had four quarrels, and like to have fought one" (42-46). Thus it is an ironic comment on the manners of the urban and civilized world, and is brought about through some striking images reflecting courtly life.

[6] Muir, *Shakespeare's Comic Sequence,* p. 9.

The spirit of many of the plays in Sanskrit is closer to Shakespearean than to Aristophanic tradition, because it does not often try to offer an explicit criticism of life. But, like Shakespearean drama, it firmly believes in a code of conduct, by which goodness ultimately triumphs over evil, and suffering is rewarded with good fortune. this may be seen with reference to Śūdraka's *Mṛcchakaṭika* in which the noble, but poor Cārudatta finally manages to secure the hand of his sweetheart named Vasantasenā, who though a courtesan, has an unfailing love for him. The Viṭa, important of this change in her attitude, coaxes her to accept Samsthānaka, and says that her house is the hospitable refuge of all youth, so that she is "like a wild flower that blooms at the side of a highway." "Your body, your caresses, are merchandise that may be bought with gold; you should, therefore, sell to all alike, and open your arms with equal abandon to the man who pleases you and to him who displeases you." He explains the meaning more clearly, and it offers a sharp ridicule on the institution of prostitution: "The wise *brahmin* and the idiot *pariah* bathe in the same lake; the flowering shrub bends beneath the crow as readily as beneath peacock; the ship that carries the *brahmin*, the *kṣatriya* and the *vaiśya* bears with equal security ignoble men. Are you not the lake, the shrub and the ship? You are a courtesan, and must minister to everyman's desire" (Act I). These three images powerfully establish the point that a courtesan should be disinterested in the manners of her customers, because her only concern is to extract money out of them.

The sordid contrast between high-flown sentiments and down-to-earth reality is a favourite topic of comic drama, and many dramatists draw fun by exploiting this phenomenon. The satire on the unintelligent indulgence in absurd fancies is a favourite topic in Shakespeare – often he cuts down the excess of romance attached to the "noble" sentiments like the romantic extravagance of Valentine in *The Two Gentlemen of Verona,* in the absurd talk of Launce:

> He lives not now that knows me to be in love; yet I am in love; but a team of horse shall not pluck that from me; nor who 'tis I will not tell myself; and yet 'tis a milkmaid; yet 'tis not a maid, for she hath and gossips; yet 'tis a maid for she is her master's maid and serves for wages. She has more qualities than a water-spaniel – which is much in a bare Christian. Here is a catalog (pulling out a paper) of her condition. 'Imprimis: She can fetch and

> carry:' Why, a horse can do more. Nay, better than a jade. 'Item. She can milk.' Look you, a sweet virtue in a maid with clean hands. (III. i. 250-75)

In this passage, Speed brings in the comparison of a water-spaniel and a horse deliberately to offer a contradictory interpretation of romance. In much the same vein are the words spoken by a high character like Titania in *A Midsummer Night's Dream,* where she is deceived into falling in love with Bottom with an ass's head. The imagery in this case renders the situation extremely ridiculous, because of the deception practiced on her: She rocks Bottom to sleep with the words: "Sleep thou, and I will wind thee in my arms ... So doth and woodbine the sweet honeysuckle/ Gently entwist; the female ivy so/ Enrings the barky fingers of the elm./ O how I love thee!. How I dote on thee!" (IV.i. 36-46).

Sanskrit comedies treat the theme of love in all its variations. The hero's sentimental exaltation of his beloved sometimes finds a parody in the Vidūṣaka's down-to-earth and even anti-romantic commentic comments, and often this becomes a comic situation by itself. An instance may be observed in Act II of *Śākuntala* where King Duṣyanta described Śakuntalā in an eloquently passionate language: "This immaculate beauty is like a flower not yet smelt, a delicate shoot not torn by the nails; an unperforated diamond; or fresh honey whose sweetness is yet untasted; or the full reward of meritorious deeds. I know not whom Destiny will approach as the enjoyer here (of this form)" (verse 10). The images in this passage suggest the freshness, beauty and the delicate charm of the youthful Śakuntalā. This speech is set off by the Vidūṣaka's answer: "Let your highness make haste, then, to rescue her, lest she should fall into the hands of some hermit whose head shine with the oil of 'ingudi; " (Act II). He further comments that the King's fascination for a hermit maid, when there are bright gems of women in his palace, is "like the fancy of a man who has lost relish for dates, and craves for the sour tamerind" (Act II). The images thus set off and act as a foil to the imagery used by the king, and serves to deflate the exaggeration of the eulogy.

Imagery in comedy is also employed for the purpose of ridicule and parody – they highlight the ludicrous aspect of a situation, and thus become a means to raise laughter and amusement. In *The Two*

Gentlemen of Verona, Speed humorously sums up the special marks of a lover and tells Valentine that "these follies shine in you like the water in a urinal, that not an eye that sees you but is a physician to comment on your malady" (I. iii. 33-36). In the same manner, Falstaff counterfeits the stately grandeur of the king and offers a self-flattery through a telling image: "Harry, I see virtue in his looks. If then a tree may be known by the fruit, as the fruit by the tree, there is virtue in that Falstaff" (II. iv. 411-14). In the same vein is Falstaff's counterfeiting of death in the battle of Shrewsbury, and it establishes him as a comic hero, because his values are diametrically opposed to that of Hal or Hotspur. To Hal, the battlefield provides an association to retrieve his lost honour – he dauntlessly pursues his duty inspite of the wounds he has received. Chance provides him with an occasion to save the king himself from danger, and the peak of his glory is achieved by the slaying of Hotspur. But to Falstaff, discretion is the better part of valour. To him, a battlefield is as cosy and cheerful a place as the tavern in Eastcheap, and so he indulges in a soliloquy on the different versions of the idea of counterfeiting: "Counterfeit? I lie, I am no counterfeit; to die, is to be a counterfeit; for he is but the counterfeit of a man: but to counterfeit dying, when a man thereby liveth, is to be no counterfeit, but the true and perfect image of life indeed" (V. iv. 116-22). Thus, the counterfeit of death by which one lives, rather than direct confrontation by which one dies, is established to be a better policy in war, and so it is a different judgement on valour. Viewed in this way, Hotspur's death becomes pointless, because it leads to the destruction of himself.

In Sanskrit drama, the Vidūṣaka is mainly responsible for promoting the ludicrous element – his traits like physical deformity, slow-wittedness and cowardice are held up to ridicule. In *Śākuntala*, the Vidūṣaka caught in the clutches of Mātali compares himself to a mouse caught in the claws of a cat, and cries out to the King that "a demon is twisting back my neck, and is about to snap it, like a sugar-cane" (Act VI). His cowardice, thus, off-sets the valour of the hero, who saves the vidūṣaka from Mātali. In this context, the Vidūṣaka's use of imagery has a tinge of self-mockery, and so it establishes him as a complex personality. In *Uttararāmacarita* even a noble person like Sage Vasiṣṭha is brought down to ridicule. In Act IV, the disciples at Sage Vālmīki's hermitage rejoice at the arrival of "the grey-bearded folks of various descriptions", who are the cause of the holiday for them. During the course of their talk. Vasiṣṭha is compared to a tiger on a wolf, on a poor, tawny calf". The image in this context is in striking contrast to the accepted view of the character of the Sage, and is solely intended to promote the humour of the play, This topsy-turvyism, which is a typical feature of comedy, is re-inforced through the use of imagery.

The imagery used by low characters suggests their social background, as well as underscores the humour of the situation. For example, in the case of the cowherds in *Pañcarātra* who employ images from dairy-products to describe a battle scene, the imagery is suggestive of their profession and it also renders them comic. In *Cārudatta*, the encounter between Maitreya and Vidūṣaka who guards Vasantasenā's jewel-box and Sajjalaka who has come to rob the house is humorously conceived. The robber, seeing the impoverished condition of the mansion, prepares to leave, when Maitreya talks in his sleep and, mistaking the robber for Cārudatta, asks him to take the golden casket. When the burglar hesitates whether he should accept it or not, Maitreya threatens to curse him if he does not do not, Maitreya threatens to curse him if he does not do so, and after handing over the treasure, he says that he can sleep soundly like "a trader who has sold all his wares" (Act III).

In Bhāsa's drama, imagery is not confined in the strict sense to metaphors and similes that evoke a pictorial image, but is integrated with the content of the drama. Bhāsa has put imagery to a variety of uses. In some plays, an image seems to illustrate the central concept of a play. This may be seen with reference to plays like *Madhyamavyāyoga*, *Svapnavāsavadatta* and *Pratimānāṭaka*. In *Madhyamavyāyoga*, the word "madhyama" is suggestive of the dramatic context and the underlying mood of the play. The *brahmin* boy who offers himself up to the demon Ghaṭotkaca as a sacrificial victim, thereby saving the other members of his family, becomes a symbol of devotion and courage, so that even Ghaṭotkaca is moved to wonder and respect for him. Ghaṭotkaca asks for an appropriate term of address for the *brahmin* boy, and gets the reply that he is "madhyama", middle one. Ghaṭotkaca sarcastically replies that madhyama is the most suited word for him, thus hinting at the callous indifference with which his kinsfolk have rejected him. The demon's address to the boy as "madhyama" brings Bhīmasena, Ghaṭotkaca's own father, to the scene and so this word becomes the key to hasten the play to its happy conclusion, the meeting between Hidimba and Bhīmasena. The arrival of Bhīma brings in another level of interpretation to the madhyama-image. Bhima boasts of his valour and might be declaring that he is the "madhyama" of the invulnerable and mighty. He is madhyama or the middle one also because of the fact that he belongs to the middle species, the human race. His definition of "madhyama" includes a combination of all these qualities. This image is used in *Pañcarātra* also to suggest Bhīmasena's valour. For example, Abhimanyu says that madhyama is he, who "before bound Jarāsandha by the neck, with hands like huge ropes, and thus achieved something that even Kṛṣṇa found a difficult task to do" (II. verse 57). Thus the key image of madhyama deepens the imaginative significance of the play.

In *Swapnavāsavadatta*, the image of the dream conveys an experience that is too deep to be conveyed otherwise. The dream-image which gives the play its title occurs as an incident in Act V, where King Udayana sees in a dream his beloved wife Vāsavadatta, who he thinks has perished in a fire. Udayana talks in his sleep to Vāsavadatta. The comic irony of the situation arises from the fact that Vāsavadatta herself is a spectator to the whole drama, witnessing with increasing joy the evidence of her husband's deep love for her, and even replying to his passionate addresses. In this case, strong emotional experience is stored up in the image of the dream, and so this image seems to stand for the play itself. In *Pratimānāṭaka*, the image of the statue reflects the theme of the play. The play gains its title from Bharata learning about his father's death by seeing the statue put up at the sculpture-gallery. Bharata's grief and his father's death is so overwhelming that he follows Rāma into the forest and requests him for permission to stay on in the forest. Rāma with great difficulty convinces Bharata of the necessity to go back to Ayodhya and rule the country effectively till he gets back and assumes power. But Bharata argues that he will not do so for himself, but will rule only on behalf of his brother. He asks for the sandals on Rāma's feet, so that he can substitute them for Rāma and act as the custodian of the country. Just as the statue represents a semblance of the original person, the sandals stand for Rāma and his right to the throne of Ayodhya. Here the imagery continues as a covert symbol which seems to justify the title of the play.

In some plays of Shakespeare, imagery becomes so dominant an element that the deeper significance of the play seems to be conveyed through it. In *The Tempest*, the imagery of the sea-storm in the scene becomes significant for interpreting the whole play. Shakespeare's imagery of storm and wreck are not descriptive comparisons, but they become the central theme of the play. About the imagery in *The Tempest*, Caroline Spurgeon notes that "it is not expressed through any one single group of images... but rather through the action itself and background, reinforced by a number of images from many groups, all illustrating or emphasizing one single sensation."[7] The play has many images relating to sound, images from such varied areas as the roaring of waters and sweet songs of the fairies. The images relating to the depth of the sea, the corals and pearls, the tempest and supernatural powers establish the setting and reveal the closeness of the region to that of magic. Caliban's words "As wicked dew as e'er my mother brush'd/ With raven's feather from unwholesome fen/ Drop on you both" (I. ii. 321-23) suggest the haunted atmosphere of the island. The song "Full fathom five thy father lies..." (II. ii. 396) is also a typical example of the use of imagery to establish the central theme of the play. In the next scene, the sea is invoked from a different angle – Francisco describes Ferdinand's struggling with the deep sea, in which the destructive aspect of the sea is revealed. Clemen observes that "this aspect of nature which threatens man's existence is repeatedly emphasized through imagery."[8] Thus an impression is created that nature is controlled by hostile and adverse forces.

Bhāsa's drama employs imagery to embellish the visual effects in the theatre. In *Dūtavākya* and *Bālacarita*, Kṛṣṇa's weapons are personified and they appear in human form. In *Bālacarita*, Kātyāyanī's retinue also assumes human form and directly addresses the audience. The play also includes a dream-scene which is powerfully

---

[7] Caroline F.E. Spurgeon, *Shakespeare's Imagery and What It Tells Us* (1935; rpt. Cambridge: Cambridge Univ. Press, 1961), p. 300.

[8] Clemen, p. 185.

conceived, in which Kamsa sees Chaṇḍāla maidens hovering in black in Kamsa's bed-chamber, haunting him and urging to be wedded to him. These maidens are personifications of Misfortune, Death and Adversity. Later, Imprecation who has also taken a human shape enters and asks permission to enter Kamsa's heart. Seeing her, Royal Fortune makes way and Imprecation establishes herself upon him. The action seems to take place inside the mind of Kamsa rather than outside. The scene symbolically suggests the ruin and fall of Kamsa and the impending calamity of his death at the hands of Kṛṣṇa. This scene seems to be unique in Bhāsa, because of its powerful imagery and theatric effect.

In the theatric representation of Kūṭiyāṭṭam, the text of the drama is subjected to an elaborate mode if *abhinaya*, and so even the imagery employed in the text provides material for improvization. This may be observed in the theatric production of the third Act of Bhāsa's *Pratijñyaugandharāyaṇa*, named *Mantrānka*. The main character is the Vidūṣaka, who appears in the guise of a jesting beggar engaged in incoherent speech. In the text, the context is as follows:

> (Enter the Jester disguised as a beggar) Jester. (Gesticulating) Well now, I put my bowl of sweetmeats in the temple steps, then I counted the gold pieces of my donation and tied them up. Now I turn round and I can't see the bowl of sweets. (Reflecting). That fellow who was hanging about, and I satisfied him with one sweetmeat – he has not followed me. The wall is too high for dogs and to get in. The sweets were unbroken as they were cooked and would not attract passers-by. Is it possible I ate them myself? I'll just bring them up again. Ha, ha! Like an old hog's bladder I am bringing up nothing but wind. Or perhaps Śiva has annexed it thinking that what belongs to the Red Goddess belongs to him. (More gestures). Now this young celibate is misbehaving in several ways. Well, I'll just have a look. Why, this is my bowl of sweets set at Śiva's feet. Well I'll take it back.

Though this speech of the Vidūṣaka appears as a ridiculous and incoherent prattle on the superficial plane, it has an implied meaning, in which the image of the bowl of sweetmeats (mōdaka) symbolically corresponds to Udayana the Vatsa King, as well as Yaugandharāyaṇa, the minister of the Vatsas. The hidden meaning of this passage is given by D. Appukuttan Nair thus: "The beggar having 'deposited the sweet balls at the feet of the Deity' implies that Udayana is safe in the hands of Vāsavadattā. His 'counting the gold pieces received as gift, implies that the instruction he received in the execution of the plan for release of Udayana, have been checked up. 'When he looked back, the sweetballs are missing' implies that after checking up the plan, when he arrives at the meeting place for further discussions, the Chief Planner is missing."[9] Similarly, in the rest of the passage, "I have satisfied the fellow with one sweetmeat, and so he will not follow me" means that since Pradyota Mahāsena has captured Vatsa Raja, he will not attempt to capture Yaugandharāyaṇa. "The wall is too high for the dogs to break in" suggests that the intelligence of Yaugandharāyaṇa is too deep for the ministers of Mahāsena to overpower. In the same manner, the whole passage has a deeper layer of meaning embedded beneath the obviously superficial. The term "modaka" in this context is the name of a sweetmeat. But literally, the meaning of the term is, "anything that gives delight". According to the context involved, the image of "modaka" refers to both King Udayana and Yaugandharāyaṇa. Thus it is not a static image, with only one layer of meaning. In the process of augmentation of the text, it becomes capable of numerous variations, and attains multi-dimensional significance.

---

[9] D. Appukuttan Nair, "Abhinaya in Kutiyattam ", *Theatre India* (1977), p. 35.

CHAPTER VIII

THE USE OF LANGUAGE IN COMEDY

THE EFFECTIVENESS OF language as a medium of expression even in *dṛśyakāvyas* or visual and performing arts is recognised by theorists in both Indian and Western traditions. The correlation between "sound" and "sense", that is, between the word and its meaning, has been subjected to detailed analysis by rhetoricians in India as well as the West. In *Raghuvamśa*, Kālidāsa compares the union of Pārvatī and Parameśvara to the inseparable state of word and meaning.[1] The question of the inter-connection of form and content in poetry is discussed by I.A. Richards in his *Practical Criticism* – a good critic, according to him, is one who has a perception of both the sense and the sound of a poem.[2] The interrelation between sense and sound can be in the nature of *vācya* and *vyaṅgya*, the former standing for a direct and the latter for a suggestive statement. When the meaning is put of the speaker/writer, the expression by the result of which the context is revealed is called *lakṣaṇa*. The third power in poetry, called *vyañjana* is an extraordinary significative power which all works of art possess. S. Kuppuswamy Śāstri equates it with the word "suggestion", and borrowing a phrase from Jespersen's *The Philosophy of Grammar,* he says that it is "impression through suppression".[3]

In India, there have been several theories regarding the exact nature or essence of poetic pleasure. While Bramhā stresses the importance of *alamkāra* (metaphor) in poetry, Vāmana pointed out that *rīti* (style) constitutes the soul of poetry. *Rīti*, according to Vāmana, applies to both the sense and the sound, and is classified under three heads: *gauḍī, pañcālī*, and *vaidarbhī,* the first standing

---

[1] Kālidāsa, *Raghuvamśa*, Sarga I, Śloka i.

[2] I.A. Richards, *Practical Criticism* (London: Routledge & Kegan Paul, 1964). p. 172.

[3] S. Kuppuswamy Sastri, "Highways and Byways of Literary Criticism in Sanskrit", in *Kuppuswamy Sastri Birth-Centenary Commemoration Volume, I* (Madras, Kuppuswamy Sastri Research Institute, 1981), p. 129.

for a vigorous and heroic style, the second for a graceful and decorative one, and the third for a combination of these two styles (*Kāvyalamkārasūtra*. I. 6-11). According to Ānandavardhana, who is an exponent of the *dhvani* school, poetic experience is conceived in terms of a power "which makes manifest, unexpectedly and with noticeable bridge, a new sense, independent of the conversational sense."[4] Thus in a *kāvya* or poem, the primary meaning and the sound suggest another level of meaning which exists in a veiled condition – this is called *dhvani*. This is responsible for poetic charm. In a poem, *rasa* is made manifest by the effective communication of this suggested sense, called *rasadhvani*. Supporting Ānandavardhana's thesis, Gnoli comments that poetic language is different from that of prose: it arouses in the reader echoes and feelings – in a word, aesthetic experience – foreign to prose, whose value is purely informative and didactic.[5]

In Western drama, the word "dramatic language" has a two-fold implication – it may refer to the language employed by the dramatist in the play, and it also signifies dialogue, or the exchange of words between characters in the play. The language employed by the dramatist sets the tone of the play, imparts information and establishes the setting. It reflects the dramatist's style of writing – for example, Shaw often employs lengthy, discursive prose, while Goldsmith and Sheridan have a brisk or vigorous style. Allardyce Nicoll distinguishes between two kinds of language – "ordinary speech" which is more or less a reproduction of the speech of ordinary life and "patterned language" which makes use of a conventional form of language to suit a particular occasion.[6] Even in realistic drama, the dramatist has to select, arrange and heighten the speech, to make it effective in the theatre. In nonrealistic plays, the language has a sharp deviation from ordinary speech – this ranges from the oversimplified and even ludicrous conversation of Beckett's *Waiting for Godot* to the highly poetic language of Eliot's *Murder in the Cathedral.* Eliot defends rhetorical style in his essay on "Rhetoric

---

[4] Raniero Gnoli, "Introduction", in *Aesthetic Experience According to Abhinavagupta* (Roma: Is. M.E.O., 1956), p. xxvi.

[5] ibid.

[6] Allardyce Nicoll, *The Theatre and Dramatic Theory* (London: George G. Harrap, 1962), p. 145.

and Poetic Drama": "At the present time there is a manifest preference for the 'conversational' in poetry – the style of 'direct speech', opposed to the 'oratorical' and the rhetorical, but if any convention of writing is inappropriately applied, this conversational style can and does become a rhetoric – or what is supposed to be conversational style..."[7] Thus, speech in realistic drama is as stylized or remote as that of poetic drama because, the medium of prose is as conventional a literary form as verse.

Speaking about the language of comedy, L. J. Potts says that in the dialogue of comedy, the aims of the writer are different in much the same way as speech differs from written language. Good comic dialogue is vigorous and rapid, with the manner of each speaker clearly differentiated.[8] Eloquence in speech is of greater importance in comedy than in tragedy. In comedy, language is often assisted by other visual and aural effects. For example in Commedia dell'arte, the comic appeal is not through the verbal medium alone. The actors resort to stylized acting, improvisation and acrobatics. When prose is employed as a medium of comedy, a degree of stylization is necessary to make it effective on the stage. For example, Eric Bentley speaks about the dialogue routines of Commedia dell'arte which Molière uses in plays like *The Miser (Life of the Drama,* p. 86). In the same vein is the pattern of catechism employed by the actor in Kūttu, because it is a method consciously adopted to focus the attention of the Vidūṣaka in Cākkyārkūttu follows a fixed pattern in his rendering a *śloka* in praise of *karma*. The superiority of *karma* is established because even the *trimūrtis* – Brahma, Viṣṇu and Śiva – are not exempt from the course of *karma*. After reciting the *śloka*, the Vidūṣaka begins his catechism on *karma* between two imaginary persons, both parts here being spoken by the Vidūṣaka himself.

> "I worship that karma." "um ... what? What do you say? It's to you I'm asking. Whom do you worship?" "I worship karma." "Karma? What's it, this karma?" "You are so old, and still you haven't heard about karma!" "No! I have seen many religious-minded people – those who are up before dawn, and after completing the morning rites, go down on their knees, chanting 'glory to Vishnu' etc. But I've never seen anyone prostrating oneself before karma." "That's exactly why you are so perverted." "Is this karma so sacred, that you

[7] T.S. Eliot, "'Rhetoric' and Poetic Drama," in *The Sacred Wood: Essays on Poetry and Criticism* (1920; rpt. London: Methuen, 1969), p. 79.

[8] L.J. Potts, *Comedy* (London: Hutchinson, 1949), p. 83.

> worship him so ardently? I've never known one such." "In that case, you must be stupid. I can convince you about the merits of karma." "Let me hear them. Is it holier than the *trimūrtis*?" "At least so much. You have respect for them, haven't you?" "These *trimūrtis* are Brahma, Viṣṇu and Maheśvara." "Yes". "You think that this karma is greater than all of them?" "Oh yes, to think of that, all the rest are insignificant before karma." "Shut up, don't talk nonsense." "O yes, but karma is still superior." "I can't believe it."

The language in such a context is interesting because of the method of catechism. This hilarious method courts comparison with Boyet's letter-reading scene in *Love's Labour's Lost* in which Berowne is rendered ridiculous. The language characterised by self-dialogue increase the comic effect of the situation:

> He came, saw, and overcame? He came, one; he saw, two; overcame, three. Who came?—the king. Why did he come—to see. Why did he see—to overcome. To whom came?—to the beggar... Shall I command thy love? I could. Shall I entreat thy love? I will. What shall thou exchange for rags?—robes, for titles?—titles, for thyself?—me. Thus expecting thy reply, I profane my lips on thy foot, my eyes on thy picture, and my heart on thy every part.
>
> (IV. i. 69-79)

When language is thus employed for comic purposes, sometimes it abounds in contemporary references, and so it tends to get dated. But because of this, it highly appeals to a contemporary audience.

In the comedies, Shakespeare employs a language that reflects his broad sense of humour. B. Ifor Evans comments that there is a subtley in the comic language which is not to be found in the passages of sentiment and romance.[9] There is a jumbling of prose and verse – as a rule the high comedy scenes are a mixture of prose and verse, while the low comedy scenes are mostly in prose. Shakespeare's language has many levels – the language that is used in the serious scenes is that spoken in the King's Court. The high-flown, pedantic language of scholars is depicted in *Love's Labour's Lost.* There are many dialects used by different characters in different situations. Besides these, the language of the rustic and that of characters like Dogberry and Verges have great comic appeal.

In Sanskrit drama, the importance of language as a medium of expression is highlighted by writers on choreography as well as literary critics. *Vācika* or the verbal medium, along with other

---

[9] B Ifor Evans, *The Language of Shakespeare's Plays* (1952; rpt. London: Methuen, 1966), p. 108.

nonverbal media like gesture, mime and dance, cohere and constitute drama. Sanskrit drama is also multilingual in the sense that it employs Sanskrit, as well as its dialectal variation called Prakrit. The high-born characters like sages, brahmins and kings are entitled to speak in Sanskrit, women and low characters have to resort to Prakrit. But the comic character of Vidūṣaka, even if he is a *brahmin* by birth, speaks not in Sanskrit, but in Prakrit. Thus the use of language is an indication not of social differentiation by birth alone, but also of good breeding, education and wisdom.

In Sanskrit comedy, language seems to establish the setting of the play. The language employed by the dramatist reflects the mood, atmosphere and character-types in the play. For example, Viśākhadatta's *Mudrārākṣasa* has brusque, realistic language, in keeping with the theme of the statecraft and political intrigue. This is in sharp contrast to the language of Kālidāsa's *Śākuntala*, which abounds in highly sensuous poetry, as befitting its pastoral background and romantic setting. Bhāsa's language is devoid of the poetic embellishments that characterise other dramatists like Kālidāsa and Bhavabhūti – his dialogue is often short, dramatic and witty, with many voids to be filled in by action on the stage – there are stage-directions in his plays like "they dance" etc. In *Madhyamavyāyōga*, Ghaṭotkaca, while fighting with Bhīma, thinks about hitting his opponent with an uprooted tree, and in the next speech, he wonders: 'why, I cannot kill him with this.' In between those who speeches there is provision for elaborately depicting the action of uprooting the tree and striking Bhīma with it. Thus the rapidity and directness of the action of the plays is reflected in his language also.

In Shakespeare, the language in situations of high comedy is full of witticisms, repartee and jests. Ludwig Borinski writes that images and jests are the two elements of Shakespeare's style: Everything gives rise to an image, a jest, and allusion of some sort, hardly a sentence is free of them.[10] In such situations, the intellectual element of Shakespeare's wit is reflected in the language that he uses. The speech between Benedick and Beatrice in *Much Ado About Nothing* and between Celia and Rosalind in *As You Like It* are the examples. Beatrice declares that she likes to remain unmarried, and Benedick

[10] Ludwig Borinsky, "Shakespeare's Comic Prose", *Shakespeare Survey*, 8 (1955), 58.

expresses his happiness at the decision because some gentleman or other shall escape a predestinate scratch'd face. To this, Beatrice replies that "scratching could not make it worse an 'twere such a face as yours". The conversation continues in this strain:

BEN: Well, you are a rare parrot-teacher.

BEAT: A bird of my tongue is better than a beast of yours.

BEN: I would my horse had the speed of your tongue, and so good a continuer. But keep you way a God's name, I have done.

BEAT: You always end with a jades' trick; I know you of old.

(I. i. 133-39).

Repartee is more than a linguistic device here – it is a verbal battle between two characters having "a mutual witty antagonism, which has evidently long continued and seems destined to go on.[11] Similarly, Rosalind and Celia engage in a light banter about Orlando's new-begotten love for Rosalind:

ROS: I could shake them off my coat: these burs are in my heart.

CEL: Hem them away.

ROS: I would try, if I could cry "hem" and have him.

(I. ii. 16-19)

In these Shakespeare's comic prose gets such clarity and subtlety that it justifies Potts's observation that "... dramatic and pregnant plainness marks highest level of Shakespeare's comic style."[12]

In Sanskrit drama, the language of Bhāsa's play is suited for the advancement of the comic spirit. In comedies of situation like *Madhyamavyāyoga* and *Pañcarātra*, the language expresses subtle humour and wisdom. Ghaṭotkaca, intending to address his victim, the middle one among the brahmin boys, calls out to him, and Bhīmasena – the middle one of the Pāṇḍavas – appears in response to his cry. During the course of their talk, Bhīma comes to know of the parentage of the Ghaṭotkaca and his attitude becomes one of loving indulgence. When Ghaṭotkaca asks him if he knows that Ghaṭotkaca is his own son. This enrages the demon, but Bhīma pacifies him by saying that warriors address all people as their sons.

[11] Brian Vickers, *The Artistry of Shakespeare's Prose* (London: Methuen, 1968), p. 176.

[12] Potts, *Comedy, p. 97.*

The mildly humorous and playful speech of Bhima is tinged with comic irony because he knows the fact about Ghaṭotkaca's parentage.

There are examples of brilliant dialogue in *Dūtavākya* and *Dūtaghaṭotkaca* in the verbal battle between Duryodhana and Kṛṣṇa in the former and that between Duryodhana and Ghaṭotkaca in the latter. In *Dūtaghaṭotkaca*, Ghaṭotkaca delivers Kṛṣṇa's message that Arjuna would destroy the *kṣatriya* clan because of his wrath at his son's murder. Upon this, Śakuni sarcastically replies that it would be possible, if one were to overcome the world with the power of more words alone. This sarcasm provokes Ghaṭotkaca who retorts that playing a false game of chess and fighting bravely on the battle-field are not the same, because the latter involves proficiency in warcraft. Similarly in *Dūtavākya*, when Kṛṣṇa comes to the Kaurava court as an envoy from the Pāṇḍavas to demand their rightful share in the kingdom, Duryodhana asks him about the well-being of the Pāṇdavas in a language that suggests their illegitimate origin and his unwillingness to part with the kingdom: "I hope my brother (Yudhiṣṭhira) son of Dharma, Bhīma the son of Vāyu, Arjuna the son of Devendra and the well-behaved twins, the sons of Aśvins, all of them with their dependents, are doing well" (verse 19). But Kṛṣṇa replies with an equally clever hint about the illegitimacy of Duryodhana himself: "This kind enquiry is worthy of you, the son of Gāndhārī. Yes, they are all very well", and proceeds to ask for the share of the Pāṇḍavas in the inheritance. But Duryodhana makes the former suggestion more explicit, and denies their right, when Kṛṣṇa refers to the family history of Duryodhana also: "Vicitravīrya, being a voluptuary, died of consumption (without leaving any issue). Then how could your father Dhṛtarāṣṭra, born of Vyāsa and Ambikā succeed to his kingdom?" (verse 22). Thus the valid antagonism and speciousness of logic are effectively conveyed in the language, in which each one tries to cap the remark of the other and turn it to his own advantage.

There are occasions in Western drama where language itself is made a subject of comedy, and humour is derived out of it. For example, in *Frogs,* Aristophanes parodies the tragic diction of Aeschylus and Euripides, and the result is highly comic. In Shakespeare also there is a burlesque of high-flown style, in plays like *Love's Labour's Lost* and *A Midsummer Night's Dream.* For example, Titania is enamoured of Bottom with an ass's head, and her entreaties expressed in rich, sensuous poetry, have a ludicrous appeal, because the audience is aware of the deception practised on her:

> I pray thee, gentle mortal, sing again.
> Mine ear is much enamoured of thy note;
> So is mine eye enthralled to thy shape
> And thy fair virtue's force perforce doth move me,
> And the first view, to say, to swear, I love thee.
>
> (III. i. 125-29)

In the same way Shakespeare sometimes employs long-winded rhetoric in verse with the purpose of increasing the comic appeal of the situation. For example, Hotspur's speech of defence against the charge of disobedience of the king's order is tinged with humour. The speech has a vivid description of a certain lord who comes to deliver a message to Hotspur from the King. Hotspur describes how he was himself "breathless and faint and leaning upon my sword immediately after the battle when/ Came there a certain lord, neat, and trimly dress'd/ Fresh as a bridegroom, and his chin new reap'd/ Show'd like stubble-land at harvest-home" (I. iii. 33-5). The description continues in this strain, till

> he smiled and talk'd
> And as the soldiers bore dead bodies by
> He call'd them untaught knaves, unmannerly,
> To bring a slovenly unhandsome corps
> Betwixt the wind and his nobility.
> With many holiday and lady terms
> He question'd me. (41-47)

The speech is so full of metaphors and images, and is rich in comic irony, so that the ridiculousness of the situation immediately registers on the reader's mind.

The Falstaff scenes in *King Henry IV* reveal Shakespeare's ability to highlight through language the comic potential of the comedy of character. These scenes have subtle, realistic prose which is in keeping with the atmosphere of revelry in the tavern. Falstaff's role as the object and subject of laughter is the source of comic pleasure in the play, and he himself comments on this duality of his nature:

"I am not only witty in myself, but the cause that wit is in other men". (2 *Henry IV* I. ii. 10-12). Ruth Nevo observes on the vivacity of his character that "He is witty intelligence itself in all its agility, speed, versatility and resourcefulness. He cannot be victimized, and this is what is irresistible. It carries us through the counterfeit death, through the counterfeit triumph, through the press-gang. It is why he has us on his side in the honour speech."[13]

The interest of some of the early plays like *The Taming of the Shrew* and *The Comedy of Errors* is more on situation than on character, and so the main function of language is to provide information regarding the progress of events. In comic contrast to this direct realistic language is Petruchio's language which is poetical – the elements of the poetical and the satiric are effectively blended in Petruchio's speeches and it is appropriate to his character and to the role which he assumes. For example, his praise of Vincentio as a most beautiful woman is full of rich poetry: "What stars do single heaven with such beauty/ As those two eyes become that heavenly face?/ Fair lovely maid, once more good day to thee" (V. i. 31-33). But it is a deliberate mask to subdue the shrewish Katherina, and so its effect on the audience is comic.

Evans calls *Hamlet* "a tragedy... of wit."[14] In the play, there is a constant reference to language – Hamlet, Polonius and Osric are themselves conscious of language. The affected and decorative vocabulary of Osric and Hamlet's comic imitation of it is a good example of the linguistic satire in the play:

OSRIC: Sir, here is newly come to court Laertes; believe me, an absolute gentleman, full of most excellent differences, of very soft society and great showing: indeed, to speak feelingly of him, he is the card or calender of gentry, for you shall find in him the continent of what part a gentleman would see.

HAM: Sir, his definement suffers no perdition in you.

(V. ii. 110).

In Kālidāsa's *Śākuntala*, the conversation between Śakuntala and her friends in Kaṇva's hermitage has youthful vivacity and friendly charm. In Act I, Śakuntala and her friends are introduced as water-

---

[13] Ruth Nevo, *Comic Transformation in Shakespeare*, p. 149.

[14] Evāns, *The Language of Shakespeare's Plays*, p. 116.

ing the plants, and Priyamvadā affectionately muses that the *kesara* tree with Śakuntalā standing near it looks as though it is possessed of a creeper. Śakuntalā gracefully accepts the compliment saying "here indeed, you are properly named Priyamvadā" (one who speaks good words). Similarly, while Śakuntala admires the beauty of Vanajyōtsnā, a creeper united to a tree, Priyamvadā mischievously comments:

PRIYAMVADĀ:	(Smiling). Do you know, my Anasūyā, why Śakuntalā is gazing so intently at Vanajyūtsnā?
ANASŪYĀ:	No, I cannot guess. Pray, tell me.
PRIYAMVADĀ:	"As the Vanjyotsnā is united to a suitable tree, thus, may I too, hope for a bridegroom to my mind."
ŚAKUNTALĀ:	This is, indeed, what you want for yourself.

Thus in this context, the dialogue is rich and sparkling, and is suited for the occasion of friendly intimacy.

In the scenes of low comedy in Western as well as Indian drama, there are a few stock devices repeatedly employed to make the language lively and humorous. For example, there are characters who indulge in verbal errors like malaproprism, misquotations etc. Dogberry in *Much Ado About Nothing* is made a butt because of his affected but wrong expressions like "comparisons are odorous" (III. v. 19) and "out watch, sir, have indeed comprehended two suspicious persons" (III. v. 49). Mistress Quickly who has very distinct speech-habits provides another instance where the language is wrongly used. She calls Falstaff "a honeysuckle villain" when she means "a homicidal villain" (2 *Henry IV.* II. i. 49). She has many other erroneous words like "detest" for "protest", "infection" for "affection", "courageous" for "outrageous" etc. Shakespeare, in conceiving her, has manipulated these errors in such a way as to promote the humour of the play. Such linguistic "errors" are not infrequent in Bhāsa – in *Cārudatta*, the very name of the character "Śakāra" is derived out of his faulty pronounciation of the voiceless palatal fricative sound "ś" for the voiceless alveolar fricative "s". His language is full of comparisons and attempts at scholarship, but his allusions and comparisons are full of errors. For example, he says that "Like Viṣṇu am I, the lord of the corpse bazaar, or Janamejaya,

Kuntī's son. I shall catch thee with my hand in thy hair and carry thee off as Duśśāsana did to Sita." (I. verse 12).

There are many instances in Shakespeare's plays where parody is used for the purpose of mockery or criticism. In *Twelfth Night,* Feste parodies the use of pedantic jargon, when Malvolio tries to tell him that he is not mad: "Madman, thou errest. I say that there is no darkness but ignorance; in which thou art more puzzled than the Egyptians in their fog" (IV. ii. 41-43). Similarly when Silvius in *As You Like It* recites the feelings of a true lover, Touchstone parodies them with the words "I remember when I was in love, I broke my sword upon a stone, and bid him take that for coming a night to Jane's Smile..." (II. iv. 37-39). Similarly, in the exchange of words between the maid and the Vidūṣaka and Cārudatta, there is a parody of the highly romantic courtship between Cārudatta and Vasantasenā. When the lovers exchange apologies for the mutual transgression of propriety, the Vidūṣaka remarks that "these two are worrying each other like a pair of ill-trained bullocks pulling a cart in opposite directions." Therefore he confronts the maid and says, "Radanikā, I beseech your ladyship to pardon me."

Another device by which Shakespeare enhances low comedy is the deliberate repetition of a word, making it appear comic. For example, Mistress Quickly says in *The Merry Wives of Windsor,* "Shall I vouchsafe thee the hearing" (II. ii. 36-39). In *Twelfth Night,* when Sebastian uses the phrase "Vent my folly: he has heard that word of some great man, and now he applies it to a fool... tell me what shall I vent to my lady? Shall I vent to her that thou art coming?" (IV. i. 10-16). Similarly, pun or play on words also frequently appears in the plays. In *Romeo and Juliet,* in the words of Mercutio, "Ask for me tomorrow, and you shall find me a grave man" (III. i. 95-96), there is a deliberate pun on the word "grave". In his plays, Bhāsa also seems to be fond of using linguistic devices like pun. There are accumulations of similar sounds, as in "sajalajaladhara", "saniranīrada" etc. He has also used pun to increases the comic effect of the situation. In Act III of *Avimāraka,* the Dhātrī, while coming to Avimāraka's apartment to convey Kuraṅgī's love for him, finds him pondering over Kuraṅgī's beauty, so that he fails to notice her. When he sees her, he feels abashed and explains that he was ruminating over the Yogaśāstra, by which he means a system of philosophy. The Dhātri smilingly replies that she too has come hoping for a "yoga" or union. Thus the double meaning of the word is cleverly manipulated to provide a comic effect.

The language employed in low comedy is Prākrit. In *Pratijña*, the scene between the soldier and Gātrasevaka who appears as the elephant-keeper, but who is actually a spy employed by Yaugandharāyaṇa, has lively and humorous language. For example, the soldier asks Gātrasevaka to bring the elephant Bhadrāvati:

SOLDIER:	Stop that irrelevant chatter. Bring the elephant at once.
GĀTRASEVAKA:	Let her come, let her come. The trouble is, I have pawned her hook.
SOLDIER:	What do you want to hook for? Bhadrāvati is so gentle by nature. Go and bring her at once.
GĀTRA:	Let her come, let her come. The worst of it is, I have pawned her half-moon necklet.
SOLDIER:	Bhadrāvati could be bound with flowers, what does she want a half-moon necklet for? Bring her at once.
GĀTRA:	Let her come, let her come. Only, alack-a-day! I have pawned her bell.
SOLDIER:	She wants to play about in the water, what do you want a bell for? Bring her at once.
GĀTRA:	Let her come. Alack, but I have pawned her whip.
SOLDIER:	What do you want a whip for? Bring her at once, I say.
GĀTRA:	She shall come, but alack!
SOLDIER:	Alack what?
GĀTRA:	Alack, I've been and-
SOLDIER:	You've been and -?
GĀTRA:	Alack-a-day! Why Bhadrā-
SOLDIER:	Bhadrā-?
GĀTRA:	Yes, alack! Bhadrāvati.
SOLDIER:	What about Bhadrāvati?
GĀTRA:	I've pawned her too.

The dialogue appears absurdly comic, and shows Bhāsa's power of delineation of low comedy. Equally amusing is the scene in Act II of *Pañcarātra* which depicts the conversation of the cowherds.

Shakespeare reveals a keen interest in using bawdy language, and often this becomes a source of humour. There are many instances in Shakespeare's plays where he employs dialogue having an obvious ordinary meaning, but also having an implicit layer of meaning which has a bawdy connotation. One such example is in *Romeo and Juliet,* when the Nurse asks if it is late enough to say "good den" or "good day". Mercutio replies that it is, "because the" "... hand of the dial is now upon the prick of noon" (II. iv.109-9). In Shakespeare's bawdy, Eric Partridge observes that "in his general outlook and in his attitude towards sex and bawdiness, he shows that he was both an idealist and a realist, a romantic and a cynic ..."[15] and so in his spirit, he strove to reconcile those opposites that made him such a complex dramatist.

In *Henry IV,* especially in the scenes in which Falstaff appears, Shakespeare uses the device of exaggeration, thereby rendering them comic. In a deliberately exaggerated way, Falstaff insists that he fought with fifty travellers at the Gadshill robbery. Similarly, when Prince Hal challenges the claim that he owes Falstaff a thousand pounds, Falstaff replies: "A thousand pound, Hal. A million. Thy love is worth a million: thou owest me thy love" (III. iii. 137-39). Thus in low comedy, Shakespeare employs all these devices to increase the comic effect of the plays.

---

[15] Eric Partridge, *Shakespeare's Bawdy* (London: Routledge & Kegan Paul, 1968), p. 4.

CHAPTER IX

THE COMEDIC VISION OF LIFE

IN *DAŚARŪPAKA*, DHANAÑJAYA observes: "As for any simple man of little intelligence who says that from dramas, which distil joy, the gain is knowledge only, as in the case of history (*itihāsa*) and the like – homage to him, for he has averted his face from what is delightful."[1] This statement implies that unlike many other forms of literature, the experience in drama is one of pure joy or delight. This experience has been analysed by Butcher in his interpretation of the function of tragedy according to Aristotle: "the poets found out how the transport of human pity and human fear might, under the excitation of art, be dissolved in joy, and the pain escape in the purified tide of human sympathy."[2] This transportation into joy is perhaps applicable not merely to tragedy, but to comedy also. Comedy has essentially an affirmative approach to life. In comedy, there is a fundamental harmony derived out of the confrontation and the final reconciliation between the opposing forcces in nature. The milieu of comedy accepts the condition of present existence. The emphasis is on freedom, spontaneity and the continuity of life. But beneath this, an attitude that goes far beyond the temporality of life is discernible. It offers an escape from the cares and anxieties of daily life in the pursuit of an ideal state in which ordinary impulses like the comic and the tragic have no more relevance. According to Indian thought, this is a condition of calm repose or serenity, derived out of the expulsion of all selfish desires and the attainment of *ānanda* or ultimate bliss. This experience has been the goal of the *ṛṣis* or sages in ancient India. This has correspondence with aesthetic experience. At this exalted level, the experience may be termed as one of "comedic gladness". This is the final experience in all art, and is described by M. Hiriyanna as "a

---

[1] Dhanajaya, *Daśarūpaka,* trans. George C.O. Haas (New York: Columbia Univ. Press. 1912). p. 3.

[2] S.H. Butcher, *Aristotle's Theory of Poetry and Fine Art,* p. 273.

kind of joy which is pure and untainted by even the least pain". According to him, "the aesthetic attitude stands higher than that of common or everyday life which is invariably characterised by more or less of mental tension".[3]

In the Indian philosophical tradition, the experience of this "higher pleasure" is not an idealized myth, but depending on one's capacity and striving, it is a practical possibility. This may be seen with reference to a Sanskrit *śloka* which throws light on the conception of a man with a comprehensive vision, an opposed to the partial vision of an ordinary man. According to the *śloka*, Kṛṣṇa, the *bhogi* (one immersed in wordly affairs). Śuka, the *tyāgi* (one who has renounced material life), Janaka and Rāma, the kings, Vasiṣṭha, the priest – all of them have reached this level.[4] This *śloka* suggests that irrespective of their action or *karma,* all of them are *jīvanmuktas* – they are joyfully impersonal in their *karma*. This supreme level of experience corresponds to Frederich Schiller's observation on the ultimate end of comedy: "The aim that comedy has in view is the same as that of the highest destiny of man, and this consists in liberating himself from the influence of violent passions, and take a calm and lucid survey of all that surrounds him, and also of his own being ... and ultimately smiling at the absurdities than shedding tears and feeling anger at the sight of the wickedness of man."[5]

In the entire range of Sanskrit dramatic repertory, Bhāsa's drama perhaps best embodies this spirit of comedic gladness. Bhāsa's drama deals with life in its diversity – it has a variety of themes and employs people with varied reactions on the human condition. But beneath this diversity, a mode of projecting certain values having a particular view of the human condition is discernible. Bhāsa in his drama reveals a broadly comic and genial understanding of the

---

[3] M. Hiriyanna, *Art Experience* (1954; rpt. Mysore: Kavyamala Publishers, 1978), p. 46.

[4] The Sanskrit version of this anonymous *śloka* is given below:

Kṛṣno bhōgī Śukah tyāgī
Nripau Janakarāghavau
Vasiṣtho karmakartā ca
Teṣām muktisthitiḥ samāḥ

[5] Frederich Schiller, "On Simple and Sentimental Poetry" in *The Comic in Theory and Practice,* p. 23.

world. He is not attached to any particular system of philosophy, but he seems to have assimilated the basic experience in Indian philosophic thought, a level of peace and spiritual calmness (*śānti*). He seems to have made some of his characters the protagonists for communicating the experience by which they transcend the merely personal and narrow, and attain a higher perspective.

In order to express his comedic perception of the world, Bhāsa has selected some episodes from the *Rāmāyaṇa* and the *Mahābhārata*, and freely interpreted them to suit his own imagination, so as to encompass the world-view of the dramatist himself. The two plays *Karṇabhāra* and *Ūrubhaṅga* are examples of a higher level of comedy in which Bhāsa's vision reaches a philosophical dimension. In *Karṇabhāra*, Karṇa, the main character, becomes the protagonist engaged in the quest for spiritual salvation. This one-act-play is a psychological study of the development of Karṇa's character. Karṇa undergoes a transformation in the drama, and is purged of his narrow, limited self, to achieve a level of philosophic detachment from the effect of his action. At the outset, Karṇa is depicted as eager to confront Arjuna and defeat him in war, but all circumstances are contrived to be against his success in the battlefield – he sees bad omens, and due to his preceptor's curse, the craft of archery fails him at the critical moment. More than this, Indra appears in the guise of a *brahmin*, and begs him for the divine ear-rings and armour that shield him from death. Though Karṇa sees that this is Indra's treachery to afford protection for Arjuna, Indra's own son, he gladly gives away the divine ornaments, because he is not willing to go back on failure in the battlefield, through them Karṇa grows in stature. To Śalya, his charioteer, he says that there is not cause for grief because if one meets with death in war, he ascends heaven, and if one wins, he gains in reputation in this world. Since both are desirable, war is not a calamity. During the course of the play, he becomes aware of the imminent success of the Pāṇḍavas in the battle, but he stoically perseveres in his duty to fight the Pāṇḍavas, especially Arjuna. At this stage, he is not tainted with jealousy or malice, but is content with his lot, because he is aware of the fact that by losing in the battlefield and accepting a hero's death, he gains spiritual glory.

The play *Ūrubhaṅga* idealizes the last moments of Duryodhana's life. Duryodhana is credited with heroic dimensions by Bhāsa's conceiving him as being better skilled than Bhīma in war and also by stressing the fact that Bhīma has to defeat him by resorting to deceit. His noble qualities like being a dutiful son, good husband and loving father are also brought out. At the moment of his fall, Duryodhana's perspective changes from enmity to reconciliation, and even forgiveness. He reaches a region of perfect calmness, where he can perceive with complete detachment the absurdity and waste of all that has happened. He pacifies the indignant wrath of Balarāma by saying that "Bhīma has fulfilled his promise, my brothers have ascended the heaven and I have come to this state: what is the point in continuing the war now?" He also states that their mutual hatred and feud have become a story of the past, and so he wants the Pāṇdavas to live, to perform the funeral rites for all the kinsfolk who have perished in war. He instils courage and soothes his wives by saying that his death, being a hero's death, is not to be lamented. Moreover, he is at peace with himself, because, while he lived, he "supported my friends by bestowing all favours on them, ruled my kingdom effectively and also had command over a vast force of army". Thus he has lived in the highest royal grandeur, and his death also, being a hero's death, is equally commendable. Aśvatthāmā, who is enraged at Bhīma's violation of martial decorum, threatens to destroy the Pāṇdavas, but Duryodhana again tries to pacify him. Aśvatthāmā does not understand Duryodhana's sudden change of heart, and asks if Bhīma has also robbed him of his self-respect. But Duryodhana's personality is thoroughly transformed; he has undergone a purgation of the soul, and reached a level of serene calmness, where petty quarrel and strife do not matter anymore. Thus in the end, he is depicted as surmounting the ego-centric self and attaining the region of bliss and quietude.

Indian drama, according to Wells, attempts at delineating humanity at its repose.[6] The device of happy ending in comedy celebrates the acceptance of a moral code which is not harsh or vituperative. *Daśarūpaka* speaks of five stages of dramatic action –

---

[6] Wells, *The Classical Drama of India*, p. 9.

ārambha, *yatna*, *prāptyāśa*, *niyatāpti* and *phalāgama*.[7] Between the second and the third stages, there is *apāyaśaṁka* or fear of failure, but it is set right by the prospect of success. In a rough way, this seems to correspond to Leone di Somi's observation on action in a comedy, quoted by Salinger: "The first act of a well-constructed comedy should contain the argument exposition, in the second we should see various disturbances and hindrances, in the third some adjustment must be made, ruin and disaster must threaten in the fourth, while in the fifth a solution is to be reached, bearing all to a joyous and happy ending".[8] In Shakespearean comedy, the device of happy ending is a way of looking above misery and accepting the existing order of things with the affirmation of life in its own terms.

Shakespeare experiments with the dramatic medium of comedy by adopting diverse perspectives. Basically, his drama seems to be an attempt to adopt an affirmative approach to life through a broadly comic understanding of the world. His comedy celebrates the spirit of freedom and offers a way of transcending despair by reaching a level of harmony and reconciliation between the opposing elements in human nature. In order to express this comedic awareness of the world, Shakespeare uses the tools of romance, wit and humour against a backdrop of humane wisdom.

Shakespeare's mature comedies and the last plays are the finest expression of his comedic vision of life. Though evil, strife and suffering appear in the plays, these are transcended through adopting an attitude of reconciliation or spiritual composure. The dominant notes in these plays are those of forgiveness, affirmation and rejuvenation. Some of the characters in Shakespeare and endowed with the power to view life in its totality – Rosalind in *As You Like It* and Prospero in *The Tempest* best embody this spirit. Rosalind exhibits the multiple layers of her personality in the role-playing with Orlando, and in this, she seems to rise above the common level of humanity. In her disguise, she is endowed with the capacity of acting to be in love, and also looking beyond it to mock the illusions of romantic love, at the same time herself being deeply in love with Orlando. Here she seems to assimilate within herself

---

[7] *Daśarūpaka*, Book I, verse 28.

[8] Salinger, *Shakespeare and The Traditions of Comedy*, p. 201.

the experience of all men – the wide diversity of joys and sorrows of men in the infinitely varied world. Prospero also has this comprehensive vision – according to G. Wilson Knight he is Shakespeare's conception of a superman, a composite of many Shakespearean heroes. Wilson Knight observes that Shakespeare "spins his plot from his own poetic world entirely, simplifying the main issues of his total work – plot, poetry, persons; whittling off the non-essential and leaving the naked truth exposed. *The Tempest*, patterned of storm and music, is thus an interpretation of Shakespeare's world."[9] Prospero is a patron and lover of humanity. He holds the thread and directs the action to suit his own end. His forgiveness is based on an awareness of the truth that the rarer action is in virtue that vengeance (V. i. 27-28). According to Wilson Knight, he is a god-man, or perhaps the god-in-man, causing yet negating tragedy for his purpose as he draws man towards vision despite inertia and retrogression."[10] Thus he represents a level of high wisdom attained through overcoming selfish desires – in other words, it is a level of spiritual harmony through philosophic detachment.

In his plays, Shakespeare displays a humane and tolerant attitude towards the foibles of the world. The motif of forgiveness in Shakespearean drama is analysed by Robert Grams Hunter, who labels four comedies – *Much Ado About Nothing, All's Well that Ends Well, Cymbeline* and *the Winter's Tale* – as romantic comedies of forgiveness, because in them "the *humanum genus* figure offends the woman who loves him and is forgiven by her."[11] The sin of this figure arises from his failure to trust his love absolutely. The plays invoke the impulses of love and strife, but equilibrium is restored by means of charity or forgiveness. For example, in the world of *Much Ado,* Claudio falls in love with Hero on seeing her lovely looks and modest manner, but when he is deceived into believing that Hero is unfaithful, he falls out of love with her. But once the treachery of the villain Don John is exposed and Hero's innocence

---

[9] G. Wilson Knight, *The Crown of Life: Essays in Interpretation of Shakespeare's Final Plays* (London: Methuen, 1965), p. 204.

[10] ibid., p. 242.

[11] Robert Grams Hunter, *Shakespeare and the Comedy of Forgiveness* (New York: Columb[illegible] Univ Press, 1965), p. 87.

established, Claudio repents, and "is unreservedly forgiven".[12] The audience is expected to participate emotionally in the happy finale of the plot, and share the comic experience of the characters and also of the dramatist himself. This same method applies to the other comedies also. In *All's Well,* Helena loves Bertram and wants to be loved by him. But Bertram is portrayed as wicked and vicious, in need of regeneration, so that he becomes unworthy of Helena's love. In order to promote the play to its happy conclusion, Helena resorts to trickery, because she substitutes herself in the place of Diana. She manages to secure the ring from him and also become pregnant by him, and thus fulfills the task imposed on her. Thus Bertram is reformed into self-knowledge, his sins are forgiven, and he is united to Helena. In *Cymbeline,* Posthumus, though by deception, attempts to murder Imogen, and thus becomes the sinner. But the play is an example of the means by which God's grace operates and sets the action through the right path. In *The Winter's Tale,* Leontes's sin is sexual jealousy for he baselessly suspects his wife of infidelity. The bond of love and trust breaks, the Leontes attempts to destroy three innocent people, his friend, his wife and his new-born son. Once the oracle declares the chastity of Hermione and the innocence of Polixenes, Leontes repents, but he has to suffer the pangs for his past crimes. Hermione symbolically seems to represent God's grace, and her return to Leontes marks his attainment of divine grace. The same idea may be applied to some of the comedies in Sanskrit also. For example in *Śākuntala,* Duṣyanta falls in love with Śākuntalā, the hermit-girl, and marries her secretly according to the rules of *gāndharva* marriage. By the time he returns to his palace, Śākuntalā is subjected to a curse by Sage Durvāsas, by which Duṣyanta loses memory of the relationship, and so when she approaches him, he repudiates her. Śākuntalā in her secret marriage has behaved contrary to the decorum of the hermitage, and so she has to suffer the consequences of her action. The curse is revoked by the discovery of the ring which restores the king's memory, and he repents his fault. His repentence and his longing for Śākuntalā are so intense that he once again gains in divine grace, and the couple is reunited. His past

---

[12] ibid., p. 104.

misdeed is explained away as the result of the curse, and he is unreservedly forgiven.

The concept of a whole man with a comprehensive view-point, as opposed to the partial vision of ordinary human beings, is brought out by Bhāsa in his portrayal of the personality of Kṛṣṇa. Bhāsa is not primarily a poet of *bhakti* or devotion, but he celebrates the nobility of Kṛṣṇa in the two plays *Dūtavākya* and *Bālacarita*. Kṛṣṇa, as seen from the two plays, is a composite figure with many-sided virtues, but he is thoroughly humanised – in *Dūtavākya*, he is referred to as "Puruṣottama", the best among men. Kṛṣṇa is conceived by Bhāsa as embodying a perspective from which *karma* or action in this world becomes not only meaningful, but also an indispensable activity. He is depicted as a patron of *dharma* or piety and an opponent of *adharma* (impiety). In *Dūtavākya*, he is sent by the Pāṇḍavas an envoy to the Kaurava court to demand the rightful share of the Pāṇḍavas in the kingdom. In this situation, Kṛṣṇa carries out the task entrusted to him with full sincerity, but it fails to succeed because of Duryodhana's unwillingness to part with the kingdom. Side by side with exalting Kṛṣṇa, Bhāsa makes Duryodhana offer an alternative judgement on Kṛṣṇa's character, by projecting his less glamorous side, that of being a coward in the battle with Jarāsandha and also his supposedly low origin as a cowherd. But in the verbal battle, Bhāsa establishes Kṛṣṇa's superiority over Duryodhana because he stands for *dharma*, as opposed to Duryodhana's *adharma*. Towards the end of the play, Kṛṣṇa assumes *viśvarūpa* – that is, he encompasses within himself the experience of all the world – a symbolic expression of the unity behind the diversity of the universe. In *Bālacarita* also, Kṛṣṇa is an agent of retribution, because he is engaged in the task of destroying evil-doers like Kaṁsa and supporting pious people. He is conceived as a true *karmayogi* who performs action, but is detached about its result – even while indulging in life, he has an attitude of poise and calmness towards all experience.

Thus, in Shakespeare and Bhāsa, the ultimate aim of comedy is not the irresponsible hilarity of laughter nor even the irrepressible zest for life characterised by the figure of Falstaff. The ideal is a state of serene calmness, which the deeper spirit of both the Indian and the Western traditions has aspired to achieve. In this respect, the comic mode in Shakespeare stands far apart from the calculated satire of Aristophanes or Ben Jonson or the social criticism of Bernard Shaw. Wells's observation on the concept of Indian theatre stands justified in relation to the spirit behind the drama of both Bhāsa and Shakespeare:

> The theatre is conceived as functioning much as music, at once artful and therapeutic, for it is not only a means of relieving or obliterating pain but of confirming well-being or happiness proceeding from an image of spiritual health and strength. The play is to induce us to feel through the harmony of its art the harmony presumed to reside equally in man's soul and the religiously conceived universe. The end of its art, to repeat, is neither mimetic nor rationalistic, neither strictly moral nor intellectual, but a pervasive awareness of an inner harmony, with the refreshment from an experience in which the spirit is at the same time active and serene, an experience valid far beyond the games and toys of childhood and yet as gratifying and smooth in its operations as a game played with complete mastery of the conditions encompassing it.[13]

---

[13] Wells, pp 53-54.

GLOSSARY

Abhinaya Literally means "to lead towards". The word stands for dramatic action. The texts on dramaturgy have a detailed account of *abhinaya* or dramatic communication.

Ānanda means "happiness" or "enjoyment". In Vedāntic perspective, *ānanda* refers to the pure and untainted joy derived out of the perception of *brahma* or the unity behind the apparent diversity of the world.

Aṅka literally means "lap". In drama, it refers to the Act of a play. According to the *Nāṭyaśāstra*, aṅka is called so because it consists of actions with *bhāvas* and *rasas*, comprising different layers of meaning or interpretation.

Anukaraṇa is "imitation". According to *Nāṭyaśāstra* nāṭya or dramatic art is in the nature of *anukaraṇa* of the ways of the world.

Bharatavākya is the concluding verses or verses of a play, the denouement.

Bhāva is primarily a condition or state of mind. In Indian aesthetic theory, *bāhava* signifies a state of mind which through the operation of other forms of *abhinaya* develop into *rasa*. According to *Nāṭyaśāstra,* there are eight *sthāyībhāvas* or permanent mental conditions which develop into their corresponding *rasas* with the assistance of other ingredients like *vibhāvas, anubhāvas* and *vyabhicāribhāvas*.

Bhoga means "pleasure" or "delight". The word suggests an epicurean adherence to the pleasures of the material world. One who gives himself up to voluptuous luxury is a *bhogin*.

Brahmānanda. See under "*ānanda*".

Cākkyar-kūttu is a variant form of Kūṭiyāṭṭam or the traditional Sanskrit theatre of Kerala. *Cākkyarkūttu* is a one-man-show in which the *cākkyar* or the actor-protagonist orally cites *ślokas* or verses from well-known mythological treatises and subjects them to verbal elaboration.

Dharma is the ethical precept or code of conduct enforcing moral discipline.

Dhvani may roughly be defined as the suggestive element in poetry. Ānandavardhana, in his *Dhvanyāloka,* considers *dhvani* as the soul of poetry.

Gāndharva relates to the form of marriage which requires only mutual agreement.

Guṇa is associated with the philosophic system of Sāṁkhya. It is an ingredient or constituent of *Prakṛti,* the chief quality of all existing beings. According to its nature, *guṇa* is divided into three types: *satva,* the superior, *rajas,* the middling and *tamas,* the inferior varieties.

Hāsya, which evokes laughter and merriment, is one of the eight *rasas* discussed in Indian aesthetics. It relates to the comic element in man's disposition.

Jīvanmukta, according to Indian philosophic concept, is a person who, while still alive, has emancipated himself from the strains and stresses of the mundane world. In other words, he is a person who, while indulging in action, practises detachment from it.

Karma stands for action. It also signifies one's occupation in the material world.

Kathakali is the sacred dance-drama of Kerala. It incorporates stories from *purāṇas* and other mythological legends and subjects them to an elaborate mode of *abhinaya.*

Kavya means "a poem." More accurately, it is a poetical composition with a coherent plot composed by a single author.

Kramadīpikā and *āṭṭaprakāraṁ* are detailed texts on choreography which have been preserved by the cākkyars or actors of

Kūṭiyāṭṭam, or the traditional Sanskrit theatre of Kerala. Kramadīpika is a practical guide which illustrates facts ranging from theatrical setting to the remuneration offered to actors. In *āṭṭaprakāraṁ*, the method of elaboration of the text of the play is vividly depicted.

Kūṭiyāṭṭam is the traditional form of Sanskrit theatre which is supposed to have been prevalent in Kerala for approximately the past two thousand years. This theatric form treats the *aṅkas* or Acts of well-known plays as fullfledged dramas and subjects them to a stylised mode of elaborate acting. This dramatic form is performed in temple-theatres called *kūttampalams* by a hereditory group of actors called *cākkyars*.

Lokadharmī and *nāṭyadharmī* are terms in the *Nāṭyaśāstra* which correspond respectively to the realistic and stylised modes of representation.

Nāndī is eulogium or praise of a deity which usually marks the beginning of a drama.

Nāṭaka is a kind of play, the first of the *rūpakas* or dramatic forms. According to its definition, *nāṭaka* is a play consisting of a well-known plot and a noble hero. It has a well-constructed body consisting of five or more Acts or *aṅkas*, consisting of five stages of development of the plot.

Prastāvanā is an introductory dialogue spoken by the Sūtradhāra or stage-manager and one of the actors. It is usually a dramatic prologue.

Rasa literally means "taste" or "flavour". In Indian aesthetics, *rasa* constitutes the pure and untainted delight derived out of poetry and drama. It is the summit of aesthetic rapture.

Rīti is a term which literally means 'the style of writing.' In Indian aesthetic, Vāmana describes poetic pleasure in terms of *rīti* or style.

Sādhāraṇīkaraṇa is a term used by aestheticians like Abhinavagupta, Bhaṭṭanāyaka and Bhaṭṭatauta by which they describe the nature of aesthetic experience. According to them, the experience in poetry and drama has no personal significance because it is in an idealized or exalted form. This state of experience is called *sādhāranīkaraṇa* because it is the perception of the universal element in aesthetic experience.

Śānta is a state of mind characterised by the absence of desire and other passions, and the attainment of peace and tranquillity.

Sphoṭa relates to the connection between sound and sense. According to Bhartṛhari, *sphoṭa* is the eternal and imperceptible element in sound which flashes into sense after the sound is uttered.

Sūtradhāra literally means a "string-holder." In Indian dramaturgy, *sūtradhāra is* the director or stage-manager of a play. He recites the invocatory stanza, welcomes the audience and introduces the play, the setting and the characters. Thus he is a leading person in a dramatic performance because he superintends the whole play.

Tauryatrika means a triple symphony of song (*gīta*), dance *(nṛtta)* and instrumental accompaniment *(vādya)*.

Vidūṣaka literally means "one who is engaged in ridiculous speech." In drama, it refers to a comic character who is a combination of a wit and butt.

Viśvarūpa is a form adopted by Kṛṣṇa depicted in the *Mahābhārata*. It is a symbolic manifestation of the unity in the diversity of the universe.

BIBLIOGRAPHY

I Primary Sources

A. SANSKRIT

Bhāsa. *The Thirteen Trivandrum Plays Attributed to Bhāsa*. Trans. A.C. Woolner and Lakshman Sarup. London: Oxford Univ. Press, 1930.

——. *Avimāraka and bālacarita.* Trans. Bak Kunbae. Delhi: Meharchand Lachhmandas, 1968.

——. *Ūrubhaṅga of Bhāsa*. Trans. C.R. Devadhar. Poona: Oriental Agency, 1940.

Bhavabhūti. Uttarāmacarita. Trans. G.K. Bhat. Surat: The Popular Publishing House, 1955.

Buitenen, J.A.B. Van. Ed. *Two Plays of Ancient India.* Delhi: Motilal Banarsidass, 1971.

Harsha. *Śrī Harśha's Plays.* Trans. Bak Kunbae. Delhi: Asia Publishing House, 1964.

——. *Rātnavalī*. Trans. P.V. Ramanuja Swamy. Madras: Sastrulu, 1936.

——. *Priyadarśikā* by Harṣha. Trans. G.K. Nariman., et al. New York: Columbia Univ. Press, 1923.

——. Kālidāsa. *Works of Kālidāsa*. Vol. I. trans. C.R. Devadhar. Delhi: Motilal Banarsidass, 1966.

Kulasekharavarman. *Subhadradhanamjayam*. Trans. Attur Krishna Pisharoti. Trichur: R.C. Bhattaraka, 1969.

Mahendravikramavarman. *Mattavilasa Prahasana of Mahendravikramavarman*. Trans. N.P. Unni. Trivandrum: College Book House, 1974.

Śaktibhadra. Āścaryacūḍāmaṇi. Trans. K.P. Narayana Pisharoti. Trichur: Sangeeta Nataka Academi, 1967.

Wells, Henry W. ed. *Six Sanskrit Plays*. Bombay: Asia Publishing House, 1964.

B. WESTERN

Aristophanes. *The Comedies of Aristophanes.* 2 vols. Trans. William James Hickie. London: G. Bells, 1910.

Congreve, William. *The Way of the World,* 1700; rpt. London: J.M. Dent, 1967.

Corrigan, Robert W. Trans. *Greek Comedy.* New York: Dell Publishing Co., 1965.

Goldsmith, Oliver. *Two Plays of Goldsmith.* Ed. Guy Boas and Margaret Willy. London: Edward Arnold, 1962.

Jonson, Ben. *The Complete Plays.* 2 vols, 1910; rpt. London: Methuen, 1965.

——. *Every Man in his Humour.* 1923; rpt. London: Methuen, 1965.

Moliere. *Comedies.* 2 vols. Trans. H. Baker and J. Miller. 1929; rpt. London: Everyman, 1962.

Oates J. Whitney, Eugene O'Neill Jr., ed. *The Complete Greek Drama.* New York: Random House, 1938.

Sheridan. Richard Brinsley. *Sheridan's Plays.* Ed. Louis Gibbe. 1906; rpt. London: Everyman, 1966.

————. *The School for Scandal* Ed. Norman Jeffares. New York: Macmillan, 1967.

II Secondary Sources

A. SANSKRIT

Ānandavardhana. *Dhvanyālokaṁ*. Ed. E.V. Damodaran, Kottayam: National Book Stall, 1973.

Ayyar, A.S.P. *Bhāsa*. Madras: Ramaswamy Sastrulu, 1957.

Banerji Sastri, A.P. "Bhāsa: His Age and Māgadhi". *Journal of the Bihar and Orissa Research Society* (1923), 49-113.

Barnett, L.D. "Who is the Author of Swapnavasavadatta?" *Journal of the Royal Asiatic Society* (1925), p. 99.

Bhat, G.K. *The Vidushaka*. Ahmedabad: The New Order Book, 1959.

——. "Bhāsa and Bharata: The Problem of Tragedy", *Journal of the University of Bombay* (Sept. 1953), 27-35.

Bhattacharya, Biswanath. *Sanskrit Drama and Dramaturgy*. Varanasi: Bharata Manisha, 1974.

Bowers, Faubion. *Theatre in the East: A Survey of The Asian Dance and Drama*. London: Thomas Nelson, 1956.

Byrski, Christopher M. *Concept of Ancient Indian Theatre*. Delhi: Munshiram Manoharlal, 1974.

Chaitanya, Krishna. *A New History of Sanskrit Literature*. Delhi: Manohar Book Service, 1977.

Chakkyar, Mani Madhava. *Nāṭyakalpadrumaṁ*. Cheruthuruthy: Kerala Kalamandalam, 1975.

Coomaraswamy, Ananda K. *The Transformation of Nature in Art*. London: Munshiram Manoharlal, 1974.

De, S.K. *History of Sanskrit Poetics*. 1960; rpt. Calcutta: Firma K.L.M., 1976.

Ghosh, Manmohan. *The Nāṭyaṣastra: A Treatise on Indian Dramaturgy and Histrionics Ascribed to Bharata Muni*. Calcutta: Manisha Granthalaya, 1967.

Ghosal, S.N. *Kālidāsa: An Estimate of his Literary Merit*. Calcutta: The World Press, 1971.

Gnoli, Raniero. *The Aesthetic Experience according to Abhinavagupta*. Roma: Is M.E.O., 1956.

Haas, George C.O., Trans. *The Daśarūpaka of Dhanaṁjaya*. Delhi: Motilal Banarsidass, 1962.

Hiriyanna, M. *Art Experience*. Mysore: Kavyalaya, 1954; rpt. 1978. London: Luzac, 1955.

Janaki, S.S., ed. *Kuppuswami Sastri Birth-Centenary Commemoration Volume*. Madras: Kuppuswamy Sastri Research Institute, 1981.

Kale, Pramod. *The Theatric Universe: A Study of the Nāṭyaśāstra*. Bombay: Popular Prakashan, 1974.

Keith, A. Berriedale. *The Sanskrit Drama in its Origin, Development, Theory and Practice*. 1924; rpt. London: Oxford Univ. Press, 1970.

Krishnachandran, V.R. Purusharthakkoothu. Trichur: Kerala Sahitya Akademi, 1978.

Levi, Sylvain. *The Theatre of India*. 2 vols. Calcutta: Writers Workshop, 1978.

Mirashi, V.V. *Kālidāsa*. Nagpur: Suvichar Prakashan Mandal, 1934.

———. *Bhavabhūti*. Delhi: Motilal Banarsidass, 1974.

Mukherji, Ramaranjan, *Literary Criticism in Ancient India*. Calcutta: Sanskrit Pustak Bhandar, 1966.

Nambiar, P.K. Narayanan. *Mantrankam*. Trichur: Kerala Sahitya Akademi, 1980.

Pisharoti, K.P. Narayana. Trans. *Bharatamuniyuṭe Nāṭyaśāstraṁ* 2 vols. Trichur: Kerala Sahitya Akademi, 1979.

Pusalker, A.D. *Bhāsa: A Study*. Delhi: Munshiram Manoharlal, 1968.

Raghavan, V. and Nagendra. ed. *An Introduction to Indian Poetics*. Madras: Macmillan, 1970.

The Number of Rasas. Madras: Adyar Library, 1940.

Rangacharya, Adya. *Drama in Sanskrit Literature*. Bombay: Popular Prakashan, 1967.

Sastri, Pancapagesa P. *The Philosophy of Aesthetic Pleasure*. Annamalai Nagar: Annamalai Univ., 1940.

Schuyler, Montgomery. *A Bibliography of the Sanskrit Drama*. Delhi: Asia Publication Services, 1977.

Sekhar, I. *Sanskrit Drama: Its Origin and Decline*. 1960; rpt. Delhi: Munshiram Manoharlal, 1977.

Tarlekar, G.H. *Studies in the Natyasastra: With Special Reference to the Sanskrit Drama in Performance*. Delhi: Motilal Banarsidass, 1975.

Vamana. *Kāvyālaṅkārasūtra*. Trans. V.V. Sarma. Valiasala: V.V. & Bros., 1949.

Varadpande, M.L. *Traditions of the Indian Theatre*. Delhi: Abhinav Publications, 1979.

Varma, Balarama. *Bālarāmbhāratam*. Trans. V.S. Sarma. Kottayam: National Book Stall, 1982.

Viśvanātha Sāhitya Darpaṇam. Trans. K.V.M. 2 vols. Trichur: Kerala Sahitya Academi, 1971.

Winternitz, M. "Bhāsa and the Mahābhārata and Kṛṣṇa Plays". *Bulletin of the Ramavarma Research Institute* 5 (1974), 1-15.

B. WESTERN

Arnott, Peter D. *An Introduction to the Greek Theatre.* London: Macmillan, 1961.

Barber, C.L. *Shakespeare's Festive Comedy: A Study of Dramatic Form and its Relation to Social Custom.* Princeton: Princeton Univ. Press, 1959.

Bentley, Eric. *The Life of the Drama.* London: Methuen, 1965.

————. *Bernard Shaw.* London: Methuen, 1960.

————. *In Search of Theatre.* New York: Vintage Book, 1957.

Bergson, Henri. *Laughter: An Essay on the Meaning of the Comic.* London: Macmillan, 1911.

Berry, Ralph. *Shakespeare's Comedies: Exploration in Form.* Princeton: Princeton Univ. Press, 1922.

————. *A Shakespearean Metaphor: Studies in Language and Form.* London: Macmillan, 1978.

Boas, Frederick S. *An Introduction Eighteenth Century Drama: 1700-1780.* Oxford: Clarendon, 1965.

Bogard, Travis and William I. Oliver. Ed. *Modern Drama: Essay in Criticism.* London: Oxford University Press, 1965.

Bradbrook, M.C. *The Growth and Structure of Elizabethan Comedy.* London: Chatto & Windus, 1973.

Bradbury, Malcolm and David Palmer., ed. *Shakespearean Comedy.* London: Edward Arnold, 1972.

Brockett, Oscar G. *The Theatre: An Introduction.* San Francisco: Rinehart, 1964; rpt. 1969.

Brown, John Russell. *Shaw and His Comedies.* London: Methuen, 1957.

————. *Shakespeare's Plays in Performance.* Loncon: Penguin, 1969.

Burns, Elizabeth. *Theatricality: A Study of Conventions in the Theatre and in Social Life.* London: Longman, 1972.

Butcher, S.H. *Aristotle's Theory of Poetry and Fine Art.* London: Macmillan: 1970; rpt. Ludhiana: Lyall Book Depot, 1967.

Cameron, Kenneth M. and Theodore J.C. Hoffman. *The Theatrical Response.* London: Macmillan, 1969.

Charlton, H.B. *Shakespearian Comedy.* 1938; rpt. Loncon: Methuen, 1977.

Chute, Marchette, *Shaw and His Stage.* 1953; rpt. London: Univ. of London Press, 1964.

Clemen, W.H. *The Development of Shakespeare's Imagery.* 1951; rpt. London: Methuen, 1977.

Coleridge, Samuel Taylor. *Shakespearean Criticism.* 2 vols. Ed. Thomas Middleton Raysor, 1907; rpt. London: Everyman, 1964.

Collins, Lucas W. *Aristophanes.* London: William Blackwood, 1897.

Crane, Milton: *Shakespeare*'s *Prose*. 1951; rpt. Chicago: The Univ. of Chicago, 1968.

Crompton, Louis. *Shaw the Dramatist: A Study of the Intellectual Background of the Major Plays.* London: George Allen & Unwin, 1971.

Dover, K.J. *Aristophanic Comedy.* London: Batsford, 1972.

Duckworth, George E. *The Nature of Roman Comedy: A Study in Regular Entertainment.* Princeton: Princeton Univ. Press, 1952.

Eliot, T.B. *Selected Prose of T.S. Eliot.* Ed. Frank Kermode. London: Faber & Faber, 1975.

————. *The Sacred Wood: Essays on Poetry and Criticism.* 1920; rpt. London: Methuen, 1969.

Eric, John J., Elizabeth T. Foster, Alvin Whitley., ed. *The Comic in Theory and Practice.* New Jersey: Prentice-Hall, 1960.

Evans, Bertrand. *Shakespeare's Comedies.* London: Oxford Univ. Press, 1960.

Evans, Ifor. *The Language of Shakespeare's Plays.* 1952; rpt. London: Methuen, 1966.

Fermor, Una-Ellis. *The Frontiers of Drama.* 1945; rpt. London: Methuen, 1967.

Foakes, R.A. *Shakespeare – The Dark Comedies to the Last Plays: From Satire to Celebration.* London: Routledge & Kegan Paul, 1971.

Freud, Sigmund. *Wit and its Relation to the Unconscious.* London: Kegan Paul, 1922.

Gascoigne, Bamber. *Twentieth Century Drama.* 1962; rpt. London: Hutchinson, 1974.

Gordon, George. *Shakespearean Comedy and other Studies.* 1944; rpt. London: Oxford Univ. Press, 1965.

Gruber, William E. "The Wild Men of Comedy: Transformations in the Comic Hero from Aristophanes to Pirandello." *Genre* XIV (1981), 207-227,

Malliday F.E. *The Poetry of Shakespeare's Plays.* 1954; rpt. London Gerald Duckworth, 1964.

Hoizknecht, Karl J. *The Background of Shakespeare's Plays.* New York: The American Book Co., 1950.

Howarth, W.D. *Comic Drama: The European Heritage.* London: Methuen, 1978.

Huizinga, Johan. *Homo Ludens: A Study of Play-Elements in Culture.* Boston: Beacon, 1955.

Hunter, Robert Grams. *Shakespeare and the Comedy of Forgiveness.* New York: Columbia Univ. Press, 1965.

Kaul, A.N. *The Action of English Comedy: Studies in the Encounter of Abstraction and Experience from Shakespeare to Shaw.* Connecticut: Yale Univ. Press, 1970.

Knight, Wilson G. *Shakespearian Production: With Special Reference to the Tragedies.* London: Routledge & Regan Paul, 1964.

————. *The Golden Labyrinth.* London: Methuen, 1962.

————. *The Crown of Life: Essays in the Interpretation of Shakespeare's Final Plays.* London: Methuen, 1965.

Koestler, Arthur.*The Act of Creation.* 1964; rpt. London: Hutchinson, 1969.

Lea, Katherine M. *Italian Popular Comedy.* Oxford: Oxford Univ. Press, 1934.

Lerner, Lawrence. *Shakespeare's Comedies.* London: Cox & Wyman, 1967.

Lever, Katherine. *The Art of Greek Comedy.* London: Methuen, 1956.

Lucas, F.L. *Greek Drama for the Modern Reader.* London: Chatto & Windus, 1967.

Mayne, Fred. *The Wit and Satire of Bernard Shaw.* London: Edward Arnold, 1967.

Mc Bride, Robert. *The Sceptical Vision of Moliere : A Study in Paradox.* London: Macmillan, 1977.

Mc Farland, Thomas. *Shakespeare's Pastoral Comedy.* North Carolina: Univ. of North Carolina, 1972.

Merchant, Molewyn. *Comedy: The Critical Idiom.* Ed. John D Jump. London: Methuen, 1972.

Meredith, George. *An Essay on Comedy and the Uses of the Comic Spirit.* London: Arichibald Constable, 1903.

Moore, W.G. *Moliere: A New Criticism.* Oxford: Oxford Univ. Press, 1949.

Muir, Kenneth. *Shakespeare's Comic Sequence.* Liverpool: Liverpool Univ. Press, 1979.

Nicoll, Allardyce. *The Theatre and Dramatic Theory.* London: George Harrap, 1962.

————. *British Drama.* London: George G. Harrap, 1925.

Nevo, Ruth. *Comic Transformations in Shakespeare.* London: Methuen, 1980.

Oreglia, Giacomo. *The Commedia dell 'Arte.* Trans. Lovett. F. Edwards. London: Methuen, 1968.

Palmer, John. *The Political and Comic Characters of Shakespeare:* London: Macmillan, 1964.

Palmer D.J. *Shakespeare's Later Comedies.* London: Penguin, 1971.

Partridge, Eric. *Shakespeare's Bawdy.* London: Routledge & Kegan Paul, 1968.

Potts, L.J. *Comedy.* 1949; rpt. London: Hutchinson, 1963.

Radcliff-Umstead, Douglas. *The Birth of Modern Comedy in Renaissance Italy.* Chicago: The Univ. of Chicago Press, 1969.

Richards, I.A. *Practical Criticism: A Study of Literary Judgement.* 1929; rpt. London: Routledge & Kegan Paul, 1966.

————. *Principles of Literary Criticism.* 1923; rpt. Bombay: Allied Publishers, 1967.

Rodway, Allan. *English Comedy: Its role and Nature from Chaucer to the Present Day.* London: Chatto & Windus, 1975.

Salinger, Leo. *Shakespeare and the Traditions of Comedy.* London: Cambridge Univ. Press, 1974.

Shank, Theodore. *The Art of Dramatic Art.* California: California: Dickenson Publishing Co., 1969.

Snyder, Susan. *The Comic Matrix of Shakespeare's Tragedies.* New Jersey: Princeton Univ. Press, 1979.

Spurgeon, Caroline F.E. *Shakespeare's Imagery and What it Tell Us.* 1935; rpt. Cambridge: Cambridge Univ. Press, 1961.

Styan, J.L. *The Dark Comedy: The Development of Modern Comic Tragedy.* Cambridge: Cambridge Univ. Press, 1968.

Swinden, Patrick. *An Introduction to Shakespeare's Comedies.* London: Macmillan, 1973.

Thorndike, Ashley. *Shakespeare's Theatre.* New York: Macmillan, 1943.

Torrance, Robert M. *The Comic Hero.* London: Harvard Univ. Press, 1978.

Turnell, Martin. *The Classical Moment: Studies of Corneille, Moliere and Racine.* London: Hamish Hamilton, 1960.

Vickers, Brian. *The Artistry of Shakespeare's Prose.* London: Methuen, 1968.

Vulliamy, C.E. *The Anatomy of Satire.* London: Michael Joseph, 1950.

Wain, John. *The Living World of Shakespeare: A Playgoer s Guide.* London: Penguin, 1964.

Willeford, William. *The Fool and His Sceptre: A Study in Clowns, Jesters and Their Audience.* London: Edward Arnold, 1969.

Willet, John. *Brecht on Theatre: The Development of An Aesthetic.* 1957; rpt. New York: Hill & Wang, 1964.

Wilson, Elkin Calhoun. *Shakespeare, Santayana and the Comic.* London: George Allen & Unwin, 1973.

Wilson, John Dover. *The Fortunes of Falstaff.* 1943; rpt. Cambridge: Cambridge Univ. Press, 1964.

——— *Shakespeare's Happy Comedies.* Evanston: Northwestern Univ. Press, 1962.

Wimsatt, W.K. *Dr. Johnson on Shakespeare.* Baltimore: Penguin, 1969.

Worcester, David. *The Art of Satire.* Cambridge: Harvard Univ. Press, 1910.

C. COMPARATIVE

Bhat, G.K. *Tragedy and Sanskrit Drama.* Bombay: Popular Prakashan, 1976

Chaitanya, Krishna, *Sanskrit Poetics: A Critical and Comparative Study.* Bombay: Asia Publishing House, 1965.

Jackson. A.V. Williams. "Certain Dramatic Events in Sanskrit Plays with Parallels in English Drama". *American Journal of Philosophy* 19 (1898), 242-47.

Jefferds, Keith N. "Vidushaka Versus Fool: A Functional Analysis". *JSAL* XIV. 1 (Winter, Spring 1981), 61-73.

Pandey, K.C. *Comparative Aesthetics.* 2 vols. Varanasi: Chaukhamba Sanskrit Series, 1959.

Rao, Hanumantha G. *Comparative Aesthetics: Eastern and Western.* Mysore: Mysore Printing & Publishing House, 1974.

Singal, R.L. *Aristotle and Bharata: A Comparative Study of Their Theories of Drama.* Punjab: Visvesvaranand Vedic Research Institute, 1977.

INDEX

Abhidhā 21
Abhijñānaśākuntalā 10, 12, 63, et al.
Abhimanyu 73, 81
Abhinavagupta 4, 20, 21, et al.
Abhinavabhārati 21
Abhinaya, see also under
Theatric Communication 11, 12, 30, *et al.*
_______, mode of 12
Abhinayadarpaṇa 31
Abhiṣekanātaka 46, 72, 74, et al.
Absolute Self 4, 27
Absurd, Concept of 42
Action 24, 133
Actress 10
Acts 46
Adam 39
Adbhuta 12
Adharma, see also under
Impiety 139
Ādiparva, see also under
Mahābhārata, first book of 93
Aeschylus 35, 125
Aesthetic enjoyment 21
Aesthetics, Indian 11, 18
Aesthetic, Sanskrit 14, 31
Aesthetic, Western 14
Aestheticians, Indian 19
Āhārya 31, 43, 83, et al.
Alakāpuri 47
Ālambana 12
Alamkāra, see also under
Metaphor 119
All's Well That Ends Well 138
Ambikā 125
Amphitrayon 39
Amphitruo 75
Ānanda - see also under
Bliss 27
Ānandavardhana 3, 17, 120, et al.
Andrew Aguecheek 84, 98
Āṅgika 31, 43, 48 et al.
Āṅgikābhinaya 31
Aṅgulīyānka, see also under
Ring, Act of 46
Aṅkas, see also under
Acts 46
Anne Page 64
Antonio 67
Anubhāva 11, 12, 17, et al.
Anukaraṇa, see also under
Imitation 21
Anumāna, see also under
Inference 25
Anumiti, see also under
Inference 21
Apahasita 16
Apāyaśaṁkā, see also under
Fear of failure 28, 136
Ārambha 136
Arbitration 37
Arden, forest of 64, 78, 97, et al.
Ariel 70, 87
Aristophanes 16, 35, 62, et al.
Aristophanic tradition 111
Aristotle 8, 18, et al.
Arjuna 58, 68, 125, et al.
Armin, Robert 98
Arms and the Man, see also under
Shaw, Bernard 41
Arnolphe 39
Arnott, Peter D 71, 72 (F.N)
Artaud 5
Artha, see also under
Wealth 69
Aśana, see also under
eating 69
Āścaryacuḍāmaṇi 46
Aśoka 62
Aśokavanikāṅka, see also under
Aśoka Garden, act of 46
Asura 56
Aśvaghoṣa 1, 57
Aśvatthāmā 135
Aswins 125

As You Like It 14, 77, 91 et al.
Athenian passion 35
Athens, ancient 1, 35
Atihasita, see also under
Laughter 16, 17
Ātman, see also under
Real Nature 27
Ātmānanda, see also under
Bliss Supreme 27
Ātmaṣtha 16
Attainment of Result 28
Āttaprakāraṃ 45
Audrey 84
Avimāraka 37, 38, 56, et al.
Ayodhyā 115
Ayyar, A.S.P. 99

Bacchus 109
Bahrukalpa 52
Bālacarita 56, 106, 72, et al.
Baladeva 80
Balarāma 135
Bālivadhānka 46
Barbanan 71
Barber, C.L. 4, 5,
24 (F.N) et al.
Barrymore, John 43
Bassanio 67
Baudelaire, Charles 11
Beatrice 14, 65, 81, et al.
Beckett 42, 120
Benedick 14, 65, 81, et al.
Bentley, Eric 18, 25, 89, et al.
Berowne 122
Bertram 138
Bhadrāvatī 85, 130
Bhagavadajjukāya 45, 51, 52, et al.
Bhakti, see also under
Devotion 139
Bharata 9, 16, 22, et al.
Bhartṛhari 2
_, theory of word 2
Bhāsa 1, 38, 65, et al.
_, comedies of 6
_, date of 6
_, thirteen plays ascribed to 7
Bhat, G.K. 55
Bhaṭṭalollaṭa 20
Bhaṭṭanāyaka 20, 22, 25, et al.
_, Commentator 4
Bhaṭṭatauta 4, 12
_, Commentator 4
Bhāva 11, 14
Bhavabhūti 32, 73, 74, et al.
Bhāvakatva 21, 22
Bhayānaka 12
Bhīma 66, 78, 125, et al.
Bhoga, see also under
Enjoyment 27
Bhojakatva 21, 22
Bhūta 46
Bībhatsa 12
Bīja, see also under
Germ 28
Bliss 27
Bodhāyana 51
Borinski, Ludwig 123
The Braggart Warrior 37
Brahmā 9, 119
_, the Creator 13
Brahman, see also under
Absolute Self 4, 27, 106, et al.
_, Creator of Nāṭya 29
Brahmānanda 4
Brāhmin 56
Brandt, George 42 (F.N)
Brecht, Bertolt 5
Bṛhannala 81, 82
Bṛhatkathā 72
Brighella 51
Brook 66
Brown, John Russel 98
Buddhi 26
Buddhism 51
Buitenen, J.A.B. Van 2, 70
Bullough, Geoffrey 91
Burlesque 15
Burns, Elizabeth 60
Butcher, S.H. 4,
8 (F.N), 18, et al.

Cakki 13, 58
Cakkyār 36, 56
Cakravāka bird 48
Cāṇakya 38
Candrahāsa, Sword 48
Candida 41
Carnival 55
Cārudatta 36, 57, 63 et al.
Catharsis 4, 18, 23 et al.
__, ideal of 18
Cause 12
Celia 97
Cervantes 35
Cesario 84
Chanḍāla 117
Charisus 37
Chaitanya, Krishna 38
Chandragupta Maurya 38
Christopher Sly 77
Chitraturaganyāya, see also under Idea of painted horse 21
Claudio 15, 108, 138 et al.
Clemen, W.H. 104, 105, 116 et al.
Cleon 35
Clouds 35
Coleridge 89
Colins, Lucas 35
Comparison 25
Comedic Vision of Life 132
Comedy 8
__, aesthetics of 8
__, Aristophanic 35
__, Attic 34
__, Characterization 89
__, Comic element in 10
__, Greek 34
__, Imagery in 104
__, Italian 75
__, Old 32, 35
__, Origin of 8
__, Roman 76, 94
__, Sanskrit 112
__, Sentimental 41
__, Shakespearian 37, 62, 78 et al.
__, Situations in 71
__, Theatre of 29
__, Themes of 60
__, Use of language in 119
Comedy of Errors 64, 66, 70
Comic 12
__ Character 13
__ modes 14, 15
Commedia dell'arte, Italian 8, 50
Commentators, Aristotelian 19
Comus 33
Coomaraswamy, Ananda 3
Cooper, Lane 8, 19
Cyclops 33
Cymbeline 138

Damaka 107
Damodaran, E.V. 3 (F.N)
Dance 5
Daśarūpaka 28, 51
Delight 11
Desdemona 87
Desire 69
Deva 56
Devendra 125
The Devil of Miracle Play 39
Devotion 139
Dhanañjaya 11
Dhārini, Queen 95
Dharma, see also under Piety 2, 69, 125 et al.
__, accepted code of 2
Dharmaputra 49
Dhātri 101
Dhṛtarāṣṭra 125
Dhvani 3, 120
Dictionary, Sanskrit-English 24
Dictionary, Oxford English 8, 55
Dionysus 33, 35, 71 et al.
__, worshippers of 8
Direct perception 25
Dogberry 34, 84, 89 et al.
Don Pedro 108
Drama 1, 50, 30 et al.
__, Classical Greek 72
__, Classical Indian 30

__, Classical Western 71
__, Elizabethan 34, 35
__, Greek 5
__, Indian 5, 33, 35 et al.
__, in England 39
__, Italian 76
__, Latin 39, 40
__, medieval English 39
__, medieval French 50
__, Sanskrit 1, 9, 34 et al.
__, Sentimental 41
__, Western 1, 62, 80 et al.
Dramatic 36, 60, 81 et al.
__, Criticism, Sanskrit 60
__, irony 81
__, repertory, Sanskrit 6, 24, 61 et al.
__, repertory, Western 6
Dramatists 83
__, Indian 83
__, Western 83
Dramaturgy, Sanskrit 28, 73
Draupadi 74
Dromio brothers 98
Droṇa 73, 92
Duḥkha 26
Duncan 84
Durjaya 88
Durvāsas 93, 138
Duryodhana 49, 73, 74 et al.
Duḥśāsana 129
Duṣyanta, King 20, 63, 138 et al.
Dūtaghaṭotkaca 72, 73
Dūtavākya 72, 74, 125 et al.
Dvija, see also under
Brāhmin 56

Eccesiazusae 35, 62
Efforts 28
Egyptians 129
Elizabeth I, the reign of 39
England 78
Enjoyment 27
Entertainment 69
Ephesus 75
Epic Theatre 5

Euripides 33, 35, 91 et al.
Europe, Western 51
Evans, Bertrand 80
Evans, B Ifor 122
Every Man in His Humour 40

Falstaff 5, 6, 24, et al.
__, figure of 5
The Famous Victories of Henry V 91
Fear of failure 28
Feast of foods 55
Ferdinand 70, 16
Fermor, Una Ellis 105
Feste 97
Final Truth, perception of 27
Firth, Felicity 51
Foakes, R.A. 104
Ford 66
France 39, 50
Francisco 116
Freud, Sigmund 11, 18, 19 et al.
Frogs 35, 90, 109, et al.
Frye, Northrop 61

Gadshill robbery 6, 81
Gammer Gurton's Needle 40
Gāndhārī 125
Gaṅgā 47
Ganymede 83, 87
Gātrasevaka 79
Gaude 119
Gautama 95
Genet 42
Germ 28
Gesture 44
Ghaṭotkaca 66, 73, 78 et al.
Gīta, see also under
Music, vocal 5
Glendower 14
Gl 'Ingannati' 75
Glycera 37
Gnoli, Raniero 60, 120
Goldsmith, Oliver 40, 41, 120 et al.
The Good Natured Man 40
Gopālaka 103

Gordon, George 84, 98
Greece 8, 32, 33 et al.
Greek 18, 33, 55 et al.
__ influence 33
__, Kathairo 5
Grotowski 5
Gruber, William E 5, 93, 54 et al.
Guṇa 26
Guṇāḍhya 72
Gupta, Damodara 32, 107
Guru 53

Haas, George C.O. 11, 51
Hal, Prince 24, 68
Hamlet 43, 87, 101 et al.
Hanumān 46, 101
Herlequin 32
Harṣa 32, 38, 80 et al.
Hāsa, see also under Laughter 6, 16, 17 et al.
Hasita 16
Hāsya, see also under Comic 6, 12, 16 et al.
__, *anubhāvas* of 13
Hāsyarasa 11, 51
__, *Vibhāvas* of 13
Helena 138
Hercules 71, 91
Hermione 138
Hero 108
Hiḍimba 66, 73, 79, et al.
Hiriyanna, M 132
History 132
Homer 33
Honeywood 41
Hostspur 14, 68, 69 et al.
Howrath, W.D. 23, 24 (F.N), 42 et al.
Hudibrastic 15
Huizinga, John 9
Humour 18
Hunter, Robert Grams 137
Iago 87
Ideal Beauty 3
Illusion 27
Illusory Sītā, act of 46
Imitation 21
Impiety 139
Indian Society, ancient 2
India, theatrical practice of 30
Indra 102
Indradvaja festival 33
Inference 21, 25
Interpretation, different Schools of 20
Invective 15, 16
Ionesco 42
Irāvati 109
Iris 71
Italian plots 64
Itihāsa, see also under History 132

Jacques 14, 97
Jagannatha 27
Janaka 66
Janamejaya 128
Jane Smile 97
Jarāsandha 115
Jaṭāyuvadhānka, see also under Murder of Jaṭāyu 46
Jayadeva 78
Jespersen 119
Jest 14, 15
Jew of Malta 92
Jīvanamukta, see also under Final Truth, perception of 27
Jīvanamukta 133
Johnson, Ben 140
Julia 75
Juliet 87
Jump, John D. 15

Kailāsa 46
Kaikeyī 92
Kālapriyanātha 32
Kale, Pramod 10, 30
Kālidāsa 34, 38, 46 et al.
Kāma, see also under

Desire 69
__, Diety of Pleasure 61
Kāmadeva 80
Kamsa 49, 117
Kaṁsabhṛtya 103
Kānci 51
Kaṇva 20
Kapālin 52, 79
Karma, see also under
Action 24, 133
Karmadīpikā, text on
Choreography 45
Karmayogi 139
Karṇa 67, 68, 102
Karṇabhāra 67, 68, 102
Karuṇa 12
Kathakali 16, 44, 48
Katti, facial make up 49
Kaundinya 59
Kaurava 73, 74
Kauṭilya 67
Kāvya 120
Keith, A.B. 1, 55, 73 et al.
Kempe, William 98
Kerala 13, 16, 32 et al.
Kinesias 62
King Henry IV 5, 14, 68 et al.
King Lear 96
Knight, Wilson 137
'Komos', Greek, see also under
Comedy 8
Kṛṣṇa 24, 49, 78 et al.
__ cult 33
Kṛṣṇāṭṭam 32
Kṣatriya 125
Kulaśekharavarman 45, 57
Kuntibhoja, King 83
Kurangi 63
Kurukṣetra, Battle of 73
Kūṭiyaṭṭam 13, 32, 36 et al.

Lakṣaṇa 119
Langer, Susanne K. 8, 61 (F.N)
Laughter 6
Launce 98
Lea, K.M. 49
L'Ecole des Femmes 39
Legends, Greek 71
Leontes 138
Lever, Katherine 37, 76
Levi, Sylvain 33
Lindenau 55
Lingi, ascetic 56
Lokadharmi 31, 43
Lord of Misrule 91
Louis XIV 39
Love 12
Love's Labour's Lost 122, 126
Lucenti, Bianca 39, 75, 76 et al.
Lydia Languish 41
Lyly, John 40
Lysistrata 62

Macbeth 84
Machiavelli 35
Madanikā 99
Madhyamavyāyoga 66, 72, 73 et al.
Mahābhārata 24, 30, 33 et al.
Mahāsena 67
Mahāvīracarita 57
Mahāvrata ceremony 53
Mahendravikramavarman 51
Maheśa 48
Maitreya 35, 57, 69 et al.
Mālatīmādhava 57
Mālavikāgnimitra 38, 59, 62 et al.
Malayalam 57, 58
Malvolio 80, 97
Man and Superman 41
Māṇavaka 95
Mantrānkam 45
Maria 80, 99
Mātali 113
Mattavilāsa 51, 52, 53 *et al.*
Maurya 67
Māyā, see also under
Illusion 27
Māyasītānka 46
Māyāsītānka, see also under
Illusory Sītā, act of 46

Mayne, Fred 41 (F.N)
Measure for Measure 101
Menaechmi 75
Menander 37
The Merchant of Venice 67
Mercutio 15, 87, 105 et al.
Meredith, George 11
The Merry Wives of Windsor 64, 66, 67 et al.
Midsummer Night's Dream 70, 80, 105 et al.
Miḻāvu 45
Mime, Roman 55
Minister 56
Miranda 70
Mirashi, V.V. 57
Mock Poem 15
Modaka, see also under Sweetmeat 117
Moha 26
Mokṣa, see also under Salvation 69
Molière 35, 39
Mṛcchakaṭika 33, 35, 57 et al.
Much Ado About Nothing, see also under Shakespeare 14, 15, 64 et al.
Mudrā, see also under Gesture 44, 48
Mudrārākṣasa 38, 57, 63 et al.
Muir, Kenneth 62, 67, 110 et al.
Murder in the Cathedral 120
Murder of Jaṭāyu, act of 46
Moschion 37
Music, Vocal 5
Myrrhine 62

Nāgānanda 80
Nāgasena 51
Nair, D. Appukuṭṭan 118
Nala 49
Nanda 38
Nandagopa 107
Nāndi, see also under Prayer 28
Nandikeśvara 31, 48
Nārada, the mythical sage 17, 56, 101 et al.
Narmasaciva 56
Nāṭaka 72
Naṭi, see also under Actress 10
Nāṭya, see also under dramatic art 9, 10
__, concept of 9
Nāṭyadharmi 31, 43
Nāṭyarasa, see also under dramatic art 17
Naṭyaśāstra 9, 13, 56 et al.
Nāyaka, dhīroddhata 72
Neptune 71
Ruth, Nevo 75, 95, 127 et al.
Nicoll, Allardyce 50, 120
Nirvahaṇa 45
Nirveda, see also under Renunciation 17
Niṣpatti 19, 20, 22 et al.
Niyatāpti, see also under Success, Certainty of 28, 136
Nṛtta, see also under Dance 5
Nyāya School 25

Oldcastle, John 91
Olivia 80, 97
Oneness 52
Oreglia, Giacomo 50
Orgon 39
Orientalists, European 33
Orlando 64, 78, 83 et al.
Orsino 97
Othello 87

Pacca 49
Padmāvati 64, 84
Palmer, John 96 (F.N)
Pañcālī 102, 119
Paññcarātra 73, 74
Pāṇḍava 66, 73, 78 et al.
Pandey, K.C. 25

Pantalone, Doctor 32, 51
Parameśvara 46, 47, 119
Parastha 116
Paraxagora 62
Parody 15
Pārvatī 46, 47, 119 et al.
Partridge, Eric 131
Pāśupata 52
Patelin, Lawyer 50
Perdita 61
Period, Elizabethan 83
Petruchio 76, 127
Phalāgama, see also under
Attainment of Result 28, 136
Phebe 84
Philosophy 45, 53, 25 et al.
__, Buddhist 45, 53
__, Indian 25
__, Nyāya System of 25
__ of Grammar 119
Pierre Patelin 50
Piety 69
Pischel 33
Pisharoti, K.P. Narayana 9 (F.N)
Pithetaerus 71
Plato 4, 35
Plautus 34, 37, 40 et al.
Poetics 18
Polixenes 61, 138
Polonius 87, 101
Polymon 37
Ponty, Merleau 2
Poor Theatre 5
Portia 101
Posthumus 138
Potts, L.J. 89
Pradyota, King 82
Prahāsa 52
Prahasana, dramatic
category of 51, 53
Prākrt 57, 123
Prakrti 26
Prāptyāśa, see also under
Success Prospect of 28, 136
Prastāvanā, see also under
Prologue 10
Pratijñāyaugandharāyaṇa 45, 56,
63 et al.
Pratimānātaka 65, 66, 95
Pratyaksa, see also under
Direct perception 25
Prayer 28
Prīti 20
Priyadarśikā 32, 38
Priyamvadā 128
Prologue 10
Prospero 70, 81
Proteus 67
Puck 77, 87
Pun 14
Purāṇa 72, 74
Puruṣa 26
Puruṣārtha 45, 69
Puruṣottama 103
Pusalker, A.D. 6, 7 (F.N)
Puṣpaka 47

Quietism 17

Rājajīvi, see also under
Minister 56
Rajas 26
Rājasevā, see also under
Service under a King 69
Rākṣasa 38, 39, 46 et al.
Ralph Roister Doister 40
Rāma 21, 74, 86 et al.
Rāmāyaṇa 30, 33, 74 et al.
Rao, G. Hanumantha 2
Rasa, see also under
Delight 3, 11, 12 et al.
__, experience of 4
Rasānubhava 4
Rasānubhūti, see also under
Rasa, experience of 27
Rasānumittivāda 21
Rasāsvādā 3, 19, 20 et al.
Rasotpatti 20
Rati, see also under
Love 12, 20

Ratnavali 32
Raudra 12
Rāvaṇa 46, 48, 49 et al.
Real nature 27
Renaissance 55
Renunciation 17
Repartee 14
Ṛg Veda 55
Richards, I.A. 3, 119
Ring, act of 46
Rīti, see also under
Style 119
The Rivals 41
Robin Hood of England 78
Romeo 15, 87, 105
Romeo and Juliet 15, 91,
101 et al,
Rosalind 14, 64, 78 et al.
Rumaṇvaṇ 65

Sabastian 97
Śabda, see also under
Verbal testimony 26
Sādhāraṇkaraṇa 22, 23, 61 et al.
__, theory of 4
Sāhityadarpaṇa 3, 56
Sahṛdaya, see also under
Spectator 22, 27, 44 et al.
Śaivite Kapālin 51
Sajalajaladhāra 129
Sajjalaka 99
Śakāra 100
Śaktibhadra 46
Śakuni 125
Śakuntalā 12, 20, 34 et al.
Salinger, Leo 62, 66, 75 (F.N) et al.
Salvation 69
Śalya 134
Samia 37
Saṁkarṣaṇa 78, 107
Sāṁkhya 25, 26, 27
Samkīrṇa, see also under
Type, mixed 51
Samyoga 19, 20, 22 et al.
Sanḍilya 52, 53, 56 et al.
Sangītaratnākara 31
Saniranīrada 129
Saṅkuka 20, 21, 25 et al.
Śānta 17
Śānti 3, 134
Santuṣṭa 57
Sarcasm 14
Śārīputraprakarana 57
Śārṅgadeva 31
Sārūpya, see also under
Oneness 52
Sastri, Ganapati 1
Śastri, K. Kuppuswamy 119
Sastri, P. Pancapagesa 6, 20 (F.N)
Satire 15
Sattvaguṇa 22, 27
Sāttvika 31, 43
Sāttvikabhāva 11
Satyr play 33
Scaramouche 51
Schiller, Frederich 133
The School for Scandal 41
Schuyler, Montgomery 1
Sekhar, I 56
Shakespeare 5, 7, 34 et al.
__, comedies of 34
Shaw, Bernard 41, 43, 120
Sheridan 41, 120
She Stoops to Conquer 41
The Shorn Lady 37
Shrewsbury, battlefield of 6,
68, 69 et al.
Shrovetide 55
Shylock 92
Silvius 129
Sir Toby 84
Sir Walter Blunt 6
Śiṣya 56
Sītā 74, 83, 86 et al.
Śiva, Lord 13, 47, 52 et al.
__, statue of 36
Śloka 36, 49
Smita, see also under
Smile 16, 17, 51 et al.
Snvder. Susan 61. 83

Socrates 35
Spectator 44
Speed 98
Sphoṭa 2
Spinchorn, Evert 50
Spurgeon, Caroline 116
Sṛṅgāra 12, 13, 14 et al.
__, Vipralambha 63
Stage manager 10
Sthayibhāva 12, 17, 20 et al.
Stimulus 12
Stoll, E.E 81
Styan, J.L. 42
Style 119
Subhadrā 101
Subhadrādhañjaya 13, 57, 58 et al.
Success, certainty of 28
Success, Prospect of 28
Śudhā, see also under
Type, Regular 51
Śūdraka 1, 57
Sukha 26
Suppositi 75
Śūrpaṇakha, Act of 46
Śūrpaṇakhānka, see also under
Śurpaṇakha, Act of 46
Sūtradhāra, see also under
Stage manager 10, 32, 52 et al.
Svakarma 56
Swapnavāsavadatta 57, 72
Swapnavāsavadattā 57, 63, 72 et al.
Sweetmeats 117
Sydney 39

The Taming of the Shrew 75, 127
Tamas 26
Tanner 41
Tapatīsaṁvarana 57, 69
Tarleton, Richard 98
Tartuffe 39
Tatvajñāna, see also under
Supreme Truth,
perception of 17
Tauryatrika 5, 43
The Tempest 70, 81, 87 et al.
Terence 34, 37, 40 et al.
Terentian 77
Theatre 1, 5, 56 et al.
__, Dravidian 56
__, Indian 5
__ of Cruelty 5
__, Sanskrit 1, 2, 13 et al.
__, Western 1, 32
Theatrical Practice of West 30
Tolan 45
Tony Lumpkin 41
Toraṇayuddhānka 46
Torrance, Robert M 6, 54
Touchstone 84
Travesty 15
Trivandrum 1
Tṛṣnākṣayasukha 17
Truth, Supreme 52
Twelfth Night 34, 64, 70 et al.
The Two Gentlemen of Verona 75, 95,
111 et al.
Tyagi 133
Type, Modified 51
Type, Regular 51

Udall, Nicholas 40
Udayana 63, 65, 82
Udipane 12
Ujjainy 33
__, King of 100
Upahasita 16
Upamāna, see also under
comparison 26
Ursula 108
Ūrubhanga 88, 91
Urvaśi 38
Utpatti 20
Uttararāmacarita 32, 57, 74 et al.

Vācika, see also under
Oral speech 32, 43, 57
Vācya 119
Vādya, see also under
rhythmical accompaniment 5
Vaidharbi 119

Vaiśravaṇa 47
Vākyapadīya 3
Valentine 67
Vālmīki 73, 74, 113 *et al.*
Vāmana 119
Vanajyotsnā 128
Vañcanā, see also under
Deceit 69
Vāsana 22
Vasantaka 56, 65
Vasantasena 36, 63, 100 et al.
Vāsavadatta, Princess 38, 63,
65 et al.
Vasiṣṭha 86, 113
Vāyu 125
Vedānta 25, 27
Vedas, dialogue hymns of 33
Verbal testimony 26
Verges 34, 84, 98 et al.
Vibhāva, see also under
cause or stimulus 12
Vibhāva II 17, 20 et al.
__, Ālambana 13
__, Uddīpana 13
Vice of the Morality 39
Vickers, Brian 124 (F.N)
Vidūṣaka, see also under
comic character 13, 34, 35 et al.
Vihasita 16
Vikramorvaśīya 34, 38, 95 et al.
Vikṛta, see also under
Type, modified 51
Vincentio 127
Vinoda, see also under
Entertainment 69
Viola 83, 84, 97 et al.
Virarasa 63
Viśākhadatta 38, 57
Viṣṇu 128
Viśwarūpa 139
Viṭa 80
Vṛnda forest 78
Vṛṣakapi 55
Vyabhicāribhāva 11, 12. 17 et al.
Vyaṅgya 119
Vyañjana 22, 119
Vyāsa 73, 125

Waiting for Godot 42, 120
Wasps 35
Wealth 69
Weber 33
Wells, Henry W. 2,
28 (F.N), 135 et al.
Willeford, William 94
Williams, Monier 24
Wilson, Elkin Calhoun 16, 81, 100 et
al.
Windisch 33, 55
Winternitz, M 86
The Winter's Tale 61, 66
Wit 14
Worcester, David 16

Yatna, see also under
effort 28, 136
Yaugandharāyaṇa 56, 65
Yogaśāstra 130
Yogin 6, 53
Yorick 88
Yudhiṣṭhira 59, 73, 125 et al.

Zanni 51
Zeus 71

NĀG SEN

OF

Milind Panhö

Dr. P.K. Kaul

EASTERN BOOK LINKERS

DELHI : : INDIA

Publishers :
EASTERN BOOK LINKERS
5825, New Chandrawal, Jawahar Nagar,
Delhi-110007 Ph.: 2520287

First Edition : 1996

ISBN : 81-86339-18-3

Price BOOK EASTERN EBL LINKERS Rs. 400-

Laser- typesetting & Printing at :
UNIQUE PRINT MEDIA
Phone : 7252362

PREFACE

Rivers whether in India or elsewhere in the world have always played a prominent role in the evolution of various civilizations and cultures. Himālyan middle mountains and Shivālik hill region of Jammu, drained by mighty river Chinab and its various tributaries, which have carved out many mountain valleys, provide adequate material for the study of history and culture of the people inhabiting them, but unfortunately, very little efforts have so far been made in this direction.

Chinab and Marwā rivers of Kaśtwāṛ find mention in *Rigveda* by the name of Asikanyā and Marutvridhā. Asikanyā literally means, the daughter of the sword. The historians of Alexander have named it Arkisine i.e.river of ill omens.This Greek word for this river is no doubt derived from the Vedic term Asikanyā and as the history confirms, it proved to be a river of ill-omen and the daughter of the sword, not only for Alexander, who during his invasion of India had a tough time in the hill region drained by Chināb, but also for another Indo-Scythian King Menānder, who was defeated in a historic religious discussion with Nāg Sen, the illustrious son of the Chināb Valley, and who's biographical sketch forms the subject-matter of the present study.

Ptolmy (A.D.150) calls this river by the name of Sandalbal which indicates, that around this time , the river had begun to be called as Chandrabhāgā, the etymological meaning of the term still remaining un-explained. By the time of 7th or 8th century the term 'Chandrabhāgā' for the river seems to have become quite prevalent, as we find this term being used in Neelmat Purāṇa, with a Brahmanic etymological explanation. It has been recorded there that its waters are cool like the rays of the moon and torn forth by the God moon चन्द्रमा सुशीतला जला; चन्द्रेन विभिन्ना

In Muslim period, the Sultāns, Mughals and Pathān Kings remained mostly confined to the plains of Punjab, where the river was known by the name of Chināb. Muslim kings did not move beyond Shivālik hills, where the river was known by the name of Chandrabhāgā? Traditional fear of this river seems to have prevented Muslim Sultans and Mughals to penetrate into the interior mountains, and accordingly we find it named as Chināb, presuming it to be water coming from the Chinese territory.

Vigne (1839 A.D.) calls the river by the name of Chināb and Foster who came to Kashmir around 1783 A.D. calls it Chanānu, derived as it appears from Chānāb. Vigne prefers to derive the present appellation of Chināb from Chāndāb (i.e. water from the moon) rather than Chināb (i.e.water from China), probably as it does not flow from any territory in China. Vigne's Chandāb has a clear co-relation with *Neelmat Purāna's* etymological explanation of the word, and Vigne seems to have been informed about Chandāb by some Kashmiri Brahmin. Whether Chāndāb or Chināb, the river is popularly known by the name of Chināb everywhere now.

However the nomenclature Chandrabhāgā in recent times has a new etymological explanation to the term and an interesting geographical account of the mountain region through which it flows. The river is formed by the confluence of two Himālayan streams, namely,

MAP SKETCH NO---1

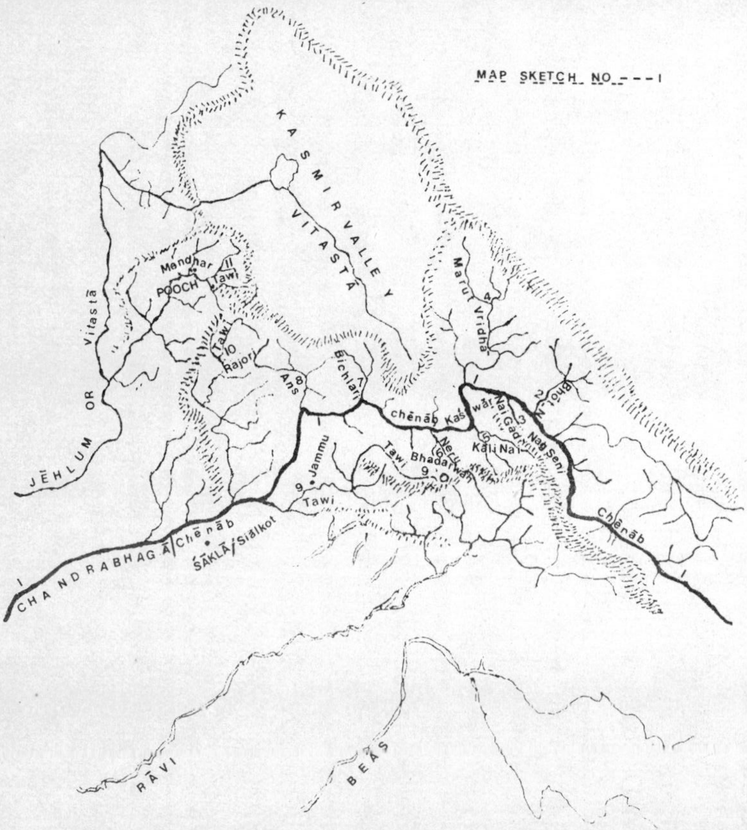

Chandra Bhāgā Valley in The Hills oF Jammu

(MOUNTAIN TRIBUTARIES OF CHENĀB)

1. chenāb
2. Bhōt Nallā
3. Nai Gad
4. Marut Vridhā (maṛvā)
5. Kālī Nāi
6. Neru
7. Bichlaṛi-Banihāl
8. Ans -

(1–8: Guarded Slopes)

9. Tawi - Jammu
10. Tawi - Rājouri
11. Tawi - Poonch

Chandrā and Bhāgā, which originate from the Himālyan heights of Bārā Lāchā (16000′ or 4879 mts), separately from its two opposite water-sheds, in the Lāhul region. The Chandrā stream circumscribes the Bārā Lāchā mountain slopes for 200 kilometers before joining Bhāgā stream at Tāndi, and before doing so Chandrā joins a high altitude mountain lake, called Suraj Tāl, near the Bārā Lāchā Pass, at one of its ends and re-emerges at the other. The Bhāgā covers a distance of about 90 kilometers before joining Chandrā.

After traversing a distance of about 200 kilometers in the Pāngi Valley, the river enters the Pādar region of Jammu near Alwās,having an altitude of some 1800′ meters, and then passing through the Nāg Senī region of Kaśtwāṛ Jangalwāṛ, Dodā Sirāj, Rāmban and Reāsi the river looses much of its turbulance from Akhnoor onwards. During the course of the journey of this river from Alwās to Akhnoor, some half a dozen tributaries join the river in the mountains of Jammu. Some of these tributaries have themselves carved out very beautiful and charming highland valleys and mountain pastures in the region through which these flow. Among the right bank tributaries of Chināb in Jammu, mention may be made of Bhutnā, Maṛusonder or Maṛiv Sind,Golan Nāṛ, Lidderkhol, Bichlari-Bihāltā or Biśāltā and Rojouri Tawi. Bhutnā near Pāḍar means Bhot-Nā or rivulet of Bhots, Maru Sonder is a joint name for Marutvridhā and Sonder or Sindhu of Kaśtwāṛ mountains, Golan comes from the syṁthan side and Lidder Khol drains the mountain slopes of Sirāj and Desā area. Ans is its tributary from the Gulāb Garh area, while Biśāltā drains the Banihāl valley and its adjoining slopes.

The left bank tributaries of the Chināb in Jammu form many Tawī's and Devikās of Jammu region, the

Anji of Reāsi, Pinktā near Rāmban (Maitrā), Basī Nālā of Batote, Riggī of Khasāl, Neru of Bhadarwāh, Kalī Nai of Bhales and Nai Gad of Nāg Senī region. These rivers and streams have carved out many small highland valleys and hanging mountain pockets, on these Himālayan slopes, which had been very safe places to live in peace and without fear, of being plundered by medieval despondants. These were also ideal places for meditation, hermitage and peaceful living for the men of sprituality. Some of these places, streams and valleys have found mention in the ancient and medieval literature also. To quote a few examples we may mention the name of Tawī of Poonch and Rājouri which finds mention in *Neelmat Purāna* as Taushit Bhāskrā. Some feel that Ans of Gul Gulābgārh and Mariv of Kaśṭwāṛ stand for Ajikiyā and Marutvrindhā of Vedas. We have some nine Tawīs, four Devikās and three Sindhus, following through this mountain region. The nomenclature of almost all mountain valleys of Chināb and its tributaries in Jammu has a strong Sanskrit base. Marutvridhā (rendered old and barren by the winds), Kaśṭwāṛ (that which has been subdued after encountering difficulties), Bhadrāvakāsh (a fine place to rest), Khaśāl (the inhabitance of Khaśās, Rāmban (the Jungles of Rāmā), Banihal (derived from Banśālā), Chanderkot, Maitreyā (if after Maitrāyinī?), Sunder Banī, Rājā Purī, (Rajouri), Parṇoṭsvā (the festival of leaves or greenery etc. All this indicate the existence of a strong Brahmanic tradition, prevalent in the region, in the ancient and medieval times.

But prior to the coming of this Brahmanic tradition, the Jammu mountain region must be expected to have some Buddhist religious foundation. It has been observed that one of the enigmas of Jammu's religious history has been the absence of any Buddhist foundation in the province. The puzzle was all the more surprising in the light of the fact that Buddhism had one of its prominent seats in the vicinity of Jammu, i.e. at Siālkot and Akhnoor.

The positive evidence of a Buddhist establishment at Ambārān, near Akhnoor, 20 miles west of Jammu, was brought to light by Charless Fabri only a few decades ago. He was an art critic and had made a detailed examination of the site and the remains that were found. He came to the conclusion that there had been a large monastery and a stūpā at the place. Among the terracottas found, were Buddha heads, Toros of bodies and pieces of drapery, belonging to Buddha figures, or figures of monks and laymen and women, profusely decorated. He considered the terracottas from Akhnoor as superb pieces of art, closely related to the terracottas found at Ushkūr (near Bārāmullā) in Kashmir, and assigned them a date of 5th to 7th century A.D.

Buddhism was prevalent in these mountain valleys at one time is indicated by some of the place names also. According to the author of Tāiekh Rājgān-e-Jammu, Thakur Kāhn Chand Billāwariā, Udhampur was known as Budhpur till 1846 A.D. when Māhārajā Gulāb Singh renamed it after his son. Village name Bādwāni in Sāmbā is said to have been derived from Budhwānī and the place names Devā, Sangaldān (gift to Sanghā), Dhammkund are also Buddhist in character. Sh.J.N.Ganhār in his recent book "Temples and Shrines of Jammu" has expressed his deep curiosity over "the striking resemblance which the name Nāg Senī region of Pāḍar Kaśtwāṛ bears to the celebrated monk Nāg Sen of 2nd century B.C., who defeated the great Indo-Scythian King Menānder in a meta-physical discussion"

According to him, one is tempted to think that the name Nāg Senī is derived from Nāg Sen. But this particular presumption is not a new one. Such doubts were expressed earlier also.

Around 1954 A.D. some Kashmiri writer in an article published in Daily Mārtand Srinagar had mentioned that King Menānder's Guru Nāg Sen resided at Kaśtwāṛ, but when called upon by another Kashmiri intellectual hawk to adduce proof in support of his contentions he failed to do so. Probably Kashmiri intellectual class wanted to have the credit of Nāg Sen belonging to the valley, as they claim that the celebrated work Milind Panho had been first written in Kashmiri and then translated into Pāli and Sinhāli.[2] Gulām Mustafā Ishrat Kashmiri, Mohi-ud-din Hājni and Ratnākar Pandit in their works pertaining to the history of Kaśtwāṛ have also expressed similar doubts.

And it was a sheer chance, while on an examination duty of the University of Jammu at Kaśtwāṛ, that I had an informal chat with one of the local Education Officers, namely D.C.Sharma, who informed me about Nāg Senī region of Kaśtwāṛ as a place of great Archaeological and antiquirian interest in the area. He also expressed his doubts about the place being the probable site of birth and education of Nāg Sen, about whom he had just read a passing reference in Mr. Fidda Mohd. Hussnanin's booklet titled Buddhist Kashmir. But he too could not provide any logical or supportive evidence to prove his contentions. Being inspired and finding some urge arising within my soul, I travelled the mountain country thoroughly in the coming years, investigated the sites, collected the relevant records and other reference material and felt assured that Nāg Senī region of Kaśtwāṛ and its adjioning slopes were place of Nāg Sen's birth, education, learning and meditation beyond any shadow of doubt, as discussed in this book. The famous work Milind Panhō assigned to his discussion with King Menānder forms one of the books of famous indological series entitled "Sacred Books of the East" translated and commented by learned Indologists under the guidance of German Sanskrit scholar MaxMuller. "Milind Panhō" has been translated and edited by Rhys David as well as by V.Treneckner but lacks details about Nāgsen and his biographical sketch.

Nāg Senī in Kaśṭwāṛ is not a particular village but a group of villages, slopy tract between the villages Chhichhā and Dūl, the site of the present 690 megawatt Dūl Hasti Project, the slopes drained by Naigad and some other small mountain streams. Some places of archaeological interest and antiquirian value, pertaining to the medieval times, still exist in the region.

Buddhism in ancient India seems to have travelled from its seat of political power in the West (i.e.Śākalā or Siālkot) farther up along the course of Chandrabhāgā and its tributaries, through Ambārān (Akhnoor) to Sangaldān, Dhammkund, Maitreyā, Chamalwās, Banshālā (Banihāl), Sirāj, Udhyānpur, Barshilā (Brahmshilā), Kānini, Ajāl, Jakyās, Kaśṭwāṛ, Nāg Seni Alwās, Machel and further up into Lāhul, Pāngī and many other Himalyan mountain valleys of Jammu and Chināb. To reach the interior mountain regions of Ladākh and Tibet it must have used other routes passing through Kashmir also.

In the present monograph an attempt has been made to evaluate the ancient antiquity of the mountain valleys of Chināb in Jammu and their contribution to the evolution of Buddhism in the light of Nāg Sen's biographical sketch and other related developments. The monograph is the 1st of the series in the antiquirian evaluation of the region. The other few are just to follow.

I hope this humble presentation of mine will cordially be received by the intellectual world.

Sādhnālyā **—P.K.Kaul**

9th November 1994.

---

1. In addition to Tawī of Jammu, we have Sukh Tawī, Munāwar Tawī, Rajouri Tawī and Later Bārekh Tawī of Sunder Banī, Nikkī Tawi and Kāli Tawī in Jammu, Tawī of Poonch and Taushī or Tawī of Chambā near Rāj Nagar. The four Devikās of Jammu region are that of Sudh Māhādev, Udhampur, Purmandal and Uttar Bani and three Sindhus are those of Ladākh, Shādipur in Kashmir and Sonder in Maṛwā (Kaśtwaṛ).
2. *Kashmiri Shāiri* - Sahitya Academy, New Delhi.

TABLE OF CONTENTS

Preface		iii
List of illustrations		xiv
Abbreviations		xvii
Chapter-1	**Introductory**	**1**
	Milind Panhō	2
	Menānder	2
	Capital of Menānder as per Milind Panhō	4
	Nāg Sen as per Milind Panhō	5
	Summary of Milind Panhō	7
Chapter-II	**Identifications**	**18-69**
	Greeko-Bactrian Kings and Menānder	18
	Menānder's	22
	time, and place of his birth	23
	Marriage of Menānder	25
	his career	26
	Warrior Menānder	26
	Territory of Menānder	28
	Social aspect of Menānder's rule	30
	Menānder's conversion	31
	Later years of Menānder	32
	Times of Menānder and the end of Indo-Bactrian empire	33
	Modified genealogy of Menānder's ancestors	34
	Time of writing of Milind Panhō	35
	Author of the work	35
	Milind Panho's account of persecution of Buddhists	36
	Fierceness of Indo-Greek wars	38
	Nāgsen	39
	Time of his birth	40

later years of his life 42
places and persons of Milind Panhõ. 43

(a) Persons : **48**

i) Milinda ii)Devmātya iii) Nāgsen
iv) Śukā v)Assāgutth̤ vi) Mahāsen
vii)Sonuttur viii) Rohan ix)Āyu Päl

b) Places:

i) Jumbū Dvīp ii) Sāglā iii)Kañjaṅgal
iv) Yugāndhār v) Vattanīya Hermitage
vi) Demzī vii)Guarded slopes
viii) Vijyam Vothu ix)Vejanta Palace
x) Ketumatī Mansion xi) Pātlīputra
xii) Sānkheya Hermitage
xiii) Route of Travellage
xiv) Buddhist Holy Land.

Chapter III : Conclusion **70-85**

A) Historical Evidence 70
B) Geographical Evidence 72
C) Archeaological Evidence 74
D) Numismatic Evidence 75
E) Ethenic Evidence 76
F) Linguistic Evidence 76
G) Religious Evidence 77

a) Sacred Crops 78

i) Siūl
ii) Phulan
iii) Bajar Bhang
iv) Drov
v) Chini

vi) Kodrā

b) Wild Fruit 78

i) Zom

ii) Kulāñch

iii) Ṭhānki

iv) Wild Wlnuts

v) Neozei

c) Sacred Trees 79

i) Brahmā Tree

ii) Gug

iii) Krain

H) Cultural Evidence 82

Conclusions

Chapter iv: Connected sites, monuments and their archeaological details. 86-113

A) Kāninī Jañgalwāṛ 87
B) Sarthal 90
C) Barshilā 91
D) Sai Draman 91
E) Bhāttan 94
F) Demzī 94
G) Rām Kund 96
H) Sakhī Maidān 99
I) Shāh Derā 103
J) Loh Devtā 104
Annexure I 114--125

Jambū Dvīp

Bibliography 126-127
Index 128

LIST OF ILLUSTRATIONS & MAP SKETCHES

Plate No.I	The table land valley of Kaśṭwār.
Plate No.II	The North Eastern Slopes of the township with Panditgām in the Centre.
Plate No.III	Sāi Draman Archaeological site at Siāh (Nāgsenī). General view from a distant place 100′ x 100′. The site of Assāgutth̤'s religious deliberations and discussions.
Plate No.IV	Siāh temple No.3 8′ x 8′ x 16′ (approx.). All stone construction ceiling with Ashat Kamal.
Plate No.V	Temple No.2, Siāh or Sāi Draman - General view.
Plate No.VI	Carved panels of flying celestials on the two sides of the Arch. Temple No.3 Siāh/Nāgsenī carved Ganeshā also visible on the gate beam.
Plate No. VII	Carved stone Arch with pair of carved lions on the two sides. Temple No.2.
Plate No.VIII	Stone slab with an inscription in Shārdā script 9-12 century. Siāh Nāgsenī.
Plate No.IX	A close up view of the same inscription.

Plate No.X	Statue of Garuḍa 9-10 century. Grey stone. Siāh temple.
Plate No.XI	Statue of Vishnu with Laxmi, in White stone.
Plate No. XII	General view of the Archeaological site at Demzī Nāgseni.
Plate No.XIII	Carved panels at the site Demzi Nāgsenī. Carved Ganesha, (probably) Nandi and 24 petalled lotus structure.
Plate No XIV	A heap of carved stones, structures and statues, Demzī Nāgsenī.
Plate No.XV	A fully blossomed field of Drove corn in the month of May. Nāg senī.
Plate No.XVI	Author on his way back from Demzī
Plate No XVII	site of Sānkhey Pariven and Milind vihāra of Milind Panho, Kriḍārāma vihārā of Lalitā Ditya. The present Sakhi Maidān in Mendhar.
Plate No.XVIII	The beautiful and enchanting Mendhar Valley.
Plate No.XIX	Do
Plate No.XX	Kālāban Side-valley in Mendhar, probable location of Kuvān vihārā of Kaniśkā's time.
Plate No. XXI.	Unexcavated and unidentified great archeaological site at Sakhi Maidān Mendhar.
Plate No. XXII	Central mound of the archeological site with stairs leading to it, still visible.
Plate No. XXIII	Outer wall of temple structure/vihārā made from massive stone blocks.

Plate No.XXIV	Centuries old Ziārat of Chotai Shāh close to the Archaeological ruins of Sānkhey Parivien.
Plate No. XXV	Newly constructed mosque (1982) close to the Ziārat of Chotai Shāh.
Plate No. XXVI	Front view of a stone fragment nicely carved and beautifully decorated.
Plate No.XXVII	Back view of the same stone structure- Sakhī Maidān
Plate No. XXVIII	A fragment of stone pillar Sakhī Maidān.
Plate No. XXIX	Carved stone pillar base Sakhī Maidān.
Plate No.XXX	The Hidden pocket valley of Narol Topā. The site of Sānkhey hermitage, Āshram of elder Āyū Pāl of *Milind Panhō*.
Plate No.XXXI	Topā the beautiful ridge top at Rāmkund Mendhar.
Plate No.XXXII	The ancient temple at Rāmkund 8-9th century.
Plate No. XXXIII	The three springs at the site. Rāmkuṇḍ and the Sitā Kuṇḍ. The third Lachman Kuṇḍ is at the lower end.
Plate No. XXXIV	Ancient Bodh Gumpā at Chasotī Machel/Kaśṭwāṛ.
Plate No. XXXV	Coins of Menānder.
Map Sketch No.1	The Chandrabhāgā valley in the hills of Jammu.
Map Sketch No.2	Empires of Śuṇgās and Menānder.
Map Sketch No.3	Jambū Dvīp of Ancient Literature.
Map Sketch No.4	Guarded Slopes, the Buddhist Holy land and Nāgsen's travel route

	from Vattaniya hermitage to Sānkheya Parvien.
Map Sketch No. 5	Jambū Dvīp of Purānic period-Medieval times. As also the other seven Dvipas.

ABBREVIATIONS

A.I.	Ancient India by V.D. Mahajan.
A.I.U.	The age of imperial unity -D.C. Sircar
B.K. Fidda	Buddhist Kashmir - F.M. Hussanain
B.K. Sarla	History of Buddhism in Kashmir - Dr. Sarla Khosla
Budh	Buddhism - Copleston D.D.1882.
C.H.I.	Cambridge History of India Vol.I -E.J. Rapson
E.H.C.K.	Early History and Culture of Kashmir - Dr.S.C. Ray
Excel	The Daily Excelsior, Jammu (N.P.)
G.B.I.	Greeks in Bactria and India - W.W.Tarn
H.R.F.B.	History of rise and fall of Buddhism in India—S.C.Dutt
I.G.	Indo-Greeks—Prof. A.K. Narain
I.G.C.	Indo-Greek Coins- Mehta Vishisht Dev Mohan
J.A.S.B	Journal of Asiatic Society of Bengal
K.C.A.	Kashmir and Central Asia - P.N. Kaul Bomzai
K.T.	Kashmir Times Jammu (Daily N.P.)
K.T.A.	Kashmir through the ages- Gausha Lal Kaul
M.K.	Monuments of Kashmir - R.C. Kak
M.P.Vad	Milind Panho— R.D. Vadekar
M.P. Treck	Milind Panho - V.Treneckner
M.P. Rhys	Milind Panho - Rhys Davids
M.P.Bhikśu	Milind Prashan Bhikshu - Jagdish Kashyap

N.W.I.	North West India 2nd century B.C. Vishishit Dev Mohan
Poliby	Polibius Historiae. Ed. & Trans. - W.R. Paton
P.H.K.	Political History of Kashmir - K.S. Sexena
R.T.	Rajtrangini - M.A. Stien
T.H.Beal.	Travels of Huen Tsang, Samuel Beal
T.S.J.	Temples and Shrines of Jammu.Ganhar J.N.
T.S.W.	Tree and Serpent Worship. Furguson
T.K.Mohi	Tariekh Kaśtwāṛ - Mohi-ud-Din Hajni
T.D.D.	Tariekh Dogra Des N.D. Nargis
T.K.Ish.	Tariekh Kaśtwāṛ - Ishrat Kashmiri
T.H.	Tariekh Hassan- Mohd.Din Faug.

Other Abbreviations

Ch.	Chapter
F.n.	Foot note
c.f.	Carried from
§	Sub-head
	Sign expressing closed vowels.

CHAPTER 1

INTRODUCTORY

The main contents of the celebrated work *Milind Panho* (questions of King Menānder) is a religio-philośophical discussion between Nāg Sen and King Menānder, which incidentally provides a lot of information about the Indo-Scythian ruler of Sākalā and other socio-religious conditions of the people in the mountain country of Jammu and Kashmir around second century B.C. The dramatic intellectual encounter between the contemporary political and religious giants is well narrated in *Milind Panho,* but it dos not furnish the much desired information about Nāg Sen, the hero of the whole episode and his native country. Students of Buddhist religion and thought had taken him as a Kashmiri,[1] but now he turned out to be a Kaśṭwāri, a mountain region of Jammu, the physical features and topography of which, fairly tallies with the description of the country of Nāg Sen's birth and learning, as mentioned in the outer story of the celebrated work. Before the subject is taken up for detailed study, it will be advisable to mention hereunder, some of the introductory informations pertaining to the celebrated work, and the scholar, and his famous discourse with equally scholarly Greeko-Bactrian King Menānder of Śākalā, as described in Milind Panho.

Menānder :-

After Ashokā (273-236 B.C.) Buddhism suffered a temporary eclipse during the reign of his successors, Jālukā and Dāmodrā. King Jālukā of Kashmir waged a ruthless war against Malecchās who probably were the Greeko-Bactrian hords trying to establish their kingdom in the territory bordering Kashmir. The history of Kashmir after Dāmodra is not certain till we come to the later Kuṣāṇas.[2] In the interregum North West India once again passed under the sway of foreigners including Greeks[3]. Tārn suggests that for a few years Demetrius was the lord of a realm which included southern Kashmir. A fragment in ptolmy gives the names of the two provinces on Menānder's home kingdom, east of Jehlum, of which Kasperiā, the Upper Valley of Jehlum, Chināb and Rāvi would correspond to Southern Kashmir[4].

Menānder was thus the Indo-Greek ruler of Gandhārā (North West India_). Eleven coin of certain kings including those of king Menānder have been located from Kashmir[5], and Kharośtī inscriptions and statues found from Lolāb Valley (North Western Kashmir) have also been preserved by Srinagar Museum[6]. He ruled over a considerable territory with his capital at Śākalā (Siālkot).

Menānder who is believed to have ruled towards the end of second century B.C. was a great scholar and an enquirer of truth. He used to spend his spare time in philosophical discussions with eminent scholars and thinkers of his time and in these discussions he invariably got the better of his adversaries . He was well versed in Purāṇas and philosophy (Darshan)

All the learned persons were afraid of him in religious discussion. In logic he was unsurpassable. His was a great personality and had won acclaim to the affection of the posterity. His genial treatment of Buddhist communities led to his characterization in Buddhist literature. He had come under the influence of Nāg Sen, the great Buddhist philosopher and thinker and was then converted to the Buddhist fold.

The Indo-Greeks , appear to have accepted the doctrine of Buddhism, and Kharośti inscriptions found at Swāt, Texilā and Kashmir (lolāb) prove the existence of Buddhism there during that period. These kings erected stūpas, constructed Vihāras and installed images of the Śākya Muni[7]. Greek writers tell us that Menānder was a great conqueror also. He is stated to have conquered more nations than Alexander himself. Surely he was the greatest of the Indo-Greek kings of India[8].

Other Indologists have recorded following observations about Menānder:

(i) "He was first a lay devotee of Buddha but afterwards left his throne, joined the Sanghā and at last became an Arhat."[9]

(ii) "He silenced the Buddhist priests in argument and drove them across the Himālays (to Rakshit Tal and Manasarovar" .[10]

As regards his political and historical career, a lot of information is available. The Greek writers tell us that Menānder was a conqueror . He is stated to have conquered more nations than Alexander himself.[11] From the variety of his coins and the wide area of their distribution , it is concluded that he was the ruler of many Kingdoms. We have come across a large number of his coins from the western districts of Uttar Pradesh. His coins are also known to have been current in Kathiāwār.[12]

According to D.C. Sircar the dominion of Menānder appears to have comprised of the Central parts of Afghānistān. north West frontier province.

Punjab, Sindh Rājputānā Kāthiāwār and probably a portion of Western Uttar Pradesh.[13]

Prof. Rapson has pointed out that the fame of Menānder as a great and just ruler was not confined to India alone. Some two centuries after his time, Plutarch recounted to the Greek world the story, how after his death in a camp, the cities of his realm contended for the honour of preserving his ashes.[14] It is thus as a philosopher and not as a mighty conqueror that Menānder like Janmejaya, the king of Kurūs and Janaka, the king of Videha in the Upanishads has won for himself an abiding fame.[15]

Milind Panho pays the following tribute to Menānder; "As a disputant he was hard to equal, harder still to overcome, the acknowledged superior of all the founders of various schools of thought. As in wisdom so in strength of body, swiftness and valour, there was found none equal to Milinda in India. He was rich, too mighty in wealth and prosperity and the number of his armed hosts knew no ends".

Capital of Menānder:

Although Menānder ruled over a great country and attacked and penetrated as far east as Mathurā, his capital was at Sāglā or Śākalā, the present Siālkot in Pakistan. According to Tarn, Sāglā in the eastern Punjāb was Menānder's capital.[16] Capleston states that Sāglā is at a distance of 12 yojans from Kashmir and 200 yojans from Kālsi.[17] We are fortunate in having the following description of the capital of Menānder's kingdom,Śākalā in the work of Minind Pahno. Siālkot finds mention in ancient and medieval history and literature as 'Śākal Dvīp , Śākalā and Siālkot. It had been a seat of political power, trade and commerce for quite a long time. In *Milind Panho* also it has been described in great details and appreciated for its geographical location and scenic beauty.

"There is in the country of Yonkas, a great center of trade, a city called Sāglā, in a delightful country well watered and hilly, abounding in parks, gardens, groves, lakes and tanks. A paradise of rivers and mountains and woods,wise Architect have laid it out and its people know of no oppression, since all their enemies and adversaries have been put down. Brave in its defense with many and various strong towers and ramparts with superb gates and entrance arch-ways, and with the Royal Citadel in its midst, white walled and deeply mounted. Well laid out are its streets, squares, cross-road and market places, well displayed are the innumerable sorts of costly merchandize with which its shops are decorated. Its streets are filled with elephants, horses, carriagesand foot passengers and crowded by men of all sorts and conditions.[18]

In Milind Panho Sākalā has been repeatedly mentioned as situated in Jambu Dvīp, which probably indicates the antiquity of the region.[19]

Nāg Sen:

Nāgsen was a great Buddhist saint, scholar and philosopher, to whom credit goes for having defeated King Menānder, in a religious discussion (which was held at a place near Śākalā, and at who's hands he accepted Buddhism and became a convert.

We know very little about the life and teachings of the philosopher, except that recorded in *Milind Panho*, according to which Nāg Sen was the re-incarnation of Arhat Māhā Sen of Ketu-Mati Mansion, and the cycle of rebirth,[20] had been accepted by Mahāsen after repeated requests of Śukā and the personal request of Assāgutth - the Sangh Nāyak or the leader of the order, for saving the faith (Buddhism): probably after the persecution of Buddhists by Indo- Bactrian invasion, and challenges from the North West as well as from Śungā Kings (Pushya Mitra and his lineage), Kashmiri orthodox Śaivites and other aggressive Brahmanical sects around the country.

Nāgsen as per *Milind Panho* was born at Kanjaṅgle village[21] to Brahmin Sönuter after ten months of conception. Some strange things are said to have happened at the time of his birth . His father was a learned Brahmin who inspired him to learn the three Vedas which he learnt by heart and mastered them and when there was no more to learn from his father and the teacher , he became philologist and grammarian. Later he underwent Buddhist studies from Assāgutthḥ and Dharmādhikāri. There were in his personality sings of great receptivity as a student. He learnt all Vedas in just one reading, mastered grammar and Lokāyat, and later all Pītkas in just seven months . From insight he saw the uselessness of Vedas indicating his preference for Buddhist thought over Brahmanic culture, or his preference for Indian way of life of non-violence, over the Āryan way of aggression and violence. He was, then admitted as a novice to the order, at the age of 20 years.

He was then asked by his Guru Rohana to go to Śākalā and overcome King Menānder in his arguments otherwise he would not be able to earn the forgiveness of his Guru. Nāgsen obeys Rohana and discussions were held in which King Menānder is defeated and he is said to have attained Arhathood.

Milind Panho : Milind Panho or the questions of Menānder, is a Buddhist canonical work, a religio-philosophical dialogue between Nāgsen and King Menānder, in almost the Platonic manner, held at a place only twelve Yojans from Kashmir.[22] *Milind Panho* was originally written in Kashmiri and subsequently translated in Pāli and Sinhalese.[23] A Chinese version of the book is also referred to.[24] Presently three critical studies with translation of the book, two in English and one in Hindi, are available.[25] However, there are some other references to the book and the philosopher in other celebrated works also.

Milind Panho contains a graphic account of how Menānder's arguments are overcome and his doubts resolved one by one, and finally he seeks refuge in Buddhist faith and becomes a disciple of the great teacher, who was a thorough going rationalist. *Milind Panho* is the best source of information on the history of Buddhism of Kashmir. It informs that Menānder built the Milind Vihāra and joined the Sanghā as a monk and finally attained Arhathood.

Milind Panho has mainly two portions or volumes. The first part or outer story mainly pertains to Nāg Sen's birth, education and preparation for the historic episode. The second portion is the final discourse between Nāgsen and the King Menānder. As the subject matter of this research is the location of the place Nāg Sen's birth and education and the place of his final discussion with Menānder, we put down in the following pages a summary of *Milind Panho's* account of Nāg Sen's birth story and his education at various places and hermitages, as translated by V.Trenecker in 1880 A.D.

Summary of Part I/or outer story of Milind Panho

"King Milinda at Sāglā, the famous town of Yore, Nāgsen the world famous sage repaired. King Milinda accompanied by 500 yonkas (mounted Greek soldiers) silences all learned men of Śākalā and for 12 years the city of Sāglā had been devoid of learned men. They had departed hither and thither and brethren of the order went for most part,to the Himālayan mountains (1/15). Milinda thought, "all India is an empty thing. There is no recluse, Brahmin, Samana, monk or laymen left, who could dispel my doubts" (1/16).

Now at that time there dwelt on the mountaneous region of Himālayas on the guarded slopes, an innumerable company of Arhats and venerable Assāgutth. By means of divine power of hearing, Assāgutth̤ heard those words of King Milinda and convened an assembly of the order , on the submit of Yugāndhāra mountain and asked if any member of the order could face the challenge of Milinda and resolve his doubts.

Then he told the assembly about Mahāsen, east of Vejayantā palace /Ketumati mansion in the heavens of thirty three (Vedic Gods). The Arhats then vanished and reappeared at the Yugāndhāra sumit. Seeing them, Śukā went to Assāgutth̤ and after paying his respects asked him if he could do anything for the service of the order . Assāgutth̤ replies about the superiority of Milinda (king Menānder) in argument. Śukā suggests that Mahāsen of Ketumati be requested to beseech to suffer himself, to be reborn into the world of men. Śukā goes himself to Ketumati and requests Māhāsen for rebirth: When repeated requests of Śukā are not accepted by Mahāsen, Assāgutth̤ makes a personal request for saving the Buddha order and therefore Mahāsen agrees(1/18).

Then all the brethren reappeared on the guarded slopes on Himālayan mountains except Rohana, who a week before had become buried in meditation. Rohana instantly (by devine yogic powers?) appeared at the spot , and Assāgutth̤ said to Rohana that:-

"There is a Brahmin village called Kañ,añal.[27] (Treneckner Kajjaṅgala) and there dwells a Brahmin called Sô**nutur**. He will have a son called Nāg Sen. Go to that house for alms for seven years and ten months. After the laps of that time thou shall draw away the boy from the worldly life and cause him to enter the order.[28] When he shall have abandoned the world, only then shall thou be free from atonement of the fault.[29]

Mahāsen passed away and was reborn to the wife of Brahmin Sonutur. At the time of conception of Nāg Sen three strange things happened.[30]

- All the arms and weapons became ablaze.
- Tender grains became ripe.
- Great rain came.

Rohana went for alms to Brahmin Sonutur's house for seven years and received nothing; nor even a word from the Brahmins house. On that occasion he received a spoonful of rice but mostly got taunts. The Brahmin was ashamed for his earlier bad behaviour with Rohana, whom he befriended and respected later.

Nāgsen learnt all the Vedas by heart , at the inspiration of his father, and Guru and later mastered them, became philologist and grammarian (1.13/27). When there was no more to learn from his father, and teacher, he wanted to go to a place of solitude, where he could do meditation.

From insight he saw the uselessness of Vedas , indicating his preference to Buddhist thought over Brahmanic culture.[31] Rohan again came to Nāg Sen at Kañjaṅgal.

He takes him to Vattanīya's heritage, to Vijam-Vothu[32] and then to the guarded slopes, and Nāgsen is admitted as a novice into the order at the age of 20 years.

On reaching at the guarded slopes, Nāg Sen thinks low and wrong about his teacher. Rohana, who reads Nāg Sen's mind, tells him that was unwarily of a good pupil and would earn his pardon, only on going to Sāglā and overcoming King Milinda in argument (1/1/10). Rainy season was due to commence and accordingly he could not go to Śākalā. Rohan asks him to go to Vattaniya hermitage where Assāgutth the Sangh Nāyak dwelt. Nāgsen did as he was told. He swept out the teacher's cell at the Vattaniya hermitage, put the drinking water and tooth cleaner ready , which the elder Assāgutth swept again, threw away the water and tooth cleaner without saying a word. The Sangh Nāyak asked him some questions which were replied by Nāg Sen. The teacher and pupil behaved in the same manner for 6 days. On the seventh day he was again asked the same questions and same reply came, and the teacher gave him the permission to stay and pass three months at Vattanīya hermitage[33]. Now a distinguished lady follower of the faith had for 30 years administered to the wants of elder Assāgutth. At the end of the rainy season, she came one day and invited him and Nāg Sen for next day to take midday meals with her. Accordingly both of them took food at the lady's house and after doing so Assāgutth asked Nāg Sen to give thanks giving to the lady, after leaving the place himself. The lady asks Nāgsen for deeper things of the faith. Nāgsen dwelt on the profounder side of Abhidharma, relating to Arhatship, and as she sat listening, there aroused an insight in her as well in Nāg Sen's mind (like that of Arhatship). Assāgutthฺ became aware of it at his hermitage and he said well done! Well done Nāg Sen! (1/1/11).

Assāgutth now sends Nāgsen to Pātlīputra which is 100 yojanas.[34] away, and where Dharmādhikāri dwelt in Ashoka park for learning the words of Buddha. Nāg Sen complains of greatness of distance but later agrees to go.[35]

On the way he meets a merchant with 500 wagons. After having a discourse, he is pleased with Nāg Sen and serves him well and leads him to Pātliputra.

After meeting Dharmādhikārī at Pātlīputra Nāg Sen learns by heart all the three pītkas (Baskets of Buddhist knowledge) and Buddha in recital, and in three months more, masters the deeper meaning,and at the end of that time (6 months), one day while discussing these with Dharmādhikārī attains Arhatship, a four fold power of that wisdom, and all Gods showered their approval on him.

Now, at that time, the innumerable company of Arhats at the guarded slopes in Himālayan mountains sent him a message to come, as they were anxious to see him, and when he learnt about the message, Nāgsen vanished from the Ashoka Park and reappeared before them . And they said that the King Milinda is in the habit of harassing the brethren by knotty questions and by argumentation, this way and that way. Do then Nāgsen go, and master him.

Then all the elders went to the city of Sāgalā lighting it up with their yellow robes, like lamps and bringing down upon it the breeze from the height's where the sages dwelt.

At that time Āyu Pal was living at the Sānkheya hermitage well versed in three baskets and all the traditional lore. Seeing the pleasantness of the weather and inspired by it, Milinda goes to the Sānkhey hermitage , exchanges pleasantries, and in the discourses silences the elder Āyu Pāla and in excitement exclaims that "All India is an empty thing. It is very like chaff". At the same time he felt that, some other must be able to answer his questions.

At that very time Nāg Sen making his Alms tour through the villages, towns, cities, had in due course of time arrived at Sāglā, attended by a band of Samananas (Buddhist monks), at the head of a body of disciples and teacher of a school, famous and reknowned, and highly esteemed by the people, master of three Baskets and erudite in Vedic lore. He was in possession of the highest Buddhist insight and a master of all that had been handed down in the school, by which the most abstruse points could be explained. He knew by heart, the nine fold divisions of the doctrine of Buddha to the perfection. He was

i) a great orator or discussioner, unable to equal,

ii) A dispeller of darkness and diffuser of light,

iii) honoured and revered by brothers and sisters of the order.

(and similar other great praise of Nāg Sen follows on P.35 of the translation 1/1/15).

Nāg Sen dwelt at the hermitage of Sānkhey, with a numerous company of brethren, appearing in the Sānkhey grove like the lion of the hills.

Then Devmātya, councellor of Ṃilinda, tells the King to wait for some time, as there is an elder named Nāg Sen, learned, able and wise, who could refute objections to perfection. " you should go great King to him and put your questions to him. He is able to discuss things with you and dispel your doubts". On hearing the same of Nāg Sen, the King was seized with a fear and anxiety and hairs of his stood on ends. And now Milinda asks Devmātya to send a message to Nāg Sen , that he is coming for a discussion. Nāg Sen sends word back that he might come. And he did so, attended by 500 Younkas, he reached the hermitage.There Nāg

Sen was also sitting in the central place surrounded by his followers in a Mandal Mālā. The King Milinda recognised Nāg Sen in the gathering of his followers and a feeling comes to his mind and he expresses it to Devmātya.

"Many the talkers I have, many the conversations I had had, but never yet, till now today, has fear so strange, so terrible overpowered my heart. Verily now defeat must be my lot victory his; so trouble in, my mind."

Here ends the secular introductory

narrative of the Sinhalese version,

"Bahirī Kathā" or Ist part of *Milind Panho*. (1/1/15)

As is evident from the above the Ist Vol.of *Milind Panho* pertains to a very brief sketch of Nāgsen and his confrontation with Menānder. Vol II of the book mainly concerns with philosophical discussion between the two and the details of Buddhist School of thought, and does not tell us in details about the life of Nāg Sen, his parentage , his education, his place of birth, its location and his other biographical details.

Footnotes :

1. B.K.Fidda - P.2.
2. K.T.A. - Kaul P.25-26.
3. Ibid.
4. G.B.I. c.f. Bomzai K.C.A. P.54.
5. B.K.Fidda. P.54.
6. Ibid.
7. Ibid.
8. I.G. Narain P.100.
9. E.H.C.K. P. 159.
10. T.S.W. P.64; Cunnigham-Bhilśā Topes. P.311. c.f.B.K. Sarla p.42. .f.n.11. Also.

11. N.W.I. P.114, 16 .c.f Starbo, who in turn qoutes Apollodorus, the author of History of Parthiā.
12. A.I. P.325.
13. Ibid.
14. Ibid.
15. Ibid. c.f. Rapson on coins of Greeko Indian Sovereigns and the Scythian and Parthian Invaders.
16. G.B.I P.133.
17. Budh. 1822 P.37 c.f. B.K. Sarla. P.42. f.n.9.
18. A.I.P. 325c.f. M.P. Treck.
19. The term JAMBŪ DVĪP and its location is being discussed separately in Annexure-I of this book.
20. Compare with the rebirth story associated with Nehru and Buddha.
21. For probable site of village Kanjaṅgle see chapter III.
22. M.P. - Treck.
23. Kashmiri Shāiri - Sāhitya Academy, New Delhi. c.f. B.K.Fidda. P.18.
24. M.P. Bhikśu -P.25-26,, Also
    F.W Cowell in his translation of Buddhist Mahāyān Text Part IInd has recorded following comments on this Chinese Edition ; No."358; very interesting dialogue between Greek King Menānder and Bhikhu Nāgsen." The Pāli text is far more interesting and fuller than Chinese. This Chinese version has many alterations and therefore must be a composition of much later date; may be of Huen Tsāng's time. According to Jagdish Kashyap the book contains only [26] pages and is different from Pāli version of *Milind Panho* in the following:-

    I) The Purva yoga is quite different.

    II) The book in narration is only upto the 3rd chapter of the Pāli edition. However the question and answers are almost same in shape and number as in Pāli edition.

    III) In Chinese editions Nāgsen is called Zo, because at the time of his birth a calf was also born to an elephant. As the term Nag means an elephant also , he was given the name of Nāg Sen. Rohan has been described as the maternal uncle of Nāg Sen. This

Chinese version may be the product of an Indo - Chinese intercourse, as observed by R.C. Majumdar in his advanced history of India; "In the early centuries of Christain era we have an epigraphical as well as literary references to this intercourse with China, the Hellenic world, Ceylone and farther India. They are recorded in Nāgārjunkondā Inscription and the *Milind Panho*", P. 136.

The summary of the Chinese version cf, *Milind Panho* as given by Bhikśu Jagdish Kashyap is as under:-

"Lord Buddha while staying at Śrāvasti (Sy-o-a- ki)felt tired of the continued company of Bhikśūs, Nuns ,disciples and admireres day and night, and decided to live in seclusion. Accordingly he left all of them and went to a forest named (Ka-Lo-Chong-Su) and there sat under a tree for meditation. Close to this very forest there lived an elephant with 500 members of his herd. He also felt detached, deserted his herd , and came to the place where Buddha was meditating. Lord Buddha showed his affection to the animal and as a result of it the elephant rendered his service to the Lord for many days. But when Buddha left the place, the elephant was greatly pained and could not forget the Lord throughout his life, and always remembered him. In the next life this very elephant was born in a Brahmin family. On coming of age he became a recluse and resided in mountain country where another recluse was residing. Both of them became friends. One day during conversations the latter told the former that he had become a recluse only to attain Nirvāna, because the world was full of sorrow and pain, but the former told him that he had adopted this mode of life only to become a great king and conqueror in the next world. Consequently one of the recluse in the subsequent life was prince Mihan (Menānder/Milinda) born near a sea shore while the other was born in Ki-Pin_Kun (Kañjańgal). The child because of his predominant wish for Nirāan appeared as if he was wearing Kāśeya i.e Yellow robes. On the very day of his birth a calf was born to an elephant also and accordingly he was named Nāgsen".

As compared to the above mentioned Chinese version of the Nāgsen's rebirth story Bhikśū Jagdish Kashyap's Hindi version of the Purva Yoga or the story of the deeds of earlier life of Nāg Sen and Milind is as under:- "In Buddha's life time, a Buddhist Sangha lived in an Aśram near the Ganges. Bhikshus of this Aśram were well learnt and led a life of piousness. They would get up early in the morning and clean the hermitage, remembering always Buddha and chanting his name in prayers".

One day it so happened that one of the Bhikśu called upon a Śramaṇa to come and throw away the dirt he had collected. The Śramaṇa ignored the call of the Bhikśu and did not respond even after being called upon for the 2nd and the 3rd time. Taking the Śramanar as very discurtious, the Bhikśu became very angry and struck him with the sweeper. The Śramanar got terrified and weepingly he took out the dirt and threw it away; at the same time affirming in his mind that he would continue to perform this very deed as a duty till he attains Nirvāna, because of the merit of this deed ; and that wherever may he be reborn, he would attain the vigour and strength of the mid day sunshine. After throwing away the dirt he went to have a bath in the river Ganges and on seeing the charm of the waves, made another affirmation,that wherever he is reborn, he may attain the wisdom and intellectual superiority akin to the speed of the Ganges.

The Bhikśu after keeping the sweeper at its place, also left for the Ganges to have his bath, and while doing so overheard the solemn resolve of the Śamaṇa. He thought that if Śramer, on being inspired by my beating of him, can have, such a hard affirmation, why should'nt I also do so. Accordingly, he also had a resolve made in his mind, "where ever am I reborn, I may attain the superiority of wisdom like the waves of the Ganges and may be able to answer all the questions and doubts raised by this Śramana. Both of them spent one Budhānter (a period of time) by being reborn in the world of Devās (Gods) and human beings (Manushya). Then our Lord Buddha also saw them there and ushered a prophecy regarding the two, just similar to the one he had made about Mogli's son named Tiśya. "After five hundred years of my salvation (Mahānirvān) both of them will be reborn and will propagate the religion I had founded, and will remove all doubts and confusion with respect to the faith by putting questions, giving answers, with similies and examples.

Among the two, the Śramner was later born as the King of the city of Sāgla in Jambū Dvīp and the Bhikśu as Nāgsen

25. Please see bibliography.
26. B.K.Fidda. P.25.
27. A famous place in Buddhist story. It is at the extreme limit to the east of Buddhist Holy land, middle country, at the foot of Himālyan mountains. For the village see Chapter III of the book .
28. Indicates his conversion to Buddhist faith from Brahmanic fold at the hands of Rohan the Arhat and Śramana.
29. For having left the place of hermitage a week before and got himself burried all alone in meditation, and reaching late at the assembly of the order.
30. M.P.Treck. The fact that Brahmin Saonutur, father of Nāgsen, taught three Vedas to Nāgsen again points out to the probability that the highland valleys of Chinab were the lands of Vedic seers and sages.
31. Or his preference for his native Indian thought of non-violence over the aggressive Āryan thought and culture of violence.
32. For identification of Vijamvothu see places, persons and terms in M.P. Chapter III.
33. M.P. Treck. P.30.
34. Ibid - Yojan = League of seven miles.
35. Ibid - P. 33-34.

CHAPTER II

IDENTIFICATIONS

1. GREEKO - BACTRIAN KINGS AND MENĀNDER

As indicated earlier, in the interregum, between Maurya and Kuśāṇa periods North West India once again passed under the sway of foreigners, including Indo-Greek.[1]

Bacteria and Parthiā, the two states that greatly influenced the history of North West India, threw off the Seleucid Yoke of Antiochus III, about the middle of third century B.C. and established themselves as independent states. Antiochus III was the Seleucid Satrap of Syria. He had , in the initial stages curbed the expansionist ambitions of Euthydemids, the rulers of Bactria, but he himself got involved on his Western frontiers, leaving Euthydemus the King of Bactria (220-192 B.C.) free to extend his kingdom in such directions as were open to him, without inviting a fresh attack by the Selucid Antiochus. After the death of Antiochus around 206 B.C., he was completely independent and carried on extension of his territory freely and fearlessly. By 190.B.C. the power of Antiochus regime had been broken[2] and Euthydemus had also died and his son Demitrius had started to extend his powers south of Hindu Kuś and accordingly he invaded India.

Demitrius, who finds mention in the Indian classics is said to have carried two invasion of India

.The first during the life time of his father i.e. Euthydemus, before 190 B.C. During the life time of his father, Arācosiā, Sindhu, Sauvirā and probably Gandhāra were added to Euthydemus Kingdom, and consolidated his rule in these parts. He probably advanced in Panjāb also, as far as the ancient city of Śākalā (modern Siālkot) and renamed if after the name of his father as Euthydemia.[3] But as the name never came in vogue, the occupation of Śākalā by Demitrius must have been of short duration.

If Demitrius had left any Garrisons in Panjāb then they were soon expelled by the Mauryan ruler of Panjāb and Kashmir. King Jālukā of Kashmir, who is said to have been a contemporary of Demitrius, freed the country from an invasion as far as Kanauj.[4] The Malechās most probably were the IndoGreek Garrisons left behind by Demitrius at Śākalā and Gandhāra after his first attack of India. However Demitrius had acquainted himself, with the type of resistance he was to face in his second assault of North India, which he had now planned.

Around 190 B.C. Demitrius commenced his second raid into India.Though he had earlier been repelled from southern Kashmir and Panjāb, he still held the country of Arācosiā, Gandhāra, Sindhu and Sauvīrā. He consolidated his rule in these parts. Around this time he is said to have founded two cities both named after him as Demitriās.

Demitrius seems to have conducted his 2nd raid on India in two phase and with two pincers. In the 1st phase, he seems to have occupied Afghānistān, Sindh and Takśilā. Apollodotus his brother [6] and General was appointed as his Sub-King to govern these regions and also to assist him in his second compaign of invading

North India. He mainly exerted to improve and overhaul the Greek war machine.

In the second phase, around 186 B.C.[7] he dreamt of conquering the whole of North India and led a two pronged attack on Sāketa, Vidiśā and Pātlīputra, the strongholds of, otherwise, shattering and decaying Mauryan empire. He penetrated through Pānipat gap into the Gangetic valley and laid siege to the city of Sāketā in Kośāla. Śungā Chief who had overthrown the weak Mauryan ruler Bridhāratha and seized power himself, gave him a tough resistance and Sāketa could not be subdued, but the temptation to capture reknowned city of Pātlipura proved irresistible and Demitrius by-passed Sāketa thereby committing a fatal blunder. When he reached the mud walls of Pātliputra, Pushyamitra, who after the assassination of Bridhārtha was in full control of his forces, threatened his rear by attacking the base of Demitrius forces at Mathurā. This lead to his disastrous retreat in the Napoleonic way. The Hathigumphā inscription probably refers to this retreat.[8]

It is quite probable that around this very time Menānder as a baby King, or hostage from Apollodotus, had been stationed by Demitrius at Mathurā, along with his mother, as Strabo mentions him as one of the Generals of Demitrius.

Another pincer or attack on the Mauryan territory of North India, aimed at capturing Sāketā and Pātliputra as planned by Demitrius, was led by his brother and Sub King Apollodotus which advanced towards Vidiśā, the ancestral Kingdom of Śungas. This was meant to link with Demitrius in the Gangetic valley, but Apollodotus found his way blocked by the fortified town of Madhyamikā. He laid a seige of the town, but could neither reduce it, nor by-pass it to link up with

Demitrius at Mathurā or Sāketa. The result was a complete failure of the planned expedition. In subsquent years Demitrius seems to have lost one battle after the other. The fierce fight between Pushyamitra alongwith his sons Agnimitra and grand-son Vasumitra on one side and Demitrius and his allies and successors (Euthedemus II, Demitrius II Pantalean, Agathocles, Apollodotus and Menānder) on the other side seems to have continued for quite a long time (probably from 186 B.C. to 150 B.C.) during which the Euthydemus family seems to have lost the whole territory of North West India except, Sindh- Sauvīra, where Apollodotus was allowed to rule under the suzerainty of Śungas. The war between the two was fiercely fought and greatly devastating as revealed by so many Indian literary references[9] as well as foreign mentions.[10] Buddhists seem to have particularly been effected by this devastation, firstly because of their sympathy for the foreigners and secondly for their doctrine of non-violence and antiBrahmanic attitude, as well as their complete submissiveness.

These wars and the revolts which were probably engineered by Śungās cost Euthydemids very heavily. Demitrius and his compelete lineage, was annihilated in a matter of few years except his youngest daughter. Agathocleia, who was married to Menānder. Demitrian territory shrank to Sindhu-Sauvīra and a small chunk in Afghānistān and his crown of thorns fell upon the head of Apolloduts, his younger brother. After about a decade and a half, in which Apollodotus seems to have accepted the suzerainty of Śungas, concluded temporary peace to the advantage of both, and later became aggressive and arrogant. He too seems to have fallen at the hands of youthful Śunga Vasumitra[11] around 158 B.C. Pushyamitra (185 B.C to 149B.C.) steadily advanced towards the North West India through Panjāb. Tāranath speaks of his rule in Jullunder.[12] Divyāvdān[13] records his advance from Pātlīputra to Śākalā and thence to Koshthakā (i.e.Kahūtā near Rāwalpīndi) and thence to Takśilā[14], where he probably met Eukradites and conspired and engineered a revolt against Demitrius and Apollodotus.[15] The revolt might have been raised by other Satraps of Demitrius,and accordingly he was killed either by Pushyamitra Śungā who continuously persued him, or by one of his own probable revolting Satraps or Chiefs.

The Geneaology of Euthydemus family as compiled by Tarn[16] is as under:—

Euthydemus
(King of Bactria)

- Demitrius I
- Antimachus I Theos
  - Antimachus II Nikephoros
    - Euthydemus II
    - Demitrius II
    - Pantaleon
    - Agathocles
    - Agathocleia
- Appollodotus I Soter

MENĀNDER

From the above genealogical table as compiled by Tarn, on the conclusions of Dr.Macdonald, Menānder does not figure in the family of Euthydemus - Demitrian lineage. Doubts have been expressed about his antecedents. However recent researches indicate that he was the son and successor of Apollodotus and nephew of Demitrius.[17] He was probably the only survivor left to represent the house of Euthydemids who had been associated with the Greek invasion of India, right from very early age, as depicted by his baby King coins[18], and was the only Indo-Greek kings of India to find a favourable mention in the Indian literature. He is celebrated as a great Buddhist king and finds mention in Indian classics also.[19]

Time and place of birth:

In Milind Panho while answering questions of Nāgsen Menānder has himself mentioned his place of birth as Alsandā.[20]

अत्थि भन्ते अलसन्दो नाम दीपो ।३४।

तत्था हं जातो ति..........

अत्थि भन्ते कलसि गाम नाम ।३४।

तत्था हं जातो ति...........

Regarding Alsandā and Kalsigām, scholars have given various suggestions. Dr.D.C.Sircar[21] and Prof. Rapson[22] have identified the Dvīpa of Alsandā of *Milind Panho* as Doāb lying between Panjshir (five heads) and Kābul rivers. According to him this very Dvīp of Alsandā of Yavnās is mentioned in Mahāvaṁśa (XXIX.39). He asserts that there is no reason why the term Alsandā should not be applied to the country between Panshir and Kābul rivers, in which the ruins of (one of many) Alaxandriās (City of Alexander) have now been recognised near Chrikar. King Menānder himself describes it[23] 200 yojnas or 500 miles away from Śākalā and according to Rapson the distance between Siālkot and Charikar fairly agrees well with Menānder's statement. Rhy Davids however feels that Alsandā Dvīp was a name given to an island presumably in Indus. No identification of Kālsī village is forthcoming. Scholars however agree, whatever their difference of opinion, that this Alsandā or Alexandriā was south of Paropamisus (Hindu kuś). To me it appears that the Dvīp of Alsandā must be located somewhere in the North West India lying between river Sindh and one of its tributaries, most probably Kābul river in analogus to Sapt Dvīpas of ancient India. The Greeko-Arab prefix "A1" joins the river name to make it Alsandhā and the village Kālsī must be located lying somewhere between the two rivers and adjacent to river Sind which at present is a difficult task for an Indian of meagre resources like me to locate in the context of difficult situation of the region (Pakistān-Afghānistān). As for the time of Menānders birth is concerned, we know that Euthydemus started his attack on North West India around 190 B.C. and occupied parts of Afghānistan, particularly the Kābul Valley, (Dvīp of Alsandā), for a short spell of time only, i.e. around 190-189 B.C. The next few years were wasted in subduing the revolts of Aśvakās and consolidating his rule in Arācosiā, Sindhu and Sauvīr . So it must be during this short period of peaceful occupation of Alsandā between 190 B.C.-189 B.C.- that Menānder must have been born.[25] Around this very time Apollodotus started his career as Sub-King of Kapīśā Gandhāra.[26] This date agrees well with Menānder's early coins. In which the bust of the King is that of a boy in his teens. In 174 B.C. when his father Apollodotus succeeded Demetrius, he must have been of 16 years and was appointed as SubKing, by his father. He received the Diadem in the life time of his father.

Apollodotus, the father of Menānder seems to have been killed in action by Vasumitra about 160 B.C. By that time Menānder must have gained considerable administrative experience. He must have been of some 30 years at the time. As his early coins have been found from Sindh and Western parts of Afghānistān, it can be inferred that these parts he inherited from his father and were not as yet penetrated either by Pushya Mitra Śuṅga or his ally and also by pretender Eukradites. It is around this time that he recruited his new sturdy soldiers, from Lohitrādri i.e. (Hindu Kuś), well versed in the art of war, which resulted in fierce battles and death of Agnimitra.

Marriage of Menānder

As seen earlier, with the death of Demitrius and his sons, his direct line, but for a daughter became extinct. The legal title to the Euthydemid's throne came to Apollodotus, the seniormost living representative of that family. When the later was raised to the throne in natural course, and Agāthocleia the youngest child of Demitrius, which seems to be a very pretty girl and cousin sister of Menānder, married him. Vishisht Dev Mohan[27] assumes that Menānder had married the youngest child of Demitrius i.e. Queen Agāthocleia, on the following grounds:-

1) Queen Agathocleia and his sons Starto I immediately succeeded to the throne of Menānder as rulers of Panjāb with their capital at Śākalā.

II) Again the bust of Queen Athena Helmeted which appears on the coins of Menānder[28] is perhaps a portrait of Agathocleia. It resembles her own coins struck in association with Strato I.[29] Her husband Menānder, perhaps for reasons of her beauty or love and reverence for her, considered her appearance as God like, and this idea of self praise of Agathocleia must be at the back of her assumption of Theotropos i.e. God like, as her title on the currency during her regency of Strato I.

(III) The figure of a warrior King on the reverse of certain coins struck by Agathocleia during Strato's minority and bearing her own portrait, may be supposed to represent the late King.[30]

A similar figure occurs on the obverse type of coins of Menānder -[31] where it is most naturally explained as that of Menānder.[32]

Career of Menānder :

Menānder's career has been portrayed by various authors in diverse shades, as a king and monarch, as a politician, as a warrior, as a religious philosopher and as an administrator. He had been a man of extra-ordinary intelligence, and capabilities.

Warrior Menānder :

According to Tarn Menānder was a commoner and had risen to Demitrius generalship by dint of his ability. He carved his own way to fortune before marrying into the royal house.[33] But he has expressed his doubts also.[34] According to him, "It was one thing for Demitrius to confer the royal title and a great measure of power upon Apollodotus who was his brother and kinsmen, and quite another to confer that title upon a General Menānder". But he ventures to suggest that, "It may have been done because of some sheer necessity", when "Demitrius himself returned to fight Eukradites". Probably Tarn did not believe or knew about any relationship between Menānder and Apollodotus and hence the confusion. If we take into consideration the deduction of Vishisht Dev,[35] that Menānder was the son of Apollodotus and the title of sub-kingship was conferred on him by Apollodotus and not by Demitrius, things become somewhat clear, but Menānder's participation as a General in the attack of Sāketa by Demitrius around 185 B.C. still needs to be explained.

According to Vishishit Dev[36], quoting Strabo and Patanjalī[37] the two pincer, 2nd attack of Demitrius on Sāketa and Madhyamikā (Vidiśā), was conducted by his above referred two Generals around 185 B.C. when Menānder was very young and of tender age, and could not participate in the terrible war. (Plate xxv) But his participation is not very difficult to explain.

Actually during the year 190 B.C. to 185 B.C., when the second phase of Demitrius attack on India was undertaken, his other sons had either been killed in the revolts of newly acquired regions or appointed as sub-kings in his parent domain of Bactria. Euthydemus IInd died after a brief reign, Panteleon was killed in the revolt, Demitrius II, his own name Sake was transferred to Bactria, the parent Kingdom, and Agathocles the youngest son was appointed as sub-king of Puśkalāvatī and Kāpiśi. He must have been left with Apollodotus only, his brother, whom he entrusted with the 2nd pincer advance towards Sāketa through Madhyamikā (Vidiśā of Pāṇinī, while he himself advanced through Pānīpat gap to Mathurā and Sāketa, and laid the seige of the city. He took alongwith him Menānder, as a baby general; probably it would have been unsafe to leave him alone at Gandhāra, where his own son had already been killed and secondly, probably he thought he could use him as a hostage and secure the fidelity of Apollodotus for a quick advance towards Sāketa after reducing Vidiśā. Again the participation of very young princes in the battle field, for educating them for the future responsibilities, can be noticed in many cases of Indian history right from the earliest times to the recent days. The busts on some Indo-Greek coins depicts young princes alongwith some wild animals like cub, elephant, bull, thereby indicating their spirits of adventure. Apollodous tried hard to reach Sāketa and join Demitrius but could not do so; and when Demitrius, after laying the seige of Sāketa, by-passed it and advanced towards Pātlīputra, Menānder must have been stationed, by him at Mathurā only as a titular general, which resulted in the mention of Menānder by Strabo, Garg,[38] and Patanjali as attacking Mathurā, only as a Demitrius war propaganda campaign. Again, as the war between Demitrius forces and Śuṅgas continued till the death of Demitrius in 175 B.C., and as Demitrius returned to fight Eukradites in Bactria, during the very period of his Indian compaigns, it must have been only Apollodotus and his very young son Menānder, who had to face the brunt of these 'Śuṅga attacks, and fierceness of the wars with them. These wars between Pushyamitra, Vasumitra and Agnimitra on one side and Demitrius, Apollodotus and Menānder on the other side, raged till Agnimitra Śuṅga death at the hands of Menānder forces around 140 B.C. Menānder thus emerged as a hero of a great and persistent was between Śuṅgās and Indo-Greek rulers. And it must be some of these wars that find mention in contemporary Indian classical literature (Pāṇinī-*Garg Saṁhitā, Māhābhārtā, Malvikāginīṃitram*). These wars seem to have influenced many Indian classical writers in portraying their characters, by giving accounts of some of these wars in their literary works.

Territory of Menānder :

There have been many misconceptions about Menānder's actual empire. Tarn has given a greatly exaggerated account of his domains. According to him every place where any Greek coins are found or Greek presence is overheard, fell within Menānder's domain.[39] However, it is certain that after his assumption of sovereignty around 158 B.C., over whatever was left after shrinking of the Demitrain India, he slowly and steadily increased his territory from Arācosiā in the North West frontier India to the bank of River Rāvī in East Panjāb. Sauvīra or Sindhu region seems to have been continued to be his ancestral province alongwith all country around Sindh Sāgar Doāb. He in the life time of Apollodotus seems to have reoccupied Arācosiā and Kāpiśī. The conquest of Afghānistan may too have been an honour shared by his father also. He recruited war like soldiers from this region. It is around this time that he subdued the Śuṅga remanent King of Swāt valley (named Vijāyaka Mitra) and appointed him as Sub-King under him. The discovery of steatite casket at Shinkot in Bajaur tribal territory of Swāt, with two kharośtī inscriptions and some 200 Dracham and 721 of his coins in mint condition from the same valley[40] proves this fact. Menānder has been mentioned there as "Mahārājā Menānder" which indicates that some Śuṅga prince acted as a sub-king or Indian Satrap of that country under the Greeks, and that the Śuṅga domination of North West India had started to show a decline now. Menānder's domain possibly included some areas of North of Hindu Kuś as Plutarch called him King of Bactria.[41] He now pressed ahead South-East-wards, and occupied other regions in West Panjāb. Literary evidence from Plutarch, Apollodorus (quoted by Tarn) and *Milind Panho* and the numismatic evidence and data collected by researchers; indicates that his empire included Kapiśa, Gandhārā, Kābul, Ghaznī, ancient Puśkalāvatī or present Charsaddā Peshāwar, Taxilā, Rawalpindi (all places now in Pakistān or Afgānistān) and Swāt Valley. Annexation of Śākā and better parts of Punjab seem to be late events of his reign. Paucity of his coins in these regions, especially in Śākalā point to this fact. The death of Agnimitra around 140 B.C. gave Menānder an opportunity to reestablish his family in Western Panjāb. Menānder took advantage by attacking the new inexperienced Śuṅga King. After a bloody battle Menānder seems to have occupied Śākalā. It is possibly this battle which finds mention in *Garg Saṁitā,*[42] fought fiercely by the soldiers from Hindu Kuś.

लौहिताद्रेस्तथा जौधैर्योधा युद्ध परिक्षताः ।
करिष्यन्ति पृथिवीं शून्या रक्त घोरां सुदारुणाम् ।।

The next few lines speak of resultant weakening of Agnimitra's successors which implies the loss of Śuṅga territory to Menānder around this very time.

The war may have been fought even during Agnimitra's time. It must be remembered that occupation of Śāklā by Menānder and his conversion to Buddhism are to be related closely one after the other.[43]

Recent discoveries have brought to light few of his coins from Western U.P. and Southern Kashmir also.

Thus Menānder ruled over an extensive empire, stretching from Hindu Kuś in the North West to North of Rāvī river in the east, whole of Sindh in the West, spread to the North East including some parts of Kashmir also. (See Map Sketch No.2).

Social aspect of Menānder's rule :

In *Milind Panho* we see Menānder possessing qualities of great oration, deep learning and intelligence, tactful handling of things decisively, even in matters related with contemporary social and religious giants. He must have possessed these qualities from the very childhood which raised him in the eyes of Demitrius, who saw in him the probability of a rising Greek General, and resulted subsequently in his appointment as a SubKing. Demitrius may have even thought, in his life time, of marrying his youngest daughter

MAP SKETCH NO---2 NORTH WEST INDIA (150 - 137 BC)

Empires Of Sungās & Menader

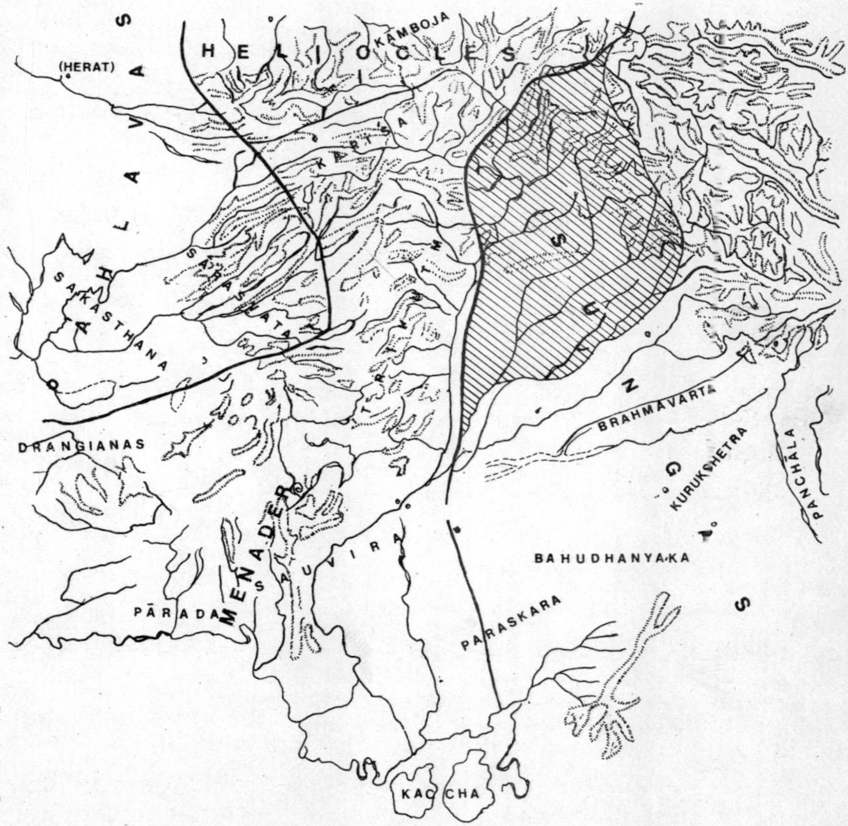

ADDITIONAL ACQUISITION OF MENĀDER CIRCA - 140 - BC

COURTSY :-

1. NATIONAL ATLAS OF INDIA-1957
2. N.W.I. P. 216.

Agathocleia to this promising young boy, who was her cousin. His social character and qualities of his person may have been the root cause for endearing him in his gallant army, Indian appreciators and foreign historians and admirers.

Menānder's conversion :

The impression that a reader gains from *Milind Panho* is that it is a mixture of fact and fiction. However, the fact of Menānder's conversion to Buddhism cannot be doubted from the numerous literary evidences from diverse sources, and from the archeological evidence as stated in the forthcoming chapter of the present work. His conversion to Buddhism was known to Plutarch who had recorded[44] and recounted to the world , how after his death his ashes were devided among the cities of his realm, each one of which raised a stūpa (Uvnuela) over its portion, which reveals that his conversion was known far and wide to the ancient world. The doubts expressed by Tarn[44] and R.D Vādekar[45] regarding the correctness of certain portion of *Milind Panho* story and levelling of allegations that its subject- matter is in keeping with the Buddhist tradition of distorting history to suit the ends of religious propaganda,[46] does not seem to be based on facts. The assertion of Tarn that conqueror does not adopt the religion and nomenclature of the conquered, may be true to Europe or Middle East countries, but it is against the basic fact of ancient Indian history and culture, and persistent long tradition of this land, full of righteous and spiritualistic forces under which most of the foreign invaders adopted Indian way of life and religious thinking. It is under these influences that we find the Besnagar inscription of Helidoras, who proclaims his Bhāgvat Dharma, and the inscriptions found in the caves of Nasik, Junnār and Kālrā recording religious gifts donated by Yavana

(Greek) Kings who bear Indian names.[47] The ancient Greek population in India is absorbed in the Indian social and religious fabric, sc much so, that today we see no trace of their separate identity. Menānder's conversion to Buddhism, as evident from Milind Panho seems to be a sincere one, and the identity of the place names in *Milind Panho* and their surface location in the Himālayan Valleys of Kashmir i.e. Poonch and Kaśṭwāṛ along with location of Archeological sites confirms the fact beyond any shadow of doubts. Menānder is the only Greek monarch widely loved and appreciated in Indian literature.

Later Years of Menānder

Not much is known about Menānder's later life. According to Milind Panho's second part Menānder handed over his Kingdom to his son (Strato I), retired from the worldly affairs, became a Bhikśu and attained Arhathood. But according to Tarn this description in *Milind Panho* is only a transfer to him of the story that Aśokā, late in his life, became an Arhat, and certain preliminaries to the meeting of Menānder and Nāg Sen as depicted in *Milind Panho* are supposed to have been taken from story of meeting of Aśokā with Tissā Moggliputtra. However it is felt that Menānder did not rule for many years after his occupation of Śākalā and conversion to Buddhism. He moved his capital to Śākalā but none of his coins have been unearthed from this famous city. According to Plutarch "he died in a camp" may be in the course of an observational pincer across Satluj or Beās upto Yamunā, or may have fallen a prey to the NonBuddhist agressive remnants of Śuṅgā rulers, or Punjab Tribal belt of Kangra or Audumbaras.

Time of Menānder and the end of the Indo-Bactrian-Empire :

According to Prof. Lāhirī, "the sudden death of Menānder demanded that the news be kept a closely quarded secret, not only from the people at large, but also from the external enemies, till the queen (Agathocleia) was able to consolidate her position. She had also to take stock of the natural dis-inclination of people to accept a woman's rule, and also guard against possible intrigues to oust her or even her child. The four coins issued by Agathocelia and Strato-I jointly indicate that for some time she was in full control of things but gradually was forced to abdicate power in favour of Strato-I his minor son[48] one of the Jugate coins issued by Agathocleia and Strato-I indicates that only the prince is wearing a diadem. However because of the teen- age of the young prince and his inexperience of life, the decisions to reduce the powers of the Queen, as well as other administrative officers seem to have been taken by the Greek court, with an India Lobby. Strato-I might have assumed full powers around 135 B.C. at the age of 15 years.

Menānder was born around 190 B.C. Around 175 B.C. he was appointed as Sub-King. On his father's (Apollodotus) death around 160 B.C. he became the King. Around 140 B.C. he is said to have occupied Śākalā, made it his capital and accepted Buddhism as his religion at the hands of Nāgsen. Around 138 B.C., on his sudden death, his wife Agathocleia is said to have assumed his powers, in the capacity of a queen. Thus Menānder ruled as a Sub-King for some fifteen years and as a sovereign for another 20 years; and in 52 years of his life he seems to have ruled for 35 years in all. He is believed to have died around 138 B.C.

The Geneological table of Euthydemus family as restructured by M.V.D. is as under :

Euthydemus-I

Ruler of Bactria (220-192 B.C.)

Demitrius-I
(192-175 B.C.)
Invaded India

Apollodotus
Succeeded Demitrius-I
(175 B.C. to 158 B.C.)

Antimachus-I
Nikephoros (?)
Sub-Kings of
under-Menānder

Menānder
M/Agāthocleiā
King of Sauvīrā,
West Panjāb,
Afghānistān,
158-138 B.C.

Apollophanes
(?)
King of
Sauvīrā
(175-160 B.C.)

Zoilus
(?)

Dionysius
(?)

Philoxenos(?)

Polyxenos (?)

Strato I
ruled jointly with Agathocleia
for 3 years 138-135 B.C. and then alone for
55 years.
(135-80 B.C.)

Strato-II died
in life time
of Strato-I.

Euthydemus II
Sub-King of
Bactria
(189-187 B.C.)

Demitrius II
Sub-King of
Kapiśā and
Bactria (186-170)

Pantaleon
SubKing of
Pushkalāvatī,
& Gandhāra

Agathocles Sub-King of
Gandhāra and Kapiśā 182-170 B.C

Agathocleia M .Menānder
ruled with Strato-I
(138-135 B.C.)

After Menander his son Strabo I assumed full powers and ruled parts of Panjāb with his capital at Śākalā, till 80 B.C. By this time Śākās led by their King Maues had spread all over the region previously held by the Indo-Bactrian Greeks.[49]

Time of writing of Milind Panho :

We see that in the very start of the celebrated work the discription of the grandeur of Śākalā starts with the words-"Sāglā of Yore" i.e. long ago, which indicates that the work *Milind Panhö* must have been written much after Ist century B.C. According to D.C. Sircar[50] it was probably written in early centuries of Christian era" but surely before 400 A.D. when Buddh Ghosh referred it in his writings.[51]

Author of the work Milind Panhö :

Milind Panhö, the religious discourse between King Menānder and Nāgsen is written in the true Indian tradition of ignoring self in all writings, and nothing is known about the author of this book.

Nāg Sen being acknowledged as a great Buddhist saint, scholar and philosopher, won acclaim in the whole Buddhist world and his name and fame travelled to far off places including China and Cylone, as their versions of *Milind Panhö* are also available. Buddhism flourished in Cylone and China from where two famous travellers Huentsang (631 A.D.) and O'Kāng (759 A.D.) came to India in pursuit of Buddhist knowledge through the ancient silk route passing through Kashmir. Nāg Sen is remembered in these countries also.

In the introductory of V. Trenekner's translation of *Milind Panhö* the author opines that the writer of questions of Milinda resided in the far North West India or Panjāb itself, and this is confirmed by the great improbability of any memory of Menānder having survived elsewhere and more especially in Cylone, where we should naturally look for our author's residence, if he did not live in the region thus suggested.[52]

Various historians, including those from Kashmir have[53] also suggested the possibility of *Milind Panhö* being basically a work in Kashmiri and later being translated into Pālī and other Indian and foreign languages. Fiddā Hussain also believes it to be a Kashmiri work.

To me it appears certain that, on the basis of the names of rivers, places and persons, that occur in *Milind Panhö* and their nearness to the Kashmir, the celebrated work must have originally been written by a Kashmiri, Kaśṭwāṛī or any outsider disciple of Nāg Sen, may be one even from Pātlīputra or Cylone at Vattaniya hermitage, in Kaśtwāṛ or Sānkhey hermitage at Sakhī Maidān or Rāmkund in Mendhar (Poonch), which the Chinese pilgrim Huentsang did not visit, as it may have been in ruins by then, but which was much celebrated for its miracles as pointed by him.

Milind Panhö's account of persecution of Buddhists :

The story of Buddhist persecution as satated in *Milind Panhö* is not without base but needs some modifications. In *Milind Panhö* it is recorded "King Milinda accompanied by 500 Yonkās silenced all learned men of Śākalā and for 12 years the city of Sāglā had been devoid of learned men.

They had departed hither and thither, and brethren of the order, went for most part, to the Himālayan mountains.[54] Here the allegation of persecution of Buddhists is levelled against Menānder which, in the light of his popularity amongst the people of his realm and his favourable mention in the Indian literautre does not seem true. Factually, around this time,

Buddhist, belonging as they were to the lower class of society, were persecuted both by Indian rulers and foreign invaders. Among the foreign invaders of the time, it had been Euthydemus, Demitrius and Apollodotus, the predecessors and compatriots of Menānder who ruthlessly killed the Indian population and from who's barbarity even women and children were not spared.[55]

It is clear from the Indian accounts that cruelity and tyrany of Demitrius had earned him a considerable hatred and bitterness of the Indian people. Purāṇas (depicting Brahmanic thought) describe Greeks/as irreligious and barbarous. *Garg Saṁhitā* also paints them in the same colour.[56]

This must have happened before 160 B.C. around which time Menānder assumed sovereign kingship. Śuṅgās and rulers of Kashmir also persecuted them. King Jalukā of Kashmir is said to have been a Śaivite and he also persecuted Buddhists. The Śuṅgā hero, who fought severe battles against the Indo-Greek rulers, is said to have been a sworn enemy of Buddhists. It appears that Buddhists had some sort of sympathy for the Indo- Greeks, and their sympathy had been all along with the Mauryās also.

Euthydemids house seems to have found a natural ally in Buddhist sections of Indian population. Pushyamitra is said to have persued fleeing Greeks in the North West India between 185 to 175 B.C. He was a Bhārdwāj Brahmin and Buddhist could not look upon a Brahman ruler of Pātlīputra with equanimity. They must have been ready to transfer their loyalities to anybody who could challenge the Śuṅgās.

It was therefore natural for an Indian prince engaged in the defence of the country to punish those who betrayed it to the foreigner. If the charge of persecution of Buddhists is levelled against Śuṅga King, especially Pushyamitra[57] (186-149 B.C.) also, it was no wonder, as the defence of the country against invading Indo-Greeks lay on him in the succeeding years. Pushyamitra is stated to have persued the Greeks throuhg Jullunder,Śākalā and right upto Indus,[58] destorying Stūpas, burning monastries and killing monks, as far as Sākalā.[59] At Sākalā Pushyamitra issued a declaration that whosoever would present him a head of a Śramaṇa would be rewarded with one hundred Dinārs.[60] This was so because Śākalā has been described in *Milind Panhö* as a resort of Buddhist monks. Thus the story of Buddhist persecution around 185-140 B.C. in North West India is correct, but *Milind Panhö's* allegations solely against King Menānder is not wholly correct. Prof. N.N. Ghosh feels that Buddhists account regarding their persecution by Pushyamitra is a correct one.[61] However being interested in Indian philosophy and relgion, Menānder may have perscuted them intellectually, by humiliating them in public discussions as recorded in *Milind Panhö*. As Menānder was the most talked about monarch of this time, the persecution, charges may have been levelled against him only, as sketched in *Milind Panhö*, with the sole aim of proving superiority of Buddhist religion and thought over all other contemporary relgions, and faiths.

Fierceness of Indo-Greek Wars :

The wars that followed the Ist and second invasion of Demitrius on India and the resultant prolonged battles between the two, were of severe nature and resulted in many unfortunate clamities for the local population. *Gargsaṁhitā* indicates a long period of strife, between the Greeks and Indians and then among the Greeks themselves.[62] Sungās too having been weakened in wars against Greeks, who's armies were largely manned by soldiers from Hindu Kuś were not allowed to rule in peace by them. All the same they are described as powerful kings.[63] In these wars men died in such large numbers as led to the predominance of women in the country's population. Men became so scarce that women had to man almost all professions from cultivation and business to that of soldiers. Men took ten or even twenty wives.[64] This long period of strife culminated in a horrible famine.[65] The Tax Collector of Demitrius having grown in number fearlessly devoured the people, since there was no authority left to bring them to book.[66]

Under such circumstances it was not only the Buddhist monks and priest of *Milind Panhö*, that fled from Śākalā region and the plains of Punjāb, but other section of populations also, who sought refuge in the Himālayan valleys.

Nāg Sen :

About Nāg Sen not much is known except what is written in *Milind Panhö*, which is primarily connected with his philosophical discussion with King Menānder. All subsequent comments about him by various authors are based on this work. However *Milind Panhö* does not furnish us the desired details of his place of birth, time of his discussions with King Menānder and other details about the celebrated work. However, one can assume that he was born in Kāṇiṅī Ajāl area of Kaśṭwāṛ, was educated in the Nāgsenī area of the same region, and undertook his deep meditation there. And finally it was at Mendhar where he held the historic discussion with King Menānder and converted him to the Buddhist fold. Nāgsenī region of Kaśṭwāṛ is still known after his name and it is only in Nāgsenī region that we still find some remnants of ancient and medieval history pertaining to this historic episode.

Time of Birth :

It has been observed previously that Menānder occupied Sāglā around 140 B.C., moved his capital to the city and around this very time had the historic discussion with Nāg Sen, and became Buddhist. As per internal evidence of *Milind Panhö*, Nāg Sen must have been of 25 year old at this time. He could have been of older age also. Before having this final discussion, Menānder had continuously defeated all learned men of Buddhist order and had exclaimed that "All India is an empty thing". If we accept above date of occupation of Śākalā by Menānder and his discussion with Nāg Sen around 140 B.C. he must have started discussing religious matters with persons of Buddhist eminence around 156-152 B.C. i.e. just after few years of his becoming Indian monarch. We know that many learned men had already deserted the country of Śākalā during the period of intense GreekoŚuṅgā War (183-160 B.C.) resulting in massive persecution of Buddhists and the country being strife torn and grief striken. It is during these years that we find Assāgutth̤, the Chief of Buddhist order of *Milind Panhö* holding an assembly of the spirtitual men for trying to salvage the brothern of the order, and moving to Vejantā Palace (Probably at Bactria) and Ketumati Mansion (Probably the residence of Eukradites in the City of Eukratida) along with Śukā (Probably Śuṅgā King Pushyamitra). This meeting[67] must have been held any time between 175 B.C. when Demitrius died and 160 B.C. (when Apollodotus territory had shrunk to only Sauvīra region.) The meeting probably concluded before 170B.C. when Eukradite the King of Bactria is said to have died. Consequently Nāg Sen must have been born any time around 170 B.C. (in confirmity with the rebirth story of Mahāsen) at Kañjaṅgal. This village at the extreme limit of Buddhist holy land in the Himālayas, can be no other place but the Nāgsenī region of Kaśṭwāṛ. Thus if the year of birth of Nāg Sen is taken as 169-70 B.C. his historic discussion with Menānder near Śākalā being held around 140 B.C. at the age of 29 years, things seem to go smoothly and there seems to be nothing wrong with the proposition[68] (regarding Mahāsen - details in coming pages) both logically, *mythologically* as well as historically.

As per *Milind Panhö* Nās Sen "met Menānder at Sāglā with all the elders, with their yellow robes like lamps, and bringing down upon it the breeze from the heights, where the sages dwelt", which clearly indicates that it must have been pleasant summer months, as Sāglā or Siālkot is just at the outlet of mountaneous Chināb valley through which the cool breeze of Himālayan heights travels down in the summer months.

Lastly it will be interesting to note, for many of us, who believe in mythology and spirituality, that Nāg Sen is credited to have possessed certain miraculous powers. Certain traditions pertaining to these powers are available from both local as well as foreign sources.

We know that Cankunā, the Turkish Magician Minister of Lalitā Ditya of Kashmir had got two images of Buddhā; one of gold he got from somewhere in Panjāb territory, adjacent to Kashmir may be from Sakhī Maidān Vihāra in Mendhar (Poonch), and the other one of stone which he carried to the Valley, and installed at his new capital Parihāspur.[69] Again we read about the origin of a most famous statue of Buddha in Indo-China (Vietnam). According to an old tradition there was a statue of Buddha of Emerald which Menānder's teacher Nāg Sen had fashioned out of Magic Emerald by his supernatural powers.[70]

Not much is known about Nāg Sen's later life and nothing more can be said in this regard over herewith authority. However some presumption about him, based on indirect references, can be considered by the students of history as under :

Nāgārjuna, a great scholar had been a student of Satya Simha who had propagated Buddhism in Kashmir 150 years before Kuśāns.[71]

This Satya Simhā may be no other person but the Śākya Simhā of Kashmirī Chronicles[72] and can fairly be identified as Nāg Sen of *Milind Panhö* on the following grounds:-

(i) In Kashmirī chronicles it has been mentioned that 150 years prior to Nāgārjuna, a Buddhist scholar Śākya Simha preached Buddhism in Kashmir and that Nāgārjuna a great Buddhist scholar and a contemporary of Kaniśkā (78-110 A.D) lived at Shāhdarhavan Vihāra (Hārwan) in Kashmir in the Ist century A.D. Since the time of King Menānder lies between 190 B.C. to 138 B.C., that of Nāg Sen's birth around 170 B.C., his discussion with Menānder around 140 B.C., the celebrated monk may have outlived the celebrated King for quite a long time, and preached Buddhism in Kashmir.

(ii) Amongst scores of names of Buddhist monks, Bhikśus and preachers, we come across only two names, who have been designated with the title of Simha i.e. Buddhā[73] (Śākya Simhā), and Nāg Sen (Lion of the hills).[74] But Śākya Simhā of *Buddh Caritā* of Aśvagosh and Śākya Simhā of 150 years before Nāgārjuna[75] must be quite different persons for obvious reasons of time in which they are said to have lived, and the nature of the work, they are stated to have performed. But the lion of the Hills of *Milind Panhö* and the Śakyā Simhā of Tariekh Hassan seem to be one and the same persons. So there is every possibility that Nāgārjuna[76] may have been a student and disciple of Śākya Siṁhā, lion of the hills or Nāg Sen; and that Śākya Siṁhā/Satya Siṁhā may be no other person but Nāg Sen himself.

Persons and Places :

Persons:

i) Milinda stands for King Menānder already described.

ii) Devamātya stands for Dev Mantrī or Kings Chief Counceller.

iii) Nāg Sen is the Central Character of this whole research work.

iv) Śukā in *Milind Panho* has been identified as Devādhipati, i.e. God of Hindu Gods, by Jagdish Kashyap and V. Trenckner. But according to Hindu mythology Śukā is the teacher, Gurū or Tutor of Asuras (i.e. Devils). In *Milind Panhö* we find him depicted as a guide and helper to Buddhist saints and learned Brahmins of Ancient India and not as that of later Purāṇic period or medieval times where he is portrayed as a tutor and helper of Asuras (foreign invaders).

Various critics and commentators of *Milind Panhö* have taken Śukā for Śukrā or Brahaspati of the Purānic literature which does not seem correct. The person needs to be traced from somewhere in the Buddhist tradition. It appears that the word Śukā in Pāli of *Milind Panhö* is the changed form of the Śuṅgā word of classical Sanskrit literature, representing the dynasty which was responsible for the downfall of Euthydemids. It appears the learned men, common masses and the Chief of Buddhist order, all may have tried to win over their persecutor, the Śuṅgā Chief Pushyamitra, and later secured his help for their salvation from the tyranny of Indo-Greek oppression. And the later with the blessings of

Buddhist spiritual Head, Assāgutth̩, seem to have engineered (through Eukradites) a revolt in the home Kingdom of Demitrius in Bactria, who as seen earlier had been a great persecutor of Indian masses. We also find the tradition that foreign invader of India and the ancient Indian defenders in their classic literature have been nicknaming each other as Asuras (Evil doers). Under such circumstances it is no wonder if Śukā of *Milind Panhö* is the Śungā Chief Pushyamitra, his son, relative or any of his prominent ambassador, who might have visited the much revered saintly person Assāgutth̩ in the Himālayan Valley of Nāgsenī for securing his blessing.

v) Assāgutth̩ is the Arhat and Chief of Buddhist order, dwelling at Vattanīya hermitage, somewhere in the Himālayas who, through some divine power over-hears the boasts of Milinda that "All India is an empty thing" and accordingly calls the assembly of learned men of the order, probably at village Siāh or Sai-Draman in the Nāgsenī region.

vi) Mahāsen : As per *Milind Panhö* is the saintly Brahmin, who lived in Ketumatī Mansion, castle of Vejanta Palaces in the heavens of thirty three (Vedic Gods). He was requested by Śukā to beseech himself, to be reborn as Nāgsen for saving the order i.e. Buddhist religion, which he turned down, but later agreed, on the personal request of Assāgutth̩. This very Mahāsen was later reborn as Nāg Sen to dispell King Menānder's doubts.

Now the above acount of *Milind Panhö*, regarding, "Vejanta Palace", "Ketumatī Mansion" and the "Heavens of thirty three", Vedic Gods pertain to Buddhist mythology but can be explained in historcial terms also.

Mahāsen appears to be the Buddhist name[78] of Bactrian pretender King Eukradites, opposed to

Demitrimus, who was instigated to raise a revolt against the Greek rulers of India. The whole conspiracy seems to have been engineered by the Śunga Chief Pushyamitra, the hero of the Greeko- Śunga war. Pushyamitra, in the beginning might have persecuted Buddhist monks for their sympathies for the Greek invaders of India, but later sought the help of Buddhist world of spirituality (Assāgutth̤) for ensuring the defeat of aggressive Greek forces. Accordingly he or any of his ambassador may have visited the great saint Assāgutth̤ at Sāi Draman in Kaśtwāṛ and with his blessings succeeded in prevailing upon Eukradites to engineer a revolt in the Demitrian province of Bactria across the Himālayan region of Hindu Kuś, which was usually considered as the heavenly abode of Vedic Gods by authors of Indian classical literautre. Eukradites later dies around 170 B.C. (killed by his own son)[79] and it is around this very time that Nāg Sen is born. The Vejanta Palace of *Milind Panhö* can very fairly be the palaces of Bactria or those of Eukradia, the city founded by Eukradites, and Ketumatī mansion where, according to *Milind Panhö*, Śukā met Mahāsen, could be the dwelling place of Eukradites, the ruler of Bactria. Thus all these mysterious terms and events can be historcially explained. The Śuṅga engineered revolt against Demitrius at Bactria is a historcial fact.[80]

And if Mahāsen of *Milind Panhö* is not the Eukradites, then he must be some remnant Mauryan Chief of the Aśokan empire, a Buddhist in faith, and an enlightened spiritualist residing around Kapiśā-Gandhāra region.

We know from Greek sources[81] that around 206 B.C. a certain person Sophagasenos (Subhagsena) was ruling over Paropamisadae, where Antiochus III of Syria met him in that year in order to renew his ancestral relationship. The reference apparently is to the relationship between the Seleucid house of Syria and the Mauryas, dating back to the time of Chandragupta. Subhag Sena therefore must be another scion of the Mauryan family ruling independently in Afghānistān.[82] His name ending in Sena suggests that he was a son or a brother of Vīrsena, who is represented by Tārānāth as a descendant of Kunāla and as ruling in Gandhāra. There is no evidence of Euthydemus of having come into clash with Subhag Sena of Kābul till the death of the later around 190 B.C., when Euthydemus took advantage of the situation and extended his sway, probably as far as Śākalā[83].

Mahā Sen could be any descendent of these erstwhile Mauryan rulers of Kapiśā-Gandhāra, with whom Śuṅga Chief might have formed an alliance.

vii) Sönūtur is the learned Brahmin living at Kaṇjaṅgal in the Himālayan mountains of the Guarded Slopes. On ordinary examination the term Sonutur has no literal meaning. Although its phonetic composition is nearer to Kashmirī-Kaśṭwāṛi language, but on close examination, the term appears to be a complex one, consisting of son+Otur. In Kaśṭwāṛī sön stands for Gold and "ötur" stands for childless person (Sanskrit-Aputra). This indicates that Sönutur, prior to the birth of Nāg Sen may not be having a child, or this might be his caste name, which started with the term "Son" or gold. He was a learned and wise Brahmin at who's hands Nāgsen learnt all the vedās and the Vedic lore. He did not behave properly with the elder Röhana, probably under compulsions of local traditions, for which he was later on sorry. Later he was a friend of Röhana, the Arhat and elderly monk at the guarded slopes and still later allowed his son Nāgsen to accompany him for pursuits of knowledge and meditation.

viii) *Röhan* was an Arhat living and meditating at the gaurded slopes. He had buried himself in meditation, and when the assembly of elders & Arhats of the order was called by Assāgutth he appeared before him at the Yugāndhār (Probably Haround Dhār or Rattan Dev peak of the Kaśṭwāṛ region). He obeys the dictates of Śukā and goes for begging of alms at the doors of Sönūtur, for seven long years and ten months, where he is always rebuffed or insulted. But he does not loose his temper and for another decade he acts as a friend of the family. He then takes away Nāgsen to the guarded slopes, where his own hermitage was situated. This specific place was probably the present Chichhā village of Nāgsenī region. Röhan sends Nāgsen to Assāgutth hermitage at Vattniya, i.e. the present Bhāttan village of Nāgsenī. In Chinese version of *Milind Panhö* Röhan is named as Löhan and mentioned as maternal uncle of Nāgsen. He is stated to be a monk of great religious merit, attainment and capability.

Āyu Pāl is the Chief elder at the Sānkheya's (Śākaya Munī i.e. Buddha) hermitage, who was defeated and silenced by King Milinda before he meets Nāgsen and enters the Buddhist fold. The name Āyu Pāl is more nearer to the plain region nomenclature than to the nomenclature of the hill region of Jammu and therefore suggests that this hermitage must be some where away from the Nāgsenī region.

The above discription of persons clearly reveals the on-going tussle between the two predominent faiths of the time i.e. Buddhism and Brahmanism and in *Milind Panhö*, an attempt has been made to show the superiority of non-violent Buddhist faith over the aggressive Brahmanic sect of the time. Rohan continuously tolerates the taunts and insults of Sönūtur Brahmin for seven years and finally succeeds in taking away his son to his own hermitage, as his disciple. Again when Śuka himself requests Mahāsen to beseech himself to be reborn for saving the order, the request is not accepted, but when the request is repeated by Assāgutth̤, the Sangh Nāyak, it is accepted by Mahāsen, which again indicates the superiority of the Buddhist monks and saints over the learned Brahmins, and their gods/lords including Śuka.

The whole story of *Milind Panhö* is like numerous Purānic tales of Dev-Asur Sangrāms (wars between the evil doers and noble men) in which success finally goes to the right doer.

b)Places :

i) *Jambū Dvīp* is repeatedly mentioned in *Milind Panhö* and the term also finds mention in other Purāṇic records. About the exact location and extent of boundaries of Jambū Dvīp not much is known. But the Śākalā of *Milind Panhö* has been mentioned to be situated in Jambū Dvīp. As Dvīp in Sanskrit means a piece of land surrounded by sea like waters, and again as Jammu has been an ancient town, Jāmbhū Dvīp must represent the area between two mighty or sea like rivers of Chināb and Rāvi with its whole catchment area which included Siālkot or Śākalā, Jammu and Duggar region of Śivālik hills. On the North East the Jambū Dvīp must have been surrounded by the only two wet rivers of Jammu i.e. Tawī and Ujj. The region thus surrounded by rivers on all sides finds geographical and terminological justification for the term Jambū Dvīp of ancient times, when sacred or holymen lived in the upper mountains. If the above explanation of Jambū Dvīp is accepted, the broad limits of King Menānder's territory in this region can be well defined and there can be no doubt that Jammu was also under his administrative control. (Map sketch No.3).

MAP SKETCH -- 3

Jambu Dvip Of Ancient India

(initial stage)

(C - 150 B.C.)

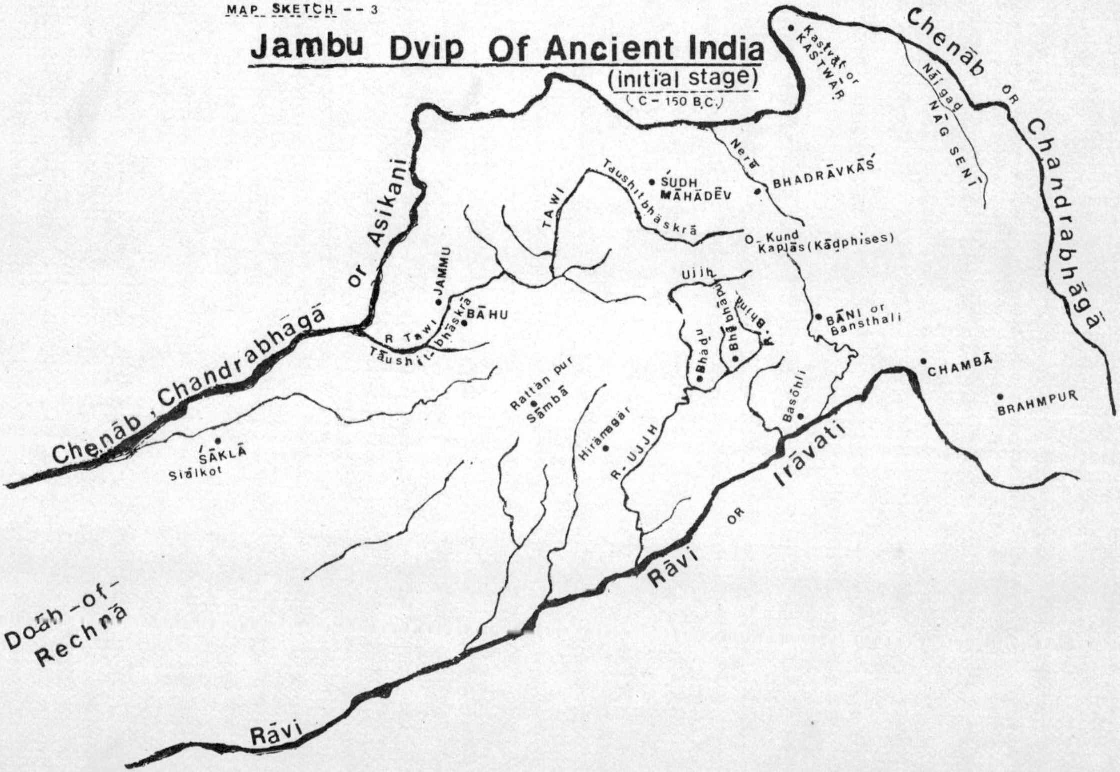

ii) *Sāglā* of *Milind Panhö* is the Śākalā of ancient Indian history or the present city of Siālkot in Pākistān, only some 30 miles from Jammu. Its grandeur of medieval times has already been described.[84]

iii) *Kañjaṅgal* of *Milind Panhö* is the birth place of Nāgsen. As per the sacred book the village is situated at the foot of Himālayan mountains, at the extreme limit of the East to Buddhist holy land and the topography of Kañgaṅgal of *Milind Panhö* tallies (on the basis of internal and external evidences)quite satisfactorily with geographical features of Kaśṭwāṛ mountaneous region. As for the specific location of village Kañjaṅgal is concerned, there are four probabilities. Village Kañjaṅgal, the place of Nāg Sen's birth can be any one of the following villages:

a) The term Kañjaṅgal is a complex one, and must be derived from the terms Kāninī and Ajāl; two village names in Kaśtwāṛ's famous pilgrim centre of Sarthal Devi.

b) Or it must be a combination of Kāṅinī - Jaṅgalwāṛ terms representing two village names lying close to Ṭhaṭhirī (Kaśtwāṛ) enroute ancient Kāngra Kaśtwāṛ route as well as Śākalā Kaśtwāṛ pedestrian route moving along the left bank of Chināb.

c) OR it must be the sacred village of Brahm Shilā (Barshilā) near Ṭhāṭhrī, and Kāṅinī in Kaśṭwāṛ.

d) OR Panḍitgām (village of Panḍits) in Kaśtwār or some other village in the very region of Nāgsenī in Kaśṭwār. In *Milind Panhö* it has been called as a Brahman village and hence the above assumptions.

v) Yugāndhāra : In *Milind Panhö* this place finds mention as under :

> "He (Assāgutth convened an assembly of the order, on the submit of Yugāndhāra mountain and asked if any member of the order could

face challenge of King Milinda" and all the Arhats vanished at the Yugāndhāra Summit".

Now this Yugāndhār is no else a place but the magestic Haround Dhār or sumit of Nāigad valley of the Nāgsenī. The term Haround is phonetically quite near to Yugāndhāra. The other name for this peak is Nāgisheru meaning the Nāg lion. Nāgsen as we know has been called in *Milind Panhõ* (1.1.15) as the lion of the hills, which clearly points to the fact that he belonged to this Himālayan mountain country and therefore the name of Nāgisheru assigned to Yugāndhār. The mountains foot is called as Rattan Dev because of a shrine assigned to Rattan Nāg. Now this Nāgīsheru or Haround Peak in Nāgsenī region is a high land mountain pasture, magestic in shape and form, and rich in summer grass, and below it, just on the slopes of Nāgsenī, lay some of the ancient archeological sites and places mentioned in *Milind Panhö*, as discussed in detail in Chapter-IV.

v) *Vattanīya Hermitage* : In *Milind Panhö* it is mentioned that Röhan asks (Nāgsen to go to the Vattanīya hermitage where Assāgutth̤ the Sangh Nāyak dwelt). At Vattanīya hermitage he did as he was told to do. This hermitage at the guarded slopes is no other a place but the present Bhāttan village in the Nāgsenī region of Kaśṭwāṛ. Situated at the foot of Majestic Nāgīsheru or Haround mountain range, in the Nāi Gaḍ valley, the village is inhabited by local Brahmins and Rajputs. Two archeological sites at Demzī and Sāi Draman are situated close by. The region is slopy and the geographic features of the region tally with the discription in Milind Panhö. The name of the village Bhāttan is a clear derivation of the term Vattanīya used in the celebrated work. The place lay on the traditional route from Kaśṭwāṛ to Pāḍar, some 12 kms away eastward. The Hermitage of

Sangh Nāyak Assāgutth̤ must have been situated in the village. A fine archeological site (Plate III) of the medievel times is still available close by, on a hill top named Sāi Draman at a distance of some two kṃs from the Bhāttan village. Again the term Sāi or Siāh seems to be an abbreviation of the first half of the term "Assā" of Assāgutth̤ and has a close relation with another important place and one more contemporary saintly person named Āyu Pāl of Sakhī Maidan. Where as Assagutth̤ Sakya and Ayu Pal were great saints, Draman and Maindān have almost the same literal meaning. The chief of the order Assāgutth̤ while living at Bhāttan village must have been having his relgious assemblies at Sāi Draman or the ground of Asāgutth̤. The location presently has a partly preserved temple ruins and a stone slab with Shārdā Inscription belonging to 9th or 10th century, some damaged stone statues still exist within the temple structure (Plates VIII to XI).

vi) *Demzī* : Some one kilometer further up from Bhāttan, in the Nāi Gaḍ Valley of Nāgsenī, we come across a beatutiful spot known by the name of Demzī. The place does not find any mention in *Milind Panhö*, but as it lies in the close vicinity of Bhāttan village, Haround or Nāgisheru mountains, and has still some archeological remains of medieval times, one is convinced that it must be associated with the Nāg Sen episode. The name of the village Demzī is a changed or Pāli form of Sanskrit word Tapsvī i.e. Hermit. The place had been an idle one for meditation. In the morning hours, the inspiring. glittering, bewitching and bewildering Brahma[85] mountain peaks just across the Chandrabhāgā gorge stands close by, shining like a cone of silver in the clear, calm and shining sky, with enchanted clouds surrounding it all around and depicting the universal truth of *Brahm*, the creator of the universe, and pouring snow white milky waters from the Himālayan heights, into the mouths of needy, hungry and thirsty people of the plains of India. The place must have been the hermitage for meditation of saintly elder Assāgutth̤ called Sangh Nāyak in *Milind Panhö*. It is probably because of the highest piousness of the place, that the Himālayan peak in front of this village is named after Brahmā, and the particular giant tree of the locality also assigned the same nomenclature.

vii) *Guarded Slopes* : This place or region has been described in *Milind Panhō* in the following words:-

"Now at that time there dwelt on the guarded slopes an innumerable company of Arhats and venerable Assāgutth̤". After the assembly of all the brethern and Śukā, and acceptance of Assāgutth̤'s personal request to Mahāsen, to save the Buddhist order" all the brethern reappeared on the Guarded slopes (Sāi Draman) on the Himālayan mountains except Rohana, who a week before had become buried in meditation. Rohan instantly appeared on the spot". Again it is mentioned that "Rohan again came to Nāgsen at Kañjaṅgal, his birth place. He takes him to Vattanīya hermitage (at Bhāttan), to Vijamvothū (?) and then to the Guarded slopes, and Nāgsen is admitted as a novice into the order at the age of 20 years. "On reaching the guarded slopes Nāgsen thinks low and wrong about his teacher".

The above version points to the probability that Guarded slopes as mentioned in *Milind Panhö* is not a single spot but more than one place. To me the whole of Chander Bhāgā Valley between Reāsī and Pāḍar in Kaśtwāṛ region can be regarded as Guarded slopes, especially the slopy lands of Nāgseni region, east of Kaśtwāṛ on way to Pāḍar. The region is encircled on three sides by the deep gorges of Chināb and on the fourth side by high altitude snow clad mountain peaks,dense Deodar forests where isolated slopy helmets, tiny hanging valleys and cultivated as well as grasy pasutre lands are inhabited by simple, noble and affectionate folk, having wisdom and experience of distant past, though lagging behind in formal education of the present times. If we have to pinpoint the area of Guarded slopes in the Nāgsenī region, it is the slopy land of Chichhā, village just above the confluence of a small rivulet with Chandrabhāgā river some 5 kms up from Paḍyārnā. The term Chichhā, also seems to have been degenerated form of Rakshital or Vijamvothū.

viii) *Vijamvothū* as mentioned above, is a place where Röhan had taken Nāgsen at the age of 20 years from Vattanīya's hermitage and admitted him as a novice. Clearly Vijamvothu must be the hermitage of Röhan on the Guarded slopes i.e. present Chichhā village. The place is also one where Röhan had probably buried himself for a week, for deep meditation, before he instantly reappeared before the assembly of the order.

The Chichhā village is a tiny slopy patch of cultivated land, presently inhabited by Gujjars. In the Nāgsenī region there is a strong tradition among the folk people that a famous Rāja of the region had his castle at this location. Geographically the place is the most secure one from all possible terror and persecution at the hands of the human cruelity and therefore assigned the name as guarded slope.

ix) *Vejantā Palace* and *Ketumatī Mansion* Finds mention in *Milind Panhö* as under :-

Then he (Assāgutth) told the assembly about Mahāsen, east of Vejayanta palace, and Ketumatī Mansion in the heavens of thirty three (Vedic Gods)" and that "Śukā suggests that Mahāsen of Ketumatī be requested to beseech to suffer himself to be reborn into the world of men. Śukā himself goes to Ketumatī and requests Mahāsen for rebirth".

The above version clearly indicates that these two places are heavenly abodes of Vedic gods, a mythological concept or some very sacred and mysterious places in the Himālayan region. The historical geopgraphy explains the places as under :

The Purāṇic concepts regarding Devtās and Asurs and their respective worlds are quite contradictory to the Pārthian and Irānian concepts. Therefore there should be no wonder, if Buddhits, who's sympathies for foreign invaders were well known, designates the handsome, well built and white complexioned North West frontier aggressive inhabitants as Devas and their land as the land of thirty three (Vedic Gods). It is also widely believed that most of the ancient Indian classical literature was composed and written in the land of Sapt Sindhu and North Western Himalayan Valleys, and other regions around it. Under such circumstances Vejanta Place of *Milind Panhö* is the Bactrian Place in the capital city of Eukratidia, which is recorded to have been founded by Eukratide.[86] The term Vejanta of Milind Panho being used as the historic term for the kingdom of Bactria in this Buddhist scripture.

Ketumatī Mansion : This place lying within Vejanta Place of *Milind Panhö* can be no other place but the mansion or dwelling place of Eukratide in terms of history. It is over here that, according to *Milind Panhō*, Śukā (and probably Assāgutthḥ) met Mahāsen and made hims to accept the proposal, which as per the story of celebrated work made him to die and as a result of it he was reborn as Nāg Sen, who later defeated Mẹnānder. Historically also we know, that the pretender Celucid King Eukratide, who occupied Bactira, in Demitrius time was assassinated around 170 B.C. by his own son brutally when he was marching homewards in triumph, after killing Agathocles.[87]

This incidentally reveals the politico-religious manures undertaken by the Buddhist monks and priests as well as Indian rulers defending their frontiers in the context of persecution of the general masses as mentioned in *Milind Panhö*.

In *Milind Panhö* the allegation of persecution of Buddhist has been levelled against Menānder and it can be explained as under :-

Firstly the persecution of common masses whether Buddhist or non-Buddhist was the result of continued war for a long time between Demitrian-Apollodotus forces on one hand and the Śuṅgā forces on the other. Menānder being the representative monarch of the Indo-Greeks, was naturally to be blamed for all the evils of his preceding lineage.

Secondly a long spell of time between the actual happening of events and their recording in *Milind Panhö,* basically a Buddhist reilgious work, may have resulted in the wrongful identification of the real persecutor.

Thirdly to quote R.D. Vādekar[88] Buddhist priests and writers had been in the practice of distorting history in such a way to suit their own religious interest.

The meeting of Bactrian King Eukratide with the Buddhist saint from Kaśṭwāṛ may look strange to the readers, but it is a historical fact, that not to speak of ordinary masses, many eminent political persons and powerful rulers from Kashmir and Afgānistān right from the ancient times to the recent past (Yāqub Shāh from Kashmir, King Shāh Shujāh-ul-Malik of Afgānistan, 1818 A.D) had taken refuge in the Himālayan Valleys including that of Kaśṭwāṛ.

Pātlīputra and **Ashöka Park** : "Assāgutth now sends Nāgsen to Pātliputrā which is 100 Yojan away, and where Dharmādhikārī dwelt in Ashoka Park for learning the Buddha word. Nāgsen complains of greatness of distance but later agrees to go".

This version clearly indicates that Pātliputra of *Milind Panhö* must be none of the places in the immediate vicinity of Kaśtwār but the world famous centre of Buddhist studies of ancient and medieval times, close to Nalandā and Patnā in Bihār. And if we assume a journey of 15 to 20 miles a day on foot in those days of lack of conveyance, it might have taken Nāgsen some one or two months to reach Pātlīputra where he stayed for six months learnt all Pītkas and also attained Arhatship, under the guidance of Dharmādhikārī. After that, on being remembered by his brethren of the order, at the Guarded slopes, he instantly vanished at Pātliputra, and appeared before them.

This discription clearly confirms that Pātliputra of *Milinda Panhö* was the famous Pātliputra of Magadha empire of Śuṅgās and Kanvas and the chief centre of Buddhist knowledge in eastern India.

Even if we believe the assumption of Nāgsen's instant disappearance from Patlīputra as baseless and impossible, it might have taken him another month or so to reach his hermitage in the Nāgsenī region. Ashoka Park in Pātliputra must be the seat of Dharmādhikārī's school of learning.

xi) *Sānkheya Hermitage : The scene of final Discussion* : As per *Milind Panhö* Sānkheya Hermitage was the scene of final discussion between King Milind and Nāgsen. The place seems to be named after Śākyā Muni Buddha and was situated 12 yojans (84-96 miles) away either from Śākalā or Kashmir. We have the following description of this event in *Milind Panhö* :-

"Seeing the pleasantness of the weather and inspired by it, Milinda goes to the Sānkhey hermitage, exchanges pleasantaries and in the discourse silences the elder Āyu Pāl and exclaims that "All India is an empty thing"; and that "Nāg Sen dwelt at the Hermitage of Sānkheya with a compnay of brethren appearing in the Sānkheya grove like the lion of the hills". Then Devmātya, counsellor of Milinda tells the King to go to him and put your questions to him". This clearly indicates that the scene of discussion between King Milinda and Nāgsen was held at Sānkheya grove away from "Śākalā". Now the important question arises as to where was this hermitage of Sānkheya situated?

The scene of discussion did not lay in the city of Sāglā is borne out also by the fact that in the very beginning of the outer story of *Milind Panhö*, it has been said that on expressing his desire to have a discussion with the teachers of Lokāyat the 500 Yonkās had provided him the names of six learned teachers of the region who they felt could dispell the doubts of the King.[89] The King went to them one by one and silenced them in the discussions. After defeating *PURAÑKAŚYAP* and *MĀKHLĪ GOŚĀL* the King is said to have exclaimed that *"JAMBŪ DVĪP"* is an empty thing". It is further recorded there that the King would immediately go to the place where a Śraman, a learned Brahman or a family holding Pandit was said to be residing, ask him questions and on not being able to satisfy the King, they would leave the place". It is therefore clear from the above that the King must have had discussion with all the learned men of the region (including those lying outside the city of Śākalā) before uttering the aforesaid boast. The name of the elder Āyū Pāl of the Sānkheya grove (Parivein), who he visited later, for the final discussion, is not mentioned in the above list. It is further recorded that "Śākalā was devoid of all learned men for twelve years and therefore the final discussion must have been held somewhere outside Śākalā.

To me Sakhī Maindān in Mendhar is the Sānkheya Hermitage of *Milind Panhō* and the scence of final discussion between the two on the following grounds:

a) The scene of discussion as per *Milind Panho*[90] was laid at a spot 12 Yojans from Kashmir[91] which on calculation comes to be around 96 miles away. This distance fairly agrees with the distance between Nāg Senī region of Kaśṭwāṛ and Mendhar in Poonch through the shortest route passing through Syṁthan (11400′) and Toshmaidān Passes (11400′).

b) The capital of King Menānder was at Śākalā but for almost all intellectual encounters that he had with the learned men of his time, he is said to have been "inspired by the pleasantness of weather", which indicates Menānder's inclination and love of nature. The pleasantness of the climate and extensive scenic beauty of the country of Sākalā as described in the celebrated work clearly points out that the scene of discussion must have been some where in the hill country, of Pir Pānchāl.

Now Mendhar in Poonch is a small but extremely beautiful valley in the foothills of Himālayas bordering Kashmir Valley and at the foot of Toshmaidān Pass. it is surrounded on three sides by mountains covered with pine trees and greenery; and traditional routes connecting the valley with the plains of Panjāb lay close to it. The place was therefore an ideal one for the establishment of a hermitage or school of learning and its scenic beauty is quite comparable to Sānkheya Parivien as described in *Milind Panhö*.

c) The historic discussion which brought to an end, by silent and peaceful means, the rule of Greeko-Bactrian rulers in North West of India, was held at the hermitage of Sānkhey and Sākhī Maidān in Mendhar has retained this nomenclature even to this day, inspite of many upheavals of last two thousand years, political change and religious transformations. The massive ruins of a temple or a Vihāra (Plate XXI to XXIII) still bear a testimony to the above noted fact. The archealogical site may have been a Vihāra which Menānder is said to have constructed after his conversion into Buddhist fold. Again it is, probably Menānder who named the site of his Vihāra as Śākyā Parivien after Śākyā Muni or Lord Buddha.

d) As the greatest among the great Indo-Scythian Kings Menānder accepted his defeat, from Nāg Sen, became a monk and attained Arhatship here at Sānkhey's Hermitage in Mendhar valley, the event must have attracted the attention of contemporary scholars, and elite section of society, as well as ruling class and consequently the place must have been remembered after him and called as Menānder, which with the passage of time, changed to Mendhar, a name retained to this day.

e) Each school of learning and the hermitage associated with some saintly person in ancient times had a residential-cum-meditational hermitage of the elder of that particular school, as seen earlier in the case of Assāgutth̤ of Vattanīya hermitage in Nāgsenī Kaśṭwāṛ. Similarly in Mendhar Valley also wẹ have two archealogical sites which seem to be connected with the Menānder Nāgsen discussion. The site of residential-cum-meditational hermitage of elder Āyū Pāl and Nāgsen was at the present Rāmkund temple site, (Plate XXX) whereas the Vihāra must have been constructed at an open place, where the great discussion was held. As per *Milind Panhö,* in additonal to 500 Yonkas, Devmātya and Menānder, 80 thousand monks, hermits and Arhats accompanied Nāgsen to the venue of the discussion, and the present site of Sākhi Maidān (Plate XVII), could very much accommodate a big gathering.

f) The pleasantness of the weather, the intellectual superiority and unconquered ego of King Menānder had inspired him to go to the Sānkhey Hermitage, where he held his first discussion with the elder of the hermitage, and only after defeating Āyu Pāl in this discussion, he was advised by his Minister (Dev Mātya) to go to Nāgsen, with whom he had a long and open discussion, in the presence of a huge gathering. Naturally the place must have been an open ground. Now when we enter Mendhar Valley from Kotlī Bhimber side (now in Pakistan occupied Kashmir), we come across a very small side valley of Rāmkund (Plate XXX). This must have been the site of elder Āyu Pāl's residential hermitage and some two kilometres further southwards we have the ancient location of Sākhi Maidān, the venue of historic discussion.

g) Heuntsang while on his way to Rājouri (C-646 A.D.) came to Poonch via Toshmaidān Pass. Why did he not go to Rājouri direct through a shorter and easier route is an important question. Probably he was attracted by some important Buddhist pilgrim centre. located in the vicinity of Poonch as recorded by him.[92] "According to his version there was a Bodh Vihāra (or Stūpa) in Parṇotsva much known for its miracles. A few decades earlier similar experience was had by King Lalitāditya in the vicinity of this very region as recorded by Kalhana[93]. The important Buddhist site of Lalitāditya's time can fairly be identified with the temple structures of Rāmkund and Sakhī Maidān in Mendhar.

MAP SKETCH ---4

GUARDED SLOPES ; BUDHIST HOLY LAND AND NĀG SEN'S TRAVEL ROUTE

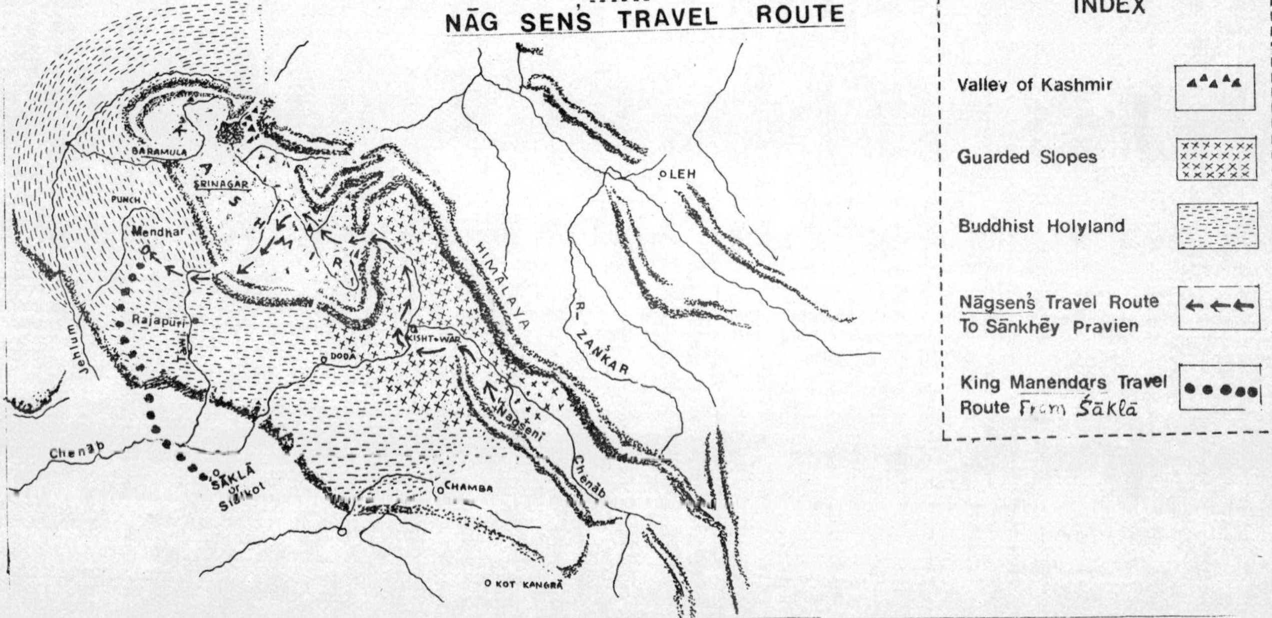

Route of Travelage : What could have been the route of travelage of Nāg Sen from Nāg Senī to Mendhar is an interesting question, but nothing can be said with authority. However, the topography of the region, location of traditional routes and the "description" of his journey indicates that he had travelled to the "Country of Śākalā" alongwith his disciples through cities, towns and villages and this journey is mentioned in the celebrated work as his Alms tour. He might have therefore travelled from his Vattaniya Hermitage in Nāgsenī region to Kaśtwāṛ town, thence over the Syṁthan or Singhpura[93] pass to Verināg and Anantnāg, to Bijbehāṛā, to Shopiān, over Toshmaidān Pass to Poonch and thence to Mendhar and Sānkeys Hermitage, across Krishanā Ghāti (Map sketch No.4). The whole distance comes round about 90 miles i.e. twelve yojans. The distance to Poonch from the valley over Toshmaidān is the shortest. Menānder's popularity seems to have travelled even to the Shupiān in Kashmir, as a village close to this Tehsil Headquarters is still called Menānder after his name.[94]

As Kashmir has not been mentioned anywhere in Menānder's domain, and as few of his coins are said to have been located from North Western or South Eastern limits of the Valley, the main valley seems not to have been under his direct rule. Nāgsen therefore might have thought it better to take shortest travel route passing through villages towns and cities of Kaśṭwāṛ, Kashmir, Poonch and Mendhar to reach Sānkhey Hermitage on his way to "Śākalā, but he happened to see Menānder at the, Hermitage of Āyu Pāl. Nāg Sen did not go to Śākalā via Kaśṭwāṛ-Ṭhāṭhrī Siālkot pedestrian route, or Kaśṭwāṛ Bhadarwāh Jammu route for the following reasons :

i) Firstly this tour of his as described in *Milind Panhö* was his Alms tour and the region along the above referred two routes had been mountaneous, slopy, difficult to traverse (Sanskrit Kaśṭwāṭ) and very rarely inhabited.

ii) Secondly most of the eastern mountainous region of Jammu Kāngṛā belt did not fall under Menānder's domain and was dominated by independent Panjāb tribes such as Audumbarās, Trigartās, Rajanyās and Kunindās.

Centuries after Menander's acknowledgment of Buddhism, his attainment of Arhatship, his becoming a Bhikśu, subsequent downfall of his empire and emergence of Brahmanism, the Sānkhey hermitage also, in due course of time seems to have undergone a change of religious order, and received the name of Rāmkund and Krishanā Ghāti after Rāma and Krishana. Still later with the coming of Mohamadan rule, the site seems to have faced distruction, with certain massive ruined structures still lying at the site.

During army operations of 1948 A.D. in the region, to flush out Pakistani invaders, some Indian army officer is said to have come across certain statues, carvings and other articles of antiquity and some of these were still lying in the residential premises of Army Officers at Poonch in 1978 when I visited them.

Buddhist Holyland

This term finds extensive use in the Holy Buddhist scriptures, including *Milind Panhö*. The Brahman village of Kañjaṅgal has been mentioned to be situated at the extreme limit to the east of Buddhist Holy land. Also it has been called as middle country at the foot of Himālyas. If Kañjaṅgal is identified as Kāṇinī- Jaṅgalwāṛ region in Kaśtwāṛ, the Buddhist Holy land must be located in the middle mountain country, immediately bordering Kashmir in the west, south and eastern directions. Actually it comprises of Himālayan mountain valleys and Shivālak hill region bordering the Valley on all side, especially its south-eastern sides (See Map sketch No.4). Rich Buddhist cultural heritage as well as influence can be noticed in Himālayan valleys all around Kashmir. In recent years the finding of Gilgit Manuscripts from Gilgit region, Archaeological sites from Sakhī Maidāṇ, Mendhar, location of Brahmī script from Śudh Mahādev, Bhadarwāh, Kaśṭwāṛ and Hārwan tiles, identification of Nāgseni region as the place of Nāgsen, and Buddhist vihar at Akhnoor, the sacredness of this Holy land of Buddhists, becomes self-evident. It is this very Buddhist Holy land of ancient times which seems to have emerged as Jambu Dvīp of ancient Brahmanic literature and which later in Purānic period assumed confusing topographical limits.

Footnotes :

1. Other foreigners occupying the North Western borders of India were Pahlvās, Śakas and Kuśāṇas, Selucids (Greeko- Bactrians).
2. N.W.I. pp.69-73.
3. Ibid. p. 102. c.f. Ptolemy VII.16 and Tarn - G.B.I. pp 140-55.
4. K.C.A.P. 5; N.W.I.P. 103 c.f. Raj. I V. pp 101; 107-08; 115-117
5. N.W.I.P. 105. The first of these Demitrias was established in Arācosiā on the main route from Seistān to Ghaznī, from where this route ran via Kābul, Puśkalāvatī and Taksilā into the interior of India. The second Demitriās was established on the Indus Delta. This city is referred to by the Kāśīkā Vrittī (Pāṇiṅī-IV. 2.7.6. as Dattamitrī among the Sauvīrās. In the Naśik Cave Inscription No. 19, a donor is described as Dattāmitrī-Yakā i.e. hailing from Dattāmitrī.
6. Around this time his own sons were appointed by Demitrius as Sub-Kings in other important areas of his

domain. Euthydemus II was appointed as Sub-King of Bacteria, and second son Demitrius II as Sub-King of Kapiśā. Euthydemus II died couple of years later and Dmitrius II was then transferred to Bacteria. 3rd son Pantaleon who was murdered during the Aśvaka revolt of Gandhāra was replaced by the fourth son Agathocles. It was this fourth son of Demitrius who tried hard to win the support and goodwill of his Buddhist subjects as indicated by his two coins with Khārośtī legend. (N.W.I. P.133-14) and again it is he who had to bear the brunt of Eukradites attacks of North West India.

7. The years between 190 B.C. -186 B.C. had been wasted in subduing the (Aśvaka) Afghān revolt and consequently delayed his 2nd invasion of Northern India.
8. N.W.I.P., 119. f.n. 42 c.f. Acta Orientalia Vol. I.P.27
9. R.T. *Māhābhaśyā* (Paṇiṁī); *Mahābhārta; Garg Saṁhitā, Divyāvdān Mālvikāganimitram,* Kālidas etc.
10. Strabo, Macrindle, Rapson and Vincent Smith etc.
11. N.W.I.pp. 167-68/30.
12. N.W.I.p. 152.
13. Ibid. c.f. Ed. Cowell and Neil p.434, Aśokavadān.
14. Ibid. p.155/0 19, p. 179/02. (VIII).
15. It is probably this conspiracy between Śuṅgas and Eukradites of Bactriā which finds mention in *Milind Panhö* in the form of Assāgutta, and Śukās visit to Vejanta (Eukradites lodge). Śukā (as a historical figure) must be the Śungā King or one of his agents, or Eukradites.
16. N.W.I.p. 79. c.f. G.B.I. pp. 75-78
17. Ibid.
18. Ibid - Annexure - Plate XIV-6.
19. Ibid. p. 135. f.n. 101.
20. M.P. Vad. III; 333-34 V.
21. A.I.U. P.113
22. C.H.I. P. 550
23. M.P. Trech. Intro. XXIII.
24. C.H.I. p.550.
25. N.W.I. p. 93/) 35.

26. Ibid. p.137/0 57.
27. N.W.I.p. 95-98 (For marriage custom with cousin sisters See Infra-Cultural Evidence, Chapter III.
28. Ibid. p. 98 c.f. C.H.I. PL VI-15.
29. Ibid. c.f. M.V.D. I.C.C. PL IV-2 & C.H.I. PL VIII-25
30. Ibid. c.f. C.H.I. P.552
31. Ibid. c.f. L.M.C. PL. VI. P.515
32. Ibid. c.f. C.H.I. P.552
    One is tempted by these and other observations to think that if it was Queen Agathoclia, from whon Kālidāsa got the inspiration for characterization of Shakuntalā.
33. G.B.I.p. 167 c.f. N.W.I. 96/0 36-37.
34. Ibid.
35. Ibid.
36. N.W.I. p. 109-114
37. Ibid f.n. 23
38. I.H.Q. XXIX 1953 pp. 180-82. An ancient reference to Menānder's invasion by Dr. V.S. Agrawala, where he sugests an amendation of महेन्द्रो into मनेन्द्रो c.f. *Mahābhāśya* (3.2.2).
39. G.B.I. pp. 22-33. N.W.I. p. 213-17.
40. N.W.I. p.215/ 8./CH. VIII.
    The Indo-Greek Dracham seems to be the parent coin of Derham circulated in some present M.East countries. See Also Select Inscriptions Vol. I. pp. 102-03. Sircar D.C.
41. Moralia, 821. D.E. (X. 276-79) in Loeb Classical Library Ed.)
42. N.W.I. p.216 and 204 c.f. J.B.O.R.S. XIV 1928. line 47-48.
43. Ibid - c.f. f.n. 65 0 4 and 8.
44. Moralia - 821. D.C. c.f. N.W.I. P.207. f.n. 16.
45. Opamma Katha. 70. M.P. Vad. P.40 c.f. N.W.I. P.6 f.n.15
46. G.B.I. P.227
47. N.W.I. P.208
48. N.W.I. P.230-232.

49. Ibid. 234-35
50. A.I.U. p.112-114
51. Ibid P.134-35
52. M.P. Trek. P.30/P-XIV-V
53. T.K. Mohi-Pre.2
54. M.P. Treck. 1-15.
55. *Vāyu Purāṇa* - 37/382-84/P. 456.—"स्त्रीणां बाल बधेनैव"
56. J.B.O.R.S. XIV. 1928, pp. 402 Sq.LL.27 Sq.c.f. N.W.I. p.152.
57. *Divyāvadāna*, Aśokāvadāna. pp. 433-34
58. N.W.I. p. 150/1.
59. A.I. p. 297.
60. Ibid. यो में श्रमण शिरो दासयति तस्याह दीनार शतं दास्यामी ।
61. Ibid. Ref. *Early History of India.*
62. *Garg Saṃhitā* op. cit. L.41. c.f. N.W.I. p. 122 f.n. 50 यवना ज्ञापयिष्यन्ति (नश्येरन्) च पार्थिवाः
63. Yug Purāṇ op. cit LL-45-46 c.f. Ibid. f.n. 55
    ततो युग वशात् तेषां यवनानां परिक्षये
    साकेते सप्त राजानो भविष्यन्ति महाबलाः ।
64. Ibid - LL. 94-103. c.f. f.n. 56
65. Ibid - LL. 111-115.c.f. f.n. 57
    देवो द्वादश वर्षाणि अनावृष्टि करिय़ष्यति
    प्रजा नाशं गमिष्यन्ते दुर्भिक्ष भयपीडिता ।
66. *Garg Saṁhitā*. L. 40., c.f., Ibid. f.n. 51
67. M.V.D. has pointed that the meeting of Śuṅgā King Pushyamitra with Pretender King of Bactria Eukradite may have been held near Taxilā. NWI. P. 189
68. Mahāsen must be either a Mauryan remanant Chief of Kapiśā-Gandhāra region or Indianized version of Eukradites.
69. R.T.
70. G.B.I. pp. 267-68 & I.G. p. 98.
71. B.K. Fidda. P.23
72. Ibid. p.11, 23 and Tariekh Hassan, Vol. II. p.42- Fauq. The two names Satya Siṁhā and Śākya Siṁhā as mentioned by the author of B.K. seems to be one and

the same person but appear to be different because of a slip of pen.

73. Buddh. Carita *Sacred Books of the East Book.* XVIII/24-31.

74. M.P. Treck.

75. Fauq-Tariekh Hassan - P.III.

76. After Nāgsen Nāgārjuna was the greastest scholar and Buddhist preacher in the valley. He is titled as Bodhisatva as also the solo lord of the land (R.T. p.78-Stien). It was due to his knowledge that Buddhists of Kashmir maintained their ascendency over other Achāryas. *Hindu History of Kashmir,* N.H. Wilson p.III. He is said to have denominated Śaka era-ibid. Nāgārjuna is said to have been a Śaivite in his early youth, for he is said to have composed CHITSANTOSH AND PARMACHANA both embodying Śavist ideas (Shrādā Peeth research series srinagar)- In religious discussion he is said to have been a Śavite R T. Nāgārjuna spring in the village Supor in Bātho, near the Hirāpur hill in Shopiān Kashmir is known upto this day -Tariekh Hassan, Vol. I, P.130.

78. Mahāsen literally means one with a great body or one who is dependent on some superior one.

79. N.W.I.P., p. 135

80. Ibid. p. 155, 186.

81. Polyby XI. 34. 11. Also J.A.S.B. 1920 . pp. 305, 310 & Tarn G.B.I. P. 10 c.f. N.W.I. p. 61.

82. N.W.I. p. 61.

83. Ibid. p. 75.

84. For Jambū Dvīp - See K.T. July 28 1991. Also Annexure I.

85. T.S.J. p. 42.
Dedicated to Brahmā, the third God of Holy Hindu Trinity is a group of five peaks, 20000 to 21000 feet high to the North East of Kaśtwār which are named after the God. Some of these peaks are so steep that they are bare of snow, while others are always clothed in it". Not only this even a particular lofty tree found in the region is named as Brahmā tree and showered reverence. Even one or two villages of the region are

also named after the God such as Barshilā or Brahma Shillā.

86. Tolmy VI.II7, c.f. N.W.I. f.n. 30 p. 186
According to Tarn G.B.I. pp. 208-9. The city has been mentioned by only Tolmy. Possibly it was Demitriās-city founded by Demitrius, earlier ruler of Bactria-renamed as Eukratidia by Eukratide, as he could not have allowed the continued association of his enemy's name with a city in the heart of his Kingdom.

87. N.W.I. p. 186. c.f. Justin.

88. M.P. Vad. Intro. c.f. N.W.I p. 206 f.n. 15.

89. i) Pūraṇ Kashyap.
ii) Mākhli Gośāl.
iii) Nigaṇṭh Nāth Pūt i.e. Son of the Nigaṇṭ Nāth.
iv) Sanjay Vālthi Pūt i.e. Son of Sanjay VālthĪ.
v) Ajit Keś Kāmbli i.e. Unconquerable wearing a blanket (of hair colours i.e. black, grey or white).
vi) Kākudh Kāchān.
The term Kāchān which contains in it the common caste suffix "an" of Bhales and Bhadarwāh and Rajori Poonch region indicates that some of these learned men must have been from Jammu hill region.

90. V. Treneckner pp. 82-83.

91. Maqbhool Ahmed - In his book *Historcial Geography of Kashmir* has mentioned various measures or distance which can be corelated with Yojan as under :-
1. Farsākh = 3 miles ; 30 Farsākh = 100 Kroh = 90 miles
Therefore one Kroh 9/10 miles.
1 Yojan has been mentioned in Hindi Shabad Sāgār as 8 Kroh. Therefore one Yojan = 8x9/10 = 7.2 miles. Therefore the scene of discussion = 7.2x 12= 86.4 miles away.
J.P.H. Vogel in *History of Panjāb Hill States,* p.101 describes 1 Kos (Kroh ?) = 4/3 miles.
One Yojan therefore must be = 4x8 = 10.66 miles and consequently 12 Yojan = 12x10.66 = 128 miles.
Again Yojan according to Capleston (c.f. N.W.I. P.371) is a very controversial measure of distance. It has been changing with time. According to him one yojan

is equal to two and a half miles, which means that the place of discussion was only 30 miles away from Kashmir.

92. T.H. Beal. p.200

93. R.T. Vol. IV. 265-76

94. The term syṁthan and Singhpur seems to have been derived from the word Scythian used for Greeko-Bactrian rulers.

95. There is every possibility that King Menānder after entering into Buddhist fold and becoming a monk might have come on a pilgrimage to the Vattanity's hermitage in Nāgsenī, named the region after Nāgsen, Syṁthan as Scythian and village near Supian as Menānder a name retained to this day. Even the very name Kaśṭwāṛ has some thing to resemble with Kathiawāṛ, the undisputed province of Euthydemid Kings for nearly one hundred years. I feel even the Rājput title of "Singh" is a changed abbreviation of Scythian-Scynth-Singh.

CHAPTER III

CONCLUSIONS

From the study of life and works of Nāgsen as mentioned in last two chapters it must be clear that he belonged to the Nāgsenī region of Kaśṭwāṛ and the following direct and indirect references provide further support and evidence to the aforesaid facts.

A) *Historical Evidence*: There is no denying the fact that serious conflicts between Buddhist and non-Buddhists had taken place, in North Western India, around early centuries of Christian era. Buddhist traditions describe Pushyamitra, the great Śuṅga King (183-149 B.C) of Pātliputra as a great persecutor of Buddhism. It is said of him that acting on the advice of his Brahmin chaplin Pushyamitra made up his mind to destroy the teachings of Buddha. He marched out from Pātliputra with a four fold army destroying stūpas, burning monasteries and killing the monks, as far as Śākala. Pushyamitra issued a declaration that whosoever would present him with the head of a Śramaṇa, would be rewarded with one hundred Dinārs.[1]

यो में श्रमण शिरो दास्यति तस्याह दीनार शतं दास्यामि।

The allegation cannot be rejected as baseless. Around this very time anti Buddhist crusade by the Kings of Kashmir, particularly 'Jālukā and Dāmodra has been recorded by various historians.[2]

Menānder occupied Śākalā around 140 B.C. and proceeded further eastward upto Mathurā. By his gallant

Scythian army, unsurpassable wisdom and scholarly discussions, he subdued all the powerful sects of the local inhabitants, whether of intellectual class warriors or religious Pandits. Those who did not submit escaped to the inner mountaneous regions. There was no way out. The dominant intellecutal class, whether Buddhist or Brahmins, being thus persecuted from the eastern, western and southern sides of the country had no option but to retreat to the inner Himālayan valleys particularly that of Jammu, as it was nearer to Kashmir, the seat of learned Brahmiṅs, as well as Rishis and Munis, centre of art and culture. The inner mountain valleys of Kaśṭwāṛ and Bhadarwāh were still nearer to Kashmir, drained by Chandrabhāgā and its tributaries, ideal places for hermitage and meditation and safe from all aggression. It is perhaps in this context as recorded in *Milind Panho* that "Sāglā had been devoid of brethren of the order, Brahmins, Śramaṇas and laymen".

The King would visit every place where a learned Pandit dwelt and put him his questions. Being unable to answer them or satisfy the King, the learned men would leave the place and move to other places.[3]

Right from ancient times to the present day, Kaśṭwāṛ as well as its adjoining hill region, have always proved to be safe refuge for all the non-submissive and disgruntled elements of the valley of Kashmir and other surrounding regions. Kashmir history, Rājataraṅgiṇi as well as other historical references pertaining to Kashmir bear a testimony to the above noted fact. People fleeing from Kashmir and Panjāb have always found a safe shelter in Jammu hills and there is no wonder if around the time of Menānder's reign, hermits, Brahmins, recluse, and Śramaṇas also escaped from Panjāb and Kashmir and sought refuge in the inner Himālayan mountain valleys of Chināb i.e. Kaśṭwāṛ, Nāgsenī,

Bhales, Pāḍar, Dachan and Maṛwā, the Guarded slopes of the Jammu Hill region.

B. ***Geographical Evidence*:**

The region of Nāgsen's activities and hermitage has been described in *Milind Panho* as guarded and slopy, mountaneous and Himālayan in character, and nearer to Kashmir and Śākalā and this can be no other place but the Nāgsenī region of Kaśṭwāṛ. A lot of geographical evidence provides support to this presumption.

Firstly, Nāgsenī region and the table land town of Kaśṭwāṛ is nicely guarded by natural topography, as it is surrounded by the mighty Chināb and its deep gorges on all the three sides and high altitude peaks and dense Deodar forests on the fourth side. At the same time it has numerous beautiful small side valleys, carved and drained by Chināb and its tributaries.These valleys, side valleys, overhanging mini valleys and other high alitude mountain hutmets, particularly those in Kaśṭwāṛ Bhadarwāh, Bhales, (also in Rajouri and Poonch mountaneous region) has been ideal places for meditation, hermitage and learning of vedic lore.

Secondly as per instruction of Rohan, Nāgsen could not go to Śākalā for dispelling the doubts of Menānder. Rainy season had commenced, and it did not allow him to move out of the gorgeous Chandrabhāgā valley, and gaurded slopes, as the region is highly vulnerable to flash floods, slips and route blockades during this season.

Thirdly we see that in the introductory of *Milind Panho* translation by V.Treneckner, famous rivers of the region have been mentioned at four places. At three places the author of the celebrated work simply repeats the names of five rivers so often enumerated in the Pitkās i.e. Gangā, Yamunā, Akhirāvatī, Sarabhu and

Māhi,which clearly indicates that the occurence of these names in *Milind Panhō* is the religious influence of the later stage of development of Pitkās on it. At the fourth place the author of *Milind Panho* has mentioned five other river names, the Sindhu, Saraswatī, the Vetravatī the Vitaṁsā and Kandabhāgā; of these the first two are well known. Max Muller suggests that Vitaṁsā is Vitāstā (i.e. Jehlum) flowing through Kashmir and adjoining region of Poonch mountains. Vetravatī is affluent of Yamuna and Kandabhāgā rises in the North West Himālayas i.e. modern Kināb.[4]

The fourth mention of river names appears more authentic. It contains the names of two important rivers flowing through the land of Nāgsen-Menānder episode i.e. Vitāstā through the valley of Kashmir and Chināb (Kināb) through Nāgsenī ; Kaśṭwāṛ Kaniṇī, Jaṅgalwāṛ, Akhnoor and Siālkot region. The name Kināb assigned to river Chināb as recorded by V.Treneckner, is so, probably because it flowed through the land of Nāgsen's birth and education i.e. Kāṅinī- Ajāl Jaṅgalwāṛ and Nāgsenī.

Nāgsen's activities pertain to the valleys of Kaśṭwāṛ Poonch and Rājouri is quite evident from numerous other indirect evidences and references about the Himālayan character of the country of his birth. For example Yugāndhār, where the assembly of the elders of the order is said to have been held, carries the common Himālayan tradition of assigning such names to the mountain pastures[5]. Dhār is a common suffix in the place names for these high mountains pastures in the valley of Chinab, in the Jammu hill region.

There is a popular tradition, possibly pretty old, as enumerated by Dr. Tarn[6] and Dr. Narain[7] on the authority of G.Gaces[8] which connects the origin of a most famous statue of Buddha, made of Emerald, with

Menānder. According to this tradition, the famous statue of Buddha had been fashioned out from a magic stone by Menānder's teacher Nāg Sen by his super natural powers. This popular tradition of Indo-China (Vietnām) can have a Geographical and Scientific basis also. The famous saphire mines of Paḍār, though officialy stands discovered only in last century, were known to the local inhabitants earlier also. This mine near Machel and Chashotī is close to the Nāgsenī region of Kaśṭwāṛ, and there is no wonder if some disciple or devotee of Nāgsen may have presented the big Greenish Gem-stone to the teacher, who as per tradition through his super natural power, or through the agency of King Menānder got it fashioned by some skilled craftsman into the aforesaid famous statue.

Again, an ancient Buddha monastery (Gumpā) with rich Buddhist literature (in manuscript form) is still lying in a village Haloti Chasotī close to the famous Saphire mines of Kaśṭwāṛ.

C) *Archaeological Evidence*: There are many archeological sites pertaining to the ancient and medieval period which reflect the richness of the antiquity and culture of the mountain valleys of Chināb in Jammu, especially that of Kaśṭwāṛ. In Jammu mountain region we have at least three Brahmī inscription sites pertaining to the times in question. According to Dr.Vasudev Sharan Aggarwal, a great Archaeologist and scholar of ancient Indian history, Kaśṭwāṛ must occupy a very important place in the cultural history of Jammu region and therefore of India. According to his observations he had the literary evidence for his convictions which must correspond with and supported by desired archeological data. He believed that certain portion of Vedas must have been composed in the Valleys of Chināb in Kaśṭwāṛ Some ten caves have been located in this region which appear to be the abodes of saints, hermits and recluse. We have identified in the second chapter of this monograph the important Archeological sites of Sai Draman and Demzī near Bhāttan village connected with Tapsvī Assāgutth and his Vattanīya hermitage in Nāgsenī region of Kaśṭwāṛ. A detailed account of all such monuments and ancient sites related with Nāgsen in one way or the other form is being given separately in the next chapter of this book.

D) *Numismatic Evidence*: According to Rhy Davids twenty two different (types of) coins, some of them in considerable number bearing the name (of Menānder) and eight of them with the bust of Menānder have been found. One of them has been found in Kashmir. It depicts the bust of the King wearing a crested Helmet. Bhikśu Jagdish Kashyap in his Hindi edition of *Milind Panho* also records that "upto this time we have discovered twenty two coins of Milind from Kābul to Mathurā, which indicates the vastness of his empire. The coin depicts the figure of Milinda clearly on eight coins. In some he is quite young and in some he is quite old which means he reigned for quite a long time. The language on two sides is Pāli and Greek.[11]

The list of coins prepared by G.B Bleazby Esq. from the Valley (Kashmir) include 15 silver coins of Menānder which are similar to the coins preserved in British Museum. They seem to have been collected by the late Accountant General of the J&K State from some where in Shupiān, though Fidda Hussain mentions them as collected from Lolāb.[12] Menānder being the name of a village near Shupiān on the traditional ancient route through Toshmaidān, the coins must belong to this area.

Again some of these coins are said to contain the figures of running horses, camels, elephants, bear or a Chakra. The coin with a Chakra (symbolic of Bodh

Dham Chakra) confirms to some extent that King Menānder had accepted Buddhism. The other side of the coin contains the word " Basileos Dikaiou Manendrou (महरजस धार्मिकस मनेन्द्रस). In Buddhist literature a King devoted to Buddhism is always called as Dham Rāj and therefore the term Dikaiou (धार्मिकस्य) on the coin confirms the influence of Buddhism on the King.[13]

E) *Ethenic Evidence*: "Sen" is a sub-caste name of many people only of Kaśṭwāṛ probably in the whole of J&K State. Mahāsen and Nāgsen are the chief characters of *Milind Panho*.

Again the Himālayan valleys formed by tributaries of Chandrabhāgā in Kaśṭwāṛ and Rājouri Poonch have much in comman in the ethnic and cultural aspects. Scores of place and caste names in the valleys of Bhales and Girgān have a common suffixal nomenclature[14] such as:-

Rajouri	*Bhales*
Girgāṇ)	Kilhotrāṇ - Places
Doḍriāṇ)	Erwāṇ (Kathuā)
Khiāṇ) Places	Deḍhāṇ)
Khulwāṇ)	Sagāṇ) castes
Knalwāṇ)	Thamāṇ)
Hussāṇ)	Khakhāṇ)
Kapran	Keśwān (Kaśṭwāṛ)
Terwān	Peswān do
Rattan Dev	Rattan Dev do

and the term ATHARWĀN of *Rigveda* used for a priest also supports the same idea.

F) *Linguistic Evidence*: *Milind Panho* is stated to have been first written in Pāli / Kashmiri and then translated into various other languages i.e. Chinese, Siṁhalese and in 1880 and 1890 into English by V. Treckner and

Rys Davids. This Kashmiri or Pāli of ancient times or early medieval times is still much nearer to the Kaśṭwāṛi and Kashmīrī of today. A study of various places and person names and words recorded in *Milind Panho* clearly support this contention. For example we have the names of persons as Sônutur and Assāgutth which are nearer to Kaśṭwāṛī/Kashmirī nomenclature, and phonetics. Names such as Kañjaṅgal, Vijamvothu, Vattanīya etc. are also nearer to phonetic peculiarities of the local dialect i.e. occurrence of closed vowels and predominance of "th" phone of Kaśṭwāṛi dialect. The term Bhatt stands for a Pandit in Kashmiri. Even today a Pandit in Kashmiri is called by the general term Buttā. A lot of village names in Kaśṭwāṛ either start or end with the term Bhāttā, such as Nāgan Bhāttā, Pullar Bhāttā, Sangrām Bhāttā, etc. depicting them as the abodes of Pandits or learned Brahmins. Again "Yār" or "ār" (like Kashmirī) is a common suffix of the Kaśṭwāṛī place names, such as Padyār/n (Bhatta Yāra) Badiār (Bad + Yar).

Again the Pālī inscription on the other side of Menānder's coin is very close to the Kaśṭwaṛī / Kashmīri i.e. on 21 coins: महरजस त्रदतस मनेन्द्रस

on 22nd coins: महरजस धार्मिकस्य मनेन्द्रस

G) *Religious Evidence*: Nāgsenī and other side valley in the Himālyan mountain ranges of Chināb and Jammu Hills had been sacred land of Vedās, Holy land of Buddhists, and pious land of Brahmanic period, is borne out by many facts pertaining to the regions. In Nāgsenī area alone most of the local agriculture and forest produce are considered pious and sacred and taken only, on religious fastings and festivities, in the whole of the surrounding country. Some of these are as under:

a) ***Sacred Crops*** :

1) *Siūl:* a kind of white mustard like grain. On a fasting day it is roasted and consumed with milk or curd.

ii) *Phulan:* Extensive crop of this grain is cultivated in the hill region and Nāgsenī valley during summer months. Its flour is used for making bread.

iii) *Bajarbhaṅg* is another small grainy crop of the region, extensively cultivated and after sorting out the husk from it, is cooked like rice or khīr, which is very tasty and entertaining.

iv) *Drov* is another kind of phulan, somewhat superior in quality. Plate XV.

v) *Chini* or *Anav* is a small ricey grain like crop, whitish in colour, cooked like rice, or with milk as khīr, and eaten on fasting days and religious festivity.

vi) *Kodrā* is yet another small ricy grain which is used as a stable food as well as for making traditional, alcoholic beverage, by the folk people. It is curious and interesting to note that consumption of one or other kind of beverage, in daily life or on special religious occasions, is a part of life style of the high landers in the entire Himālayan region, right from the ancient times. It may be Somras or Chhang; it may be vedic times, Buddhist period, Śaivism or revived Hinduism of Gupta age and style, use of beverage was a part of the Indian mountain religion. Kodrā forms the basic ingredient for making such drinks.

b) *Wild fruits* : Many types of wild fruits are also available in mountain valleys of Chināb which are not only abundant but tasty and nutritious, also:

i) *Zom* is a kind of sweet but dark brownish wild grapes, very tasty and nutritious, found in the Naigad valley of Nāgsenī.

ii) *Kulāñch* is again a small juicy, herby wild fruit extensively found on these slopes, sweet as well as nutritious.

iii) *Thānkī* a wild jungle nut found on high altitude mountain slopes.

iv) wild walnuts are also extensively found in the region.

v) *Niozei* is a fine tasty nutritive needle shaped high altitude, pine fruit found in Pāḍar region of Kaśṭwāṛ close to the Nāgsenī valley.

Most of these grains and fruits are eaten by the people on the days of fastings only, probably because of their being considered sacred as they grow in the sacred land of Nāgsen.

c) *Sacred Trees*: Certain trees are also considered to be most sacred in this region. One such tree is the Brahmā tree.

It is found in the whole of the Nāgsenī valley. It is planted at the time of a good deed, and is usually found near a water spring or a shrine. In no case is it damaged or cut. On the day of full dark moon night, it is offered Dhūpa or other incadscent.

In addition to the above named sacred trees, others whose products are used for cleansing purposes are:-

Gug: a kind of "surf" tree whose fruits are used for washing of clothes. In plains it is probably known by the name of Reiṭhā.

Krains : a similar jungle product used for the same purpose.

Thus the above religious base for considering the Bhadarwāh- Kaśṭwāṛ - Shupiān - Poonch Himālayan mountain belt as the sacred land of composition of Vedas, and Buddhist Holy land, and abode of saintly men, is confirmed. Other supportive evidence in this respect is as under:-

a) Nagsen is said to have learnt three Vedas from his father and later become Philogist and Grammarian. There is every probability of Kaśṭwāṛś mountain region and Chandrabhāgā and its side valleys being the abode of learned Brahmins, who probably composed, learnt, mastered and preserved the Vedas. Many places in the upper Chināb Valley of Pāngī, Bhales, Maṛwā and Banihāl still preserve the place names indicating these as abodes of certain Rishis, saints or seers, such as:-

i) Rikinwās; Rishi + Niwās (Dachan Maṛwā)

ii) Chamalwās; Chamal + Wās (Banihāl)

iii) Alwās; Alv + Wās (Pāḍar-Paṇgi)

iv) Darwās; Darv + Wās (do)

v) Jakyās; Jakya + Wās (Bhales)
or Yakya +Wās

vi) Bhatyās; Bhat + Wās (do)

vii) Malwās; Malv + Wās (Doda)

Even the small side valley of Bhadarwāh, drained by Chināb's tributary NERŪ which is known for its beauty, has been recorded by the name of Bhadrāvakāsh, Bhadrāshram and Bhadrakāshī.

Again the Śukā is mentioned to have addressed the assembly of the order, on the summit of Yugāndhar which reveals the sacredness and religious potential of the Himālayas of this region, especially when Śukā is taken as Devādhipatī, a *Milind Panho* innovation.

As per *Milind Panho,* Nāgsen had learnt from his father all the three Vedas and was well versed in Vedic lore, which means vedic knowledge had been a household affair for the local Brahmin population of the region, and therefore lends further support to the hypothesis.

b) Not only did Kaśṭwāṛ provide religous teachers to Kashmir and North Western India, in Buddhist times, in the person of Nāgsen, but in later periods also this *Himālayan* tradition of imparting religious teaching continued in the form of some Muslim Saints and Pīrs having moved into the land of Nāgsen and then gone to Kashmir as religious teachers. We find a small cave at Bhandārkot just near the bridge over Chināb.

Sheikh Zain-ul-din Walī of Palmāṛ in Kaśṭwāṛ, before moving to Aishmukām in Kashmir, is stated to have stayed here for many years. He was a principal disciple of Sheikh Nur-ud-din Sahib Walī, patron saint of Kashmir who's ancestors too belonged to Kaśṭwāṛ, probably from Sarthal- Kāñiṇī Ajāl and birth place of Nāgsen,(Kāñiṇī Ajāl). A Shārdā inscription lies in the cave spring, on the left bank of Chandrabhāgā, just opposite the first cave.

c) Sanskritised nomenclature of local places all along the Chandrabhāgā river and its tributaries in Jammu hills again indicates that the above region had been a seat of ancient Indian school of learning. To quote some of such names of Kaśṭwāṛ - Poonch region we may mention them as under:-

Nāgsenī, Kaśṭwāṛ Kāñiṇī, Brahmśilā, (Earśila), Drabśālā, Shīvā, Sirāj, Khaśālya, Himtā (Hiuta - Chanenī - Himavant) Buddhpur (Udhampur) Rāmban, Rāmsu, Chandarkot, Maitreyā, Desā, Rājgaṛh, Rudradhār (Rudhār), Sudh Mahā Dev, Hastī, Bindrāban (Kaśṭwāṛ), Bhadravakāsh, Kaplas (mountain named after the Kuśān King Kadphises I or IInd (15-75 A.D.), Rājāpuri (Rajouri) Surankot, Chandimaṛh, Singh Dwār (Shāh - Derā), and many others. All such names also prove the Sanskritised antiquity of the places as well as persons of the region.

d) One of the interesting co-incidental evidence and co-occurence of events in the region of Nāgsen-

Menānder episode is , that many traditions, religious observations and monuments in the Kaśṭwāṛ and Poonch valleys, the two main Himālayan regions connected with him, are almost similar in certain aspects. The monuments (temples) at Sāi Draman and Rāmkund (Plates IV & XXXII) are broadly same in shape and size. The Chaitrā Chaudashī (the fourteenth day of Lunar Bright Moon) is celebrated and considered sacred for taking Holy bath both at Rāmkund and Dodā, i.e. Sangam of Neru and Chandrabhāgā rivers. The tradition and story attributed to Pir Chotā Shāh of Sakhī Maidān in Mendhar and Pir Farid-ud-din in Kaśṭwāṛ is, broadly speaking, similar in narration, contents, and time of occurence. The elderly or spiritualy enlightened persons of the later times seem to have utilized the spiritual sanctity of these places to awaken themselves to be capable to bring political and social reforms in the overall degenerated life of the people of the region, or in other words we may say, that the spirit of aggression of foreign invaders of India, being defeated spiritually as in the Nāgsen -Menānder episode, later restored to a silent invasion, in the shape, form and person of Pirs, Faqirs and saints as shall we see in the following pages, to acquire all the meta-physical or spiritual power, from these places of ancient sanctity, probably for propagation of their own faiths.

Cultural Evidence: An interesting socio-cultural evidence indicating the Greeko- Bactrian influence on the subjects of their domain is available from an interesting custom prevalent among the Hindus as well as Mohammedan residents in certain regions of the land. We know that Menānder had married Agathocleia, his first cousin sister. This custom is not ordinarily prevalent amongst the Hindus of the land . However the custom of marrying cousin sisters can be seen amongst Hindus also (Thākur and Brahmin communities only) of certain areas of Gujrāt, Rajāsthān, Kathiāwāṛ as also around the land of birth of Nāgsen i.e. Bhaderwāh, Bhales and Pāḍar etc. The same custom seems to have been practised in the land of Menānder's home Kingdom (Sindhu- Sauvīrā) as indicated by the popular Sanskrit Ślokā (now out of my memory) which reads something like

पूर्वे ....? पश्चिमे ....?

उत्तरे मांस भोजनं दक्षिणे मातुला कन्या ।

and which indicates that the custom might have travelled Northwards from the southern country of Menānder's domain i.e. Sindh. The custom became so predominantly prevalent in the Himālayan Valley of Chināb, that from the very childhood, the boy or the girl in question was in the know of his or her probable future life companion. I still remember one interesting event of my school days at Bhadarwāh when two of my classmates, both first cousin quarrelled over a trifle and the one in a taunting voice shouted at the other "Oh you, my child (Bāichu)? You dare to quarrel with me ? Have I not to marry your sister?" And the other fellow had nothing to say but to swallow the insult. The custom seems to be the direct influence of Greeko-Kuśāṇa ethinic culture, the remnants of which can still be traced from the Himālayan Valleys, and which forms the matter of another research paper.

The main villages of the Nāgseni region of Kaśṭwāṛ and the guarded alopes of *Milind Panho* are as under:-

1. Cherjī
2. Ārchī
3. Poller
4. Chichhā
5. Tyālan
6. Dichalā
7. Wulay
8. Galhār
9. Naigaḍ
10. Sīrī

11. Demzī
12. Bhātan
13. Bhiṛā
14. Chandanānā
15. Paḍyārnā
16. Kwāṛ
17. Charol
18. Thumnei
19 Dul
20. Sumanei
21. Ghoṛnei
22. Siāh
23. Bāgnā.

All this should provide a sufficient convincing evidence to prove that the valley of Chandrabhāgā is not only rich in the field of antiquity, but is also the land of birth, education and meditation of one of the greatest sons of India, named Nāgsen, who like Buddha, without uttering even a single harsh word or abuse to anyone, silenced these foreign messengers of death and destruction, removed their biting teeth and made them humble, accommodating and peace loving citizens for centuries to come.

And the presumption of some unknown Kashmiri writer of Daily Mārtanḍ article, years ago, and the strong conviction of D. Vāsudev Sharan Aggarwal about the richness of antiquity of Kaśṭwāṛ region, now seems to have come true to some extent by surveying, locating, indentification and evaluation of the Nāgsenī region of Kaśṭwāṛ as the place of birth and meditation of one of the greatest philosopher, thinker and saints of his time and probably some other Buddhists, as well as Hindu saints and hermits. of the region, which needs further investigations and continued research.

Footnotes :

1. A.I. p.297.

2. K.T.A. p.24.
"Ashoka (273-236 B.C) exterminated Malechās root and branch. However the state religion did not draw to itself many followers from the populace, as the land was under the sway of learned Brahmins, who's fame for scholarship in Sanskrit lore had travelled to distant parts of Hindustan, Tibet , Chinā,Jāvā, and Jāpān. Low caste Hindus alone presumably adopted the new faith".

3. Fidda Mohmmad P.114 In Buddhist Kashmir recods:- Buddhist suffered untold miseries during the reign of Abhimanyu, who gave patronage to Śaivism. Buddhist were forced to renounce their religion or face anihilation. Under such circumstances many a Buddhist ran away from the Valley.

3. M.P. Treck. 1/1/3

4. Ibid X / IV-V

5. Such as Sibār-Dhār, Rudhar, Seoj Dhār, Nāglotan, Dhār, Kanṭhi-Kaṭar Dhār, Gadiāni Dhār etc. etc.

6. G.B.I. p. 267-68.

7. I.G. p. 98.

8. Bulletin de 1' Ecole francaise d' extreme orient B.E.F. ED. XXV 1925 p.112 XXX 193 p. 448.
c.f. N.W.I. 207. f.n. 17.

9. D.E.

10. R.C. KaK. *A handbook of coins of Kashmir*, p. 129

11. M.P. Bhik. P. 6-7.

12. The Valley of Lolāb also lay on the traditional route from Kashmir to N.W. frontier, the Domain of Menānder.

13. M.P. Bhik. p.6

14. This "An"suffix seems to mean "son of " or "coming from". According to Pāniṇī Sūtra (IV. 1.117) suffix "अण" is used for a son or descendent. c.f. N.W.I P. 146 f.n.8.

15. B.K. Fidda. P.

CHAPTER IV

CONNECTED MONUMENTS, SITES AND THEIR ARCHAEOLOGICAL DETAILS

The greatest achievements of ancient Indian civilization and culture was, probably its rich tradition of spirtual superiority which by the time of beginning of Gupta period had started to indicate the signs of decline and degeneration.

While Vedic India was country of nature worshipers, Upanishdas indicated a changed environment of pursuits for philosophy and intellectualism, Buddhism and Jainism stood for equality among different sections of people, tolerance, mutual love, cooperation, and coordination, Purānic Hinduism patronised by Guptas, based on mythical faiths and traditions proved to be the root cause of Indian religious and spiritual degeneration.

It is interesting to note that in many cases the armed attack of Indian soil by a foreigner was preceded by the visit of some saintly persons or some foreign spiritualist to the sites and monuments associated with some Rishi, Muni, saint, hermit, Yogi, Yatī[1] or Satī.[2] But whenever an Indian intellectual gaint or spiritualist retaliated, the foreigner had to face defeat and humiliation.

We have already seen that Nāgsen not only silenced Menānder but also converted him to Buddhism to such a stage of firmness that he is said to have later become a Bhikśu and attained Arhatship. In the times that followed we see complete shattering of his empire and liquidation of Greeko- Bactrian invasion at the hands of Śakas.

If we study the history of religious transformations and change in faiths in India, with special reference to the tract of land under study we find that scores of Pīrs, Faqīrs, saints and other pious men had started to pour in at the places of spirtual sanctity, temples, hermitages and other monuments, from the West. Every city, town or village in Panjāb and its adjoining territory is still seen to preserve one or more Ziārats or Mazārs of some particular Pīr or elderly Faqir, who in addition to the preaching of love and brotherhood among different sections of people also preached their own faith and religion. Kaśṭwāṛ, Rājourī, Poonch and Udhampur districts in Jammu also have a rich ancient tradition of Hindu saints and their hermitages followed by Pīrs and, Faqirs of the later medieval times. Many locations in the mountain valleys drained by Chināb and its tributaries seems to have been places of religious activity and spiritual merit, right from ancient times to the present day. In the following pages an attempt is being made to draw an informative sketch of some of these places of spiritualistic interest, of the ancient and medieval times from the available sources.

Nāgsenī or the Land of Nāg Sen:

In *Milind Panho* it has been stated that Nāgsen was born in the Brahmin village of Kañjaṅgal situated in the Himalayās, in the extreme east of Buddhist holy land. Now if we study the geographical features of the land tract around the valley of Nāgsenī, we come across gorgeous and slopy region only lying between the present villages of Kāniṇī and Jaṅgalwāṛ (on the present Batote Kaśṭwāṛ National Highway) which can be associated with the birth place of Nāgsen, on the following reasons:-

1. Some of the villages of the belt, such as Barshilā Sarthal and Panditgām (Kaśṭwāṛ) are still predominantly Brahmin villages.
2. The village name Kañjaṅgal, the birth place of Nāgsen is the abbreviated form of the village names of Kāniṇī (Kāndinī) and Jaṅgalwār, a region of difficult accessibility in those days, and therefore termed as guarded slopes.
3. It is really situated to the extreme limit of Holy Buddhist land, which in those ancient days included valley of Kashmir and all the Himālayan mountain valleys surrounding it especially those falling in the middle mountain range of Pīr Panchāl range on the South East of Himālayās.

Nāgsen seems to have been born in the Pandit village of Kaśṭwāṛ (Kāniṇī, Jangalwāṛ belt) and late moved to village Chhihhā (Vijamvothu) and Bhāttan (Vattaniya hermitage) for learning and meditation. In addition to various facts as stated in Chapter III, additional evidence which proves the antiquity of this region are as under:-

i) The region is located on the traditional ancient mountain route from Kāngṛā to Kashmir and was quite familiar with the ancient and medieval, political and religious personalities, travelling through this mountain route.

ii) There is a mini cave temple, containing three Shiv liñgam, on the right bank of Chandrabhāgā river near Kāndoth. On examining its location, form and structure the place seems to be a traditional ancient mini-cave shrine associated with Pāndavas.

iii) Numerous Megāliths belonging to both ancient and medieval times can still be noticed in the slopy hutments of Kaśṭwāṛ Jañgalwāṛ region. Those found at Bhellā, Kañḍot and Kaśṭwāṛ belong to 1st to 5 th century A.D.

1v) Ruins of a small fort exist on a small hillock at Bhellā Kānḍot and as per tradition the fort was built by some Chinese invader who could be none else but the Chinese appearing Hun Chief Mihirkul or any of his chieftain.[3]

v) Kāniṇī or Kāndiṇī is a small beautiful spot at the foot of Sarthal Devi shrine, on the left bank of Chandrabhāgā river. There is a folk song in Bhadarwāhī dialect depicting the sacrifice of Rānī of Kāniṇi (Kandiṇī) for the welfare of village folk, similar to one that of Rāni Shārdā of Chambā.[4] A few miles further up towards Kaśṭwāṛ, we have a place named Hastī (i.e. Elephant) which reminds us of the Chinese version of the birth story of Nāgsen, according to which Nāgsen was named so because at the time of his birth, a calf also was born to an elephant. In Sanskrit an elephant is known by the term Nāg also. The Hastī slopes of Kaśtwāṛ are at a distance of only few miles from Kāniṇī and must have something to co-relate with Nagsen, and his birth place.

vi) The Chinese version of *Milind Panho* also mentions Rohan residing at Vijjamvothu (Chhichhā) and as Maternal uncle of Nāgsen, which again makes one to believe that Nāgsen was born in some village of Kaniṇī - Jangalwāṛ belt, his mother belonged to Chichā belt and his education and meditation must have been carried out in Chichhā- Bhāttan- Demzī region.

vii) The Chief of Kanḍā (Bhellā- Kānḍot) principality in Kaśṭwāṛ, named Gabhir Singh (probably a Rānā) is recorded to have taken part in the assembly of hill

Chiefs called by Kalśā, the King of Kashmir in 1886 A.D, in which Rājā of Kaśṭwāṛ and Chamba also took part.[5]

All these things indicate the richness of the antiquity of the region. The sites and monuments connected with Nāgsen in Kaśṭwāṛ and Poonch are as follows:-

A) *Sarthal* is said to have derived its nomenclature from Shri Sthal called so because of the sacred shrine of Devi Shārika, which as per tradition and religious belief came there from Kashmir, only five or six centuries earlier but the cluster of villages of Kāniṅī in Sarthal seems to be quite old. Kāniṅī (presently called Kandinī) is some 53 miles away from Batote and from here the village Ajāl near Sarthal is seven miles up. The village is inhabited by Brahmins, and the place is a over-hanging valley at the foot of dense Deodār forest with a small hutment. The location and inhabitance is an ancient one. Now this Kāniṅī-Ajāl slopy hutment can be one of the possible precise location as a place of birth of Nāgsen. The term Kañjaṅgal is derived from Kāninī and Ajāl. Some people use the term Ajār for Agār. It is presently considered one of the most sacred places of the region because of the presence of shrine of Devi Shārikā.[6]

The place is nearer to Nāgsenī and more easily accessible from Kaśṭwāṛ) and Kashmir, from where the fine statute of Goddess Shārikā is said to have been brought at a much later date. According to J.N. Ganhar the image has come here over five and half centuries ago. Sutan Sikander popularly known as Sikander the Iconoclast (1389 - 1413 A.D.) was the ruler of Kashmir then. Under the influence of religious teachers from outside Kashmir he took delight in demolishing Hindu places of worship and destroying the sacred images therein.[7] The Shārikā temple at Hāri Parbat might have also faced an imminent threat from him and hence the image brought to the guarded slopes of Kāniṇī-Ajāl the place of birth of Nāgsen.

B) *Barshilā* is a small predominantly Brahmin village on the right bank of Chinab. Just across it on the left bank of the river can be located the villages of Hastī, Kāniṇī[8], Sarthal , Ajāl, Kanḍot[9], Bhellā, Ṭhaṭhri and Jañgalwār[10]. The place name Barshilā is said to have been derived from Bramshilā. The nomenclature being associated with Brahmā, the creator of the universe, has already been noticed with certain specific mountain peaks of the region and also with a particular kind of tree as seen earlier. The place Barshilā associated with Brahmā must therefore have something of an antiquitarian interest and importance. It may be yet another probable village of Nāg Sen's birth.

C) *Sai Draman* : The most important place connected with the Nāgsen's education and learning in Nāgsenī region of Kaśtwāṛ is the one where Nāgsen's preceptor, Gurū and well wisher Assāgutth used to convene the assembly of the Buddhist order, elders and learned men. The place is called even today by the name Siāh or "Sai" Draman, derived I believe from Assāgutth. The place is located about a dozen miles away on the traditional pedestrian route from Kaśtwāṛ to Pāḍar, or some one mile up from Padyārṇā on the present Kaśtwāṛ Pāḍar motorable road. An important archaeological site still exists at the place, which consists of three stone temples, and confirms the religious nature and sanctity of the place. The place, in the time of Nāgsen must have been, the centre of religious activity discourses and assembly of elders. The archaeological remains today at the site consist of three ruined stone temple structures, once marvelously built in this remote Himālayan mountain valley. These probably belong to any time between 8th century A.D. to 12 century as indicated by a Shārdā inscription-bearing slab 1'x 3' inscribed in the left wall of the main temple structure. The archaeological site had been hitherto undiscovered by any individual or agency. This temple structure has a lot of similarities to the temple structure at Rāmkund in Mendhar Poonch, and Pāndrethān in Kashmir. All the three temple structures at Sāi Draman are made of chiselled stone-slabs and are facing east. Two of them are adjacent to each other, whereas the third one almost completely in ruins, is some forty feet away southward on the hill top ground (Draman).

Structure No.1 is some '8x8' at the base with almost the same height. The arch beam of the gate has a carved statue of Ganesha, now almost weathered, and partially recognisable. The temple is rectangular in shape with a few stairs. No other particular feature of this temple structure, presently a heap of stone rubble, is worth mentioning.

The temple No.2 at the site (Plate v) is almost completely ruined except its base, some three feet elevated from the ground. Some portions of it seem to be buried as seen from the picture. Two carved lions (Siṁhās) decorate the eastern side of the base arch. No further details can be recorded in the absence of proper excavations, and identifications.

The third temple structure, though partly damaged still maintains some recognizable appearance. It is rectangular in shape, a stone work, probably 8x6 in size. The triangular arch above the gate has a carved panel decorated on both sides with images probably of Gangā and Yamunā (Plate IV) and so is the case with its pyramidical or conical roofing. A carved statue of

Ganesha is situated just below it, and above the entrance to the temple.

A stone slab measuring 1'x3'with early Shārdā inscription is inscribed in the left wall of this temple. If deciphered it could prove to be a big source of positive information regarding the antiquity of the place for the medieval periods. The exploration, evolution and its preservation is therefore of urgent importance.

Following statues in damaged condition still existed inside this temple structure when I visited the site in July 1991.

i) Shiv Pārvatī or Vishnū and Lakshmī in white stone (Plate XI).

ii) Vishnu or Śiva in black stone.

iii) Garuḍa in greystone (Plate X)

iv) Few other statues in fragments which could not be recognised.

v) A fine Ashat Kamal carving on the ceiling.

vi) All components of the temple i.e. walls, flooring, ceiling, roofing and doors comprise of stone slabs only.

vii) Many fragments of carved stones are scattered every where all over the temple premises which is about 100' x 100' dimensions and located on the Siāh hill top.

viii) Some long, thin, oily Deodar, wood pieces, usually used in the hill country as torches for dark night travellares, were also lying inside the temple sanctum, offered as I suppose by village folk as symbol of lamps.

ix) Remanants of a stone boundary wall can also be seen and some pieces of charcoal were also obsered there, reminding one, of the seasonal observance of some kind of festivity by the village folk of the region.

D) *Bhāttan*: Whereas Siāh of Sāi Draman had been the place of religious discourses and assembly of the elders under Hermit Assāgutth̤, village Bhāttan just 3 miles away must have been the site of his residential hutment. The name Bhāttan of the village is still preserved as an alteration of the term Vattanīyaś hermitage as recorded in *Milind Panho*. Though no archaeological site or monument around the village could be traced during the course of my short visit to the site, yet there should be no disappointment on that account, as great men of saintly nature of ancient India were usually in the habit of leading a very simple life. However the site of Assāgutth̤'s residential hutment should be located somewhere near the present damaged wooden temple structure of the village.

E) *Demzī* : The term Demzī, as stated earlier seems to be a name derived from Pālī word Tapsī, or Sanskrit word Tapasvī meaning a meditator. This village in the Nāigad Valley of Nāgsenī region has an extremely charming location at the foot of Nāgīsherū or Haround mountain in the North East of Kaśṭwāṛ. It is some three miles above the traditional route from Kaśṭwāṛ to Pāḍar and five miles up from Padyārnā on the present motorable road from Kaśṭwāṛ to Pāḍar. The height of the location is some 7000 feet. The climate in the summer is very pleasant. In the morning and evening hours the shining glitter of the Brahmā peak, just across the Chandrabhāgā Gorge is quite enchanting. The location is surrounded by a cluster of small villages namely Chandnānā some two and a half miles away, Gordash Nāg, some one and half miles away and Bhāttan the residence of Assāgutth̤ some a half mile away.

We have already seen that Assāgutth̤ was not only the Chief of order, but also a saint of highest merit and therefore it is self evident that his place of deep meditation, must have been away from his residence at Bhāttan, and place of religious discussions and discourses at Siāh Draman. This place is to be located near Demzī where the ruins of a temple structure, probably constructed later at the site of earlier Stūpa of Assāgutthฺ still exist (Plate XV and XIII). The place has a great sanctity, natural charm, purity and calmness. Even in winter months, the place enjoys a warm sunshine for a greater part of the day. A dense and beautiful Deodar forest lies on the upper slopes of the mountain, covering all the aforesaid villages of the region.

Demzī had been the seat of deep meditation for a saintly person like assāgutthฺ is proved by:-

a) The existing remnants of medieval temple containing fragments of carvings, statuary, fountain stone and 24 petalled lotus (Plate XIV).

b) Presence of a Brahmā tree.

c) Remnants of a probable small Bodh stūpa dedicated to Assāghtthฺ.

d) A boundary wall of dry stone masonary.

The stone fountain consists of a big stone slab moderately carved, the water to which must have been channelled from some adjoining source. The weathered stone statue of Vishnu (Plate XIV), a Trimurtī, the right hand face being that of lion, with its foot resting on Prithvī indicate that it should be that of Vaikunthanātha. Two small figures, probably those of Dikpālas, with deity's hands resting on their heads adore the statue on both sides. The 24 petaled lotus may have been the pedestal for a Shivalingām, as the carved panel on stone also indicates the carvings of Ganesh in the centre of the panel and Nandī on one of the undamaged side.

The above sites of Buddhist Kaśṭwāṛ (alongwith Buddhist Poonch-Rājourī) were subjected to enforced religious transformation by the later Brahmanism and still later by Mohamdanism. We find some interesting traditions pertaining to certain saints and Faquirs in Kaśṭwāṛ, and Poonch area as indicated in the last chapter.

On the left bank of Chināb at Bhandārkot there is a cave shrine and a spring with a small inscription in Shārdā still undeciphered. According to Gulam Mustafa Ishrat the inscription carries some Buddhist message.

Whereas Kaśtwāṛ has been the place of birth and education of Nāgsen, Mendhar, in Poonch probably was the centre from where he continued his religious and spiritual activities in his later life. The valleys of Rājourī and Poonch also have a rich tradition of saints and hermits, later followed by Pīrs and Faqīrs. The archeological site of Sakhi-Maidān or Pāndav temples, the miraculous vihāra at Parṇotsva (Poonch) indicates that the whole region in general and the Mendhar-Poonch in particular had remained a place of great Buddhist interest and activity and the testimony and proof thereof is provided in the following archeological sites of the region.

F) *Rāmkund:* is an archeological site in Mendhar valley of Poonch District of Jammu region. The location comprises of a mini pocket valley called by the name of Narol Topā. It is a very beautiful spot (PlateXXX). A gushing fresh water spring, a gently descending slopy water shed and a plate type hillock called by the name of Dhūn Topā or Māchigaṛh lies on its North and Eastern sides. The site is some 5 miles away from Mendhar town and some 2 miles away from Sakhī Maidān, the site of an ancient Vihāra and the present ruins of a medieval temple. A lot of tradition and folk belief are associated with Rāmkund temple site as well as with the great Archeological site of Sakhī Maidān which provide very valuable information regarding the antiquity of the region, as well as existence of some ancient hermitage at the temple site, most probably Sānkhey Hermitage of Āyū Pāl of *Milind Panho* named after "Śākya Muni Buddha, where the elder of the hermitage Āyū Pāl resided around 150 B.C. and where Nāgsen on his way to Śākalā stayed and encountered King Menānder.

As per local belief Panḍavās during the Mahābhārta time came and stayed here for some time. Later some important hermits made this place as their hermitage. King Menānder or his son Starto I later seems to have constructed a small stūpa at the site and decorated it with the gold image of Buddha, which as per Rājataranginịi[11], had later been excavated by King Lalitā Ditya and taken away by his minister Caṇkuna to Kashmir, where he installed it in a Chaitya, probably at Parihāspur. Lalitā Ditya seems to have constructed the present temple structures at Rāmkund,from where he obtained two Keśavā statues, with inscription on the base, stating them to be made by Rāma and Lakshmna[12]. The king accordingly seems to have named the place as Rāmkund towards the middle of 8th century A.D. Later these statues were taken away by the king to Kashmir. One of those was installed by him in a temple and the other by his Queen.

Still later, after some eight centuries more passed, another incidence seem to have occurred not at the venue of hidden pocket valley of Ramkund, but close to the Lalitā Dityas temples/ Vihāra at Sakhī Maidān, which gave rise to the establishment of a Ziārat of Chotai Shāh or Sheru Shāh and where now a mosque is being constructed. The style, shape and architectural structure of the Rāmkumd temple at Narol in Mendhar can fairly be compared, with temple of the same age of Kashmir or elsewhere in the region, namely Parihāspur and Pāndrethān in Kashmir and Sāi Draman in Nāgsenī Kaśṭwāṛ. The entire temple and spring structure of this shrine is made of stone slabs and is still extant. It seems to have escaped the wrath of aggressive and intolerant rulers of the times, only because of its unnoticeable location in the pocket valley of Narol at the foot of Shāh Sitār range. Even the credit for its present tracing out goes to some Indian army officer, who while expelling the Pakistanī invaders in 1948 from the region, noticed the site and brought it to the notice of others as well as outsiders. The temple presently does not possess any sculpture pertaining to the time of its construction, nor any fragment of it is found from the site. The walls are now roughly plastered with cement, probably by the temple Pujārī or some other devotee, and consequently the details regarding panels and carvings are lacking. The temple faces east, and its stairs lead down to three springs (Plate XXXII). These have been constructed from sand stone locally available and named after the legendary Rāma, Sītā and Laxmana. The temple walls, floor, roofing and stairs, all comprise of the same material. These stone blocks or slabs are some times as big as 7′. The dimension of the temple is some 8′x8′x20′.

In ancient and the medieval periods, the importance of the place seems to be immense. Presently no Hindu family is residing there because of the border location of the area with Pakistan. The entire land of the Dhūn Shāh Sitar range measuring some 650 kanals, both cultivable and non-cultivable is the property of the shrine. It is said that prior to 1948 some 40 families of

Muslim Jajwān[13] Rājput converts and few Khakhars inhabited the adjoining villages who migrated to Pakistan at the time of Pakistani raid. The region is now being mostly inhabited by Gujjars. A fair on 14th luminous day of Chaitra (Chaitra Chaturdashī) is held at the place every year, when many devotees from the adjoining region gather there.

Sakhī Maidān:

Some five miles away from the present township of Mendar, the Sakhimaidān site is really like a playground or a table land slightly elevated from the Mendhar rivulet.There are two archaeological locations presently available at the site, the one shrine of Sheru Shāh or Chotā Shāh and the other of gigantic ruins, traditionally assigned the name of Pāṇḍava temples, which indicate that the place must have had quite an ancient existence. Both of them are just half a kilometer apart. The present temple ruins, on the basis of structural evidence and construction pattern seem to belong to King Lalitā Ditya's time.The ruins still lay buried in the ground as no excavations of any kind have so far been made.However, the overground projections of the site, its shape, dimensions and size indicates a great degree of its similarity with the basement structure of Avantiswāmī temple of Avantīpurā and Martand temple of Mattan in Kashmir. The temple premises measures some 150′ x 150′ with a central structure of at least 20′ x 20′ (Plate XXI).A deep well exists at the southern corner, which is now almost covered with bushes in a betraying manner. Huge carved and uncarved stone slabs, giant stone pillars and other stone fragments lies scattered everywhere, and it is only after proper excavations and detailed evaluations of the site that some concrete conclusions can be arrived at. However the literary evidences as put down in previous chapters and the overground observations are also quite encouraging and point out towards the aforesaid assumptions, that the temple structure might have been a Vihāra, probably Kriḍārāmā Vihāra of Rājataraṇgini[14]. We have already seen that as per Rājataraṇgini, "Lalitā Ditya while receiving fruits had constructed Phalpura, while taking leafs (Parṇa) Parṇotsasva (Poonch) and while at play (Kriḍān) the Vihāra of Kriḍārāmā. Stien has identified Parṇotsva with Poonch. Regarding Kriḍārāmā Vihāra he says that "It has not been referred to again and its position is unknown". But the narration in Rājataraṇgini of the construction of Krīḍārāmā Vihāra by Lalitā Ditya is found in the chapter and place where most of the events connected with the region (Poonch-Mendhar) have been described. It can therefore be presumed that the Vihāra of Krīḍārāmā must lie in the close vicinity of Poonch, most probably at Sakhī Maidān or Śānkheya Parivien, where seven or eight hundred years earlier to Lalitā Dityas own time, King Milinda had encountered Nāgsen in a discussion, got defeated by him and constructed a Vihāra, known as Milind Vihāra[16], and probably adorned it with a gold image of Buddha as he was a very rich monarch. This Vihāra of Milinda in the course of time (some eight centuries) got damaged and buried. And after King Lalitā Dityās episode with breaking - in of the horse, meeting with the two singing and dancing girls and coming across two statues of Keśva after excavation of the site, he might have felt to pay his reverence to the sacredness of the place by constructing a new Vihāra or renovate the older one. As he played (Krīḍān) with the horse over the vast open space available there, the Vihāra might have been called as Kriḍārāma Vihāra.

Again we see that Huentsang after his two and a half years stay in Kashmir, came to Poonch via Toshmaidān Pass. While on his way to Rājouri he first came to Poonch (Mendhar). Probably he wanted to visit a "Bodh Vihāra much known for his miracles" in those days as recorded by him[17].This Vihāra in the vicinity of Poonch could be no other Vihāra but the one at Sakhī Maidān, as Lalitā Ditya and Huentsang are almost contemporary.

As seen from various traditions, right from King Menānder's time to the present day,the Sakhīmaidān site had been a seat of religious sanctity and spiritual merit and therefore there is a great probability that the fourth Buddhist council convened by Kaniśka (78 A.D.), about 200 years after King Menānder's own time, may have been held at this place, to facilitate the attendence of monks and priests coming from outside the valley, who may not have liked to cross high altitude passes leading to the valley.It is also noteworthy that the massive archaeological ruins at Sakhīmaidān is the only of its kind outside the valley and the site is extremely beautiful and pleasant.According to Sarlā Khoslā : "It is not possible to locate with certainty the place where this council was held, but it is almost certain that it must have been held either in Kashmir itself or in its vicinity[18].

Various names regarding the sight of the fourth council have been recorded by the authors, such as Kuṇḍal Van Vihāra, Karnāvatārisvan Vihāra or Kuvāna Monastery in Kashmir[19].The monastery had been specially constructed by Kuśāṇa King Kaniśka as a venue for the 4th Buddhist council, and the probability of the council meeting being held at this sight i.e. Sānkheya Parivien or Milind Vihāra cannot be ruled out. Rather it can be supported to have been held in the vicinity of Sakhīmaidān on the following grounds :-

a) The influence of the Buddhist triumph over Menānder and other higher sections of the ruling class may not have vanished as yet in Kaniśka's time as the historic episode was only some 200 years old.

b) The scholars from outside the valley, including Aśvaghosha from Benāres and others could come to this place without having to climb tiresome high altitude mountains and trekking difficult Himālayan routes leading into the valley.

c) Thirdly the Mendhar valley on the traditional route from Kashmir to the rest of the country was easily accessible.

d) The Kuvāṇa monastery appears to be none else but the Kuśān monastery named after Kuṣāṇa King Kaniśkā, and this Kuvān, Kundal Van or Karnāvatārisvan Vihāra must be traced somewhere in the vicinity of village, named after the same Vihāra and is still preserved in the place name of Kālāban, a few kilometers away, just in front of the already described historic ruins of Sakhī Maidān Archaeological site.

Therefore the detailed explorations, excavations and evaluations of other probable Buddhist sites in the vicinity of Sakhīmaidān-Kālāban area, and the preservation of those already located is all that is urgently needed for providing further material evidence to the present monograph and also to ascertain the fact, whether the enormous work of the fourth Buddhist council was deposited there[21].

Thus we feel that the hermitage of Śākya Munī changed to Sānkhey Parvein of *Milind Panhö,* and later Milind Vihāra added to its complex, the Kuvān Vihārā or Kundāl van Vihārā of Kaniṣkā's time and then changed its name to Kriḍārāmā Vihāra of Lalitāditya, which 7 or 8 hundred years later, around the time of Aurangzeb - Shāh Jehān, might have undergone further changes and emerged as a Ziārat named after Chotai Shāh, who was descendent Gaddinishīn of a saintly person named Sheru Shāh. An interesting and informative account of the history of Ziārat as given by its Gaddinashin Mulla Sufi Mohd.Sidiq Chisti Nizāmi belonging to village Behṛā Ḍhakkī is given in the foot note[22].

According to him the Ziārat pertains to Mughal times and is 3 or 4 centuries old. The original Ziārat consists of sacred graves of two children (brother and sister) named Chotai Shāh on account of his being a child. The happening at the sight (as stated in the footnote) provide some important clues to the ancient antiquity and sacredness of the place, and a close relationship and a similarity of contents of the traditional beliefs pertaining to this Ziārat and the one of Pir Farid-ud-Din and Asrār-ud-Din Sāhib at Kaśṭwāṛ[23].

Shāh Derā :

According to J.N. Ganhār the term Shāhderā is derived from Sanskrit term Siṁh Dwārā i.e. lions gate. It appears that the place was on the ancient route to Kashmir valley and led to an important Devī shrine dedicated to Devi Chanḍī. The mountain meadow higher up is even today known as Chandimaṛh and on pursing this path one comes across the Kaunsarnāg lake or Vishnū Pād on the way to Shupiān in Kashmir .

There are other probabilities also. The nomenclature Siṁha Dwāra may have something to do with Śākya - Siṁhā or Nāg Sen who while on his way to Śākya Parivien in Mendhar, from Vattanīya's hermitage in Nāgsenī, may have stayed here for some time, for this hermitage in ancient India may have some relation with ancient Shādarhavāhan Vihāra (Hārwan) of Kashmir. Distinguished archaeologist R.C. Kak had "noted five fountain springs Baulies in Shāhdārā village, the best preserved of which flows from a spout, shaped like a tiger's head (Siṁha) from the middle of the back wall. Fragments of stunted fluted columns still exist. The upper panels, are carved with figures of gods, goddesses votaries, warriors with swords and shields and bowman shouting an arrow".

In recent times, the place being situated on the old Mughal route to Kashmir gained prominence on account of the shrine of Shādrā Sharief which has grown round the tomb of a Muslim saint named Pir Gulām Shāh. Born in a Sayeed family of a village Saidā of Kasrāban (now in Pakistan) he is said to have displayed certain miracles at an early stage of life.His preceptor instructed him to move to Shāhdāra in Rajouri (it is interesting to note that, while on his way to his new destination, he stayed at Kālāban (the probable site of Kuvān Vihāra) in Mendhar, just in front of Sakhīmaidān archaeological site, where he meditated for some time and practised austerities. Then he moved to Dhundhāk and again meditated under a big stone, on a dry patch of land in the midst of a roaring stream which on being flooded did not carry him away. He then moved to the present site of Shāhdrā where he lived for seven years meditating and on his death a tomb was erected over his grave which became a centre of pilgrimage both for Hindus and Muslims". Gulab Singh the Dogra ruler is credited to have visited the sight and constructed the shrine.[24]

h) *Loh Devtā* :- It is a Shrine in Krishanā Ghātī over a hill top on the Pedestrian route from Poonch to Mendhar via Jullās. The shrine is stated to have one room of stones, statues of bull, lion and some Goddess.The shrine could possibly be the sight of

Loh - Stompā (Loh Stupā) constructed by King Megh Vāhana's Queen Amrit Prabhā" (8th century A.D.) though Govind Kaul has mentioned it to be situated at Leh[25], in Ladākh.

from the above study of the sites and monuments of the land of Nāgsen's birth,education and spiritual and religious activities, it should be amply clear that the mountain valleys in the Himālayan region of Pir Panchāl and Chandarbhāgā river, particularly those of Kaśṭwāṛ, Rājouri and Poonch had been the seats of Bhuddist meditators and men of spirituality in the early period of Indian history and later subjected to all sorts of aggression, political,religious as well as spiritual.With the change of each and every King and the dynasty, their appears some change in the boundaries and territories of each kingdom or a principality, but the basic religious spirit of sanctity, purity and piousness of this Holy Buddhist land has retained to this day, the sacred message of universal love and brotherhood from India (सर्वे भवन्तु सुखिना and वसुधैव कटुम्बकम्)in the form of dozens of ancient places of pilgrimage, temples, architectural ruins, miraculous sights and Dargāhs, present every where in these valleys of Himālayas of Jammu and are a living testimony to the above noted fact.

Footnotes :

1. Yatī: The term has two meanings. The first being that human being, who has attained a stage of highest spiritual order. The other meaning is associated with a mysterious biologically living, Himālayan mountain creature or snow man, who's physiological details are not as yet available, and who is now being considered as a living species of a higher stage of evolution as compared to human beings.

2. Satī: A female with a firm devotional faith, who persued a nobel cause, or who was compelled to die by a cruel

section of society for the sake of certain traditions, observed by an individual or a group of society as a whole.

3. P.H.K. p28 c.f. Raj., Vol.I, V-317 states that "Mihirkul the tyrant while chasing khaśās in the mountains of Kashmir perused them upto Kaśṭwāṛ".
   According to another version of traditional history the ruler of Suru (Ladakh), around 4th century A.D. attacked Chīrhaṛ (Kaśtwāṛ via Bhotcol and sub-dued the whole area upto Thāthri and named it as Bhot Nagar. (T.D.D)

4. Pritam Krishan, *Bhadawahī Lok Sāhitya* (Hindi)

5. Dr. P.K. Kaul "Rājā of Kāndā" - Daily Excelsior, Jammu dated Feb.16,1992.

6. No ancient monument is presently traceble except a temple. The temple structure is of comparatively recent origin where an extremely fine 80 kg, black stone sculpture of mother Goddess, which has a powerful bewitching effect on the beholder is of ancient origin (common belief 2000 years). The origin of shrine is shrouded in mystery. Many legends are associated with it. But the most popular and accepted version is that, "once a shepherd while grazing his livestock in the nearby forests spotted a small but extremely beautiful small girl on a rock. He was astonished to see the innocent girl at such an isolated place. Taking her as a child, who had lost her way, he lifted the girl on his back with the idea of carrying her to his own home, till her parents are traced. To her utmost surprise, the weight of the girl child on his back began to increase suddenly, so much so that he was compelled to take some rest. Accordingly he placed the girl under the shade of a Deodār tree, but after a while when he wanted to lift her for onward journey, he had to see an unbelievable. The girl was nowhere there and instead stone image of the Godess was lying before his eyes. The place was assigned the name Sri (Laxmī) by the shepherd. A simple stone structure was constructed there, by him and he began to act as Pujāri (worshiper) of the shrine.
   According to J.N. Ganhār (Jammu Shrines and

Pilgrimages) the Goddess resided at Hāri Parbat in Kashmir Valley where according to an ancient legend she had killed the great Demon of Satisar lake by throwing a pebble on his head at the place of Hārī Parbat Hillock. Later she took the form of a small girl and asked a shepherd boy standing close by to carry her on his back. The boy was perplexed but obeyẹd the devine command. As soon as he did so he was wafted into the air, till he flew to the place called Ajāl on the Sarthal mountain slopes. Here he stopped to take some rest. But as soon as he did so the divine load turned into a stone image and a spring of crystal clear water gushed out from under the spot. The local chieftain Agār Dev who heard about this strange phenomenon came early next morning to pay homage and obeisance. According to a different version, the Devi appeared before the Rājā in a dream.Next day when he went to the resplendent image, he remembered his dream over night and ordered the image to be lifted to his place, when it had been carried about a mile, to Ajāl /Agār village the men carrying it put it on the ground, to rest a while. But when they tried to lift it again, they could not do so, try however hard they might. So the Rājā got a temple made there. Short of myth, it must be clear that the fine sculpture was brought to Ajāl from Kashmir by some devotee in Calamitous times. General Zorāwar Singh Kalhuriā during his Governorship of Kaśtwāṛ (1825-35) is stated to have obtained a grant from Gulāb Singh authorising utilization of income from the surrounding forest for the maintenance of the shrine. The shrine is highly venerated. The Goddess is believed to grant every wish to her devotees and in particular she is believed to grant children to baren couples.

The historical roots of the traditions associated with Shārikā can be traced probably from Bāṇā's mention in *Harsh Charita,* wherein it is stated that the confidential deliberations of Nāga King Nāgsen were divulged by Shārikā bird and that led to his destruction by Samudra Gupta (335-375 A.D.). Now Nāgsen and Ganapatī Nāg were the rulers of Aryavarta about the middle of 4th century A.D. (A.I.P. 379-80). As per Kashmirī traditionals Shārikā is the representative bird of Devi Shārikā and nobody kills it in the mountainous regions.

7. T.S.J. P.123.

8. A small but beautiful spot near Drabshālā on the left bank of River Chināb on the Baṭoṭe Kaśṭwāṛ National Highway.

9. Kānḍot was the main village of Chief of Kānḍās territory, a strategic location between the principalities of Chambā, Kānḍot, Churāh and Kaśṭwāṛ around 1086 A.D.

10. Jañgalwāṛ is the Western extremity of Kāniṇī - Ajāl on the left bank of Chināb.

11. R.T. IV, V 201-215 and 246-64. Lalitā Ditya, while returning to Kashmir from an expedition, was helped by his Minister Caṇkuna to cross a river in Panchnad with the help of two miraculous stones, which the minister threw in the river to dry it and Lalitā Ditya crossed the river. Naturally, the King got tempted towards the miraculous stone which he exchanged with the very valuable statue of Buddha. This statue was carried to the valley of Kashmir by Cankuna and installed there in a Bodh Vihāra/ Chaityā (most probably at Parihāspur, the new capital of the King).

12. R.T. IV, V 265-76 states that once it so happened that Lalitā Ditya took a horse to break it in, as he was proficient in the knowledge of horses. There in a lonely place he saw a maid sing and another dance. After completion of their performance the two bowed slightly and went away. He came day by day to that place and saw the two girls perform exactly in the same fashion. He came up to them and questioned them in his surprise. He was told by the girls that they were dancing girls belonging to a temple. The village of Surāvar Dhamana was their home and that they performed this dancing and singing at the spot, under the direction of their mother, which their descend makes them incumbent and by which they get their living. The custom handed down by tradition had become fixed in their family and its reason they did

not know, nor any one else.

"When the King had heard from them this information he was astonished and next day had the whole of the ground dug up by workmen. Then when they had made a deep excavation,the King saw as announced (by them) two decayed temples with doors closed. On opening of the folding doors he saw there two (images of) Keśavā which as the letters engraved on the bases (Pithās) showed, had been made by Rāma and Laxman. The illustrious King after errecting a separate stone building by the side of (temple) Vishnu Parihās (Keśava) had the (image of) Rāma Swamin consecrated there. Thus the two images of Gods were put up by Queen Cakramardikā by the side of (Śivā) Cakreśvara after she had obtained it on request from the King 265-276)."

It is interesting to note that Stien has recorded no comments on these verses probably for lack of clarity or probably he did not visit Rāmkund site situated as it was astray from the main route to Mendhar Valley, and as he could not locate the place in question. Stien had visited, Poonch in 1892 A.D. and had identified certain places of Poonch as mentioned in Rājatraṅgini such as Loharkot (Loran). Attālikā (Atoli), Swarnik (suran) etc.

It is quite possible that the name Parihāspur assigned to the new capital of Kashmir by Lalitāditya might be the result of an inspiration from Mendhar, after recovering from there the Gold image of Buddhā and two idols of Keśava as mentioned above.

In verse 184 of the same book we come across the statement of Kalhaṇa that Laltā Ditya, while taking leaf (Parṇa) constructed Parṇotswa (i.e. Poonch) while at play constructed the Vihārā of Krīḍārāmā (probably Sakhī Maidān site) and while taking fruits constructed Phalpura. As these events in Rājatraṅgini are recorded with the verses and events related with Buddhā and Keśava statues, followed just after the story of construction of Parnotsva, Kriḍārāmā Vihāra and Phalpua, the aforesaid statues must have been found in the vicinity of Rāmkund Sakhīmaidān site in Mendhar Poonch.

The home of two dancing and singing girls of Rājatraṅgini narration (V 264-74) has been recorded as Surāvar Dhamana. This village by present name of Dharana can still be located near Rāmkund in the Mendhār Valley.

13. The Rājput caste Jajwān is similar to scores of caste names of Bhales valley in Bhadarwāh and Kaśṭwāṛ therefore proves some sort of ethenic relationship between the two.

14. Stien R.T., Vol1. IV-V184, Vol.III-v--1256.

15. Ibid.

16. M.P. Treck.

17. T.H. Beal. p.200

18. B.K.Sarlā. p.44-45. f.n. 26

19. H.R.F.B. c.f. Ibid.

20. Ibid. p. 134-35. Also B.K. Fidda. P.54. Aśavgosh was a resident of Saket and belonged to a Brahmin family. He was a literary giant and was well versed in grammar, four Vedas, six treatise on Vedāngas, conversant with Tripitakās, of 18 schools of Buddhism and a laureate of literature. Due to his literary genius he was invited by Kātyāyinīputra to Kashmir where he compiled the Vibhāśas.
He is also known as the third president of the Buddhist council held in Kashmir during the days of Kaniśaka. He is known as the preceptor of Kaniśka. One of his texts entitled "Sariputra Prakaraṇa have been located from Central Asia".

21. (i) B.K. Sarla PP.44-45. Vastness of Buddhist literature as Mahā-Vibhaśās of Sarvastivāda School, that was produced in Kashmir shows that this region must have had the benefit of being venue of a gathering of learned scholars of the Age".
(ii) B.K Fidda. P. 21-22. It has further been given by the Chinese sources that the final decision of the council were engraved on copper plates and deposited in a stūpa under orders of the King (Kaniska). The problem of location of these copper Plates still engages the attention of scholars throughout the world.
(iii) R.T. Vol. i. P. 144. f.n. 188- "The place where the

work of the council is deposited was identified as Uśkūr near Bārāmulā. Mr. Garrik carried out extensive excavations in 1882 but failed to get anything.

22. According to Sufi Mohd Siddiq, "One descendent from a distant spiritual elder named Sheru Shāh, resided at village Chajlā. Some 2 Kilometres North West of Chotai Shāh Ziarat at Sakhīmaidān. He had two children and a wife. The family being descendants from a saintly person possessed miraculous powers, but were for certain unknown reasons, forbidden from using them. The family at occasions talked about it, and the two children over-heard them. Although the family was desperately poor and helpless, it did not use the power of the elders to achieve worldly comforts.

One day it so happened, that the two children of this Sheru Shāh lineage, while grazing their few castles near Sat Mangat or Segi- Di-Dhab (Water Pond) had a conversasion with each other. The younger female child wished to her brother saying that had they also many castles like those of their neighbours they too would have been rich and enjoy life. But she could not understand why their parents, who possess the power of their ancestors to have anything including cattles, did not use it for removing the poverty of the family. On hearing the natural wish of the innocent sister the boy was moved and accordingly he consoled his sister by saying that he would test the powers of his forefathers and try to fulfill her wish. Accordingly the boy took few grains of a wild pomegranate fruit from nearby Trees and threw them in the pond Seri- Di - Dhab wishing that the power of their fore fathers may turn them into milk yielding buffalow; and strangely it actually happened. The brother and the sister were excited with joy and shouted in happiness pointing towards the swimming buffaloes in the pond. People from adjuring fields and pastures ran towards the children and the pond, and thence to the village of Chajlā, where they informed the parents, that the forbidden family secret stands revealed by the two children. The father in a fit of anger ran towards the site to punish the children. On the other hand the joy of the two children had also vanished, and fear of punishment had caught hold of their mind. Consequently they ran towards the site of present Ziārat. At this spot they again wished to the mother earth to accept them back, so as to spare the family from any curse for revealing the family secret. Consequently the two children disappeared at the spot. By this time the father of the children also reached there, but nothing could be done now. Instead he was all sorry for losing his temper. Feeling helpless he wished that the power of his forefathers and ancestors, which was not to be revealed by the lineage, may now be bestowed upon these children and may appear after sometime. Two graves of these children are lying at the spot which forms the main Ziārt of Chotā Shāh, the popular name for the boy. As for the details pertaining to Sheru Shāh, his family descendants and the family origin is concerned, nothing is available. But from the antiquity of the region plenty of religious tradition and association of the place with King Menānder and Bhikśu Nāgsen, it should be no wonder if we assume that the ancestor of Sheru Shāh or Chotai Shāh lineage was no else but a person associated with Nāgsen himself or if there is some difficulty for assuming Sheru Shāh as Nāgsen, whose marriage account is not known, the term Sheru Shāh of the abovereferred tradition could be a traditional title of the saintly person Nāgsen,the lion of the Hills of *Milind Panho*. Śākya Simhā of Tariekh Hassan, who is said to have preached Buddhism in Kashmir some 100 years before Kaniṣka might have also resided at Rāmkund or Sakhīmaidān, and whose lineage,in Mohammedan period might have accepted Islam, and accordingly forbidden their lineage, neither to reveal the secret power of their forefathers, nor use it in future. The village of Jhajhlā is hardly one kilometre away from Sakhī Maidān and Rāmkund temple site.

Another very interesting and curious thing pertaining to him is repeated around the same very time but at a different place, and the place is none else but Kaśṭwāṛ, the ancient links of which with Nāgsen had already been established some fifteen centuries earlier than the events of Chotai Shāh's time.

23. J.N. Ganhar - According to this tradition a Muslim elder (Shāh Farid -Ud-Din) came to Kaśṭwāṛ during the reign of Rājā Jai Singh (1656-1664 A.D.) for the propagation of Islam. Prior to his coming to Kaśṭwāṛ he had stayed at Sirāj and Dodā, where he is stated to have married himself with a Hindu girl. He finally settled at Kaśṭwāṛ where he met with success in his mission.

Shāh Faried was blessed with a number of saintly children. Two of them Shāh Akhyār-Ud-Din and Syed Anwār-ud-Din lie buried in the Ziārat in which lies the tomb of Shāh Faried himself while the tomb of his third child Shāh Asrār-ud-Din, who like Chotai Shāh died at the young age of 16 years, lies buried separately at a distance.

Many miracles are associated with Shāh Faried-ud-Din once he is said to have restored the eye sight of a neighbour. The local Rājā is said to have won against a neighboring chief, when in the midest of a loosing battle he prayed to the saint.

His third son Shāh Asrār-ud-Din Sāhib who was perhaps the youngest of all was greatly advanced in spirituality. It is said of him that he restored to life one of his playmate Hindu Youth. As he was strolling he found an Arthī (death procession) being taken to cremation ground lying close to the Chaugān (play field) of Kaśṭwāṛ. On inquiry he was told that corpse was that of his playmate and consequently he felt sad and immediately directed the Pal bearers to place the Arthī on the ground. He then touched the dead body with his stick saying, "Get up, Get up, you still owe me a game" and strange enough the dead man was restored back to his life. But the father is stated to have got annoyed which resulted in the death of Asrār-ud-Din and a separate burrial for his youngest son". Incidentally this incident conveys many things common with the Ziārat of Chotai Shāh of Sakhimaidan.

24. Daily Excelsior------------------ Aug.12th 1993.

25. B.K. Sarla, P. 87 f.n. 26.

ANNEXURE I

JAMBŪ DVĪP

The city of Sāklā finds mention not only as the capital of Menānder's kingdom, and that of many other subsequent rulers, but it finds mention also as "Sākal Dvīp" in the Buddhist literature of that time. In *Milind Panho* Śākal Dvīp is said to exist within Jambū Dvīp, thereby making the later more important.The later writers of Brahmanic literature (Purāṇās) seem to have used the term, Jambū Dvīp, in their compositions without mentioning its logical geographical limits.Their use of the term and estimations of the tract, seems to have been based on the usual traditional beliefs, and almost each of them used it in the form of a traditional popular Sanskrit saying found at the termination of every Sanskrit Purāṇic text "BHUVANKOSH VARNANODYOTE JAMBŪDVĪPE BHĀRATVARŚE UTTARĀKHANDE ETC." To me the term Jambūdvīp and the above referred popular Sanskrit saying has something more to tell us in the form of history, geography, linguistic, as well as politics of the region in ancient and early medieval times.

Actually the word Dvīp used frequently in Purānic literature seems to be a parallel for the Persian term Doab[1]. The birth place of king Menander as mentioned in *Milind Panhö* lay in the Dvīp of Alasandā or Kābul valley. Sāgardeo (Sāgar Dvīp) has been mentioned in Greek records for Saurāsṭra[2]. Again we come across two terms i.e. Jambū Dvīp and Sākal Dvīp in *Milind Panhö*.

All these references pertain to Pre-Christian era. Around the time of advent of Kuṣānas i.e. 1st century A.D. we find another mention in the name of Śāka Dvīp for the region just above Sindh delta. These terms for Dvipās are therefore the oldest records which seem to have a close linguistic identity with the Persian term Doāb.In both, Sanskrit and Persian "Dvī" and "Do" stand for two, and "P" and "Ab" stand for water.But whereas in Sanskrit Dvīp means a tract of land surrounded by water, the Persian "Doāb" means a tract of land bounded on two sides by rivers (or river water). Śākalā or Siālkot also lies between the mighty Chināb and Rāvī and therefor by it is meant Do-āb of Siālkot or Śākal Dvīp. The Śākal Dvīp of *Milind Panhö* is stated to exist in Jambū Dvīp and consequently the concept of Jambū Dvīp.

The oldest mention of the term in the Indian literature is close to the time of *Milind Panhö* when Jammu hill region and its adjoining mountains valleys attracted many religious persons, Buddhist saints, hermits and recluse for spiritual attainments, persecuted as they were by invading Greeko-Bactrain hoards (as by King Menander) from the north-west, successors of the Mauryan empire from the East (such as Pushya Mitra) and the intolerant "Śaivite and Nāga rulers from the valley of Kashmir". Consequently a lot of people moved to the Himālayan valleys close to the borders of Kashmir.The Sanskritised nomenclature of many places in these valleys clearly indicates the presence of the powerful Brahmanic tradition, and religious character of the people inhabiting this region. Rakṣhit Tal (Guarded slopes of Milind Panho). Bhadrāvakāsh (Bhadarwāh), Kaśṭvāṭa (Kaśṭwāṛ), Hiuntā (Chanenī, Himāvant of Purāṇic literature), Parṇotsava and Rājāpuri (Poonch- Rājourī of Huentsang), Rudhār (Rudra Dhār) and scores of other names point out towards this fact. The well laid out structure of medieval temples at Balor, Krimchī and Babbāpur also indicate that some religious elements had moved from Panjāb to this tract of land, now called as Dugar (Dungaṛh),lying between the two rivers Ravī and Chināb and surrounded on the north east by two rivulets of Kanḍī area namely Tawī (Taushit Bhāskrḥ) and UJJ.

This small tract of land, of the shape of a cupola "Ḍunā" derived from Ḍūn, (a well guarded valley), and enclosed on three sides by river waters gave rise to a small Dvīp of Jāmbulochana's place and was accordingly named as Jambū Dvīp, in the religious scriptures written and composed in this region of ancient India. On account of political domination by the rulers of Śāklā of the whole North Western India, and the predominant religious character of the literature that was composed during this period (Purāṇas) in this region, the whole of Do-āb of Śākalā or Śākal Dvīp, was mentioned to exist in Jambū Dvīp for all the geographical references. With the passage of time use of the term seems to have become a tradition. It is interesting to note that in the hill region of Jammu we have a similar tradition of assigning the common name to many rivers[3], many places[4] and castes.[5] More interesting is the fact that this Brahmanic class as well as its influence in Himālayan Valleys including Kashmir[6] is still dominant both in number and power.

The terms Dvīp and Do-āb have a great deal of similarity in phonetics and etymology. Probably this is the very reason that we not only find some seven geographical units of land tracts mentioned as Doābs of Muslim India[7] but find seven Dvīpas of medieval Purāṇic Hindu India also. These Muslim Doābs and

Jambū Dvīp – Sapt Sindhu - - - Sapt Dvīp Nav Khand
Of

Bharat Varsa

IN
(PURANIC INDIA & INDIA OF LATER MEDIEVAL TIME)

1 JAMBŪ DVĪP
2 DO–ĀB OF RECHANĀ
3 DO–ĀB OF JETCH
4 DO–ĀB OF SINDH SĀGAR
5 DO -ĀB OF BĀREE
6 DO–ĀB OF SHIMĀULI-KUCHEE
7 DO–ĀB OF JANOOB KUCHEE
8 DO–ĀB OF JĀLANDHAR
9 DO–ĀB OF ALSANDHĀ
10 ŚAKA DVĪP (SĪNDH DELTA)
11 SĀGAR DEO SAURASTRĀ–KUTCH

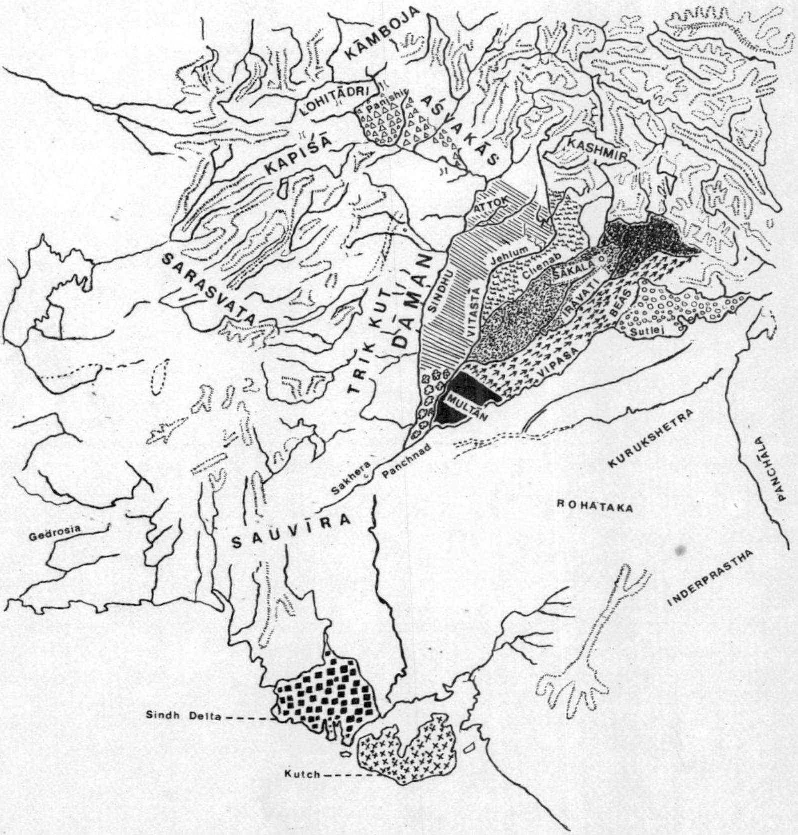

Hindu Dvīpas of North Western India can be described as under (Map sketch No.5.):-

1. Doāb of Sindh Sāgar:

It is probably the biggest of the seven Doābs of Panjāb and lies between the river Indus (Sindhu) and Jehlum and includes the regions between Attok and Rāwalpinḍi to Derā Dān Panāh. This is one of the seven Dvīpas of Purāṇic India, may be Kuśā Dvīpa of Matsya *Purāna* or Śāmali Dvīp of *Viṣṇu Purāṇa* or Patanjalīs *Māhā Bhāśya;* where butter and wine were the product of the seas (rivers) but the exact Purāṇic nomenclature cannot be traced for the time being. The lowermost portion of Doāb of Sind Sāgar forms the Doāb of Janoob-e-Kuchee.

2. Do-āb of Janoob-e-Kuchee:

This is the lowermost portion of the Do-āb of Sindh Sāgar and lies between river Sindh and Chināb (Which now includes Rāvi and Jehlum also) below Dehrā Dān Panāh, and upto the confluence of Sindh river with Panchnad (five rivers). Do-āb of Shimauli Kuchee, which is part of Doāb of Bāṛee is adjacent to it, just across the river Chināb, below Multān upto its confluence with Satluj and Beās. This may be identified with Kraunch Dvīp of *Matsya Purāṇ, Vishṇu Purāṇa* or *Pātanjaliś Māhā Bhāśya.*[8] But further identification and place locations is much needed before anything with autority can be said in this regards.

3. Doāb of Jetch:

This Doāb Dvīp or tract of land lies between the rivers Jehlum and Chināb, right from Jehlum and Gujrāt to the point of their confluence. The outer mountain valleys of Poonch, Kotlī, Mīrpur and Rājouri (J&k State) were not the part of this Doāb. These might have been part of Jambū Dvīp of *Milind Panho* and Buddhist Holy land of the contemporary period.

4. Doāb Shimaulī Kuchee:

As stated above, the further south Western portion of Bāṛi Do-āb between the rivers Sutlej (which now includes Rāvī and Jehlum also) from Multan in the North to otch in the South West. This is probably the "ŚAMALĪ Dvīp of *MATASYA PURĀṆ* or KAUNCH DVĪP of *PATAÑJALI'S MAHĀBHĀŚYA* or *VISHṆU PURĀṆA.*[9] Further investigation is much needed.

5. Doāb of Rechnā:

This is perhaps the second biggest land tract lying between the rivers Rāvī and Chināb from Jammu in the North East to Tootumbā in the South West. The land tract above Jammu in the North Eastern direction comprising of Dugar (Dūngaṛh)? Kaśṭwāṛ Bhadarwāh and Reāsī lying between these two rivers, formed part of Jambū Dvīp which included Śākal Dvīp or Doāb of Rechanā also. It is because of the central position of this Doāb in the region of seven rivers that all foreign invaders of ancient India made Śākala (Siālkot) capital of their empire, in Bhārat Varsha of ancient literature. Lahore formed part of the adjacent Doāb of Bāṛī. Jambū Dvīp must be located at the higher grounds of this region (See map sketch) adjacent to the guarded slopes of *Milind Panho* and early medieval period, which now included Kashmir also, and must therefore represent the tract of land of present Doāb of Rechnā in Pakistan, and Himālayan valleys in the outer hills adjacent to the valley of Kashmir in India, as also the valley of Kashmir itself. This region of Panjāb i.e. Doāb of Rechnā had always been the region of activity and creation (Rachnā). Most of the Purāṇic text that close with the usual dictum "Jambū Dvīpe Bhārat vershe etc". must have been composed within or around this very tract of land. This very region contains the richest folkloric traditions of Panjāb; folk tales, folk songs and folk dance. The lovesome and passionate folk songs dealing with the eternal love affairs of Panjābis mostly pertain to these two rivers, that make this Do-āb. The Śasi-Punū, Heer-Rāñja, Sohni-Mahiwāl and similar other tales are associated with the rivers of Chināb and Rāvī alone.

6. Bāṛī Doāb:

Is the tract of land lying between the river Rāvī and Satluj (or Gaṛāh as it is called near Teebhee Havalee, right from Govindpur in Panjāb (India) to Havelee Futtipoor in South West Panjāb (Now Pakistan). Its equivalent name in Purāṇic literature needs elaborate investigations of the relevant records.

7. Doāb of Jullunder:

This piece of land tract lies between the rivers Satluj and Beas right from Hoshiarpur and Nādaun in North East to Attāree in the South West.

From the above it is clear that seven Dvīpas and nine Khandās of Purāṇic India or of early medieval times, are somewhat similar to above seven Dvīpas or Doābs of recent times but more needs to be said about Jambū Dvīp which name has been included in Pātanjali's *Māhābhāshya, Vāyū Purāṇa, Vishnu Purāṇ and Varāhmihir Saṁhitā,* all of which were composed around the time of Guptas i. e. 5th to 8th century A.D.

We find mention of Jambū Dvīp even in some other later writings of recent times such as *Vāsukī Purāṇa* of 18th century. But the earliest mention of Jambū Dvīp can be traced to the time of *Milind Panho*. Prior to which time we do not find any mention of Jambū Dvīp any where. Jambū Dvip of *Milind Panho's* time must be located in the vicinity of Menander's Kingdom, adjacent to Śākala, guarded slopes, Sānkheya Parivien,

Kāñjaṅgala, Buddhist Holyland and the country of Śākalā. All this description of Jambū Dvīp of *Milind Panho's* time quite satisfactorily agrees with the location of Dungaṛh, or Balor-Krimchi foot hills through Shivālak valleys of Jammu hill region, which formed part of Menānder's empire or its borders with Suṅgās. The most beautiful and picturesque valley of Mendhar in Poonch, and the archeological ruins at Sakhī Maidān still bear a monumental testimony to such a probability. Later, with the passage of time the boundaries of Jambū Dvīp, in the subsequent writings increased. Accordingly we see that by the time of Pātanjalīs *Mahābhasya, Matsya Purāṇa* and *Vayu Puraṇa* its limits extended to the salt range, as Kshār (salt) has been mentioned as the name of its seas (i.e. rivers)[11] Now Jehlum is the river that passes close to the salt range in Panjāb and indicates the extent to which the limits of Jambū Dvīp might have extended from the time of Menānder to the time of Guptas. Patanjali assigns the name of Jambū Dvip to the existance of Jambū tree i.e. Jaman fruit tree which is predominantly found in Jammu region. By the time *Neelmat Purāṇ* was written the limits of Jambū Dvīp extended further and included Kashmir Valley in it, and in one or two centuries more i.e. by the time Alberuni came to India, the limit, of Jambū Dvīp got confused and distortions arouse so much that contradictions were noticeable in the same very single composition as noted by Alberuni also. Quoting *Vāyu Purāṇa* Alberuni says that in it the description of Jambū Dvīp is self-contradictory. There at one place it is stated that centre of Jambū Dvīp is the centre among the Nav-khand Prathmā or the primary nine parts. According to him there are angels on it which again indicates the sacredness of the region and its close relationship with the Jammu hill region.

The diagram prepared by Alberuni on the basis of various Puraṇic texts[12] to show various division of Bhārat Varsha contain in the middle of the diagram, Indra Dvīp, or Madya Deśa, Gandharva lies to the North. West of it. By Gandharva probably is meant present Gāndhāra and by Nāġ Dvīpa to the South West of it. By Gandhāra and by Nāg Dvīpa he probably means Rājasthān and Mahārīshtra where snake worship and Nāga cult finds predominance. This middle country is no else a region but Śākal Dvīp of *Milind Panho,* included in the Jambū Dvīp as mentioned there.

The last confussion about the term Bhuvankosh can be resolved if we concentrate upon the usual closing dictum of the specific Purāṇa, which states, "Bhuvankosh vernanodyote" i.e."intended to describe the particular specialities of the specific geographical region under study" and not the part of the whole world or complete Asian sub-continent as is being interpreted by various Sanskrit writers of the times.

From the above it should be clear that the Jambū Dvīp of our ancient literature should be taken as the Himālayan valleys of Shivālak range and other Himālayas of Jammu region, adjacent to the valley of Kashmir, which has richly contributed to the evolution and development of Indian civilization, thought and culture, especially in the religious fields.

Footnotes :

1. It is a strange coincidence that Prof. Rapson (C.H.I.P 550) also feels that Dvīp and Doāb are probably one and the same word (c.f.N.W.I. P 91). In trying to prove that in *Milind Panho* the word Dvīp is used in the same sense in which Persian word Doāb is used, (the land lying between two rivers), he says that for instance, the Rechanā Doāb between Chināb and Ravī was often called Śākal Dvīp.

2. Ibid. Rapson's identification of Strabo's Geographical names, among other places also identifies, Pātālene or the country of Pātāla for Indus Delta and Sarasotas for Saurāstra. Sigārdis which he does not identify seems to be a correct form of Sāgar Dvīp or Kutch.

3. We have some 8 or 9 Tawīs in Jammu Kāṅgṛā mountain region, some 4 Devikās and 3 Sindhūs in Jammu Kashmir & Ladakh.

4. We have a lot of place names not only in Jammu having common suffixes but in many cases they have similarity to the place and caste names of distant countries like Irān; such as:
Kilhotrān (- 'an' suffix) In Jammu/Bhales
Ahān— In Kashmir; Isfahān, Bazaragan - 'an' suffix, Irān.
Tehrān etc.)
"_ote" and "Kot" are other common suffixes Batote, Balote, Ratnote etc. and Surankot, Balakot, etc.

5. For similarity of caste names please see Sherāzā Hindi Cultural Academy, Jammu.
"-an" and "outra" are the common suffixes in Hudreds of caste names in Jammu and its Himālayan mountains valleys.

6. There is hardly any class of people other than Brahmins among Hindus of Kashmir and the Brahmins of Jammu region have also maintained their dominant influences in the religious and political circles of the region.

7. Alberuni has dealt with the subject of Dvīpas, as enumerated in Pātañjalī's *Mahābhāṣya, Matsya Purāṇa,* which clearly indicates the contradiction in the nomenclature of various Purāṇic Dvipās and their

geographical locations as observed by Alberunī. According to him "each Dvīp and sea has a separate name. The difference of tradition as exhibited by his table (*Alberuni's India*, p. 236) cannot be accounted for in any rational way. These can hardly have sprung from any other source but from arbitrary or accidental changes of the enumeration." To me even the term sea (Sindhu) is arbitrary or accidental. For I feel that use of the term Sapt Sindhu (For Bhārat Varśa) in Vedic India meant only the region of seven Sindhus (Sanskrit - Sindhu = Sea or Indus like rivers which flow in this region). These seven rivers of North, Western India were well known and find mention in Rigveda's Nadī Sukt also. All the invaders that entered India from the North Western direction had to cross these seven rivers one by one to reach the Gangetic plain. River Indus (Sindhu) was the first one they had to cross. As they proceeded further eastward they came across other six rivers of a similar shape and dimension as that of Indus and accordingly the whole of the region was assigned the name of (Sapt Sindhu). The same Sapt Sindhu term was later exploited by the Brahmanic class of Purāṇic period, who had no travel experience of their own, but relied upon the available verbal accounts or official version of the tract as mentioned by the ruling class and was Sanskritised by the Brahmins. By and by this land of seven rivers began to be presumed as the land of seven seas and nine parts (SAPT DVĪP NAV KHAND), as noted in *Alberuni's India* - Vol. I, Chapter XXi, pp.235-36). It is still interesting to note that the land tract lying between river Sindh and the mount Sulamān range, does not find any name associated with the term Dvīp or Doāb but is called by the name of Dāman i.e. foot hills.

8. Dr. Schau - *Alberuni's India* - p.235 - Consult tables.

9. Ibid.

10. Alberuni has also dealt with the topic Jambū Dvīp in the context of a book named Rishī Bhuvankosh and tried to examine and explain various terms mentioned therein (Chapter XXIX, pp. 294-297). The book named Rishī Bhuvan Kosh which he discusses in this chapter

could not be traced from anywhere by any subsequent authors and researchers so far in India or abroad. May be he got one in his time,but he did not discuss anything about this book in his Indica, nor mentioned anything about its author. According to him Bhārat Varsha stretches southwards from Himāvant i.e. Himālaya (I feel this Himāvant may be the Himtā or Hiuntā; present Chanenī region of Jammu; a sacred ancient Indian Tiratha of Sudh Mahadev, just below Rudra Dhār, very much within my thinking of Jambū Dvīp). According to him the inhabitants of his Indica are those to whom alone reward and punishment in another life are destined i.e. who believe in the cycle of rebirth. Again he says that Bhārat Varsha is divided into nine primary parts (Nav Khaṇḍa Prathama) as per this Rishī Bhuvan Kosh and between each two parts or Khaṇḍās (he means Dvipas) there is a sea. On verification these nine Khaṇḍās or Dvipās can be enumerated as in the text above. We have already mentioned seven Dvipās or Doābs of North Western Ancient India. In addition to these we find names of other three Dvīpas mentioned by Greeks and Turuśks. These are:

(i) Dvīp of *Alāsandā* of *Milind Panho* (probably land tract between Sindh and Kābul river or Panjshir and Kābul rivers.

(ii) Śāk Dvīp; region just above the delta of Sindh river named so probably because of the Śakās who entered this region via Drangiānā and named it after them. (It is interesting to know that the term Drangā is used in Kashmir and Bhadarwāh also where certain places of specific geographical features are termed as Drangā or Gateway (For Śaka Dvīp please see *Ancient India* -V.D. Mahajan p.344- map Sketch).

(iii) Sāgar Dio (Dvip) for Saurāstra. It is interesting to note that Rapsons identification of Strabos Geographical names in ancient India identifies Pātalene or country of PATALA for Indus Delta

(iv) Doāb of Yamuna with Ganges.

Thus we have some eleven Dvipās of ancient and medieval India. If we carefully study the above eleven

Dvipās or Doābs on the map sketch we find that Doāb of Janoob-e- Kuchee and Doāb of Shimāule nearly form one unit, and same can be said about the Doāb of Jullunder. Thus the number of these Khandās or Dvīpās can be reduced to nine only.

It should be noted here that prior to the time of *Milind Panho,* the North Western India was already known to the outsiders by the name of Sapt Sindhu, having a close resemblance to the seven Doābs of Panjāb as discussed in the text.

11. Alberunis India -p.235, Vol.I.
12. Ibid. p. 296 Vol. I.

BIBLIOGRAPHY

1. Bhikśu Jagdish Kashyap. — Milind Prashan (Hindi)- Sugat Prakashaṅ, Dr. Ambedkar Road, Nagpur, Maharashtra.

2. F.M. Hussanain — *Buddhism in Kashmir and Ladakh*, J&K Publishers.

3. G.B.Bleasby Esg. — List of coins and medals belonging to S.P. Museum Srg. M.N.S. London. 1900 A.D.

4. N.D.Nargis — Tariekh Jadid Dogra Des; Chand Press Jammu.

5. P.N. Kaul Bomzai — *History of Kashmir*.

6. P.N. Kaul Bomzai — *Kashmir and Central Asia*.

7. R.C. Kak — *Ancient Monuments of Kashmir*, Sagar Publication Janpath, Indian Oil Bhavan, New Delhi. 1971 Ed.

8. R.D. Vedakar — *Milind Panho*- Pāli text in Devnagri script. Pub. University of Bombay, 1940.

9. R.C. Majumdar — *An Advanced History of India*.

10. R.N. Dandekar — *The age of Guptas and the essays*

11. Rhys Davids T.W. — *Milind Panho* - Translation from Pāli. The Claredon Press Oxford. 1890-94. (Sacred Books of the East Series - Vol. XXXVI and XXXVII Editor Max Muller).

12. S.C. Ray, Dr. — *Early History and culture of Kashmir*,1970.

13. S.Maqbool Ahmed — *Historical Geography of Kashmir.*

14. Sachau, Edward C. — *Alberuni's India,* Vol. I & II reprint 1989 A.D. Atlantic Publishers and distributors.

15. Sarla Khosla, Dr. — *History of Buddhism in Kashmir,* 1972 Ed. Sagar Publications, 72 Janpath New Delhi-1

16. Stien, M.A. — Rājataraṅgiṇi.... Bombay 1892.

17. Vidya Dhar Mahajan — *Ancient India* Pub. S. Chand & Co. Ram Nagar ,New Delhi. Edition. 1977

18. V.D. Mahajan — *Ancient India,* S. Chand & Co. 1976 Ed.

19. V.D.Mohan Mehta" — *North West India of 2nd century* B.C." Indological research institute- Ludhiana

20. V. Trenecker — *Milind Panho* (Questions of Milinda-2 Vol. London 1880).

INDEX

A

Abhidharma 10
Abhimanyu 85
Afghānistān 3, 19, 21, 24, 25, 29, 55
Aggarwāl, Vasudev Śaran 65n, 74, 84
Agathoceles 28
Agāthocleia 22, 25, 33, 34, 35, 82
Agardev 107n
Agnimitra 25, 28, 29, 30
Alberuni 120, 121, 123n, 125n
Alberunis's India 123n, 125
Alexander 3
Alexandria 23, 24 (city of Alexander)
Alsandā 23, 24
Antimachus I 22, 34
Antimachus II 22
Antiochus 18, 45
Athena, queen 25
Apollodotus 19, 20, 21, 22, 24, 25, 26, 28, 29, 34, 37
Apollodorus 14n, 23
Arhat Mahāsen 5
Āryan 6, 17n
Arhathood 32
Āryāvarta 107n
Assāgutth̤ 5, 6, 8, 10, 44, 47,48,51,64n,91,94,95
Ashoka 2, 32, 85n, 11
Ashoka Park 11, 56
Aurang zeb 103
Aśokāvadāna 64n, 66n
Aśokan empire 45
Avantiswāmī temple 99
Aśvaghosh 42, 110n
Āyu Pāl 5, 7, 11, 47, 51, 60, 97

B

Bactria 18, 27, 44, 45, 64n
Rulers of 34
Bactrian Palace 54
Bajaur Tribal Terirtory, 29
Bāṇa 107n
Bāri Doāb 119
Beal, T.H. 110n
Besnagar inscription 31
Bhadarwah 71, 80, 79
Valley; 110n

Bhāgavat Dharma 31
Bhattan 50, 51
Bhikshu, M.P. 14n, 85n
Bhikshu, Jagdish Kashyap 14, 15, 75
Bleazby Esq. 75
Bodhistva 67n
Brahmā 67, 68, 91
Brahmanic culture 9
Brahmanical sects 6
Brāhmī inscription 74
Brāhmī script 63
Brahaspati 43
British Museum 75
Bridhārtha 20
Buddha Carita (of Aśvaghoṣa) 42, 67n
Buddha 3, 8, 11, 12, 15, 16, 59, 74, 84, 97, 108n Statue of 41
Buddhism 2, 5, 7, 30, 31, 32, 33, 42, 47, 62, 70, 76, 86
Buddhist 23, 35, 37, 38, 45, 54, 62, 63, 70, 76, 86, 88n, 91, 95, 96 101 faith 7 fold 59; monks 12, 38, 39, 45, 48, 45, 48, 55; religion 1, 44
Buddhist Sanghā 16
Buddhist school 13
Buddhist thought 9
Buddhist tradition 31

C

Cakramardika 109
Capleston 4
Cankuna 41, 108n
Chamba 89, 90
Charsada 29
Chandragupta 46
Chandrabhāgā river 71, 72, 76, 80, 81, 82, 83, 105
China 35, 85n
Chinābs valley 17n, 41, 80, 117
Chinese 14-16
Cowell, F.W. 14, 64n
Cunnigham 13n
Cylone 35

D

Dāmodrā 2
Demitrius 18, 21, 23 24, 25, 26, 27, 28, 37, 45, 55
Demetrius I 22, 34
Demetrius II 27, 34, 64
Devmātya 12, 13
Dharmādhikārī 6, 10, 11, 56
Divyāvadāna 22, 64n, 66n
Doāb; of Jetch Janoob-e-kuchee 117, 125 117; of Jullunder 119; 125 of Rechnā 118; 122 Shimauli Kuchee 119
Dvip of Sindh Sāgar, 117

Drip of Kuśa 117
Kraunch 117
Sāmli 118
Sākal 114,118
Śaka 124
Nāg 121
Jambu 114, 118, 14, 48, 59, 63, 67, 120, 121
Sāgar 122n

E

Emrald, 41
Euthydemus 19, 22, 27, 37, 46
Eukradites 40, 55, 66n, 22 44, 45, 64n
Euthydemus II 34, 64n
Euthydemids 18, 23
Eukradia 45, 54

F

Fauq; Tariekh Hassan 67n
Fidda, B.K. 13n, 14n, 17n 85n, 87n

G

Ganges 16
Gāndhāra 2, 19, 27, 29, 46, 64n
Gaṅgetic plain 123n
Gaṅgetic Valley 20
Gandhāra 24
Gaṅhār, J.N. 90, 103, 106n, 113n
Garg Saṁhitā 28, 30, 37, 38, 66n, 64n
Ghaznī 29
Ghosh, N.N. 38
Govind kaul 105
Greek 75
Greeko - Bactrian 1; invasion 87; court 33; hords 2; influence 82; rulers 59
Gujrāt 83
Gulam Mustafa Ishrat 96
Guptas 120, 85

H

Harish Charita 107n
Hāri Parbat 91
Hārwan 42
Hāthīgumpā inscription 20
Hindū 82, 83, 84, 87, 122n
Hindū Dvīpas 117
Hinduism 86
Hindu Kuś 18, 30, 39, 45
Himālayan Mountain 11, 81, 88
Himālayan region 45,52,82
Himālayan valleys 32, 39, 41, 44, 54, 55, 71, 83, 105, 115
Huentsang 60, 101, 115

I

India 27
Indo-Bactrian invasion 6
Indo china 41, 74
Indo-Greek 38; Dracham 65n; Coins 27; garrisons 19, wars 38
Indo-scythian kings 59

Indo-scythian ruler of Sākalā 1

J

Jālukā, king 2, 19
Jambū Dvīp 14, 17n 48, 57, 59, 63, 67, 114
Jammu and Kashmir 1
Jaṅgalwār 38, 73, 89, 108n, 100
Jāpān 85n

K

Kabul 23
Kadphises, King I 81
Kadphises, King II 81
Kak, R.C. 85n, 104
Kalsa, 90
Kalhaṇa 60, 109n
Kālidāsa 64, 65n
Ka-lo-Chong-Su 15
Kalsi 24
Kathiawār 83
Kaniśka 42, 101, 102, 110
Kanauj 19
Kapiśa 24, 46
Kashmir 2, 7, 9, 19, 30, 32, 35, 37, 41, 42, 55, 57, 58, 61, 63, 70, 84, 85, 88, 108n, 116
Kashmiri 7, 36, 84, 88
Kāśikāvriti 63n
Kaśṭwār Jaṅgalwār 36, 39, 41, 45, 47, 49, 58, 61, 67n, 73, 75, 76, 80, 82, 88, 91, 106n
Kastawari, 1, 46
Kaul, Govind 105
Kaul, P.K. 106n
Kaunsarnāg 103
Keśava 109n
Keśava statues 97
Ketumati mansion 44, 45
Kharośti inscriptions 2, 3, 29; legend 64n
Khakhar, 99
Khoslā, Sarlā 20, 101
Krishana Ghāti 62, 63n
Kuṣāṇas 42, 115
Kuṣāṇa periods 18
Kuvan Monastri; 102

L

Lakshmi 93
Laxman 97, 98, 109n.
Lahirī (Prof.) 32
Lalitāditya 60, 97, 99, 100, 108n

M

Maccrindle 64n
Macdonald (Dr) 22
Madhyamikā (Vidiśā) 27
Mahajan, V.D. 124n
Mahābhāṣya 64n, 65n, 117, 119, 120, 122
Mahābhārata 28, 64, 97
Mahā Sen 9, 44, 45, 48, 54
Mahāvamśa 23
Mahāvibhaśya 110

Majumdār, R.C. 15
Malvikāgnimitram 28, 64
Manasarovar 3
Mandalmālā 13
Maqbool Ahmed 68n
Martand temple 99
Mathurā 4, 20, 21, 27, 28, 75, 70
Matsyapurāṇa 117, 120, 122
Mauryas 18, 46
Mauses, King 35
Max Muller 73
Meghvāhan king 105
Mendhar (Poonch) 36, 38, 92
Mihirkul 89
Milind Vihāra 7

N

Nāgārjuna 42, 43, 67
Nāgārjunakoṇḍā 15
Nāgsenī 41, 42, 44, 47, 50, 51, 69n, 73, 77, 78, 87, 91
Nāgsenī region 39, 41, 52, 61, 63, 70, 74, 75
Nāgsenī Valley 78, 79
Nalanda 56
Narain, I.G. 13n, 73
Nasik cave inscription 31 63n
Nirvān 16
Neelmat Purāṇa 120
Neil 64n
N.N. Ghosh 38
Nur-ud-din-wali sheikh 82

P

Pandvas 97, Pahalvas 63n
Pāṇḍav temples 99
Panjshir 23
Panjāb 39, 59
Pantaleon 22
Pāli 7, 75
Pāli inscription 77
Pākistan 49, 60
Pāṇinī 27, 28, 63n, 64n
Parihāṣpur 108n
Parthiā 14n, 17
Patañjali 27, 119, 120, 122n
Patkā 56
Pāṭaliputra 10, 11, 20, 22, 37, 56, 78
Pitnas, 56
Pir Faried-ud-din 101
Pir Asrār ud din 101
Plutarch 32
Pritam Krishan 106n
Pushya Mitra 6, 20, 21, 22, 27, 28, 38, 39, 43, 45, 70
Pushkalavati 27

R

Rajouri 60
Rajasthān 83
Rājatarangiṇi 71, 97, 100, 109n
Rāma 62, 97, 98, 109n
Rāmkund 60, 92, 97

Rāmkund temple 59, 60, 97, 98, 110n
Rapson (Prof.) 4, 14n, 23, 69n, 122n
Rhys Davids 23, 75, 77
Rig-veda 76, 123n
Rohaṇ 9, 47, 52, 72

S

Sāgalā 4, 10, 11, 36, 40, 49
Sakhī Maidān 36, 41, 60, 63, 97, 99, 101, 102
Sākalā 1, 7, 10, 19, 22, 25, 33, 35, 38, 41, 57, 58, 113n
Sākal Dvīp 114
Samudra gupta 107n
Sāket 20, 21, 26, 27
Sāket, Vidiśā 20
Śākya Muni Buddhā 3, 56, 59, 97
Sākya Siṁha 42, 43
Sānkhey's hermitage 12, 36, 56, 57,' 60, 61, 97
Sanskrit 48, 51, 85n, 89, 121, 123
Sarla, B.K. 13n, 14n, 110n, 113n
Satya Siṁhā 42
Saurashtra 122n
Sauvira 40, 83
Schau (Dr.) 123n
Shāh Asrār-ud-Din Sāhib 113n
Shāh Faried 113n
Shah Jehan 103
Shārdā inscriptions 51, 92
Sharika Temple 91
Sikandar konoclast 90
Sindh 19, 124n
Sindhu 29, 83
Singhpur 61
Sinhālese 7
Sitā 98
Shiv Parvati 93
Shivālak hills 48
Siddiqui, Sufi Mohd, 111n
Sirkar, D.C. 3, 21, 23, 65
Sonutur 9, 17n, 46, 47
Stien 100
Strato I, 25, 27, 33, 34, 35, 97
Strato II 34
Śuṅgas 20, 21, 28, 37, 38, 45, 56
Śuṅga, Vasuṁitra 21, 28

T

Tārānath 22, 46
Tariekh Hassan 66n, 112
Taxila 3, 19, 29
Toshmaidān Pass 61, 101
Tisā Mogli Putra 32
Treck, M.P. 17n, 67n, 85n, 110n
Treneckner, V. 43, 72, 73, 77

U

Upanishads 4, 86

V

Vādekar, R.D. 31, 55
Vasumitra 24, 28
Varāhmi-hir Saṁhitā 119
Vattanīya hermitage 10, 36, 44, 50, 61, 69n, 75
Vāyu Purāṇa 66n, 119, 120
Vedas 6, 9, 17n, 74, 77, 79, 80
Vedic lore 11
Vihāra—
  Bodh 101
  Milind 97, 101
  Kuvān or
  Kundalvan 104
  Shahdarhāvan 42
  Sakhimaidān 41
  Kriḍārama 97, 100
Vijāyaka Mitra 29
Vijayanta Palace 45, (Enkradite lodge 64n)
Vincent Smith 64n
Vishnu 93
Vishnu Purāṇa 117, 119

W

Wilson, N.H. 67n

Y

Yamunā 32
Yonkas 12
Yugāndhāra 47, 49, 50
Yuga Saṁhitā 66n

Z

Ziārat 103
Zain-ul-din wali sheikh 81

Plate No. I The table land valley of Kaśtwāṛ.

Plate No II The North Eastern slopes of thetownship with Panditgām in the Centre.

Plate No. III Sai Draman or Archeological site at Siāh (Nāgsenī). General view from a distant place 100' x 100'. The site of Assāgutth's religious deliberations and discussions.

Plate No. IV Siāh temple No.3 (8' x 8' x 16' (Approx.). All stone construction cealing with AshatKamal.

Plate No. V Temple No. 2. Sāi Draman. General view.

Plate No. VI · Carved panels of flying celestials on the two sides of the Arch. Temple No. 3. Siāh / Nāgsenī carved Gaṇeśa also visible on the gate beam.

Plate No. VII Carved stone Arch. with a pairof carved lions on the two sides. Temple No. 2.

Plate No. VIII Stone slab with an inscription in Shārdā script 9-12 century. Siāh/Nāgsenī.

Plate No. IX   A close up view of the same script

Plate No. X Statue of viṣṇu with Laxmī, inwhite stone.

Plate No. XI Statue of Garuḍā 9-10 century. Grey stone. Siāh temple.

Plate No. XII General view of the Archeological site at Demzī/Nāgsenī.

Plate No. XIII Carved panels at the site Demzī Nāgsenī. Carved Gaṇeśa, Nandī and 24 petaled lotus structure.

Plate No. XIV A heap of carved stone structure and statues **Demzī/** Nāgsenī.

Plate No. XV A fully blossomed field of Drove corn in the month of may.
Nāgsenī.

Plate No. XVI **The author on his way back from Demzī.**

Plate No. XVII Site of sānkhey pariven and Milind vihārā of Milind Panhō and krīḍārāmā vihārā of Lalitā Ditya. The present sakhī Maidān in Mendhar.

Plate No. XVIII The beautiful valley of Mendhar, named I suppose after Menānder.

Plate No . XIX Beautiful and enchanting, the Valley of Mendhar.

Plate No. XX Kālāban side valley in Mendhar probable locat on of kuvān vihārā of kaniśkāś time.

Plate No. XXI Unexcavated and unidentified great Archeological site at sakhī Maidān Mendhar. Probably Milind Vihārā of Menānder or kriḍārāmā vihārā of Lalitā Ditya.

Plate No. XXII Central mound of the Archeological site with stairs leading to it still visible.

Plate No. XXIII **Outer walls of temple structure vihārā in ruins made from massive stone blocks (Sakhī Maidān).**

Plate No. XXII Central mound of the Archeological site with stairs leading to it still visible.

Plate No. XXIII Outer walls of temple structure vihārā in ruins made from massive stone blocks (Sakhī Maidān).

Plate No. XXIV Rear view of the same stone segment.

Plate No. XXV Front view oı nıcely carvedand beautifully decorated stone structure (Pedestal) .?

Plate No. XXVI A fragment of stone pillar - Sakhī Maidān.

Plate No. XXVII Carved stone pillar base - Sakhī Maidān.

Plate No. XXVIII Topā, the beautiful ridge topon the North of Rāmkund temple site.

Plate No. XXIX The Hidden pocket Valleyof Narol Topā. **The** site of Sānkhey Hermitage ; **Āshram of elder Āyū Pāl** of Milind Panhō.

Plate No. XXX The ancient temple at Rāmkund 8-9th century.

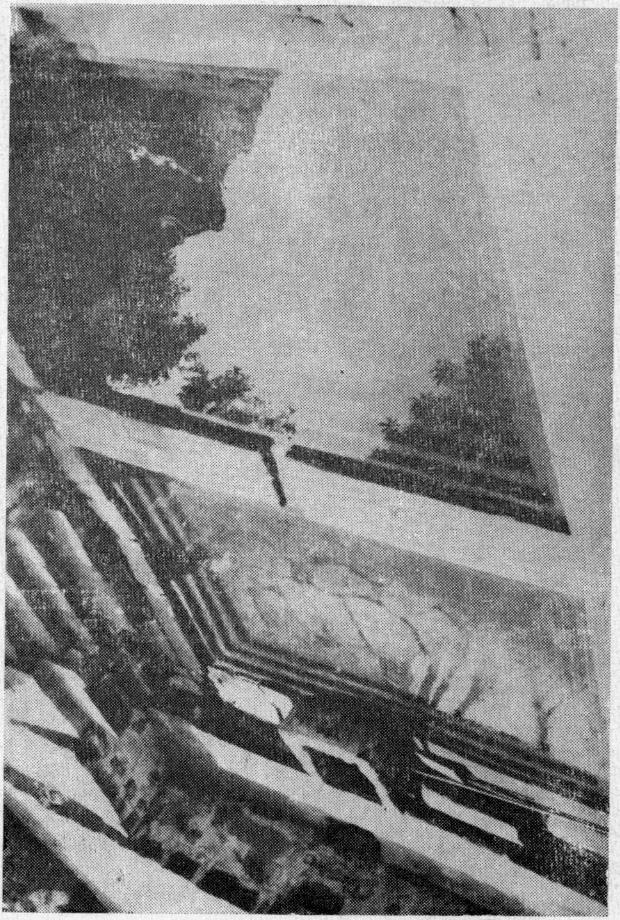

Plate No. XXXI The three springs at the site. Rāmkund and the Sītākund. The third Lachamankund is at the lower end.

Plate No. XXXII Centuries old Ziārāt of Chotai Shāh close to the Archeological ruins of Sānkhey Parivien (Sakhī Maidān) .

Plate No. XXXIII Newly constructed mosque (1982) and on going constructions work near the Ziārāt.

Plate No. XXXIV Ancient Bodh Gumpa at Haloti which is very less known till today.

Plate No. XXXV Coins of Manāndars.

1. Obverse--Draped and helmeted bust of babyking.
   Reverse--Pallas striding left, holding sheild in left hand and hurling thunderbolt with right. Silver coin.
2. Obverse--Draped bust of teenaged Manāndar. Diadum, both ends hanging stiffly down.
   Reverse-- Pallas as above.
3. Obverse--Draped bust of Manāndar-Middle age.
   Coursy --N.W.I.P. 299, cf.
   C.H.I. and I.G.C.